The Derrida Reader

The Derrida Reader
Writing Performances

Edited by

JULIAN WOLFREYS

Edinburgh University Press

© Selection and editorial material Julian Wolfreys, 1998

Edinburgh University Press
22 George Square, Edinburgh

Typeset in Bembo and Frugal
by Pioneer Associates, Perthshire, and
printed and bound in Great Britain by
The University Press, Cambridge

A CIP record for this book is available
from the British Library

ISBN 0 7486 0965 2 (hardback)
ISBN 0 7486 0964 4 (paperback)

The right of Julian Wolfreys to be identified as author
of this work has been asserted in accordance with
the Copyright, Designs and Patents Act 1988.

Contents

Preface

I would like to thank the following people for their comments, help and encouragement at various stages of the preparation of this reader.

Claire Jones, Ruth Robbins, Nicholas Royle and Jenny Bourne Taylor, all of whom offered invaluable insights and commentary at the earliest stages of preparation.

Vincent Cheng, Peggy Kamuf, James Kincaid and Peter Manning at the University of Southern California; Alison Chapman, Mark Currie, Jane Goldman, Jane Stabler and Andrew Roberts at the University of Dundee.

John Brannigan, Sun Hee Kim Gertz, Moyra Haslett, David Hearn, Brian Niro, Virginia Mason Vaughan, Leah Wain.

The Librarians at the University of Dundee Library and the British Library. The Librarians of the University of Southern California's Doheny and Leavey Libraries, for help in the latter stages of preparing the introduction and bibliography (not forgetting Homer).

Jackie Jones at Edinburgh University Press, who commissioned this reader, and who was always helpful, encouraging and enthusiastic.

Thanks are also due to Martin McQuillan for reminding me of a couple of bibliographic entries and to Peter Williams for his scrupulous efforts.

Finally, sincerest thanks to Jacques Derrida, who gave his 'blessing' to this project from the first, who was fully supportive, without reserve, to the last, and to whom *The Derrida Reader* is dedicated.

Julian Wolfreys
Los Angeles, September 1997/February 1998

Acknowledgements

Chapter 1, 'Scribble (writing-power)', by Jacques Derrida, translated by Cary Plotkin, reprinted from *Yale French Studies*, volume 58 (1979) (pp. 117–47), © 1979 by Yale University, Chapters 2 and 3 reprinted from *Of Grammatology* (pp. 107–18, 270–80) by Jacques Derrida, translated by Gayatri Chakravorty Spivak, with the permission of the publishers, The Johns Hopkins University Press, © 1974, 1976 by The Johns Hopkins University Press; Chapter 4, 'The *Retrait* of Metaphor', by Jacques Derrida, translated by F. Gasdner, reprinted from *Enclitic*, 2: 2 (1987) (pp. 5–33); Chapter 5, reprinted from *Dissemination* (pp. 330–40) by Jacques Derrida, translated by Barbara Johnson, with the permission of the publishers, The University of Chicago Press, © 1981 by The University of Chicago; Chapter 6 reprinted from *Specters of Marx* (pp. 95–105, 166–76) by Jacques Derrida, translated by Peggy Kamuf, with the permission of the publishers, Routledge, © 1994 by Routledge; Chapter 7, reprinted from *Memoirs of the Blind* (pp. 32–7, 44–57) by Jacques Derrida, translated by Pascale-Anne Brault and Michael Naas, with the permission of the publishers, The University of Chicago Press, © 1993 by The University of Chicago; Chapter 8, 'Logic of the Living Feminine', reprinted from 'Otobiographies', translated by Avital Ronell, in *The Ear of the Other* (pp. 3–19) by Jacques Derrida, edited by Christie McDonald, with the permission of the publishers, Schocken Books, Inc., © 1985 by Schocken Books, Inc./Random House, Inc./Alfred A. Knopf, Inc.; Chapter 9, reprinted from *Margins of Philosophy* (pp. 273–306) by Jacques Derrida, translated by Alan Bass, with the permission of the publishers, The University of Chicago Press © 1981 by The University of Chicago; Chapter 10, '*Khōra*', translated by Ian McLeod, reprinted from *On the Name* (pp. 89–127) by Jacques Derrida, edited by Thomas Dutoit, with permission of the publishers, Stanford University Press, © 1995 by the Board of Trustees of the Leland Stanford Junior University; Chapter 11, 'Economimesis', by Jacques Derrida, translated by R. Klein, reprinted from *Diacritics*, volume 11:2 (1981) (pp. 3–25), © 1981 by The Johns Hopkins University Press.

For

Jacques Derrida

… elle m'échappe, échappe à toute définition,
mais laisse dans mon esprit et sur ce papier
des traces, des taches informes …

Chacune de ses formes a une allure particulière;
il y répond un bruit particulier.
Le tout vit avec intensité comme un mécanisme
compliqué, aussi précis que hasardeux, comme une
horlogerie dont le ressort est la pesanteur
d'une masse donnée de vapeur en précipitation

(Francis Ponge)

Justifying the Unjustifiable:
A Supplementary Introduction, of sorts

Derrida's text leaves us with the infinite responsibility undecidability imposes on us. Undecidability in no way alleviates responsibility. The opposite is the case. (Drucilla Cornell[1])

Sentences of the form 'deconstruction is so and so' are a contradiction in terms. Deconstruction cannot by definition be defined, since it presupposes the indefinability or, more properly, 'undecidability' of all conceptual or generalizing terms. Deconstruction, like any other method of interpretation, can only be exemplified, and the examples will of course all differ. (J. Hillis Miller[2])

Viens, oui, oui (Jacques Derrida[3])

Injunction I (Double-bind): write an introduction to a collection of essays and fragments of essays by Jacques Derrida entitled *The Derrida Reader*, in which you attempt to do a number of things, in which you seek to make a number of affirmations about the writings that are signed in the name of 'Jacques Derrida'. You would have to point to a number of problems in terms of your various justifications which arise as a matter of course in making the affirmations that you do, and all of which are unjustifiable. Yet the introduction is still to come.

Where, then, to begin? Perhaps with those affirmations, or some of them, in the form of a list. A list of what? Statements such as 'There is no such thing as deconstruction' or 'Jacques Derrida is not the originator of a critical methodology called deconstruction'; or another: 'That which Jacques Derrida writes is neither abstractable nor reducible to a single methodology for the purpose of critical analysis.' Strange affirmations these, constituted as they are by negations. Another affirmation might be that 'deconstruction is nothing more or less than good reading as such'. This affirmation is not even mine, it is a citation from an essay on deconstruction by J. Hillis Miller.[4] Still, at least we've got the beginnings of a list here. But a list is just a list, unless, of course, someone mistakes the list as a series with a peculiar combinatory logic, or a collection of aphorisms. Such judgements are unavoidable inevitably. They

1

come down to a question of the list-maker's inability to control the destination or reception of the list. Whoever reads this collection, whoever takes the time to read the introduction before plunging into the selection of pieces which are gathered together under the title *The Derrida Reader*, will no doubt read, consider and even possibly interpret the list of affirmations in ways that the editor, who is also the list-maker, cannot guess, let alone direct. But that's the condition if not the nature of writing. The list-maker, that's to say me (let's not be coy about this), wants to justify what he's—alright, what I'm—doing. Yet part of what I am doing, which includes gathering these essays, chapters, fragments and excerpts together, writing an introduction, compiling a bibliography and so on, will be looked at with regard to justifications for its existence. I hesitate to make a list, any list, because I know that what I will be put in the position of doing is attempting to justify the unjustifiable. So for now, at least, let's avoid that list (those lists). Let's turn instead to the title. (Titles have been given a great deal of attention by Derrida over the years.)

The Derrida Reader. Beginning again with another negation, I want to state right from the outset that I am not going to get into all the problems which the term 'Reader' puts into place, if only because it would not be terribly original and, anyway, Peggy Kamuf has already provided an exhaustive consideration of the problems in her introduction to *A Derrida Reader: Between the Blinds*.[5] She also has the advantage over me inasmuch as her title doesn't claim to be definitive. *A Derrida Reader* suggests the possibility of its being one among many, an infinite number perhaps. *The Derrida Reader*. Now that's another matter. The definite article proposes or appears to propose a certainty with which I am not at all sure I am comfortable. At worst, it suggests that this reader is *the* reader, the one which defines Derrida readers from here on. Other readers by an extension of such tyrannical logic, such as those edited by Kamuf or Derek Attridge,[6] are merely rehearsals, dry-runs. This Derrida reader, the logic demands from one perspective, is **The Derrida Reader**.

There really is no way around this problem. Books have to be called something, all the more so, it would seem, when the book is being generated specifically for pedagogical purposes and is directed by both its editor and its publisher at a presumed or anticipated body of readers. So, *The Derrida Reader*. Be wary of this title, suspend it somewhat ironically if at all possible. Keep it in mind and try to find other ways of reading it.

Yet there's another problem: *The Derrida Reader* implies someone who claims to read Derrida. There is an implication in this title of an identity. Yet how can we tell just who the Derrida reader is? How might we recognise the Derrida reader? If you're holding *The Derrida Reader* open—as you are no doubt as you read this—you are identified as the Derrida reader. You are not merely *a* Derrida reader (always supposing that you think you know how to read Derrida), one among many, but, precisely, the one, *the* Derrida reader for whom, presumably, *The Derrida Reader* is intended, towards whom it is being directed.

How can you be sure of this, though? Is your position, your identity, that certain? And does the title refer unequivocally to this collection of essays? Is there some kind of reflection or some synecdochic correlation between this title and these essays? Do you know? Can you be sure? *The Derrida Reader* plays with unknowable or, at least, undecidable possibilities. And as a title, the certainty of which seems assigned by that definite article, it leaves itself wide open to all manner of accusations. In anticipation of some of those possible accusations, without in any way being able to limit their proliferation, imagine some other possible transformations or performances of/for the meaning of this title.

The Derrida reader is, it might be imagined—albeit a little awkwardly—a certain Jacques Derrida who reads while claiming never to have 'read' particular authors,[7] attending patiently to the contours of a text. On the other hand, the Derrida reader may name a certain collective, each member of which attempts to read in his or her own manner; this collective yet heterogeneous reader might be what Derrida describes in a different situation, and with reference to Joyce scholars, as '. . . an infinite institution of people working as interpreters and philologists . . .',[8] all of whom will never have done reading, reading remaining always ahead, always to come.

As you can see from these brief and, admittedly, somewhat fanciful speculations, far from being a particular and discernible entity, defined with certainty and even arrogance, *The Derrida Reader* is on the way to becoming an imaginary or even a mythological creature, one to be given over to a variety of narrative possibilities, whether one is talking of the possibility of a book which supposedly brings particular texts together, presented in a more or less coherent form, or whether by this title we signal one (who is also multiple, different from and within him- or herself) who, we imagine, desires or aims to read Derrida, so as to read after Derrida, so as to read with all the attentiveness and patience of Derrida, with the image of (the) Derrida (reader) always before her/him. Henceforth, *The Derrida Reader* will no longer define or designate an imagined unity, a presence or identity. Instead, this title should be taken to name that which we can barely imagine. The Derrida reader is one who, we imagine, will always have to begin reading again and again.

This is still to get no further than the title, however. There is still the problem of the introduction before me.

So let me begin, once again then, by confiding in you.

This is the third time in the last two years (as I write) that I have written something which supposedly goes under the heading of an 'introduction' to the work of Jacques Derrida.[9] You might think that, having performed the task already, albeit in different contexts and for different purposes, the task would be, if not easy, then *easier* at least than, say, the first or even the second time. No doubt this might well be the case, if it were only a question of laying out for the reader the parameters, the rules, the protocols, of a systematised methodology which could be said to operate in the same manner each and every time. Which, of course, is not the case at all when it comes to the text of Jacques Derrida, let alone so-called deconstruction, if there is such a thing.

It is, we are forced to admit, precisely the 'nature' of Jacques Derrida's writing—if 'nature' can be the appropriate metaphor or figure at this juncture—which precludes the possibility of writing an 'introduction-by-numbers'. This is so because Derrida's writing is, in all its various and heterogeneous manifestations, folds, gambits, openings and performances, not reducible to the interpretive or hermeneutic. It is this condition which makes it so challenging and radical, and why, in this local instance, the idea of writing an introduction can be so daunting.

Furthermore, what also proscribes the simple act of writing an introduction or preface is not only Derrida's text generally; it is also Derrida's discussion of the function of the preface. Derrida unfolds the problematic and, for him, the self-problematising act of writing an introduction or preface in *Dissemination*. Prefatory material, neither wholly of the book nor exactly outside the text, exists in a liminal or marginal relationship to what is considered the corpus of the text. In this strange position, the preface or introduction is nonetheless supposed to present or re-present—never simply a beginning point the preface is supposed to bring back or to be mimetically faithful—the thoughts, ideas, arguments, which occur across the chapters of the text, as though these essays and extracts were either (a) insufficient in some manner, incapable of presenting their own theses, or (b) reducible in some fashion to a neat, homogeneous, comprehensible and seemingly finite, definable range of thoughts or theories. As Derrida puts it:

> [A] *preface* would retrace and presage here a *general* theory and practice of deconstruction, that strategy without which the possibility of a critique could exist only in fragmentary, empiricist surges . . . The preface would announce in the future tense ('this is what you are going to read') the conceptual content or significance . . . of what will *already* have been written.[10]

Here we see Derrida both acknowledging the chiasmatic temporal inversion which is already at work in the form and place of the preface, and analysing its rhetorical function also. He continues:

> Prefaces, along with forewords, introductions, preludes, preliminaries, preambles and prolegomena, have always been written, it seems, in view of their own self-effacement.[11]

What Derrida shows us here is the figure of a pen which, while it traces the outline of a thought, never present as such, erases that gesture of outlining, describing, in the same moment and movement. This is the peculiar double logic of the introduction. You read this introduction and, indeed, you are enjoined to do so by the rules which govern the institutionally approved sub-genre of the 'Reader'. Yet the whole purpose in reading it is that you get to some point where the introduction has saved you in some manner from having to read what you will have to read in the body of the text, while, simultaneously, the introduction will vanish, leaving only the trace of its grin, like Alice's Cheshire cat. The introduction supposedly helps you get to that point where you can put it behind you. In contradistinction to the rules of introductions, I am therefore seeking to tell you *not* what I am going to tell you, but that I am not going to tell you what Derrida might have to tell you, even though and all the while there is that assumption that here, in this intro-duction of sorts, I *should* be telling you precisely that which I say I am not telling you, which I am not telling you and which I am telling you that I am not telling you.

And I know that I will already have failed to write an introduction, that I can't help but fail, and to betray Jacques Derrida in the process. So this 'introduction', already aware of its own problematic status *after Derrida* (so to speak, and with apologies to Nicholas Royle[12]), seeks to avoid being merely an 'introduction' while being no more than what Geoffrey Bennington describes as a series of 'programmed excuses', a possible 'point of departure' (one among many) and a '*strategic* justification'.[13]

So this introduction is not an introduction in the conventional sense (even though its excuses are wholly conventional), because it aims to be both sin-gular *and* excessive at the same time. It does not pretend to deliver a 'pocket Derrida' or 'deconstruction for beginners'. This is not—and cannot be for all the reasons discussed by Derrida—a summary or a potted version; there is not a question here of joining the dots and getting a complete picture, for there is no complete picture to be had, and, anyway, the dots can always be joined in different ways. The singularity of this unjustifiable introduction comes from its resistance to, and self-awareness of, 'what the introduction does', even as it negotiates with the 'technical' aspect of the introduction conventionally comprehended. At the same time, however, in positioning itself in a supplementary fashion, in coming 'after' Derrida (while situating the text of Derrida as a text yet to be read and always to come, at some point in the future), this 'introduction' aims at a certain excessiveness which overflows the limits of the introduction. This excess prevents this introduction (of sorts) from being either (mis)taken for a methodologically orientated version of Derrida's text or, otherwise, from being transformed into a method, process or theory for the interpretation of the literary text.

So I find myself with that injunction (where we began), which is also a double bind, spelled out above in both the first and the second epigraphs to this 'introduction' by, respectively, Drucilla Cornell and J. Hillis Miller. Cornell alerts us to the inescapable responsibility imposed by Derrida's writing because of his attention to the question of undecidability. Miller is talking about the problem inherent in any attempt to say what deconstruction is, thereby stabilising it, taming it or making it conform to some preconceived notion of a critical methodology. The problems are the same, and as acute, when one attempts an introduction to a collection of texts, the workings of which are inimical to any idea of generalising or totalising definition and which are themselves marked by the undecidable. This marking is, we hasten to add, not peculiar to Derrida's writing, Undecidability is a condition of all writing. Each essay and each fragment of an essay, chapter, lecture or book in this collection exemplifies, to use Miller's word, the writing and thought of Jacques Derrida.

Yet each 'example' differs from each and every other example, except perhaps in that shared rigour, a shared attention to details, especially those details which are all too often overlooked by those readers who approach the same texts with a disciplinary template or rigidly defined epistemological framework in mind. It may be said that readers who approach texts from within the parameters of institutionally defined and approved methods or approaches do so with an eye to the restricted economy of the text, that structure which is defined in order to produce particular meanings. The writing of Derrida on the other hand has always already moved in its responses from a restricted to a general economy of the text,[14] paying attention to both the singularity and the production of the text in excess of meaning, an excess which is not reducible merely to the effects of textual polysemy. Writing, as it is understood and given a broader definition by Derrida, is of the order of a general economy. It is that mode of excessive production which cannot be accounted for by the desire for meaning which informs hermeneutic reading practices, and which leaves in its wake excessive traces.

So, to reiterate: it is because of Derrida's response to singularity, excess and undecidability in each case, in each text, *in each example*, that writing the introduction is so impossible, so unjustifiable, even though I am seeking to justify this, to justify the unjustifiable. The essays contained herein and, by extension and in principle, this very collection, resist the idea behind any 'introduction' that these pieces can, through a process of reading, assimilation and homogenisation, become reified as typical or representative of a particular approach (such as deconstruction) and which has little to do with a complex range of writings of someone such as Jacques Derrida over a wide span of time. Each of the pieces gathered here, written over a period of nearly three decades, has a specific focus wholly typical of Derrida's writing and attention to detail. These pieces usefully bring together a number of key issues, or what might be called abiding interests or concerns, in Derrida's writing. All are self-contained enough to provide a strong focus for a teaching programme, while retaining their disparity and heterogeneity. Perhaps the first thing these essays can teach us is that, even as Jacques Derrida respects and responds to the singularity of every text, topic or trope in question, so too should we respect the singular writing performances of Jacques Derrida, the performances of the pieces which comprise this Reader. Derrida's work is singular, even though it shares certain affinities with the work of J. Hillis Miller, Paul de Man, Peggy Kamuf, Geoffrey Bennington, Nicholas Royle, or with Jean-Luc Nancy and Philippe Lacoue-Labarthe as Derrida himself comments on the question of singularity, relationship and difference:

> What I share with Lacoue-Labarthe, we also share, though differently, with Jean-Luc Nancy. But I hasten immediately to reiterate that despite so many common paths and so much work done in common, between the two of them and between the three of us, the work of each remains, in its singular proximity, absolutely different; and this, despite its fatal impurity, is the secret of the idiom . . . *The most urgent thing . . . would be to break with the family atmosphere, to avoid genealogical temptations, projections, assimilations or identifications . . .*[15]

Derrida's understanding of the respect owed to singularity is of vital importance if one is to attempt to read Derrida faithfully, if one seeks to be the Derrida reader. This question of singularity is also, as he suggests, the question of the idiom, that which is idiomatic in every act of writing, and which reading should attempt to attend to in its efforts to follow the contours of textual forms, tropes, grammars and structures. Avoiding the temptation to construct a methodology known as deconstruction from reading Derrida would be the effort to break with the 'family atmosphere', the assimilations and identifications of which he speaks, above.

At the same time, and moving on from the position articulated by Derrida regarding singularity, it should not be thought that, because of this regard for singularity, what Derrida has to say is merely self-referential and abstract, spinning its own ideas without any regard for the textual other which his writing encounters. It is to be stressed that the purpose of this Reader is to enable students to free themselves from the notion that Jacques Derrida's work is dauntingly abstract and that it has little to do with the actual encounter with the literary text, or with the literary and rhetorical aspects of the text of philosophy which Derrida has so patiently taken an interest in throughout his writing career. With this in mind, where extracts have been taken from longer, book-length studies such as *Of Grammatology* or *Specters of Marx*, these pieces have been kept quite short. While this no doubt runs the risk of doing a degree of violence to Derrida's text, it has been done in order to provide the student with a particular focus. One of the difficulties of teaching from Derrida with a view to considering the literary or what is called literary language is that the problem arises that Derrida all too often does not read the literary text in any conventional sense (as he points out in an interview in *Acts of Literature*, where he claims never to have 'read' certain authors[16]). Instead, he discusses a certain troping effect, referring to a line from a text, or touching on a text in passing, doing so in a larger context, as is the case of the references to various works of literature in the extracts from *Memoirs of the Blind*, or the 'ghostly' appearances of *Hamlet* throughout *Specters of Marx*.

When Derrida does attempt to 'read', he does so in a manner which does not seek to get to grips with a text, putting everything in order or in the right place. Indeed, his understanding of reading runs contrary to the conventional understanding of what it means to read critically. Derrida's comprehension of the reading act is marked by a sense of randomness and chance, in which performance something is always left behind. As an example of this, take the following passage from *Glas*, in which Derrida seeks the appropriate metaphor for 'reading' the text of Jean Genet:

> I am seeking here the good metaphor for the operation I pursue here. I would like to describe my gesture, the posture of my body behind this machine.
>
> . . .
>
> . . .
>
> So I am seeking the good movement. Have I constructed something like the matrix, the womb of his text? On the basis of which one could read it, that is, repro-duce it?
>
> No, I see rather (but it may still be a matrix or a grammar) a sort of dredging machine. From the dissimulated, small, closed, glassed-in cabin of a crane, I manipulate some levers and, from afar, I saw that (*ça*) done at Saintes-Maries-de-la-Mer at Eastertime, I plunge a mouth of steel in the water. And I scrape {*racle*} the bottom, hook onto stones and algae there that I lift up in order to set them down on the ground while the water quickly falls back from the mouth.
>
> And I begin again to scrape {*racler*}, to scratch, to dredge the bottom of the sea, the mother {*mer*}.
>
> I barely hear the noise of the water from the little room.
>
> The toothed matrix {*matrice dentée*} only withdraws what it can, some algae, some stones. Some bits {*morceaux*}, since it bites {*mord*}. Detached. But the remain(s) passes between its teeth, between its lips. You do not catch the sea. She always reforms herself.[17]

Here Jacques Derrida seeks, appropriately enough, the good metaphor, the most appropriate metaphor in this particular example, which best describes the process of trying to read Jean Genet's text. The metaphor of the dredging machine might seem a curious choice initially for describing *how* one reads, but its power cannot be denied, even while it is also clear that this is not some conventional figure, appropriate to the literary-analytical process which can be transformed into a figure for reading generally. The figure of the dredging machine is absolutely appropriate because it wrenches us from our complacent notions concerning reading habits. The force of the image is such that the effect is perhaps best described not as metaphorical but as an example of the way in which catachresis functions, whereby the exchange of images is so forcefully dissimilar as to estrange, defamiliarise, denaturalise, the assumed relationship. To imagine reading as dredging is to offer a wholly unfamiliar figure for a particular activity in this instance. This in itself forces us to consider the image as presented specifically through the workings of what we call literary or poetic language, rather than assuming there to be some more or less mimetic correspondence.

Derrida follows through his performative image in describing how, as the teeth scrape the seabed, so, while random particles are picked up, something is dropped, something remains, and something cannot be scooped up in the first place. This suggests that no act of reading can ever attain mastery over the object of its inquiry. It cannot do so for at least two reasons: (a) what reading 'picks up' cannot be wholly determined ahead of the event of the textual encounter, and (b) whatever the reading does gather up, there is always that which remains, which are the remains of reading, the excess or supplement beyond the act of reading. This is acknowledged through the performance of Derrida's writing, indicated above where French words appear in brackets. Each of the words carries within it a supplement to itself, another possible meaning in its sound and/or inscription, which the act of reading cannot wholly gather up, but which falls back into the play of language.

Furthermore, Derrida leaves us with that image of the sea-text reforming itself, as though untouched by the act of reading, of dredging. No theory of literature can ever account for the totality of the text. Derrida teaches us this. In addition, and among so many things, Derrida has taught us that the nature of the text is such that all the 'boundaries and divisions' which we assign a text are always already overrun by textuality itself. Attending to Derrida means, among other things, that we acknowledge in response to textuality that what Derrida calls the 'accredited concept, the dominant notion of a "text"' has to be extended and expanded.[18] Reading the following essays by Derrida should allow the Derrida reader the possibility of expanding and extending the notion of 'text' for her/himself. The text is always 'a differential network, a fabric of traces referring endlessly to something other than itself, to other differential traces'.[19] This is true equally of each separate chapter of the reader, and of the reader as a differential network itself always available for reformulation, transformation and translation, in particular ways. Responding to Derrida responsibly means acknowledging the impossible possibility of the very idea of *The Derrida Reader*. It also means that we must begin by revising our most fundamental notions concerning 'texts', 'writing', 'literature' and other concepts related in our thought, which dreaming of being the imagined Derrida reader makes possible.

All of which is presented to the student reader in order to suggest that s/he avoid, once again, the suggestion that it is possible to abstract a 'Derridean method' which can be formalised and assimilated within literary criticism, and then applied as a rubber stamp or template onto various kinds of texts. A mere roll-call of proper names, as a form of shorthand for the texts which they sign and which are discussed in the following chapters, should be able to make plain the impossibility of determining some method, whether it goes by the name 'deconstruction' or 'Derridean'. The material on which Derrida writes—Warburton, Rousseau, Lévi-Strauss, Sollers, Heidegger, Nietzsche, Valéry, Plato, Marx, Baudelaire (to indicate only the most prominent, visible proper names to be found herein)—alerts us to the diversity, heterogeneity and breadth of Derrida's interests. These proper names compose one of those lists, of which we spoke earlier, out of which only the most tyrannical logic could construct a narrative. This list is itself excessive, immune to the restricted economy of the family atmosphere. Little can be said to connect the names. Derrida's writing performances, attuned to being responsible to the singularity of each writer, offers us no means by which to assemble a normative critical methodology, even though so many commentators in the Anglo-American academy have sought to pin down Derrida and to pin on him the label 'deconstruction'.

If *anything* can be said to connect these essays—and this is a highly tentative, provisional connection, one where disconnection also occurs—then the connection can be sought in the constant raising of the question of rhetoric, of tropes, metaphors, structures of language, the poetics and grammar of a text, and all as they pertain to concepts, quasi-concepts or philosophemes which infest the history of western thought, and are then made manifest in textual form. Yet I should hasten to add that if Derrida is some kind of rhetorician, then he is a radical rhetorician, complicating our understanding of rhetoric by showing and performing the resistances of rhetoric and troping to acts of interpretation and reading, conventionally understood.

This very patient focus of Derrida's on certain movements, rhythms and resistances, to the double-logic which writing effects, attends to what Derrida has described as 'the tension between disruption . . . and attentiveness'.[20] From this, Derrida's attention is given to what he himself refers to as an 'analysis which tries to find out how their thinking [that of the writers already named among others] works or does not work, to find the tensions, the contradictions, the heterogeneity within their own corpus'.[21] To enact this analysis, Derrida works with, expanding and transforming in the process, the meaning of a number of terms, several of which are to be found throughout the chapters of this collection, all of which are never quite reifiable into domesticated operative concepts which can be applied to the reading of literature. The terms employed or, rather, *deployed* and considered by Derrida in these essays—trace, *trait*, *retrait*, *revenant*, metaphor, writing, text, supplement—and others elsewhere—*différance*, dissemination, deconstruction, hymen, *archi-écriture*—all act as potential counterparts or substitutes for one another, wrenches and levers applying torque and displacement in the textual machinery, even while they are not to be considered synonymous. Indeed, they are described by Derrida as 'nonsynonymous substitutions'.[22] The terms have a singularity and also a proximity to one another. They cannot be reduced to a restricted economy of interpretive functionality which operates with a predictable consistency. They do not remain constant, and they do not retain constant meaning-value in the general economy of Derrida's text. They are, instead, excessive (even within themselves), non-identical, supplementary. Their performance is dictated by Derrida's own response to and transaction with a particular text in a given context which Derrida does not choose, over which he does not have complete control (any more than any of us in our acts of reading). This non-identical heterogeneity, in which no one term is presumed to take precedence over another in Derrida's writing (certainly not the term 'deconstruction', which is not a Derridean neologism but an archaic French word, chosen by Derrida in a specific context as a possible translation/transformation of Heidegger's *destruktion*), is indicated in Derrida's use of *différance*. The word is modified by that silent *a* which is substituted for the more conventional *e* of *différence*. Signalling deferral and differentiation, difference and repetition, *différance* thus has inscribed within in it in a non-vocalisable graphic mark, an excessive production which proscribes the possibility of assigning a single meaning or identity.

All of which still gets me no further. I still have in front of me the unjustifiable act, that injunction *and* double-bind, of writing an introduction, of sorts, to Derrida, in the face of everything which mediates against such a generalising gesture. Like some character from a novel by Samuel Beckett, I can't go on, I'll go on.[23]

So . . .

Injunction II (Double-bind): write a supplementary introduction of sorts, after all I have said so far, in which you paraphrase without paraphrasing, in which you delineate, and thereby transform, the essays and fragments by Jacques Derrida which are gathered together here under the title, *The Derrida Reader*. Remaining faithful to the essays and fragments which are signed in Derrida's name, you betray his thought in the attempt to be faithful to the contours of that thought. It cannot be helped.

Already in writing, I am situating myself—another signature, another proper name, another act of filiation *and* betrayal—between. Between the reader and the text, for example. This impossible, deplorable situation of being *between* in which this so-called introduction finds itself, reveals it as a being-between, if not a between-being, an intertext which is also an *inter-est*. What interests me (among others) 'in Derrida', to use a shorthand frame, are issues pertaining to the conditions and economies, the rhythms and transformations, which are effected in, through, by writing as these appear to relate to conceptual frameworks of comprehension.

In each of these writings, in which, as I have said, Derrida responds to the contours and rhythms of already existing texts, you'll see an interest in writing, text, trace, rhetoric, rhythm, narrative, genealogy, structure. He attempts to open up to view the in-between: between what a writer consciously intends or desires to say, to control, and what cannot be controlled by the writer but which is produced from some other location.[24] This situation is perhaps most apparent in Chapter 10 of this reader, where Derrida traces the difficulties Plato encounters with the idea of *khōra*; but we also see Derrida at work in the 'in-between' of Warburton's, Rousseau's, Lévi-Strauss's and Heidegger's texts, to name only the most obvious here. What we see in reading Derrida is that even as he respects the contours of a particular text and the protocols which attend such acts of analysis, another trace of the text in question comes into view. In each piece Derrida writes as though dictated to from some other place, some place in the other text, the other of the other text. And each piece is itself, in all its singularity, an example of that singularity (exemplary singularity, we might say), whereby what one comes to understand, as one reads Derrida carefully, diligently, is that the example is always singular; you cannot take the example as a figure for some greater whole. The example is only exemplary of singularity, it is not exemplary in that it might be taken to have some possible metonymic or synecdochic relationship to 'the works of Jacques Derrida'. This Derrida reader does not assemble some jigsaw puzzle.

I have employed the term *piece* a couple of times now, knowingly, with the figure of the jigsaw puzzle firmly in mind. Yet the puzzle which I seem to see is not some neat unity, a whole gathered together from any number of pieces composing a recognisable identity. That's just not possible for all sorts of reasons I don't have time to go into now but which several of Derrida's commentators have spelt out. No, the puzzle I imagine is one where pieces are clearly missing. The pieces we do have don't all belong to the same image. They offer a series of traces which retain their heterogeneity in the event of their being gathered, and in the event of their being read, or in the event of this response, this writing which is never quite a reading, never a reading as such.

The pieces don't fit together then. At least, not in the way in which the pieces of a puzzle are supposed to interact. But what does this idea, this figure of the puzzle made up of pieces from assorted images, suggest? It might well be the case that there are certain chance connections, so that if and when pieces might come together in different and unexpected relationships, a wholly different figure could emerge. Like those children's books, if you'll forgive the illustration, where the pages are divided into three and—for example—by turning the different parts of the different pages at different speeds, at any given time you may well find yourself with a gorilla's head on a ballerina's torso, with either a policeman's or an emu's legs. The permutations are not entirely predictable. Sometimes funny, sometimes sinister, always disruptive and disjointing, where identity is transformed endlessly through little acts of figural catachresis.

The idea of the reader, *The Derrida Reader*, is something akin to the child's picture book where there is a constant remaking and remodelling, always immanent as part of the resistance against what Rainer Nägele calls, with reference to Brechtian theatre, 'identification and absorption'.[25] To go back to the jigsaw analogy once more, when pieces don't fit together properly so as to provide a clearly identifiable portrait, then there appear gaps, differently shaped spaces between the pieces. And of course these are not all the pieces: these are set adrift, while others are left behind.

This does not mean to suggest, however, that the pieces of the reader might not set off new resonances, signposting other possible orientations, other directions in which we might head. And, equally, the act of reading and writing in response to the traces found here might indicate that there are always already echoes and resonances between the gathered fragments and essays. There are no guarantees. But the chances are that this is not so much a *reader* as an echo chamber, in which resound conflicting signals. Whatever you may take from this, there is always something of writing, *in writing*, that remains. Which is why writing is our principal concern, why we can only acknowledge a few of the traces imaginable, and why we turn to . . .

. . . Scribble (writing-power) . . .

From *Of Grammatology* onwards (see the selections in Chapters 2 and 3, below), Jacques Derrida has insisted on the necessity of considering writing in a broader sense than that of mere graphic inscription, conventionally understood. Writing is not to be considered merely as a technical, mechanical, figural or metaphorical device by which reality is represented in the absence of the subject of writing. 'Scribble (writing-power)' is one possible supplement in Derrida's works to the contentions concerning writing put forward in *Grammatology* (as he acknowledges in passing at the opening of the present essay).

Written as a preface of sorts (one of those 'introductions' which are never quite what they should be) to a French translation of a section of Bishop

William Warburton's *The Divine Legation of Moses Demonstrated* (1742),[26] 'Scribble' returns to writing as writing, to the mark or trace itself, its operations and movements. Through extended paraphrase and quotation of Warburton, Derrida sets out to explore the inextricable, though hidden ('encrypted') relationship between writing and different forms of power. In so doing, he also shows how writing is capable of performing its own statements (thereby collapsing the distinction between constative and performative statements, as he does in his study of Francis Ponge, in the essay 'Psyche: Inventions of the Other', and, in different ways, in 'Qual Quelle: Valéry's Sources' and '*Khōra*' (Chapters 9 and 10, below).

Beginning with the questions 'Who can write? What can writing do?', Derrida proceeds to raise the question of the politics of writing, a politics later described in the essay as a 'cryptopolitics', for reasons which we will explain. The questions asked as the opening gambit of the essay are positioned strategically, so as to raise the very issue of politics *in writing*, both in the writing of this preface and in writing in general. 'Who can write?' is, therefore, not merely—only—a question of ability, but is already a double question concerning who is authorised to write, who can write on the subject of (the power of) writing. The second question similarly concerns itself with the writing-effect, and with power-effects in writing. Involved in the question of the politics of writing is the implicit consideration of the roles of writing and intellectuals', academicians' and priests' control of writing in what Derrida terms the 'ideological apparatus'.[27] One of the figures raised in Warburton's writing which interests Derrida is that of 'nature'. Derrida argues for an understanding of 'nature' in discourse as a metaphorical device which deploys the economy of analogical reference. This gesture serves to hide what writing does, and what one can do in/with writing. Writing, it can be seen, hides its powers in the figures, metaphors, tropes and economies of nature, the voice of nature, and so on. Yet, if we are to be attendant on the 'nature' of metaphor with regard to metaphors of nature and the natural, we will understand how the natural, far from guaranteeing or promising the confirmation of presence as part of a general phonocentrism, in fact unveils the limits of the natural within writing.

This leads Derrida to ask: 'why must the question of *power . . .* be worked out today, urgently and insistently, as a question of *writings?*' Instead of seeing writing as that which simply supports abstract and conceptual notions of power, Derrida inverts the relationship to suggest that powers are themselves written, articulated performances based upon the circulation and withholding of knowledges in an inscribed manner, the decoding of which is not available to all.

Turning to Warburton's essay, the economy of the metaphor is explored through Egyptian hieroglyphs principally, although also with brief detours into the area of Mayan or Aztec pictograms and Chinese ideograms. The movement between forms of inscription is perceived as a double one, of abstraction and abridgement. This double movement occurs as symbols are required which serve to figure more and more complex concepts, forms of knowledge, and abstract ideas and concepts. This movement thus *encrypts* knowledge within the sign which, in turn, requires the power of a particular knowledge to decode, explain or make meaningful. The meaning of the sign or symbol is guarded and controlled in writing by those whose power determines the value of the sign and its dissemination in its particular forms.

The hieroglyph is understood to represent not something beyond itself in a so-called reality. Instead, it is comprehended as figuring the condition of writing in general, its function and purpose, its modes of operation. Thus the hieroglyph can be said to anticipate all writing in its ability to signify, before any mimesis, its own gesture. In this double mode of pronouncement and performance, the hieroglyph, as read by Warburton, figures for Derrida the event of writing. From this, Derrida reads the 'historical' movement of writing *in writing* as it arrives at the letter and the alphabet, not as necessarily distinct and separate from hieroglyphs but as only the latest in a discontinuous line of glyph-like functions. In the letter the hieroglyphic function has become more abstract, more abridged, its sign-function more encrypted, made more secret. Thus, moving from the hieroglyphic 'representation' of nature and the natural voice as the necessity of a writing to prolong the duration of voice in the absence of the speaker, Derrida observes that 'it is not natural that nature naturally likes to encrypt itself'. He then proceeds to show how, while Warburton relies on a conventional distinction between physical and metaphysical, the author in fact undermines the assumed primacy of the metaphysical by showing it to be an effect *of/in writing*. All the while, Derrida follows the contours of the other writer's argument and, in doing so, shows the workings of writing through unveiling the limits of Warburton's discussion, which limits are marked by the maintenance of the distinction between physical and metaphysical, and to see the encryption of written language as 'normal', and not a power-effect, a question of writing's cryptopolitics.

When Derrida, in tracing Warburton's reasoning, points to the example of the apologue and its function, he is also directing our attention to the example of his own essay as a preface for Warburton's text. Of the apologue, he suggests, after Warburton, that it is a 'kind of discourse which acts a symbolic displacement'. It stands in for the essay, text or book which it discusses, *in other words*. The apologue, and, by extension, Derrida's preface, perform the arguments of their 'principal text, to which they act as supplements' (as does this discussion of 'Scribble'). In so doing, they may be understood to collapse distinctions between constative and performative utterances, while also uncovering a certain otherness within the 'principal text' in question by transforming its gestures and manoeuvres, creating an ironic distance in tracing the textual contours and detours. This in turn suggests the preface, introduction or apologue as a symbol *in writing* not only *of writing*, of what writing does, but also as a symbol *in writing*, a metaphor, metonym or synecdoche, which refigures the other text in graphic form, while encrypting the contours of that other text within its own graphic movements and rhythms.

Such encryptions are actively engaged with by Derrida in both his title in French, 'Scribble (pouvoir/écrire)' and, at one point, with the verb 'devoir', as translator Cary Plotkin explains in his brief preface to the essay and in note 8 (see below). Of 'Scribble' Plotkin writes the following:

> Derrida points out . . . that it refers back to the language of the original, 'to scribble' meaning to write hurriedly for a living as well as to card wool (hence, to *separate* fibers; in French, *scriblage*) . . . Pronounced Frenchly, the word yields *crible*—screen, sieve, and riddle (that is, both a grid, which organized, and a device for sifting, winnowing, separating)—and *scribe*, each functioning *critically* . . . to select, to discern, to hierarchize. Superimposing one upon the other produces the stenographic nonce word *scrible*, which is intended to epitomize the system shadowed forth by such questions as 'how to read?' and 'how to write on writing?' . . . Yet if a question already bears within it the protocol of its answer, if it screens and programs it in advance, if it establishes or reflects the power of a critical apparatus (*pouvoir/écrire* means both 'power/to write' and 'to be able/to write'), might it not also identify with and appropriate to itself that power, whether political, technical, or religious?[28]

Thus 'Scribble' carries in its graphic form two contrary meanings encrypted within its sign. The power of the sign—specifically the graphic glyph, but, arguably, traceable in the effect of/in writing—comes from the mystery and the encryption it maintains through its semantic undecidability, the ability to maintain several, sometimes contradictory meanings in the same mark or trace (as in the example of 'scribble', the undecidability of which is multiplied between French and English). Hence the power of those who control writing effects over those who have little or no access to the word or sign.

As writing becomes less pictographic, less *representative* in any straightforward sense, and more abstract and arbitrary, so its power increases, argues Derrida. Writing thus involves what Derrida calls a veiling-effect in the service of power(s). To draw attention to this effect in writing is to demonstrate what Plotkin describes above as the power of a critical apparatus, but, as he correctly observes in following Derrida, this leaves writing open to the chance of appropriating to itself the form of power in question. Bodies of knowledge are involved in the veiling-effect of the encryption or the *scrypt* (to use Derrida's term: writing-as-crypt, inscription-as-encryption). But the effect or effort of veiling is doubled as the use of words results in the wearing away of the veil, to paraphrase Derrida, which threatens with use to become transparent. Writing's powers must therefore involve themselves in the reduplicated effort of encryption in order to maintain mastery/mystery. It is this doubling, the veiling and unveiling, which is described by Derrida as the cryptopolitics of writing. The power(s) of/in writing 'results from the necessity of "representing something else"; and it appears at the threshold of representation'.

Derrida concludes by suggesting that there is no *one* power, abstractable or conceptualisable as a general figure of power. There is not one power of writing, and not all writing serves the same purpose, to the same ends, all the time. Similarly, there is no *one* knowledge. There are knowledge*s* and there are power*s*. There is no unity to power or knowledge, and writing, that in which powers are encrypted, reveals *in writing* the 'nature' of power through writing's unveiling of 'what writing can do'. Yet how *can* writing do what it does in its various ways? What might we take as an example of the work of writing? One of Derrida's recurring interests has been explored in . . .

. . . The Battle of the Proper Names . . .

. . . in which is considered the proper name, and our understanding of the proper name, its functions and effects. The proper name is typical of the effect of writing-power, of its ability to veil and unveil. This section and the next are taken from Part II of *Of Grammatology*, 'Nature, Culture, Writing', this text being perhaps Derrida's most well-known work. In the second part of *Grammatology*, the author elaborates a reading of Rousseau's assessment of writing as a 'supplement to speech', to borrow Peggy Kamuf's phrase.[29] The supplement, or supplementarity in language, is that which both 'substitutes' and 'supplants' a term or concept (of which more with regard to the next extract, 'The Originary Metaphor'). Part of Derrida's concern in *Grammatology* is the function (and impropriety) of the proper name, as we will see in the extract below on anthropologist Claude Lévi-Strauss. How might we understand the proper name, as both supplement and an effect of or in writing?

Proper names belong to the possibility of nominal effects in any system of writing, even though proper names supposedly function outside language. As Derek Attridge points out in a comment from his Derrida reader, *Acts of Literature*, within language the proper name is only ever supposed to refer and not to mean.[30] The supposed uniqueness of the proper name is discussed and unveiled in its relation to writing by Geoffrey Bennington in his 'Derridabase':

> [The proper name] . . . is precisely the keystone of logocentrism . . . [yet] what is called by the generic common noun 'proper name' must function . . . in a system of differences: this or that individual rather than another and thus marked by the trace of these others, in a classification . . . We are already *in writing* with proper names.[31]

and

   . . . the so–called proper name is already drawn into a system of differences . . .[32]

The proper name is supposedly absolutely unique and singular. My name is mine, yours is yours and there is no similarity between the two. Yet there is a degree of play in the proper name between singularity and generality, between my name as my name and no one else's, and my name as a proper name which, like all other proper names, only signals me in terms of a nominal difference between me and all others. Thus, as Bennington suggests, the proper name functions as do all words, as does writing, there being the trace of difference in the name.

   Furthermore, for the proper name to have its function, it has to be repeatable in order for it to function through the generation of meaning according to difference. The proper name therefore operates as though it were already *in writing*. In addition, the proper name operates improperly in that it can still operate in the subject's absence or even after the subject's death. My name, which is supposedly properly mine, can be written or uttered after my death, and is not dependent on my being or my presence. The proper name, then, performs in accordance with a semantic function which is not proper to it. Its use erases its propriety, the proper name being improperly marked— outside of its alleged singularity—by a doubleness, a doubling-effect. As are all acts of writing. This doubleness of the proper name marks it with a textual quality, in that it both performs and defines. Hence its exemplarity for Derrida in relation to writing.

   The proper name would not be possible without the possibility of its iterability. To paraphrase Derrida, what goes for the proper name, any proper name, also goes for any literary text. The only universal truth about any text or name is their singularity *and* iterability:[33] 'There is no pure singularity which affirms itself as such without instantly dividing itself . . .'[34] In its paradoxical condition, the proper name accords not to its own uniqueness but to the economy of difference and writing.

   In the light of his reading of Rousseau's understanding of writing as an inescapable evil opposed to the good of the voice (good because it supposedly guarantees self-presence, presence to the self who speaks and to those who hear), Derrida turns to a consideration of an example of use of the proper name in Lévi-Strauss's work. Through the analysis of Lévi-Strauss's thinking on the proper name as used by the Nambikwara tribe, Derrida considers the possible relation between violence and writing, the violence generated in writing. Derrida highlights Lévi-Strauss's insistence on the Nambikwara's apparent lack of writing, and his mis-recognition of the function of proper names within the tribe. Derrida's understanding of the impropriety of the proper name and its relationship to writing is expressed here through the example of the tribe's use of proper names which, for Derrida, unveils a degree of ethnocentric violation *in writing*, in the writing of Lévi-Strauss, which, Derrida claims, is marked by an inheritance of certain gestures from Rousseau's texts concerning anthropology and European culture. Derrida not only connects Lévi-Strauss to Rousseau but also, in his comprehension of the speech/writing binarism, to Saussure, to whose model of structural linguistics Lévi-Strauss's anthropological discourse is indebted. In this, Derrida points to the way in which Lévi-Strauss's conception of writing 'according to a model' limits his comprehension of the Nambikwara people as a people who cannot, do not write, who do not have written language. In contradistinction to this, Derrida raises the very subject of the proper name and the tribal prohibition concerning its use.

As Derrida suggests in this extract, and as we have already signalled, the proper name is not proper at all. Despite the assumption that the proper name supposedly carries in it a 'transparent legibility' as Derrida calls it, nonetheless it erases its own legibility in being used. It erases itself because it functions as a form of singular classification which does not admit to classification as type. The idea of the proper name is, at one and the same time, suggestive of classification, yet it does not function in the way in which it should. The type—proper name—is erased in the singularity of a given proper name. Yet the singularity is only guaranteed in the name's reiteration, as we have suggested.

Derrida highlights Lévi-Strauss's anecdotal recounting of his efforts to have two children give away not only each other's names, but, also, importantly, those of the adults of the tribe. Lévi-Strauss's writing is read by Derrida as a typically ethnocentric violation of the other, driven by the desire to find a 'hidden good Nature' which is governed by the 'dream of a full and immediate presence' and the 'suppression of contradiction and difference', hidden in the secret names. The goodness of the Nambikwara is related to the apparent lack of writing, from the anthropologist's perspective. Yet the proper name only reasserts contradiction, difference and otherness, and Lévi-Strauss's desire to uncover the proper name demonstrates for Derrida an act of penetration which connects writing and violence in a particular fashion.

Just prior to 'The Battle of Proper Names', Derrida asks the question 'why Lévi-Strauss *and* Rousseau?'[35] This has been acknowledged briefly above but, before turning to . . .

... The Originary Metaphor ...

. . . which is taken from the much longer reading of Rousseau's texts on the subject of writing in *Of Grammatology*, we should remind ourselves, as does Derrida in his text, of the importance of Rousseau, a certain Rousseau, certain texts signed by the proper name, Rousseau, for Lévi-Strauss, or, at least, the Lévi-Strauss read by Derrida. Rousseau is, for Lévi-Strauss, the 'founder' of modern anthropology, and it is Rousseau's *Essay on the Origin of Languages*,[36] which connects metaphoricity to human passion, which is so important to Lévi-Strauss's conceptions of speech and writing. It is to Rousseau's *Essay*, then, after Lévi-Strauss, that Derrida turns. In the section entitled 'The Originary Metaphor' (reproduced here, and taken from Part II, Chapter 4 of *Of Grammatology*, 'From/Of the Supplement to the Source: The Theory of Writing'), Derrida gives particular attention to the two chapters of the *Essay*—Chapters 5 and 6—which treat of writing, and which come the closest to offering a Rousseauean theory of writing (albeit an incomplete one).

It is in this where Rousseau 'opposes speech to writing as presence to absence and liberty to servitude'.[37] Writing is a debased form of speech, a necessary evil to be used only in the absence of the speaking subject. Derrida's starting point is to wonder why Rousseau was so troubled by the thought of writing. Writing is, for Rousseau, something which both disturbs and is to be feared. In this he is hardly alone, as Derrida points out here and in other writings (on Plato, for example, in *Dissemination*). The transaction with Rousseau undergone by Derrida is part of his greater understanding of writing as a theme within metaphysical thought and within the history of metaphysics. In Western philosophy, writing as a theme always insistently returns and is, equally, always marginalised, 'debased, lateralized, repressed, displaced' as a theme. Writing is feared, suggests Derrida, because its gesture promises to erase the promise of presence or the guarantee of the self-same supposedly available in and to vocalised language. It is this situation concerning writing that Derrida finds so interesting.

What is of special interest in Rousseau's *Essay* for Derrida is that interest in the so-called 'origins' of language. Rousseau comprehends writing as a degenerate and degenerating form of language. Derrida argues that Rousseau comprehends the origin of writing in language as that point where articulation emerges from a cry or other vocalised sound. As soon as the cry becomes articulation, becomes words, the gesture of writing is already there *in speech*. As writing supplements speech so speech is the supplement to the expression of passion. This movement is marked by the insufficiency of language to express itself 'properly'. Language always signifies something other than itself, its operation or performance is always figural in some manner. The plenitude of the cry—its promise of passion and immediacy, presence and propriety— is forever lost for Rousseau in language which both obliterates or effaces and, simultaneously, substitutes or supplements the passion of the inarticulate sound; writing comes to redouble this process. Given this, given the figurality at the heart of language, all language, even speech is traced by the movement of writing. Speech is nothing other than a form of writing, subordinate to it rather than being writing's antecedent. This is so, Derrida shows us in his engagement with Rousseau, because, Rousseau reveals, despite his model of the degeneration of speech into writing, that language is originarily metaphoric, figural in its articulation.

Yet what we understand as metaphor, by the term metaphor and by metaphoricity in general, is what comes to be questioned elsewhere by Derrida, in his essay 'White Mythology',[38] and in a supplement to that essay entitled . . .

. . . The *Retrait* of Metaphor . . .

. . . which is the next chapter in *The Derrida Reader*. In 'White Mythology', Derrida had concluded that 'Metaphor, therefore, is determined by philosophy as a provisional loss of meaning . . . a certainly inevitable detour . . . within the horizon of literal proper meaning'.[39] Philosophical discourse has, in its history, a problematic recourse to metaphor, given the transport or movement within language which metaphor automatically activates, a movement and displacement of meaning which in effect is similar to that of writing, of *différance*, the trace. Hence the problem of metaphor for philosophy, perceived by Derrida. In the present essay, Derrida considers further the effects, movements and actions of the concept of metaphor within the Heideggerian text, as a specific example of the ambiguous relationship between philosophy and metaphor.

Like 'Scribble', 'The *Retrait* of Metaphor' opens with some apparently straightforward questions, questions which themselves institute what may be comprehended as a metaphorical displacement and detour, to which Derrida returns at the close of the essay. The questions, put in two languages, are:

What is happening, today, with metaphor?
Qu'est-ce qui se passe, aujourd'hui, avec la métaphore?
And without metaphor what is happening?
Et de la métaphore qu'est-ce qui se passe?

These questions treat in particular ways the subject of this essay and I wish to stay with them a while, rather than providing merely a paraphrase of the essay itself.

The first question appears to concern itself simply with the present fate of the metaphor in general, metaphorical language, let us say (as opposed to what? literal language, supposing for the moment that such a thing exists?). The second question adds a certain twist to the question. It is not merely a negative rephrasing but supposes, albeit momentarily, that we can get along without metaphor, that one can ask what is happening without metaphor, what occurs in language were there to be no metaphor. Can one ask what happens, what comes to pass, without recourse to metaphors? Is the question 'what is happening/Qu'est-ce qui se passe?' without metaphor? Is such a thing possible?

You'll notice that the questions are asked in two languages at least, English and French. There is already installed here a certain transferential drift, a slippage between tongues, so to speak, the one, to paraphrase a line from an as-yet-unpublished essay by John Leavey, in the mouth of the other.[40] But that's to speak metaphorically, isn't it? Certainly, we seem to have a problem, if not the issue of translation, from one language to another and even within the same language, on our hands here. The reduplication *of* different languages and the reduplication of the questions *in* different languages, or different tongues, as we said just now, is of great importance to Derrida. These questions are not merely constative utterances, rhetorical questions standing outside the question of metaphor, as though metaphor could be questioned as to its activity in language, from some metalinguistic position, by and in a language which is metaphor free. (Language is not, after all, like petrol; you cannot remove the movement of metaphor as you would subtract lead, hoping to produce an uncontaminated voice.) The questions themselves certainly perform a movement, a movement which is, moreover, double, occurring not only between what we call languages or tongues, but within each language. There is, as Derrida's opening paragraphs indicate and consider, the double question of translation and transport, translation *as* transport and vice versa (but that's to use a metaphor surely, and to double its activity? perhaps it is a question of being economical, of the economy of metaphor).

Paying close attention to these questions, particularly those given in French, it might be suggested that, in a certain manner, the entire subject of 'The *Retrait* of Metaphor' is contained in the movement within French of the verb(s) *passer/se passer*, the meaning(s) of which is (are) never stable or stationary from the outset, but which shuttle(s) back and forth, determined only by a virtually inexhaustible range of contexts. The reflexive form *se passer* is employed in the questions, but the play of *passer*—the give and take or torsion if you like, to employ somewhat economic or mechanistic metaphors—is still very much in operation. Possible translations might include:

> to cross, to go or get through, to pass or go past, to pass on, to take or to sit (an exam), to spend (time), to skip or pass over, to go over something or to place something, to play or to show, to pass or run by, to pass or go through, to come before or after, to leave or to move from, to be handed down between generations, to be promoted, to go on or into, to die (to pass away), to fade, to happen, to take place, to go, to do without, to pass between or exchange . . .

The various movements of *se passer* and *passer* can be read as effectively performing for us Derrida's comprehension of writing, of the difference at work within meaning. Were we to spend time substituting the various translations I've offered here for the obvious 'happening' in the two questions which begin 'The *Retrait* of Metaphor', we might see just how language 'skids' or 'slides', and why Derrida, in having recourse to various figures or metaphors pertaining to movement, journeying, transport in his opening statements, is not merely playing word-games (if in all seriousness he could even be accused of doing so); instead he may be read as demonstrating economically the metaphorical ebb and flow of language, where the metaphor hides itself in the very movement of the discourse, while returning repeatedly in that same movement, hiding and disclosing itself at the same time, withdrawing and returning simultaneously.

When Derrida describes his discourse as a 'floating vehicle' in the opening pages, he is not only employing a more or less suitable metaphor. He is also pointing up what we need to comprehend about language in general: that all language is more or less metaphorical or quasi-metaphorical (never quite metaphorical and never quite not- or a-metaphorical). This is enacted by Derrida in the passage or changing places of subjects and terms in a constant circulation (as we would say of blood or, equally, traffic) or transport (as again we might say of traffic or the cartridge in which we place a CD); all of which is performed *in passing, en passant*, in that/those verb(s) (*se*) *passer*, and elsewhere (in a different manner) in the title and throughout the essay in the word *retrait/re-trait*, which has the dominant meaning of withdrawal, but also carries in it its own *trait* or mark and also intimates the *return*—and the doubling—of the *trait*. That *re-* marks economically the withdrawal of the withdrawal, the veiling and unveiling of the *trait*, as the double (re)marking of fraying, splitting, division and disjunction, and, at the same time, if not connection, then the mark as border between places which makes possible the transport as that which *takes place* within the (withdrawal of the) *trait*.

Of course it is not Derrida only who 'performs' such movements. To suggest this is to miss one of the points that he is making. The verb *passer* is always already available for transference; the transport—in two directions at once—is always already in operation in both *trait* and *retrait*, in the *trait* in *retrait*. We are already underway before we've begun, and, as Derrida suggests, in changing tack and changing metaphors, 'we are not in metaphor like a pilot in his ship'. The speaking subject does not control, command or master the metaphorical drift in language. This drift or slippage is always already, if not *in place*, then what *takes place* as the condition of writing, of *différance*. This is apprehended in the verb(s) (*se*) *passer*. We have no control over the drifting, so we may as well give ourselves over to it.

In his own statements and questions, Derrida points to the intractable problem of discussing, discoursing on, metaphor without being able to stand outside (metaphorically passing) the domain of the metaphorical. At the same time however, the very pervasiveness of metaphoricity as a figure for figurality in all language hides itself within language. (In understanding this it should be comprehended how even what we take to be the most literal language is never a form of direct representation; language is never mimetic). Metaphor retreats. It is simultaneously everywhere, overflowing all the limits of the discussion of what language does while it is nowhere immediately visible, leaving only its mark in its withdrawal.

However, this is only to allow ourselves a detour from the specific example of the essay and its consideration of metaphor in the Heideggerian text, even if this detour does seem to be dictated by the very same essay. Derrida turns his focus onto the use-value of metaphor, working through a family of words which incorporate notions of economics, the house, usury, wear-and-tear, and in so doing turns our attention to the relatively few mentions of metaphor in Heidegger's writing. He does so, first, in order to respond critically to Paul Ricoeur's reading of 'White Mythology'[41] and, second, to expand on the issue of metaphor and metaphoricity as it pertains to the philosophical questioning of Being, with specific reference to the Heideggerian text.

The links between metaphor, metaphysics and the concept of Being are explored through the polyvalence of *retrait* which is neither properly literal nor metaphorical, as Derrida demonstrates. Derrida shows how in the Heideggerian text that which is termed metaphysics corresponds with this so-called 'withdrawal of Being'. Metaphor, defined as a metaphysical concept, corresponds to a withdrawal of Being. Yet Being is not a metaphor, for it does not designate a 'determinate being'. Being is quasi-metaphorical in that not only does it not designate some being, some existent, but also it is never revealed as such but only through indirect tropes, through figures such as will, work or subjectity. Being has already withdrawn (quasi-)metaphorically. And as Derrida suggests, the phrase 'Withdrawal of Being' 'cannot have a literal and proper sense to the extent that Being is not something'. Again, to quote Derrida, 'Being being nothing, not being a being, it cannot be expressed or named *more metaphorico*'. What complicates the withdrawal, the *retrait* is the return of which we have already spoken: 'as this withdrawal of the metaphoric leaves no place free for a discourse of the proper or the literal',

> it will have at the same time the sense of a re-fold (*re-pli*), of what retreats like a wave on the shoreline, and of a re-turn (*re-tour*), of the overcharging repetition of a supplementary trait, of yet another metaphor, of a double trait (*re-trait*) of metaphor, a discourse whose rhetorical border is no longer determinable according to a simple and indivisible line, according to a linear and indecomposable trait. This trait has the internal multiplicity, the folded-refolded structure of the double trait (*re-trait*).

The simultaneous, double withdrawal and return, the doubling gesture suggests for Derrida that the *trait* is never a secondary effect. It does not emerge as the *trait* of some thing or some subject but is what in splitting, disjointing and bordering 'brings together and separates'. This withdrawal is neither literal nor figurative, because withdrawal is 'neither thing, nor being, nor meaning'.

Thus Derrida concludes in the final paragraph of the essay the *retrait* is always *retraits*, always plural within itself, always already marked by division *and* assembly. In closing he returns to where he had begun, in passing, multiplying the figures of passage and happening, playing on the play in (*se*) *passer*, between *le passe* and *pas*, the path and the step which is not, playing on that which passes by the path, that which causes us to take the detour. In doing so, he marks the return to a certain opening gambit, while inscribing all the while the division and the difference in language/*in language*. For, as he states at one point, and as the language of the essay plays out, 'there is always more than one language in language'. As if to give itself over to this understanding more completely, 'The *Retrait* of Metaphor' returns in/to two languages at least.

Which performs a double opening, dispelling the idea of any simple, single location from which to begin. This is also one of the concerns in . . .

. . . The Time before First . . .

                . . . in which, albeit in a very different manner, it becomes apparent that there is no absolute starting point. The idea of a beginning is, pure and simple, a fiction, a myth, or a 'make-believe', as George Eliot says at the outset of her last novel, *Daniel Deronda*.[42] (This is, by the way, yet another reason why this 'introduction' presents me with such problems. Knowing this, how can I continue to begin—or even to begin to continue?) Narratives conventionally require (the make-believe of) some starting point as a kind of programmed excuse, although even the most conventional novel always begins by jumping into the midst of a range of details concerning the narrative's principal protagonist, some prior problem or event pertaining to the narrative as it stands, or the context which allows the narrative to unfold as it does. Beginnings—an introduction for example—involve retrospective considerations after the event. They are arbitrary incisions, cuts into the text, which lead back to a point of departure or otherwise fold back the text for the reader, folding the text onto itself.

Of all the chapters and extracts reprinted in *The Derrida Reader*, 'The Time before First' perhaps requires the most patient rereading, as Derrida plunges us into the middle of the text of French novelist Philippe Sollers, particularly the novel *Nombres*, but also *Drame* and *Le Parc*, among a range of other texts which are acknowledged briefly.[43] As in the essays 'Qual Quelle' and '*Khōra*',

Derrida here considers questions of form and undecidability, along with the issue of the myth of origins and starting points, which the writing of Sollers effectively deconstructs.

This essay is both aptly and ironically titled, offering an ironic folding on Derrida's part. There is both a doubling and a distancing at work. A reiterative structure is put in place in the book's form, which may be understood as having either three principal sections or two, with an 'interlude'. 'The Time before First' 'begins' or 'introduces' the final section of *Dissemination*. The first section of *Dissemination* is entitled 'Plato's Pharmacy'. The middle section is 'The Double Session', an equally apt, alternative title for *Dissemination*'s disparate, yet interwoven parts. In the first part, Derrida elaborates on the double figure of the *pharmakon* in the text of Plato. The pharmakon is that substance which is, doubly, both poison *and* cure. It thus obeys the double logic of the trace which confounds single identity and self-presence. The final part of *Dissemination*—which 'begins' with 'The Time before First'—is entitled 'Dissemination'. The title of the text is itself doubled, being folded into the body of the text. The title displaced, so also is the identity of the book.[44] This final section, 'Dissemination', is itself divided into two sections, numbered I and II, as are both previous sections. These may well be considered as a pair of vertical columns standing side by side, as much as they might be understood to be sequential, readable horizontally from left to right, as is the custom in the history of reading in the West, among European languages at least. This point pertains to Sollers' *Nombres*, with which 'The Time before First' interests itself and into which it folds its text, even as it finds itself folded, unfolded and refolded by that text (but we will return to Sollers). The two sections or columns are subsequently subdivided numerically, with accompanying titles, as Derrida explores the structures and concerns of *Nombres*.

Derrida's text appears to be stitched together, woven through with a number of slices taken from Sollers' *Nombres* as well as from other texts. These citations and grafts are more or less proper or improper, according to the law of citation, some being placed in quotation marks while others stand free of all diacritical marks. This, once again, may be read as echoing that which Derrida shows to be occurring in Sollers' text, where *Nombres* picks up on 'themes' or even lines from *Drame* and *Le Parc* (the text of Sollers has what Derrida describes as a thematic matrix). As Derrida suggests almost at the start of 'The Time before First', everything 'begins' by a certain repetition or reiteration. Thus the beginning is never a beginning as such. Structurally, it appears as a starting point, but it is also a continuation as well as a return, always already destined to duplication and displacement. As Derrida later reminds us in the essay, *Nombres* does not in fact 'begin' at all, but continues, the 'first' sentence of the novel opening with a triple dot ellipsis and a sentence already in process.

'The Time before First' demonstrates Derrida's comprehension of textual complexity through the most particular enumeration of writing's performance in the textual theatre (a figure used by Sollers in both *Drame* and *Le Parc*, and which finds itself taken up in 'The Time before First'). Simultaneously, it is clear from observing Derrida proceed that the attention of the reader must be given over to the details of the text in question in such a manner that no method or general theory of reading may be extracted from this textual engagement. This can be shown furthermore because everything on which Derrida comments is to be found already there in Sollers' writing. This does not mean in any simple sense that the writing of Philippe Sollers is *the* source (or even *a* source) for Derrida's comprehension of writing and text, any more than it would be accurate to suggest as a source Paul Valéry, Plato, Jean-Jacques Rousseau or Sigmund Freud. Instead, writing and text have histories within western culture which both Sollers and Derrida explore, each in their own manner, both men giving attention to that which contradicts, disturbs or disrupts the dominant comprehension of the work of writing as being mimetically reproductive.

Hence the citation or epigraph, the text before the text, which in itself is an allusion to an equally complex textual matrix, from *Through the Looking-Glass and What Alice Found There*.[45] Derrida's citation of this has not only to do with that brief mention of the park which you'll read there and which acts as a chance citation of or reference to one of Sollers' novels. Carroll's novel is also, like the work of Sollers, particularly interested in issues of spatiality and geometry. It is concerned also not with depth and character psychology (traits of the novel which Sollers actively works to abandon and rid narrative of[46]), but, instead, with planes, surfaces, arithmetico-graphic relationships, where spatial concerns displace temporal or psychological imperatives. Derrida's citation of Carroll points up, albeit obliquely, a certain interest among a number of Parisian intellectuals during the 1960s, particularly those associated with *Tel Quel*. This interest has to do with the critical investigation of the history and politics of mimesis in western thought as that politics pervades aesthetic thinking in both philosophy and literature, from Plato and Aristotle to the present day. Sollers' writing reveals strategic uses of indeterminacy and geometry as part of the critical response to the dominant politics of mimesis, and as part of what Malcolm Pollard calls 'a questioning of representation . . . established at the centre of the writing practice'.[47]

We may question the figure of the centre as a metaphor somewhat, if not entirely, inappropriate for discussing Sollers' writing practice, for, as Derrida shows in 'The Time before First', if there is no 'beginning' as such then, certainly, there is no centre to the textual matrix either. There is only and always a complex geometrical relationship at work. However, it is not to be denied that Derrida's interest overlaps with Pollard's where it is a case of showing how in *Nombres* the 'western dynamic of writing [the horizontal, linear movement from left to right] . . . can be questioned internally' through the performance of/in writing.[48] This internal questioning is also effected through Sollers' use of numbering, as well as in the shifts from horizontal to vertical textuality, the graphic disruptions caused by punctuation and other silent marks, and the use of Chinese ideograms. Derrida's own attention to the vertical and the vestige is signalled in the opening two paragraphs, and begins his own consideration of Sollers' performative critique of the conventional mimetic uses of writing. As Pollard suggests, the interruption of linear, horizontal narrative continuity effected by the insertion of verticality into the text, causes the disruption—we might perhaps call this the deconstruction—of 'the representational function of language'.[49]

Sollers, then, can be understood through Derrida's essay, as concentrating on writing as trace, as *trait* (a word which appears quite often in *Nombres*), rather than as a mimetic tool. Writing is for Sollers, as it is for Derrida, a figure in excess of representational and psychological modes of production which in the history of western thought have tended towards the production of the illusion of presence and identity rooted in the self-same. Derrida pursues the multiplying and disseminating effects of what he calls Sollers' 'arithmetical theater' by giving his attention to the numerical structure of *Nombres* and to Sollers' reiteration of his own texts within the square-like structure which is produced by the numbers. For the text of *Nombres* is 'made up of one hundred sequences which are grouped together in fours'.[50] The four groups (1–3 written in the past tense, 4 written in the present tense) number the four sides of the geometrical figure and the stage, as well as numbering the axes and vertical columns, all of which are designed to disrupt linearity and representation, foregrounding the graphic and writing in general over the voice, the subject and the conventional transparency assumed of narrative. Through such devices, Derrida sees Sollers' text as expropriating the proper, which writing makes possible through the constant disseminating return of the other, text, *différance*. The text folds and unfolds, says Derrida, in an 'undecidable process of opening/closing that reforms itself without letup', where there is 'no secret' no depth of 'beyond', no simple *a priori* before to which *Nombres* refers, and where 'everything happens in the intertext' or the 'between', as we suggested earlier. For Derrida, all notion of the prior, the *pre-text*, is dissolved because in Sollers' text writing performs the division and multiplication beyond any notion of polysemy that is the condition of writing in general. Sollers' text exemplifies the differential dissemination always already in writing.

The 'always already', the wholly other which haunts our perception and with which we become obsessed is one concern for Derrida in the two extracts . . .

... from *Specters of Marx* ...

                                    ... which are included in *The Derrida*
Reader. They are taken from Chapters Four and Five, 'in the name of the
revolution, the double barricade (impure "impure impure history of ghosts")'
and 'apparition of the inapparent: the phenomenological "conjuring trick"'.
To be precise, I have chosen the beginning of Chapter Four and the end of
Chapter Five, as Derrida considers, across both chapters, the motifs or tropes
of the spectre, the spectral and spirit in the text of Karl Marx (across *The
Eighteenth Brumaire of Louis Bonaparte*, *The German Ideology*, and *Capital*, in these
extracts) and the spectres of Marx which haunt the twentieth century. The
original presentation of this text was as a lecture given over two days in 1993
at the University of California, Riverside, at an international colloquium on
the possible futures of/for Marxism, entitled 'Whither Marxism?'

    The inaugural gesture on Derrida's part is one of return, response, recircling
and revolution, which movement dictates the rhythms of the passage included
from Chapter Four. The concluding movement is one of an opening, Derrida
still responding as he opens himself, his text, his readers and Marx onto the
future returns of the spectres of Marx, anticipating the unanticipatable and
awaiting a wholly other, unpredictable spectral return; hence the use of the
word *revenant* throughout these extracts, signifying in French (and very old
English) a certain ghost who only ever arrives in the act of returning, making
the movement of a revolution. This opening on to the spectral other to-come
is remarked in the 'context' of acknowledging the necessity of a certain messianic structure,[51] already discernible in the text of Marx as Derrida argues in
the second fragment, without which messianic spirit neither the Marxist nor
the Derridean text in their hope for justice 'have a ghost of a chance', as John
Caputo quips.[52] Having explored the relationship of the spectral to Marx's
analysis of the commodity as fetish, Derrida moves to consider the spectres
to come in the context of certain messianic structures in the Marxian text.
The fetish is but one dematerialised, disembodied spectral effect of a market
economy; in being so, it is understandable by Derrida as having a relation 'to
the ideological and the religious'. Having drawn out this spectral logic, Derrida
then considers the return of religion today, observing connections between
this return and the proliferation of spectres through tele-technology.

    The first extract appears to begin with a certain return of Marx, an antic-
ipated rather than an actual return, but a haunting nonetheless: Marx, as
spectre, as *revenant*, perhaps even as spirit, the return of which—the spectre is
not a 'who', not a person, as Derrida cautions us to remember at the conclusion of Chapter Five by invoking the words of Marcellus from *Hamlet*[53]—
Derrida observes disturbing certain political thinkers and commentators in
the recent past, following the dissolution of the Soviet Union, and prior to

the conference on Marxism. These commentators are seeking to 'conjure away' this spectre or spirit (and the two are not equivalent, as Derrida shows elsewhere in *Specters*).[54] Indeed, this clamour, this jubilation and celebration at the so-called 'death of Marxism' or 'death of communism' is precisely what gives Derrida pause. The volume and the general air of triumphalism should make us suspicious of all the fuss. For, Derrida's argument goes, if something is dead, why be disturbed by it? Why draw the attention of so many to a corpse, and why make such a noise about it?

This is merely the beginning of Derrida's complicating performance. In proposing to surrender himself to the return of the plural specter(s) of Marx and their indelible, haunting *traits*—the marks of Marx, we might suggest, playfully, or the indelible Marx—Derrida observes the contradictory gesture of attempted exorcism on the part of some at the same moment when the death of Marxism is supposedly celebrated. In the face of this, Derrida insists that 'the dead must be able to work'. In the opening of the lecture, Derrida resuscitates the idea of the work of mourning, which is not, as he suggests, merely one type of work among others, but 'work itself'. Already discussed in *Memoirs for Paul de Man*, the work of mourning involves a delicate balance of remembering/forgetting. Derrida points to the necessity of a certain continuation which is not a domestication. Those of us who are alive have to work to remember the spirit of past thinkers, such as Marx, to carry the *trait* of this thought within our thinking as a necessary condition of the work of mourning. Yet we must, simultaneously, strive to acknowledge and respect the alterity of the *revenant*. This work of mourning, considered in the second of the two extracts presented here in relation to a certain messianic structure in *Capital*, in which the spectres of the dead come to work on us, is the necessary, ineluctable ethical response to the *revenant* on our part. It is a response to the 'injunction of justice' which is owed to whoever is not living, those who no longer live and those who do not yet live.

Clearly the notion of the spectral is complicated by Derrida, who sees the spectral not only as the *trait* or manifestation of those who have already died, but also as a certain spirit of the other yet to come. This complicates the notion of the ghostly as merely the trace of a simple *a priori* existent. Indeed, Derrida insists on the temporal disjointing which occurs as an effect of the spectral. 'Untimeliness and disadjustment': spectrality, properly thought, is, quite literally, 'anachronistic', not of this, or any other, time. But, as Derrida demonstrates, this does not mean that it is simply from a past, discernible as a moment in time. The time—or, more correctly, *times*—of the spectre is always already multiple. Spectrality thus disrupts all conventional notions of time and presence or, even, time conceived according to the logic of the binarism, presence/absence. For, as Derrida suggests, 'the *revenant* may already mark the promised return of the specter of living being'. In considering the return and the promise of the return as the displacement of a simple, linear and progressive temporal structure (adhered to by those who dance on the grave of Marxism), Derrida also implicates the very notion of 'revolution' which, as its name suggests never happens only for the first time but also, always, figures a certain return of, response to, and inheritance from the dead.

This temporal displacement is one figure of a general displacement figured in Derrida's writing and in the title *Specters of Marx*, which, as Derrida suggests in the first extract, points not only to those Marxist and Marxian spectres who haunt both the twentieth century and the commentaries of recent political commentators, but also to the spectres which haunt Marx himself and which are to be found everywhere in his writing. (The first line of the *Manifesto of the Communist Party* is only the most obvious example.) Once again, as in other texts by Derrida, the movement of displacement and multiplication is at work here. What Derrida develops through his analysis of the figures of spectres and spirit in the text of Marx is a *spectropolitics* (which is also a *spectropoetics*) as a counter-discourse which serves to allow the spirit of Marx to return, while countering those who claim Marxism is simply dead.

One of the points made by Derrida is that 'Marxism' has left a decentring *trait* in humanist thought in the twentieth century, a *trait* which, as is proper to the trace which is also a cut, has opened an aporia in that thought, where the spectre is discerned as being '*of the spirit*'. This is merely one effect of the spectres of Marx. (This is not an isolated critical gesture. Elsewhere, Derrida also criticises humanism and its possible effects: in 'Economimesis', the essay which concludes this reader, and in *Of Spirit* and 'White Mythology: Metaphor in the Text of Philosophy'.[55]) The spectres leave a number of traces in our century, haunting particular systems of thought and institutional manifestations. Another example of this is demonstrated through Derrida's consideration of the idea of the 'party', along with the suggestion that we cannot analyse what is happening to the idea of the state today without considering 'the Marxist inheritance' as part of 'a reflection on what will become of Marxism tomorrow', as Derrida puts it. Spectres return frequently, and it is frequency which determines our comprehension of the spectral.

Of course, we don't simply *see* the spectre; we feel ourselves to be under its surveillance, to be observed by the other, to be subject to its gaze. The issue of sight occupies Derrida in another context in . . .

. . . Memoirs of the Blind . . .

. . . which provides the two extracts which comprise Chapter 7. *Memoirs of the Blind* was written by Derrida to accompany —and supplement—an exhibition of the same title held at the Louvre (October 1990–January 1991), the first in a series of exhibitions at the Louvre entitled 'Taking Sides'. Derrida was invited to choose and organise the drawings and paintings for the exhibition and write the accompanying discourse. Derrida's essay concentrates on issues of blindness, memory, writing, (self-) representation and drawing. The extracts given here consider the possible relationship between blindness and writing, blindness and drawing, blindness and memory (in each of these formulations we should perhaps invert the terms and substitute *and* with *as*, in order to initiate a preliminary and elliptical understanding of Derrida's essay). The essay *Memoirs of the Blind* (the title is also translatable from French as *Memories of the Blind*) suggests from its very title a link between autobiographical writing *as* blind and memory itself as that which is also blind: memory does not see, it recalls to itself that which is not present, that which is not representable to perception, that which cannot be put on view. This essay and catalogue is, then, the blind recall of that which we can no longer see, the exhibition.

The first extract begins with an autobiographical reminiscence in which Derrida (responding to an interlocutor we cannot see) recalls the invitation to curate the exhibition while remembering also a temporary viral illness which left one side of his face paralysed, his sight on that side affected by the disease. Derrida uses the memoir/memory to suggest a link between blindness and writing and the difference between sight and knowledge which seem to be connected (one says 'I see' when in fact one means 'I understand', sight in this case being the metaphor for the blind act of comprehension). In considering the relation of writing to memory, writing in this case being the inscription of memory as a blind act, from a place of blindness, Derrida highlights his text briefly with a number of authors who relied on memory because of their blindness. Pairing Homer with Joyce, and Milton with Borges, Derrida gestures towards the theme of sight and blindness in *Finnegans Wake*—drawing our attention, we might say, by the merest sketch of a reading—in order to turn to a passage from Jorge Luis Borges' text, 'Blindness', which also invokes Homer and Joyce, among others.

From this consideration of writers, writing, memory and blindness, Derrida then directs our gaze back to the beginning of the passage from Borges. It is Oscar Wilde, not Homer, with whom we began, and it is towards painting, specifically the painting of Dorian Gray in *The Picture of Dorian Gray*, and towards the act of writing on painting that Derrida wishes to direct us. Linking this image to one from the work of Edgar Allan Poe, Derrida considers portraiture, or self-portraiture to be exact. As the example from *Dorian Gray* demonstrates, the subject gazes upon an image of himself while the image presents the figure of a spectator gazing back on the gazing spectator who becomes the subject of the gaze. What interests Derrida here is not so much the issue of painting—indeed he is at pains to point out on a couple of occasions that he is concerned principally with drawing, not with painting at all—but the figure of sight turned on oneself, that double movement traced within the *trait* of drawing, and within the different meanings of *aspect / aspectus*. (Derrida discusses 'three types of powerlessness', the first two of which are included in the second fragment from *Memoirs of the Blind*.) *Aspectus* is, Derrida informs us, that which is both gaze and object of the gaze, spectator and spectacle. This doubleness is, in drawing, also a disjunction or break, a hete-rogeneity as Derrida puts it, between the drawing *trait* and that which is represented in drawing.

In considering the *trait*, Derrida turns to the figure of *anamnesis*, recalling to the mind (though not to the mind's eye; let's not confuse matters by a figure of speech). Memory is not sight, a memory is not a seeing, any more than is a knowing. Drawing, and, specifically, representational or supposedly mimetic drawing, Derrida argues, proceeds not directly from the model, not from perception or vision of the model, but from the indirect and blind access of memory. Drawing is always a drawing—and a writing of sorts—from the memory of the model. The drawing *trait* is the memory of the model or object, it is the mark or trace of *anamnesis*, and never simply a representation. There is an irreducible gap between the *trait* and the representation. Memory makes possible the *trait*, even as the *trait* is the *trait* of memory. Memory is both invisible *and* blind: it does not see and cannot be seen.

From these considerations, Derrida turns to an essay by Charles Baudelaire, in which the poet concerns himself with the issue of 'representative drawing' as an example of what has been stated. Through quotation, Derrida demon-strates how Baudelaire understands drawing as an art which subordinates per-ception to the order of memory. Representative drawing is thus understood as a form of writing, a writing written out of (the) blind(ness of) memory, rather than visual perception. The *trait* of the drawing is blind and free from the tyranny of the ever-present present of perception, of what appears as presence to visual perception in the moment of the present. This is itself given the lie, says Derrida in reading Baudelaire, in the wink of an eye, that move-ment which divides the moment from itself. The *trait* is that movement or mark which announces *différance* within identity, within presence, and which installs the heterogeneous, spacing and deferral within identification.

From here, Derrida is brought to remember briefly Rousseau's *Essay on the Origin of Language*, and, marginally, his own *Of Grammatology* (see above), before turning in a deft movement to Maurice Merleau-Ponty's phenomenological essay, *The Visible and the Invisible*.[56] All of which leads to the consideration of the *retrait* of the *trait*. (*Retrait*, to recall the discussion of 'The *Retrait* of Metaphor' above, can mean withdrawing or retreat but clearly is marked by *trait*, by the *trait* within *retrait*, while also implying the return of the *trait*.) Derrida pauses to ask, what occurs not in the tracing of the *trait* but after it has been marked, after the tracing of the *trait* begins to withdraw? The *trait* is a mark of divisibility and doubling. Neither inside nor outside, a figure and that which

is not the figure, the *trait* is still that which makes impossible pure identification. The *trait* retreats once it is withdrawn because it never refers to itself in
being drawn, but only to that which it divides and marks. The *trait* signals
towards that which surrounds the *trait*. Its tracing makes the surroundings
appear and it disappears, becomes invisible in gesturing towards what never
belongs to or is part of the *trait*.

Drawing is thus comprehensible, in the movement of difference and divisibility, doubling and disjointing, as a writing. The *trait* of drawing is concerned
with borders, margins, limits and, simultaneously, exceeding those very same
limits, leaving in its wake, its retreat, an excess. It is with such marginal effects
and the question of borderlines that Derrida concerns himself in the next
chapter of this reader . . .

. . . Logic of the Living Feminine . . .

. . . which is taken from the first part of
Otobiographies, a reading of Nietzsche and the proper name. The borderline
and its divisible *trait* is once more that which interests Derrida, the 'divisible
borderline [which] traverses two "bodies", the corpus and the body', or the
work and the writer, in this case philosophy and biography. In this opening
section, we read Derrida taking an interest in marginal moments from
Nietzsche's *Ecce Homo*,[57] the first paragraph of the preface and a brief exergue
inserted between the preface and the 'beginning' of the book. Examining
these passages, Derrida gives himself over to an investigation of what he calls
the dynamic border between work and life through an understanding of the
borderline mark of the proper name or signature, which as he suggests in
reading Nietzsche, is not reducible to the biological self. Nietzsche is, for
Derrida, that signature which most complicates the supposed division
between life and work.

The identity given to Nietzsche by his readers, reflected on by Nietzsche
in the passages in question (as well as in the writing of *Ecce Homo*), is analogous,
suggests Derrida, to a line of credit extended to Nietzsche by himself because
of the imposture of his signature, taken to signify not just the biological
person but the works which are signed by that name. The consequences for
'Nietzsche' after his death are an extension of this credit, as the name returns.
After Nietzsche's work then, after Nietzsche (which two are not necessarily
the same, though never absolutely distinct), we can no longer easily suppose
the distinction between biography and philosophy while, at the same time, we
can also no longer simply assume the location of some origin or source for
philosophy in the life of the philosopher, and this occurs because of the
complications installed by Nietzsche's own considerations of who he is.

Whenever one seeks to consider or determine starting points, origins or sources, one is seeking to determine and fix in place the movement of the border between identities and identifications, that very movement which Nietzsche in his writing plays up and plays with.

From here Derrida considers the problematic of dating an event. Dating is also a signing, says Derrida. It is that gesture which seeks to fix or figure the singular as singular and unique, yet which is reiterable, the credit of the signature extended infinitely by the eternal return. This is seen, as Derrida points out, in Nietzsche narrating to himself his life within his own text, always already receiving himself as the gift to himself. Only ever returning through the I of the narrative, as another Nietzsche, Nietzsche no longer simply exists. No moment is ever static or present simply. It is only an 'instantly vanishing limit' which returns constantly. The moment the author signs always slips away, the signature being the instance or example of this impossible moment, never present as such yet always to come and always already having been: to return again and again, already dead and always living. The date and the signature therefore obey a double logic. Both prefigure one's own death, inscribing the fact of one's death in the possibility of their iterability. However, each also figures a living on, figured in Nietzsche's writing through the double figures of what Derrida calls 'the dead man and the living feminine'. It is in the signature that there is (counter)signed this double logic.

We move from the signature to another concern of Derrida's, the source or origin in . . .

. . . Qual Quelle: Valéry's Sources . . .

. . . in which we find Derrida foregrounding the myth or narrative of sources, points of origin, genesis or departure, once more. He does so through responding to the issue of the source and its relationship to identity or consciousness in the writings of Paul Valéry, in which, Derrida insists, source is found to be a profoundly textual affair; it is a question yet again of writing as the singular example of Valéry's text gives us to comprehend. As Derrida makes clear through this singular example, there is never access to the source as such, it is always already irretrievably cut off from any reflection on or return to it. Any thought of the source can only ever be a copy of that which is not available. Consciousness, similarly, before any reflection, phenomenological or otherwise, remains inaccessible, even to itself (which, as Derrida suggests, is so remote, so cut off as to be almost nothing, practically non-consciousness). As with *khōra* which follows, the concern here would appear to be with the formless form, that which only comes to be possible and to be known through the shaping that occurs in what we will, no doubt too hastily, call 'context', as well as on reflection as this impossible possibility assumes the guise of a singular example already detached and at a distance from what we might otherwise call a 'source'.

But let's pause briefly at the title, or the first part at least (for Derrida will explain why there is never *a* source but only the thought of *sources*, plural, already multiplied and divided). There is installed in the curious title 'Qual Quelle' the disseminative movement of writing, the endless rhythm of *dif-férance*, to which Alan Bass, the translator of this essay, helpfully alerts the reader in note 1, referring also to Derrida's own note (n. 12). We would draw the reader's attention to these notes and the issues raised elliptically through the title, in order that the reader might comprehend how, contrary to what some of Derrida's detractors have said, the author does not indulge in mere punning or word play for its own sake. Where Derrida does activate the unde-cidability (which to a certain degree is always already at work) within the semantics of a given word or phrase (or even his own name), this always has at least two purposes: (a) to make available to his readers at the levels of writing and text the contradictory, paradoxical and undecidable within con-cepts, philosophemes, systems of thought, discourses, institutions, structures and even ideologies (as more recent publications have made clear[58]); and (b) to demonstrate how writing always already performs its own 'deconstruction' (using this word with all possible caution); how pure, full meaning (presence or identity) is never simply available to us as such, but is always at the most apparently 'fundamental' levels traced abyssally by the performance of *différance* and—to use a phrase of Derrida's from 'Qual Quelle' to which we will return presently—'the difference of the other'.

Were Derrida merely interested in the pun, in word games, the title of any given essay, chapter, lecture or book would soon exhaust itself and its interest for the reader in facile polyvocality. However, as Alan Bass points out in that first footnote, the effects of the performative trace are to be found across languages, within a single language—whether this happens to be what I call 'my' language, English, Derrida's language, 'French', or Plato's Greek—and across this lecture of Derrida's. Bass also comments on a similar disseminative effect caused by undecidability in n. 7, in which it is pointed out that the French phrase *point d'eau* is both incalculable in its effects and untranslatable (even within French) because it means both 'source of water' and 'no water at all'. Derrida puts the double meaning to work throughout 'Qual Quelle' as part of the tracery of watery tropes, figures, metaphors, in relation to the subject of the source. As the French *source* makes plain in its double meaning (it can be translated as either origin or spring, fountain), contradictory movement is always already found. Even when what we think we understand as a 'context' appears to determine meaning, the difference of trace of the other is still at work, haunting meaning. Thus it is to *source*, as it concerns identity or consciousness in the text of Paul Valéry, that Derrida turns the closest attention in all that term's turns, returns, detours and displacements.

Beginning at the beginning we note therefore that the beginning is marked multiply by a certain division already installed in the beginning. No simple bifurcation, these divisions are themselves multiple, and are remarked not least in the French *marque* which remarks immediately both the singular and the plural, as does (as do) *multiplie*, which here is rendered as 'multiply (multiplies)', but which, in French, is already multiplied within itself / itselves. This performative gesture of Derrida's circulates, flows and reiterates or comes to the surface throughout the movement of the essay. This is inscribed nowhere more so, and as a kind of differential punctuation, picked up by Derrida from Valéry, in that very sign—I—which supposedly remarks and signs (guarantees?) one's presence to oneself, one's identity or consciousness reflected upon and (re)turned back as though the detour of the turn had never occurred. Yet 'I' operates as a form of marker or trace of *différance* within identity everytime it is uttered or inscribed. The movement of 'I' in the inscription or articulation traces the return and so amputates the act of inscription—inscription cuts itself off from itself—from the source which we mistakenly recognise in the return. This remarking of 'I', which installs a distance from the self, dividing the (idea of the) source from the source, also multiplies one's 'self'. Identity is not a self-reflexive and self-fulfilling essence, but is of the order of writing: a discursive, textual construct. If there is a pure 'I', as 'source of all presence' as Derrida puts it, this is so removed as to be inaccessible and to have no meaning as such. The self is never simply that; it is, says Derrida, always 'multiplied or divided by the difference of the other'.

And we should pause at this phrase, 'the difference of the other'. This remark seems to be particularly considered on Derrida's part, or at least we might imagine it so, especially if we recall its French counterpart ('original' seems hardly appropriate, given all that has been said so far to counteract any belief in the idea of origins), which reads: *la différence de l'autre*. In this there is readable partly, and albeit in somewhat submerged fashion, the concerns of 'Qual Quelle', Derrida's interests, that *inter-est* precisely *between* form and content, *between* text and context or text and concept, *between* literature and philosophy. Implicated in this phrasing there is discernible the flow of the essay, with its strategic, watery troping (over)flow, in which Derrida goes with the flow, sometimes submerged, sometimes on the surface, more or less, precisely to avoid the solidification of the response to Valéry into a thematics of the source. There is in the French a multiplication and a division at the level of homophony. The sentence (re)sounds particularly within itself as a performance of division and the other within, the trace of division, as we hear in *la différence de l'autre* the following: *la différence de l'eau*—the difference of water. This is not to say that water is difference; such a definition would be nonsensical inasmuch as, similarly to definitions which aim at pinning down 'deconstruction', any definition of difference would miss the point. Yet there is in the movement of writing that trace of the other which, in the case of 'Qual Quelle', comes to be announced by Derrida through the recourse to the course of the watery flow cut off from its source.

However, we should avoid letting ourselves 'be carried along with the flow . . . towards a thematics of water', as Derrida cautions us. For the source is always already heterogeneous, other and plural. The flow of the other never stops but, as other, cannot be traced to some simply identifiable source. The other is never simply the other (of identity, for example) but other *than* identity, leaving its trace on and in the text, and erasing itself as such in the same gesture. The source can never become thematised, as is pointed out, and it can never be 'reassembled into its originary unity . . . [b]ecause . . . it has no proper literal meaning', no 'determinable character'. With such *caveats* in place, Derrida proceeds to connect the idea of source to the notion of a 'pure I' which 'does not amount to the individual'. In a passage which, in retrospect, may be read as predicting in a certain manner Derrida's later discussion of *khōra*, the source, the 'pure I', is described thus:

> Incapable of receiving the imprint of any characteristic, evading all predication, not permitting itself to be attributed any property, this source also will be able to lend itself without resistance to the most contradictory determinations.

Unavailable to an interpretation which would lead to a thematic reading, nevertheless Valéry's engagement with the source opens up for Derrida various performative effects of writing, of theme, meaning, figure and rhetoric. In the figure of the source and its relation to identity or consciousness, writing is discerned, to paraphrase the opening of another essay by Derrida—'writing: a nonsymmetrical division [which] designated on the one hand the closure of the book, and on the other the opening of the text'[59]—which, in turn, is pursued through the figure of the *figure*: the figure of speech and the face, the gaze, reflecting upon itself from some initially displaced other place.

The impossible figure occupies Derrida's consideration in the next chapter of this collection . . .

. . . *Khōra* . . .

. . . which addresses a number of issues pertaining indirectly to language, writing, narrative and fiction, translation and structure, through a reading of the passages in Plato's *Timaeus* which treat of *khōra* and through discussion of the difficulties of translating *khōra*, both from

Greek into another language—say French or English—or within Greek. As Derrida suggests, *khōra* names place, location, region, country, while also naming the figures of mother, nurse, receptacle, imprint-bearer. The 'translations', Derrida says, 'remain caught in networks of interpretation'. The question is what, precisely, is meant by *khōra*? Can *khōra* be given, or does it have, a meaning, to what does *khōra* refer? Can it be said to refer to anything, within any conventional representational logic? In examining the place and effects of *khōra* in the Platonic text, Derrida considers such problematic questions, problematic inasmuch as they are always already problematised by the very term *khōra* itself.

The question of narrative structures is, once again, of interest to Derrida here. As writing and text had unfolded themselves in complex, abyssal structures through the analysis of Philippe Sollers' *Nombres* (in 'The Time before First'), so in Plato's *Timaeus* does Derrida find similar concerns at work, this time around the figure of *khōra* and the problem of definition. The problem of defining *khōra* troubles the text of Plato at the very level of its form; for *khōra*, in the words of John C. Caputo, troubles definition, being 'neither an intelligible form nor one more sensible thing [the two categorial distinctions made by Plato], but, rather, that *in which* (*in quo*) sensible things are inscribed.'[60] Yet all definitions and translations of *khōra* have relied, in the history of translation of Plato's *Timaeus*, on distinctions between the sensible and intelligible; a binary distinction which the idea of *khōra* problematises by obeying a double logic, as Derrida shows us. This double logic is of the order of 'both this and that' and, simultaneously, 'neither this nor that'. Because *khōra* can, and does, function in this fashion, depending on its location within the textual structure, its value is not easily defined, and Derrida's essay works throughout its reading of *khōra* to show how *khōra* is precisely that which cannot be described or positively represented. As Derrida suggests *khōra* troubles all polarities, whether one is discussing proper sense/metaphorical sense, or whether the binarism is that of *mythos/logos*, upon which division the seriousness of philosophical discourse rests. As Derrida puts it in the essay, 'the thought of the *khōra* would trouble the very order of polarity, of polarity in general, whether dialectical or not'. *Khōra* is thus one of those figures which dismantles the logic of all binary oppositions and the supposedly discrete definition of each term in a pair on which such logic relies. To paraphrase a comment of J. Hillis Miller's, quoted above, on the impossibility of defining deconstruction, *khōra* cannot by definition be defined. Formulations of the sort '*khōra* is/is not . . .' miss the point and are neither true nor false inasmuch as *khōra* is not determinable according to the conceptual framework which posits such questions in the first place.

Khōra, suggests Derrida, appears to function as a proper name. It does not operate according to the logic of identification *and* exclusion, by which logic meaning is conventionally generated and guaranteed. Instead, *khōra* announces equivocality, ambiguity, undecidability, by bearing in it the other of meaning, as well as other meaning which effectively destabilises its location, translation and definition. *Khōra* names what cannot be named. Thus its excessive function is aporetic. Irreducible to any paradigm or 'thing', it opens up in its 'name' an aporia in the logic of definition, and in structures such as binary oppositions which aim at producing meaning. Irreducible to any paradigm, *khōra* opens in its naming the logic of meaning. For such reasons, among others, *khōra* draws Derrida's attention. The essay on this quasi-figure in the text of the *Timaeus* is specifically concerned with what appears never to have been addressed in the entire history of critical/analytical/philosophical responses to the text of Plato. It is to be noted, by the way, that Derrida makes an important distinction between, on the one hand, 'the philosophy of Plato' and, on the other hand, 'the text of Plato'. This distinction helps us understand both Derrida's interest in *khōra*, and, at the same time, the philosophical neglect of *khōra*. For Derrida, 'the philosophy of Plato' defines that abstractable, conceptual body of thought which can, and has, been raised above the text, the writing, so as to provide philosophemes and a system of thought. 'The text of Plato' is the network of traces wherein is to be observed the residue in writing for which philosophy cannot account, that which is both singular *and* excessive, in this case, in the *Timaeus*.

In Derrida's understanding then, *khōra* is that which troubles interpretation while performing a certain opening of the text right at its heart. For, as Derrida observes, *khōra* first appears at the middle of the *Timaeus*, figuring a textual abyss where there should be a centre. Thus the text of Plato performs its own abyssal structuring. To quote John Caputo once more, 'Derrida identifies the text of the *Timaeus* as itself having a "*khōral*" structure.'

> For the *Timaeus* is structured like a vast receptacle, as a series of mythic or 'narrative receptacles of receptacles' . . . a string of myths containing myths—the very structure of which (containing receptacles) mirrors *khōra* itself. Which contains all.[61]

Derrida's essay is therefore implicitly concerned with that which resists being appropriated under the rubric of translation, interpretation, reading as such. Similar concerns are of course at work in Derrida's understanding and use of 'writing', 'trace', 'text', 'différance', to name only a few of the non-hermeneutic quasi-concepts which are to be found in his text. *Khōra* is another of those 'nonsynonymous substitutions' which produces and performs the effect of *différance*. We can never say what *khōra* is, we can only refer to it *in other words*.

Khōra does find itself implicated in the question of narrative, however. The number of relational narrative structures in the *Timaeus*—such as the story told by Critias, or Socrates' reference at the 'beginning' of the *Timaeus* to a discussion not in the text—is elaborated by Derrida. Their frequency is such, argues Derrida, that it is impossible to locate the Platonic thesis and thereby extract from 'the text of Plato' 'the philosophy of Plato', in this particular case. The literary or rhetorical, whichever you choose to call it, but certainly the textual, figures the *khōral* displacement of any simply definable, locatable philosophical content. As the figure of the source had been impossible to thematise in the text of Valéry, so the 'logic' of *khōra* is impossible to formalise, for it neither is an existent, nor does it name some thing, some other existent. Its undecidability troubles philosophy, Derrida argues. Momentarily inscribed, *khōra* is also the place of inscription. Although it appears to function as a proper name, yet it is (appears to be) a 'reference' without a referent. In its undecidability, *khōra* names for philosophy that which philosophy is unable to name except indirectly and by analogy—improperly—as that which precedes philosophy, makes philosophy possible. The text of philosophy can only describe *khōra* improperly and imprecisely through recourse to fictions, through narrative—that is to say textual—unfolding and interweaving within philosophy.

Narrative takes place endlessly then, redoubling, dislocating and redefining itself each time through the moment of narrative differentiation and deferral. Therefore, to take the *khōral* rhythm as an example, we can never say precisely what narrative is. There can be no general theory or concept of narrative because each singular example will always disrupt the general definition. We can only point to examples of narrative, each of which—in *khōral* fashion— define themselves only in their singularity and through that which remains before and beyond any narrative theory. The various folds and contours of narrative are organised, Derrida shows us once more through a faithful tracing of the *Timaeus*, into a woven textual complex. This structure, like that of Sollers' *Nombres*, disorganises any notion of binarism or polarity (as has already been suggested), while also displacing any idea of an 'origin', 'source' or 'beginning' (for there is always another narrative to which the present narrative defers). Once again citing Caputo's admirable introduction to *Khōra* (by which I mean to suggest Derrida's essay, although that troublesome figure in the text of Plato finds itself caught up in this sentence . . .), we understand that '*khōra*, which can be spoken of neither properly nor metaphorically, pushes up against the very limits of naming'.[62] This impossibility is not, as Caputo reminds us[63] (reminding us of that which Derrida reminds us, and of which I am now reminding you), a 'failure' on Plato's part. It's not a question of Plato being a poor philosopher. Instead the question is one of coming to terms with a 'structural' feature of writing, the trace of undecidability. And, as Derrida has pointed out elsewhere, '[t]here is no beyond-the-undecidable'.[64]

We find ourselves, in one sense, at the 'final' section of this 'introduction' and the 'final' piece of this reader . . .

... Economimesis ...

           ... although we wish to stress that the order is there only to be disorganised. This collection does not constitute a polite *corpus*. So it is appropriate, then, that we 'conclude' with an article given over to an extensive critique of Kant's consideration of mimesis and aesthetic theory in which Derrida concludes with a figure acknowledging expropriation, exteriorisation, *excorporation* rather than incorporation: vomit.

    The 'vicariousness of vomit' is that figure which, in Derrida's exhaustive critique of Kant's aesthetic theory in the *Critique of Judgement*,[65] is absolutely other, excessive of all mimetic or domesticating incorporation. 'Vomit' figures the 'between', the border which is also an 'over-board', an 'overflow', the *parergon* which defines the limits of the Kantian system of aesthetics.[66] In an essay which examines extensively the use, figures and laws of analogy, the violent figure of vomit resists and undoes 'the hierarchizing authority of logocentric analogy'. Beginning, for the moment, at the conclusion of the essay, we understand how Derrida reads so as to comprehend the function of that which is excluded in any system—in this case, the Kantian critique of judgement, and the related issues of aesthetics and taste (moral judgement allied in the Kantian text to good taste). Derrida reads after, and locates, those excluded figures or terms which a system or structure of thought cannot accommodate according to its own terms, and yet with which it is fascinated and even controlled, as Geoffrey Bennington suggests.[67]

    But let's consider briefly the title of the essay. *Economimesis* is a Derridean neologism which brings together, thereby giving us to consider, the possible relationship between the concepts of economy and mimesis. The point for Derrida is to 'exhibit the systematic link between the two' through what Peter Fenves has described (with reference to another essay of Derrida's on Kant) as a 'transformative critique'.[68] This phrase perhaps best describes what it is that 'Derrida does' when he encounters another's text. Reading for the excluded, the marginal, the barely mentioned, Derrida traces the contours of the text of the other in a way which, while absolutely faithful to that textual system, exhibits (to use Derrida's own word) how the supposedly coherent discourses of the system rely on the excluded other. One term which fascinates Derrida in this reading is *salary* which hardly appears in Kant's third critique, yet which is crucial in making hierarchical distinctions between types of artistic production, between what Kant describes as 'free' and 'mercenary' art, that which is produced for pleasure and that which is produced for money or otherwise takes part in some exchange mechanism. It is, Derrida informs us, the scarcity of reference to *salary* which should draw our attention and interest us.

    Derrida pursues an analysis of the connections and distinctions made by

Kant concerning art and nature. As Derrida shows, Kant's comprehension of mimesis is worked out throughout the third critique through a persistent movement between the two concepts of 'art' and 'nature' which aims at generating a hierarchical model of production, organised from instinctual production on the part of animals, through the various arts of human society, to the work of God.

Yet as he explores the various concerns of Kant's text, including issues of genius, the production of poetry, and the role of the various senses, which are themselves hierarchised, privileging those which lend themselves more readily to abstraction, as opposed to those which are perceived as more 'organic', such as smell and taste,[69] so Derrida unfolds the 'political' work of aesthetic theories. Kant's aesthetic theory is part of, and articulated from, the implicit 'political' assumptions at work in humanist systems of thought. Particularly important in the text of Kant is the understanding of what Bennington describes as 'nature as a unitary event'.[70] 'Nature' is, though, not a unitary or originary event at all, as we have already seen in earlier articles in the reader (particularly those which discuss Warburton and Lévi-Strauss); it is not something, some absolute origin or presence, from which all other productions spring. 'Nature' is, within humanist philosophy, what Derrida terms a 'philosopheme'. The philosopheme is a unit of knowledge within the structure of a system or body of thought which functions and maintains its mystified power. In the example of 'nature' the work is achieved through the operations of analogy, according to the various hierarchies on which Kant relies, and even though every effort is made to to keep the various categorial distinctions separate.

Yet, as we've suggested and as Derrida makes plain, no philosopheme has an originary identity external to its functioning. Derrida unpacks this in the opening paragraphs of 'Economimesis', where he discusses the figure of the political within aesthetic discourse, pointing out that the political is transformed by being folded into the aesthetic, while the aesthetic is mutually and reciprocally 'contaminated' by the political. In the example of Kant's critique, the political is defined as a double question concerning both 'pure morality and empirical culturalism'. From such a double question comes the generation of hierarchical distinctions concerning the production of art which are, in turn, part of 'the inexhaustible reiteration of the humanist theme' where the 'concept of nature . . . functions in the service of that ontotheological humanism'. Contrary to the politics of humanism as given expression in Kant, the work of Derrida's reading is to disclose the performative operations of what he calls 'analogical mimesis' at those various moments throughout the text of Kant where a category such as Fine-Art is supposedly discerned as detached and discrete. The exhibition of analogical mimesis shows repeatedly the interdependence of categories and modes of production. Far from being an independent, self-defining and self-evident category, 'Fine-Art' belongs to

a productive network which is not spelled out. Its value as a categorial definition can be produced and the term can function because its meanings are
assumed to be unique. Yet, like 'nature', 'Fine-Art' has no unitary totality, no
absolute identity.

Derrida's efforts in 'Economimesis' are, then, aimed at exploring the system
of effects of which the text of Kant is the immediate example. His concerns
too are with the question of what regulates the system, what hierarchises and
borders it, what gets assimilated and what remains unassimilable, what gets
excluded. That which is excluded is an 'irreducible heterogeneity', defined by
Derrida, in response to Kant's consideration of the senses as they pertain to
questions of taste, as vomit, as we announced in beginning this final section.
This essay is, simultaneously, absolutely singular and yet typical in its attention
to detail, as an example of Derrida's 'reading work', to use Geoff Bennington's
phrase, or as 'transformative critique', to recall the expression of Peter Fenves.
It is certainly a writing performance, a response to the event of the other's
text, a response which is responsible to the demands made on the reader by
the other. Derrida's writing demands an equally responsible response, a
response which doesn't decide ahead of the event of encountering the text of
Derrida what we might find there. Reaching this point in this 'introduction'
I cannot begin to find a way to conclude; the only way to close is to open
onto Derrida's writing. I find myself (leaving you) with the injunction to read
(to do justice to) Derrida, an injunction which is, still, a double-bind and also
a necessity, with the essays—and the Derrida reader—still before us, while
hearing Derrida say, all the while giving us the slip, . . .

– viens, oui, oui …

Notes

1. Drucilla Cornell, *The Philosophy of the Limit* (New York: Routledge, 1992), p. 169.
2. J. Hillis Miller, *Theory Now and Then* (Hemel Hempstead: Harvester Wheatsheaf
   1991), p. 231.
3. Jacques Derrida, *Parages* (Paris: Galilée, 1986), p. 116.
4. Miller, *Theory Now and Then*, p. 231.
5. Peggy Kamuf, 'Introduction: Reading Between the Blinds', *A Derrida Reader:
   Between the Blinds*, ed. Peggy Kamuf (New York: Columbia University Press,
   1991), pp. xiii–xlii.
6. Derek Attridge, ed., *Acts of Literature* (New York: Routledge, 1992). Hereafter
   referred to as *Acts*.
7. Attridge, ed., *Acts*, p. 62. Of Joyce, Celan and Blanchot, Derrida has said that,
   while he has mobilised a word or two, here or there, as an analytical fulcrum, he

would never claim to have read these authors. More recently, he has said of Plato and Aristotle: 'I have constantly tried to read and to understand Plato and Aristotle and I have devoted a number of texts to them . . . I think we have to read them again and again and I feel that, however old I am, I am on the threshold of reading Plato and Aristotle. I love them and I feel that I have to start again and again and again. It is a task which is in front of me, before me'. Jacques Derrida and John D. Caputo, *Deconstruction in a Nutshell* (New York: Fordham University Press, 1997), p. 9. All further references to this text will be indicated in the notes as *DN*, followed by the page number. As Derrida's remarks suggest, reading is something which is always ahead of us.

8. *DN* p. 26.
9. Readers might refer to my essay 'An "Economics" of Snow and the Blank Page or, "Writing" at the "Margins": "Deconstructing" "Richard Jefferies"?' in *Literary Theories: A Case Study in Critical Performance*, eds Julian Wolfreys and William Baker (New York: New York University Press, 1996), pp. 179–244, and *Deconstruction • Derrida* (Basingstoke: Macmillan, 1998).
10. Jacques Derrida, *Dissemination* (1972), trans. Barbara Johnson (Chicago: University of Chicago Press, 1981), p. 7.
11. Derrida, *Dissemination*, p. 9.
12. Nicholas Royle, *After Derrida* (Manchester: Manchester University Press, 1995). See Royle's discussion of the figure of 'after' in the phrase 'after Derrida', pp. 2–5.
13. Geoffrey Bennington, 'Derridabase', in *Jacques Derrida* (1991) by Geoffrey Bennington and Jacques Derrida, trans. Geoffrey Bennington (Chicago: University of Chicago Press, 1993), pp. 8, 15.
14. See Derrida's essay, 'From Restricted to General Economy: Hegelianism without Reserve', in *Writing and Difference* (1967) trans. Alan Bass (London: Routledge & Kegan Paul, 1978), pp. 251–77. George Bataille, whose work influences Derrida and who is considered in the essay just named, defines 'general economy' as the production of excess which overflows strictly useful material or intellectual production. For further discussion of this, and Derrida's work, see Arkady Plotnitsky, *In the Shadow of Hegel: Complementarity, History, and the Unconscious* (Gainesville: University Press of Florida, 1993), pp. 10–30.
15. Jacques Derrida, 'Introduction: Desistance', trans. Christopher Fynsk, in Philippe Lacoue-Labarthe, *Typography: Mimesis, Philosophy, Politics*, trans. and ed. Christopher Fynsk (Cambridge, MA: Harvard University Press, 1989), pp. 6–7, emphasis added. For an interesting discussion of Derrida's work in relation to Lacoue-Labarthe and Nancy which respects singularity and distance, see Joan Brandt's *Geopoetics: The Politics of Mimesis in Poststructuralist French Poetry and Theory* (Stanford: Stanford University Press, 1997). Brandt's work situates Derrida, along with Lacoue-Labarthe and Nancy, in relation to the Parisian intellectual scene of the late 1960s in general, and in relation to *Tel Quel*, a prominent radical review of the period. See also the discussion of Derrida's work in the milieu of *Tel Quel*, in Suzanne Guerlac, *Literary Polemics: Bataille, Sartre, Valéry, Breton* (Stanford: Stanford University Press, 1997), pp. 216–22. For further discussion of *Tel Quel* and the development of what is referred to as poststructuralism in the Anglo-American academy, see Jonathan Culler, '"Beyond" Structuralism: Tel Quel', in his

Structuralist Poetics: Structuralism, Linguistics and the Study of Literature (London: Routledge & Kegan Paul, 1975), pp. 241–54.

16. Refer to n. 7, above.

17. Jacques Derrida, *Glas* (1974) trans. John P. Leavey, Jr, and Richard Rand (Lincoln: University of Nebraska Press, 1986), pp. 204–5b. The lower case 'b' refers here to the layout of *Glas*, which is presented in two columns, left and right on the page. The lower case letter refers here to the right-hand column.

18. Jacques Derrida, 'Living On • Borderlines', trans. James Hulbert, in *Deconstruction and Criticism*, Harold Bloom, Paul de Man, Jacques Derrida, Geoffrey Hartman and J. Hillis Miller (New York: Continuum, 1987), pp. 83–4.

19. Derrida, 'Living On • Borderlines', p. 84.

20. *DN*, p. 8.

21. *DN*, p. 9.

22. Kamuf, ed., *A Derrida Reader*, p. 65.

23. Samuel Beckett, *The Unnameable* (1958), trans. from the French by the author, in *Three Novels by Samuel Beckett* (New York: Grove Press, 1965), p. 414.

24. On this definition of a 'deconstructive reading', see John Caputo's commentary (*DN*, p. 78).

25. Rainer Nägele, *Echoes of Translation: Reading Between Texts* (Baltimore: The Johns Hopkins University Press, 1997), p. 14.

26. William Warburton, *The Divine Legation of Moses Demonstrated* (1742) (New York: Garland, 1978).

27. This phrase has clearly Althusserian overtones, reminding us of Althusser's well-known (and well-worn) phrase, 'ideological state apparatus'. It also allows us a degree of speculation concerning what is encrypted in this essay. There is readable in this preface a certain imminent critique of certain then-contemporary trains of thought among Parisian intellectuals, which is perhaps why Derrida points to what interests him in Warburton *today*, signalling the contemporary moment. At a number of points in the essay Derrida resists the notion of power as a unitary figure, favouring the plurals, *powers, knowledges, writings*, and draws on Warburton's own analysis to point, albeit briefly (as a preface must necessarily do), to relationships and differences between writings and the powers they operate. Such gestures on Derrida's part suggest a critique of, if not Michel Foucault's own analysis of power, then, at least, a particular trend in the analysis of 'power' in the wake of Foucault's own writing. This critique appears to come to a head in the question: 'But if one does not believe in the (political) simplicity of the epistemological-break [a model of the history of the movement of knowledge favoured in Foucault's writing], is there not something to read, for us today, in this interpretation of the "art of interpreting dreams"? in what it says about the relations between the science of dreams, writing, knowledge in general, power, the hegemony represented by a priestly caste, etc.?' Derrida's act of questioning, and giving the question a specific and, arguably, polemic orientation in that *today*, which conjures possible readings of Freud, is given added weight in the phrase 'a priestly caste, etc.' The indefinite article allied to the adjectival description is readable as offering a metaphorical symbol for the hegemony of specific—though unidentified—academic-institutional-ideological groups.

28. Cary Plotkin, translator's note, *Yale French Studies*, 58, 1979: 116.

29. Kamuf, ed., *A Derrida Reader*, p. 33.

30. Attridge, ed., *Acts*, p. 19.

31. Geoffrey Bennington, 'Derridabase', p. 105.

32. Bennington, 'Derridabase', p. 107.

33. Attridge, ed., *Acts*, p. 65.

34. Attridge, ed., *Acts*, p. 66.

35. Jacques Derrida, *Of Grammatology* (1967), trans. Gayatri Chakravorty Spivak (Baltimore: Johns Hopkins University Press, 1974), p. 105.

36. Jean-Jacques Rousseau, *Essay on the Origin of Languages*, trans. with Afterword by John H. Moran and Alexander Gode, intro. Alexander Gode (Chicago: University of Chicago Press, 1986).

37. Derrida, *Grammatology*, p. 168.

38. Jacques Derrida, 'White Mythology: Metaphor in the Text of Philosophy', in *Margins of Philosophy* (1972), trans. Alan Bass (Chicago: University of Chicago Press, 1982), pp. 207–72.

39. Derrida, 'White Mythology', p. 270.

40. John P. Leavey, Jr, 'French Kissing: Whose Tongue is it Anyway?', in *French Connections: Jacques Derrida and French Literature*, eds John Brannigan, Ruth Robbins and Julian Wolfreys (Albany: State University of New York Press, forthcoming).

41. Paul Ricoeur, *The Rule of Metaphor* (1975) trans. R. Czerny (Toronto: University of Toronto Press, 1977).

42. George Eliot, *Daniel Deronda* (1876), ed. Barbara Hardy (Harmondsworth: Penguin, 1967), p. 35.

43. Philippe Sollers, *Nombres* (Paris: Éditions du Seuil, 1968); *Le Parc* (Paris: Éditions du Seuil, 1961); *Drame* (Paris: Éditions du Seuil, 1965). Readers interested in Sollers' work should refer to Roland Barthes, *Writer Sollers* (1979), trans. Philip Thody (Minneapolis: University of Minnesota Press, 1987), who discusses in Chapter Two (pp. 39–69) Sollers' efforts to inscribe the subject as always already divided within him/herself and the novelist's attempt to rid the novel form of the bourgeois concern with character psychology. As Barthes suggests in this chapter, Sollers' novels are concerned primarily with the structures and forms of language. Another highly useful and comprehensive introduction to the work of Sollers is that by Malcolm Charles Pollard, *The Novels of Philippe Sollers: Narrative and the Visual* (Amsterdam: Editions Rodopi BV, 1994). Any references to this study will be given by author's surname and page number.

44. As this introduction has already suggested, one of Derrida's abiding concerns is the space of the 'between' or the 'in-between', and what can take place in this negotiable, non-fixed space. The sections of *Dissemination*, concentrating as they do on the discourses of 'philosophy' and 'literature', on the texts of Plato and Sollers, can be read as opening up that space between, in which Derrida enacts the performance of writing. Although *Dissemination* is laid out more or less conventionally, its reiterative bipartite structure does, along with the interests of the sections (or, more properly, the *inter-est*, literally the being-between which is always named when we speak of 'Derrida's interests'), appear to anticipate the

interests of a later work, *Glas*, which is set on the page in two columns, left and right. The left-hand column offers the reader an analysis of Hegel, while the right provides a commentary on Jean Genet, once again creating a performative and transformative space between the texts of philosophy and literature.

45. Lewis Carroll, *Through the Looking-Glass and What Alice Found There*, preface and notes James R. Kincaid, ed. Selwyn H. Goodacre (Berkeley: University of California Press, 1983); on issues of spatiality and structure see also, Gilles Deleuze, *The Logic of Sense* (1969), trans. Mark Lester with Charles Stivale, ed. Constantin V. Boundas (New York: Columbia University Press, 1990), and Ch. 1 of my *The Rhetoric of Affirmative Resistance: Dissonant Identities from Carroll to Derrida* (Basingstoke: Macmillan, 1997), pp. 35–69.

46. Again, see Barthes (n. 43, above) and, also, Pollard, pp. 85–102.

47. Pollard, p. 85.

48. Pollard, p. 86.

49. Pollard, p. 87. See also pp. 88, 93 and 99.

50. Pollard, p. 90.

51. On the messianic in Derrida's thought, see John Caputo, Ch. 6, in *Deconstruction in a Nutshell* (pp. 156–80), and also Caputo's, *The Prayers and Tears of Jacques Derrida: Religion without Religion* (Bloomington: Indiana University Press, 1997).

52. DN, p. 159.

53. *Specters of Marx: The State of the Debt, the Work of Mourning, and the New International* ((1993), trans. Peggy Kamuf, intro. Bernd Magnus and Stephen Cullenberg (New York: Routledge, 1994)) is doubly haunted, by both the texts of Marx and a 'reading' of the spectral in *Hamlet*.

54. Derrida works through the various translations and terms used both in Marx's German and in French translations which separate spectre from spirit, even though the latter resounds with the sense of the former. 'Spirit' refers in general to a sense of national identity or 'the spirit of the people', as Derrida has elsewhere discussed with reference to the relative absence of the figure of *geist* (meaning both ghost and spirit) in the writing of Martin Heidegger (*Of Spirit: Heidegger and the Question* (1987), trans. Geoff Bennington and Rachel Bowlby (Chicago: University of Chicago Press, 1989)). Derrida suggests that Marx has difficulty controlling the effects of these words and their difference in his text, pursuing a consideration of what appears in the aporia between the two.

55. Jacques Derrida, *Of Spirit: Heidegger and the Question* (1987), trans. Geoffrey Bennington and Rachel Bowlby (Chicago: University of Chicago Press, 1989); 'White Mythology: Metaphor in the Text of Philosophy', in *Margins of Philosophy* (1972), trans. Alan Bass (Chicago: University of Chicago Press, 1982), pp. 207–72.

56. Maurice Merleau-Ponty, *The Visible and the Invisible*, ed. Claude Lefort, trans. Alphonso Lingis (Evanston: Northwestern University Press, 1968).

57. Friedrich Nietzsche, *Ecce Homo*, in *On the Genealogy of Morals and Ecce Homo*, ed. and trans. Walter Kaufmann (New York: Vintage Books, 1967).

58. See, for example, *Specters of Marx, The Politics of Friendship* (1994), trans. George Collins (London: Verso, 1997), and 'Foi et savoir: les deux sources de la «religion» aux limites de la simple raison', in *La Religion*, sous la direction de Jacques Derrida and Gianni Vattimo (Paris: Seuil, 1996); see also an interview from 1996,

'oui, mes livres sonts politiques: Entretien avec Didier Eribon', in *La Nouvel Observateur*, 1633, 22–28 February, 1996: pp. 84–6.

59. Jacques Derrida, 'Ellipsis', in *Writing and Difference*, p. 294.

60. *DN*, p. 84. Geoffrey Bennington provides a useful discussion of *khōra* in the text of Derrida in 'Derridabase', pp. 207–12.

61. *DN*, p. 87.

62. *DN*, p. 91.

63. *DN*, p. 95.

64. Jacques Derrida, *Memoires for Paul de Man* (1986; French edn 1988), revised and augmented edition, trans. Cecile Lindsay, Jonathan Culler, Eduardo Cadava and Peggy Kamuf (New York: Columbia University Press, 1989), p. 137.

65. Immanuel Kant, *Critique of Judgement* (1790), trans. Werner S. Pluhar (Indianapolis: Hackett Press, 1987).

66. On the *parergon*, see Derrida, *The Truth in Painting* (1978), trans. Geoff Bennington and Ian McLeod (Chicago: University of Chicago Press, 1987), pp. 15–147.

67. Bennington, 'Derridabase', pp. 283–4.

68. Peter Fenves, ed., *Raising the Tone of Philosophy: Late Essays by Immanuel Kant, Transformative Critique by Jacques Derrida* (Baltimore: The Johns Hopkins University Press, 1993).

69. Peggy Kamuf, 'Introduction', in Kamuf, ed. *A Derrida Reader*, p. xxxviii.

70. Bennington, 'Derridabase', p. 238.

Chapter 1

Scribble (writing-power)

Who Can Write? What Can Writing Do?

We sense that the (advanced) form of these questions can be, already on its own, diverted. It harbors a ruse, of writing, and this is not accidental. What would it divert from?

Fostering the belief that writing *befalls* power (one can, in general, and one can write if occasioned to), that it can ally itself to power, can prolong it by complementing it, or can serve it, the question suggests that writing can *come* [*arriver*] to power or power to writing. It excludes in advance the identification of writing *as* power or the recognition of power from the onset of writing. It auxiliarizes and hence aims to conceal the fact that writing and power never work separately, however complex the laws, the system, or the links of their collusion may be.

Now what is astonishing is not writing as power but what comes, as if from within a structure, to limit it by a powerlessness or an effacement. But this was said elsewhere;[1] let us leave it at that.

Writing does not come to power. It is there beforehand, it partakes of and is made of it. Starting from which, in order to seize it—nameiy power, such as determinate power (politics, for example, which does not assume an exemplary position by accident)—struggles and contending forces permeate writings and counter-writings. For the question also led to the singular abstraction: *power, writing.* It ran the risk of reproducing that political operation which, to heap blame on something like *power* in general, assimilates all kinds of power for whatever purposes they may serve (we know the rest). Hence, *struggles* for *powers* set *various* writings up against one another [*les* luttes pour *les* pouvoirs opposent *des* écritures]. Let us not shrug our shoulders too hastily, pretending to believe that war would thus be confined within the field of literati, in the library or the bookshop. This has been treated at length elsewhere;[2] let us leave it at that. But it is true that the political question of literati, of intellectuals in the ideological apparatus, of the places and stockages of writing, of caste-phenomena, of 'priests' and the hoarding of codes, of archival matters— that all this should concern us.

What interests me first, here, today, in Warburton, is the theory of powers. I thus assume a discriminating reading and will attempt to justify it. Politically, for example. Where the *Essai* touches on language as such, on the use of rhetorical schemes in the interpretation of writing, its history, and its varying and unvarying features, in the genesis of idolatry or oneirocritical knowledge, it interests me less. All this is rich, exciting, but better pinpointed today, and fascinates only by leaving—'in order to' leave—in obscurity the theory of powers that is coextensive with them. Indeed, Warburton proposes a history and a general system of writings, which he always analyzes according to an interpretation of 'ideological' and politico-religious powers—of the ideological in general. This can be inferred from several clues.

The most general might be called *economy of action*, even if it means displacing these two words along the way. What about action, in the first place? And how is a *veil* necessarily implied, with the values of dissimulation, ruse, crypt, sexual modesty, and hymen that it always envelops?

Language and writing possess a common filiation, according to Warburton. From the very beginning it passes through 'action language.' The common genealogy authorizes a continual comparison between the two 'arts,' which must be understood as two powers, themselves already analogous to a rhetorical power (tropical or figural) evenly distributed within one family, one law of kinship, one economy: 'Comparison of these two arts, which one may, as it were, regard as brothers [*sister-art*, as Warburton himself put it], will shed light on them both' (§ 7).[3] The 'comparison' between the two arts, as well as the 'influence' of the one upon the other, will be continually re-instigated: both are powers of graphico-rhetorical 'comparison.' For this reason also, the relationships can no longer be those of auxiliarihood or ancillariness (this time between speech and writing). And yet, if auxiliarihood does not determine *ex post facto* the speech/writing relationship, a certain auxiliariness (one must once again say supplementarity) marks its first emergence.

'Action language,' the common origin of verbal and graphic powers, is indeed rendered indispensable by an essential limitation, an irreducible finitude of 'sound,'—in human communication, naturally.

The sound of the voice never carries far enough. It lacks extension. Extension fails it. The scarcely paradoxical consequence: although it belongs to duration, sound never lasts long enough—duration fails it too.

> We have two ways of communicating our ideas. The first with the help of sounds; the second by means of figures. Indeed, the opportunity of perpetuating our ideas and of making them known to people far away presents itself often; and as sounds do not extend beyond the moment and the place that they are uttered, we invented figures and characters, after having imagined the sounds, so that our ideas might partake of extension and duration. This manner of communicating our ideas by marks and figures at first consisted in drawing quite naturally the images of things.

Thus, to express the idea of a man or a horse, one represented the form of one or the other. The first attempt at writing was, as we see, a simple picture. (§ 1 and 2)

The deficiency of the word [*verbe*] is not due solely to the element of sound in which it is deployed. It also appears on the semantic or referential side. In the beginning language is said to have been, necessarily, 'rude, barren, and equivocal.' This proposition has axiomatic value in the *Essai*; it is the price to be paid for a conception of language that is massively (let us say so just as massively and without delay) evolutionistic, naturalistic, representativistic, almost linearistic.

> Language, if one judges by the monuments of antiquity and by the nature of the thing, was at first extremely rude, barren, and equivocal: so that men were perpetually at a loss, with each new idea and each extraordinary case, to make themselves mutually understood. Nature led them to obviate [*prévenir*]⁴ these deficiencies by adding to spoken words apt and significant signs. Accordingly, conversation in the first ages of the world was upheld by a mixed discourse of words and actions. (§ 8)

This 'action' is obviously an 'action language' (§ 9) already informed by an entire rhetoric, by a thorough, active, and discriminating sifting [*criblage*] of figures. Examples of this are first drawn from the Orient of Holy Scripture, either from the language of the Prophets ('When the false Prophet shakes his iron horns to mark the utter rout of the Syrians,' etc.) or from their 'visions,' which are in fact only translations, equivalents of action 'turned into vision,' the effects of a *practical* rhetoric: the vision is thus the language God speaks by 'condescension,' 'to conform to the custom of the time.'

But insofar as this rhetorical 'action' is original, insofar as it supplies the deficiencies of a natural and primary impotence of speech, nothing—neither upstream nor downstream—can overflow its realm. The entire realm is a realm of action. There follows a sort of generalized 'practicism' that offers its foundation, its place, and its meaning to a theory of writing as power. The concept of action ensures the (homogeneous or analogical) passage between action in general (physical, technical, political, etc.) and that of 'action language': manifestation through action, act of manifesting.

How will this manifestation come to the point of concealing? The question awaits us—it is that of scrypture [*écrypture*]; it is too early to formulate it.

With this generality of action only the generality of nature can contend. With its equivocalities and its powerful resources, the concept of nature presides over all of this discourse. It does so according to the rules that organize the entire historico-theoretical configuration to which such a discourse belongs.

On the one hand, this configuration permits a break with a certain type of dogmatism. Explanation no longer has theoretical recourse to revelation: 'it is nature and necessity. . . that have produced the various kinds of hieroglyphic writing and have given them currency. . .' (§ 7). 'Language, if one judges by antiquity and by the nature of the thing . . .' (§8). 'Nature led them to supply these deficiencies by adding to spoken words apt and significant signs' (*ibid.*). Even the deficiency is natural, but equally natural is the supplement to the deficiency—here, writing as action language. Nature fills up: that is history (the history of action, of language, of action language). It foreruns itself. [*Elle se prévient elle-même.*] It leads to the obviation [*à prévenir*] of those 'deficiencies' that are at first its own but that are no longer simply its own from the instant it obviates them, from the instant it forewarns [*prévient*] man in nature of them. Nature is the necessity, order, and arrangement of the world (cosmos or creation); it is essence ('the nature of the thing'), providential finality, the condition and object of knowledge.

But on the other hand, and just as regularly, the value of nature is at the service—is the very service—of a Christian apologetics, a 'true defense,' a 'reasonable defense of prophetic writings' (§ 9). Mediation here takes the form of natural language and even—it may be said without anachronism—of ordinary language. In prophetic texts, figures of action language will cease to seem absurd, odd, or fanatic as soon as one no longer attributes them to an 'extraordinary language' but rather to ordinary usage and the natural 'idiom' of a culture (*ibid.*). Figures of rhetoric active in the idiom of language, in its natural and ordinary usage, 'discourses expressed by actions,' pictography (and by natural development hieroglyphy, ideography, alphabet)—all this arises from one and the same *natural* system, from a great, universal, and analogical chain of analogies. It is the powers of 'comparing' that are being compared among themselves. This signifying practice of nature expresses itself by signs—which amounts to expressing and silencing itself at the same time. Already the crypt *en abîme* is presenting itself *naturally*:

> It is not only in Sacred History that we encounter these examples of discourses expressed by actions. Profane Antiquity is full of them, and we shall have occasion to refer to them subsequently. The first oracles were rendered in this manner, as we learn from an ancient saying of Heraclitus: 'That the King, whose oracle is at Delphi, neither speaks nor keeps silent but expresses himself by signs.' Proof that it was, anciently, a normal way of making oneself understood to substitute actions for speech. Now this way of expressing thoughts by actions agrees perfectly with that of preserving them by pictures. I have noticed in ancient history an instance that so exactly reflects discourse by action and writing by pictures [the first writing] that we may consider it as the link that binds together these two means of expression and as proof of their likeness. Clement of Alexandria tells this story in these words: 'As *Pherecydes Syrus* recounted it, it is said that *Idanthura*, King of the Scythians, being ready to do battle with Darius, who had passed the Ister, instead of a letter sent him, by way of symbol, a mouse, a frog, a bird, a dart, and a plough.' This message having to supply speech and writing, we see its meaning expressed by a mixture of action and picture. (§ 10)

Always present to itself, in one form or another, nature is self-presence, come to itself in anticipating itself [*venue à soi se prévenant elle-même*].

Action is the manifestation or the production of this nature *preserve*. The 'deficiencies' that are produced in action are still natural ones; they are the means of production proper to it. It anticipates [*prévient*] them, in this was preceding itself and as it were advancing itself.

One may speak here of an *economy of nature*. What about action? we asked above in connexion with the economy of action. What about economy, now? Economy because nature is always at home, close beside itself, not going out without preventing/advising of [*prévenant (de)*] its return. And it orders everything according to its own proper law and the law of what is proper to it: economy. But also because the natural law that presides over the modes of production and over the evolution of systems of writing is, in a more restricted sense of economy, a law of *saving* and *abridgement*. The point is always to improve the efficiency of the signifying practice and to save space in the storage of information and in the repository of the archive: *ecotoponomy*.

If nature is always present to itself, the metaphor of its self-production will tend to be vocal: the voice of nature. At this point (the metaphor of nature as a whole), auxiliarihood recovers its rights, along with phonocentrism. Contradicted, overturned, or neutralized by the affirmation according to which speech and writing belong as it were to the same generation (as one says of family relations but also of data machines), auxiliarihood reappears just as the most general metaphor expresses [*dit*] nature, lets nature express itself [*se dire*]—which is done, one thinks, as close to home as possible, only in the voice, 'the uniform voice of nature.' If there are universals in the history of language and writing, if from one nation to another the analogy of the process can be explained neither by 'imitation' nor by 'chance' or 'unforeseen event,' it is because the voice of nature carries, everywhere, without bounds, without alteration, everywhere the same, 'the uniform voice of nature, speaking to the rude conceptions of men' (§ 7).

This attentiveness [*prévenance*] of the voice can be explained, explains itself, even if only through metaphor: although the arts of speech and writing are 'brothers,' although the necessity of marks, figures, and language arose from the very beginning by reason of the (human) finitude of the word, it remains that, of the 'two ways of communicating our ideas,' the 'first' came about 'with the help of sounds': elder brother if you like or, closer to the English, elder sister who resembles more nearly her progenitor, nature, whose sex we shall leave indeterminate. 'First' way, immediately followed or accompanied, but first. If the deficiency of the human voice in its finitude is immediately supplied by action language and by the marks of writing, the 'voice of nature' everywhere and ceaselessly supplies its own deficiency in metaphors, properly, of itself.

Since nature produces, utters, and makes up for itself—in other words, *unveils itself* in its *truth* through speech and its writing supplement—how does one explain that it came to the point of *veiling* (hiding, encrypting) itself throughout history? throughout history as the history of language and writing (which is why the veiling is cryptic and the concealment encyphering), as the history of science, religion, economy, and politics, and even of a certain unconscious such as arises in dreams and in the science of 'oneirocritics'? That is the only question. Warburton poses it as such. He provides an answer. The possibility of the question, of its systematic unity, concerns us today. More than its knowledge-content, its examples, and its answer, more than the content of the answer. Not that the point is formally to isolate problematic schemas, ideal types of explanation, a certain style in the articulation of regions (the political, the economic, the linguistic or graphic, the rhetorical, the religious, the oneirocritical, etc), but rather to pinpoint, within that which links knowledge-contents to question-forms or to procedures of analysis, a system (of powers and limits) relevant to a present-day discourse, an unevenly developed discourse that the system may favor here and hinder elsewhere, in any case disorganizing every sort of hasty and comfortable periodization and simplistic determination of limits. The engrossing [*préoccupant*] relation between two (or more than two) scribbles: such will here be the 'object.' I am thus assuming my scribling selection not in order to impose it but in order to ask: why must the question of *power* (an old word that needs differentiation, an abstraction that needs analysis) be worked out today, urgently and insistently, as a question of *writings*? What must follow from this, with regard both to the powers and to the writings?

To summarize. It is as if a catastrophe had perverted this truth of nature: a writing made to manifest, serve, and preserve knowledge—for custody of meaning, the repository of learning, and the laying out of the archive— encrypts itself, becoming secret and reserved, diverted from common usage, esoteric. Naturally destined to serve the communication of laws and the order of the city transparently, a writing becomes the instrument of an abusive power, of a caste of 'intellectuals' that is thus ensuring hegemony, whether its own or that of special interests: the violence of a secretariat, a discriminating reserve, an effect of scribble and scrypt.

This perversion is described as the violent effect of a *veil* (the word recurs regularly—at least, I have determined, in the French *Essai*[5]), of a veiling: something is *veiled*, like a presence or a truth, but also like the rotation or revolution of a social wheel. Warburton often calls the course of this process *revolution*. A certain natural revolution is turning out badly. The perversion is said not to have limited its (real) effects to the cultures under study (Egyptian antiquity, mainly) but by the same token to be at the root of the errors made by Europeans (Kircher, mainly) in the interpretation of hieroglyphs, their structure, and their finality, and consequently—following this clew—in their conception of language and writing in general. 'The undertaking is extremely difficult owing to the general error into which we have fallen regarding the first use of hieroglyphs, believing as we do that Egyptian priests invented them so as to hide their knowledge from the common man. This opinion has cast over this part of ancient literature a shadow so large that one can dispel it only by unveiling the error completely.' (*Object of this paper.*) Warburton will not claim that the priests never wanted to 'hide their knowledge' by veiling it. But by demonstrating that neither this veil nor this intention was originary, he wants to 'unveil' the error that had made concealment the (secret) mainspring of writing. Kircher's mistake is itself the effect of a (real but secondary) veil: by lifting the veil and returning to the natural origin, one will unveil the error. One will even show the cause of the error, its necessity, and its law by going back to the origin or to the original ('*it will be necessary to trace up hieroglyphic writing to its original*') (sentence omitted in the *Essai*).

For such is the (extreme) difficulty of the undertaking, the riddle of the riddle and hence of history: the catastrophe of the veiling is not an accident; it remains natural. The error of deciphering that results for the science of writings is also natural and must be decipherable as such.

The dual figure of the priest and the hieroglyph occupies an exemplary position in this: apparently one among others, it is true, in a series or group of social types and types of writing, but at the same time bringing together the essence of social power *qua* power of writing or at least as an essential moment of these powers and of what is represented in them. And these two figures are inseparable; they belong to the same system and are mutually constitutive. No priests without a hieroglyphic writing, no hieroglyphics without a working priesthood. Occupying the *center* within the succession of types of writing, the hieroglyph is also, as we shall see, the elementary milieu, the medium and general form of all writing. It is twice marked, occupying a space and all the space. This is also true of the priest: this very special social agent also represents that place and function in which scientific, religious, political, technical, and economic powers are capitalized in the power of a lever of writing that overturns natural relations.

The *Essai* revolves around this critical overturning (cryptic catastrophe). It adjusts its rhythms and its composition according to it: three parts, as in Section IV of *The Divine Legation of Moses demonstrated*, are in this respect faithfully reconstituted. The first part describes a sort of ideal normality, the natural derivation of writings when they fulfill transparently their function in communication (notably of laws) and as archival instruments (of science, political history, financial accounts). The only problems—and they are solved by the technical improvement of writings—are hence economic problems of storage. The second part, a central and catastrophic moment in the natural revolution, explains the veiling of this ideal normality. The third part demonstrates that oneirocritical science and the animal cult draw all their resources from hieroglyphic writing. The existence of such a writing thus proves the great antiquity of the sciences in Egypt. It is the sought-after 'internal proof': hieroglyphic writing does not surround knowledge like the detachable form of a container or signifier. It structures the content of knowledge. This explains why, according to Warburton, when other peoples were reaching toward a more manageable and economical system of writing (the alphabet), the Egyptians should have wished to preserve, with their writing, the very treasure-house of their knowledge—a premise indispensable to the author's theses on the religion and politics of the Hebrews and the condition for a revival of Biblical studies as well, a major concern of Warburton's in his struggle against 'freethinking.'

It must therefore be explained that the accident is necessary: that the veiling, which *befalls* writing, is also prescribed for it by a certain nature, from within; and finally that this effect of writing remains at once secondary and essential: a non-accidental accident. This is not a simple matter. Prejudices, themselves provoked by the veiling, have made the undertaking 'extremely difficult.' One must go back to the origin ('*trace up hieroglyphic writing to its original*') to explain what has befallen.

From its origin, the simplest and most representative writing (representative of the thing: 'to draw naturally the images of things,' § 2) was designed to preserve laws and history. The best example of this is drawn from the Mexican Empire, whose pictography (*picture-writing*) is attested by the tax rolls of the royal treasury and by the abstract of their civil code, the most developed part of which treats, not insignificantly, *de jure patrio*.[6] From this simplest of stages onward the pictogram is scribled by an entire rhetoric. Things that had no bodily shape were represented by 'other significant characters': an-Indian-kneeling-before-a-priest signified 'I confess,' three-heads-crowned stood for the Trinity.

From the pictogram to the hieroglyph, a simple techno-economic restraint. The size of volumes had to be reduced and data storage improved. The art grew by means of three types of abridgement: the principal part for the whole, the instrument ('real or metaphorical') for the thing (the eye set on high for the science of God), one thing for another (the snake coiled in a circle for the universe). These three stenographic representations suppose knowledge, a growth in knowledge. They are the premises of the thesis, and Warburton dwells on them particularly in regard to the third type of abridgement, that which proceeds from 'some resemblance to or delicate analogy with the other.'

At the point we have now reached (the second stage, hieroglyphic writing in the strict sense), we are dealing solely with a 'method devised to preserve the memory of the deeds and thoughts of men,' nothing is being contrived with a view to 'secrecy,' everything is following a natural necessity.

This remains true when the same economic imperative forces the passage from the hieroglyph (Egyptian) to the ideogram (Chinese). But this time the economic difficulty no longer derives solely from 'the enormous size of the volumes written in pictures' (insofar as there is still some pictogram in the hieroglyph). The limited number of hieroglyphic characters also necessitates a change of system, a rejection of the images that the Egyptians still preserved, and an augmentation of the 'characteristic marks' that they were adding to them. Chinese writing thus went 'a step further.' It multiplied the 'abbreviated marks ... to a prodigious number'; 'each idea has its distinctive mark.' Independent of language, it can be spread among nations speaking different languages and thus possesses the 'universal character of picture-writing' (§ 4).

But just as the pictogram (already scribled by a rhetoric) partook *already* of the hieroglyph, so the Chinese ideogram partakes of it still. It is a 'more abbreviated and refined hieroglyph' (*ibid.*). 'These more modern characters are nevertheless *true hieroglyphs*' (*ibid.*). The hieroglyph is thus clearly the exemplary center of writing, its medium, an element, a species and the genus, a part and the whole, general writing.

It was however a writing in advance of its time—before the letter. Now, the passage to the letter ('for letters are the last step that remains to be taken after the Chinese marks' § 5) does not break with this law of the hieroglyph. The Chinese marks that 'partake on the one hand of the nature of hieroglyphs,' 'on the other partake of letters.' The last step, the alphabetic letter, completes 'the general history of writing, brought by simple gradations from the state of the picture to the state of the letter.' The advantage of the alphabet still remains *steno*graphic; it holds meaning in a narrower, *stricter* place. Chinese characters were already so 'close' to letters that the alphabet simply *restrained* their number and hence the space they occupied without altering their essential nature. It 'merely lessens the cumbersomeness of their number and is a succinct epitome of them.' What I have elsewhere proposed to call the law of *stricture*[7] would indeed manifest itself as the process of general writing. That this law does not possess the linearistic, economistic, and continuistic simplicity that it sometimes takes on in the *Essai* is only too obvious but would involve us in a problematic of which I can here only indicate the locus.

For the moment, then, in this 'general history of writing,' no recesses, no 'mystery,' contrary to what Kircher thought. The apparent and badly analyzed rupture between picto-hieroglyphic representation (representation of things or meanings, of 'idea') and alphabetic representation (of words) led to belief (which it produces by its structure) in the mystery and divine origin of the 'marvelous artifice of letters.' Whenever a new type or a new stenography arises, one believes that a rupture has occurred instead of analyzing the simple gradation: an effect of breaking and of mystery. This was already true before the alphabetic event. A little more than simply another stenogram, the letter conceals the natural necessity of its production. And its continuity.

According to Warburton, Plato and Cicero already were mistaken about this. They did not pay 'attention,' simply, to that 'natural and simple progress' which moves from the hieroglyph to the letter and to which the 'words' *sēmeia* and *sēmata* bear witness, as words, precisely, as well as natural indices, 'meaning both *images of natural things and artificial marks or characters*: and *graphō*, signifying both *to paint* and *to write*' (*ibid.*). The opposition between nature and artifice therefore has no relevance to writing.

But it is itself—insofar as it is a lure—an effect of writing. One should therefore be able to propose that if mystery and secrecy (with all their political and religious overtones) *befell* writing, the cause is external to them ('an exterior cause' and one 'foreign to their nature' (§ 6), that of stenographic progress: 'some private or peculiar cause unrelated to their general nature'), although of an exteriority that natural and hence internal laws must explain. Here lies the entire difficulty of the *Essai*. It will have to be explained that the *veil* of mystery and secrecy was necessary and inevitable, but like the exteriority of the alien, the parasite: the necessity, at once natural and unnatural, of the crypt. It is not natural that nature naturally likes to encrypt itself.

If the natural, and hence universal, necessity of this general history of writings has not imposed itself uniformly on all nations, it is because of accidents of various kinds. Warburton's explanation is here, for reasons that I have just indicated, necessarily involved. This general history of writings, as it is conceived, has small hold on history. It will prove necessary to say that the Mexican Empire was not sufficiently long-lived to pass from the pictogram to the hieroglyph; that the Chinese (another kind of explanation, less external in appearance) did not attain to letters because of their 'scant inventive genius' and *their* xenophobia.

Henceforth, in order to prove the natural necessity of the laws without recourse to choice or art, a detour is necessary, this time through the origin and history of speech. In the process, the rational and naturalistic explanation of prophetic languages will serve religion. The freethinker will no longer judge fanatical or absurd the visions of the prophets: they will be explained to him by the necessity of action language, 'a common and familiar manner of conversing' (§ 9) to which God, as well as the prophets, could or had to have recourse. The prophets were content to speak the 'idiom of their country.' This argument opposes both freethinkers and Christian authors who wish prophetic language to retain its supernatural character.

Parallel growth of the two arts: as language develops and is refined, Warburton follows the analogy with writing or action language. For example, the apologue is a kind of discourse that 'corresponds' to hieroglyphic writing: in the two cases, the 'symbol of a different thing' is 'understood' (§ 12). Not only are the same symbolic displacements comparable but the same economic condensations as well. The privilege of the economic viewpoint (the economistic mechanism) in the analysis of structures biases the attention toward condensations rather than displacements, and hence, no doubt, toward metaphorization. In this way we follow the process of the apologue which becomes 'simile' when language is refined (the economy of narrative); then the 'simile,' which would correspond to Chinese writing, produces the metaphor: by stenolexia, one might say, metaphor being a 'simile in small' (*ibid.*), exactly as the ideogram makes way for the letter, or rather becomes the more economical letter.

In its two parallel or analogous paths, this analysis can be reduced neither to the diachrony of a genetic narrative nor to the placing of structural, ahistorical relationships. One kind of writing or language may remain in use when another, later and more economical, has already imposed itself. This permits not only a more finely differentiated, suppler, and more faithful historical description, but also a more admissible explanation of the fact that matters above all else to Warburton: the Egyptians maintained their writing in spite of its relative inconvenience because it was the very treasure-house of their lore, whose antiquity is thereby demonstrated.

All those were mistaken, whether ancients or moderns, who believed that hieroglyphs were designed for secrecy, for mystery, for the cryptic concealment of knowledge. Nothing in the natural laws of their production determined them for this.

And yet this is what came about. Warburton does not contest it. That which should not have come about was to come about.[8] May one even venture, in the margins, this proposition: that such is the structure of that which comes about if it does come about—in other words, of the event? The *should-not* describes (by force and play of structuring forces) the very edges of that which is henceforth to fix itself in it, in the form of the 'unforeseeable' event. That which should not have come about, or should have not come about (an imperceptible and immediately necessary transformation of the utterance) was to come about, could come about, could not fail to come about.[9] The matter at hand is still writing and a play of power. Warburton must maintain that this—the crypt or the veil—ought not to have come about (an accident has supervened) and that it has come about nevertheless, has come about in accordance with a rigorous necessity; and that what has thus come about does not weaken—on the contrary—the premises of this explanation, according to which nothing of the sort was naturally foreseeable. This is the task of the Second Part—laborious, involved, but also richer. The entire difficulty of the crypt is sheltered in the fold between two parts: *how did this come about?* 'I hope to have shown that the opinion of the Ancients and the Moderns, regarded until now as incontestable, that the Egyptians invented Hieroglyphs in order to hide their lore and to make it mysterious, has no legitimate foundation. However, as it is certain that this nation did put it to that purpose in the end, we must examine how this came about . . .' (§ 15).

How did this come about? How did writing become *veiled* (covered and twisted, concealed and devious, masked, hypocritical)? Warburton claims to answer this question by taking up again the analysis he elaborated in the first part, by *reapplying* it, so to speak, this time to Egyptian hieroglyphics alone, the non-limiting element and milieu of writing. The reapplication is much more minute and highly differentiated; it is the solemn and critical moment of the book. A sort of battle is joined at the moment (as for the moment) that darkness has fallen over history.

After a description of the *four* kinds of hieroglyphic writing (1. *Hieroglyphic*, curiological or tropical; 2. *Symbolic*, simple and tropical or mysterious and allegorical; 3. *Epistolic*, intended for civil affairs; 4. *Hierogrammatic*, intended for matters of religion:—the first two consisting of marks of things, the latter two of marks of words), after a description of the relationships between them (sometimes of *supplementarity* (*supply*) § 18) and of the errors to which they have given rise, Warburton comes down to the question of veiling, of what veils a body or a machine or indeed a vehicle of writing that begins suddenly, veiled, to act differently and with a view to mystery. Léonard des Malpeines translates: 'Examinons présentement comment les hiéroglyphes sont devenus un voile mystérieux.' Warburton: 'Let us next enquire how *hieroglyphics* came to be employed for the *vehicle of mystery*.' If one takes into account, in addition, the role that the figures of the veil and the vehicle played in the rhetoric of rhetoric, in an impossible meta-rhetoric, the secret fold linked to superencoding manifests (or veils) itself from the very moment the question is uttered.

Everything is then re-examined, from the pictographic origins of Egyptian writing onward. The veiling is a continuous, gradual, imperceptible passage. The cryptic catastrophe seems never to have taken place in an event. Even the reversal is not apparent. This non-event should not, if such is really the case, have any proper place. *It does not take place here.* It does however manifest itself on analysis; it lets itself be located strictly, the structure producing precisely an effect of place, yet of an improper place since the 'proper place,' if one might still say so, of the catastrophe would be located very precisely between the so-called '*proper*' hieroglyph in its most highly evolved form, the *tropical*, and the so-called 'symbolic' hieroglyph in its least highly evolved form, still the *tropical*. The veil falls between the second kind of the first hieroglyph and the first kind of the second, between the two of one and the one of two—which have in common, in a common weld, being tropical. Dissimulation, ruse, and perfidy of writing, reversal of places and of history, again a catastrophe of *tristes tropiques*. A tropical revolution, inside the trope, since the first tropes served to make manifest and the second to encrypt: 'such was the progress of the two kinds of proper hieroglyphs, which, in their final state as tropical hieroglyphs, came close to being symbolic ones, of which we are going to speak. They had this in common: both represented one thing by means of another; and they differed in that the tropical hieroglyph served to divulge, and tropical symbol to keep hidden' (§ 23). The passage from one to the other was progressive, continuous, imperceptible, one of complication by refinement. A *passage*, says Léonard des Malpeines, though Warburton said a *fall*, both however stressing the 'insensible degrees.' 'The following examples will let us see how easily the tropical hieroglyph passed into the state of (*fell into*) the tropical symbol. Eternity was represented now by the sun and the moon, now by the basilisk: Egypt by the crocodile, and formerly by a lighted censer with a heart on it. The simplicity of the first figure in these two examples and the refinement of the second show that the one was a tropical symbol, intended to be known, and the other a tropical symbol, invented for secrecy' (*ibid.*). Again a continuous passage from the tropical symbol to the enigmatic symbol; and the fact that this occurs by 'insensible degrees' should not harm the rigor of the demonstration. This imperceptibility is the very condition of the occultation. The concealment must conceal itself, the crypt encrypt itself; it must never be recognized for what it is. Its power then becomes impregnable.

By the same token, these insensible degrees spreading out over all of hieroglyphic space from the first kind of 'proper' characters (curiological) up to the last kind of symbolic characters (enigmatic), the general affinity becomes unrecognizable. One believes in the rupture and the overturning. This is the origin of the common and naive mistake: blind to the continuity, one no longer understands the sense of the overturning.

In the interval of 'insensible degrees,' the veiling of writing shelters, conceals, and *produces* perhaps all of the history of metaphysics. Let this be translated: of a certain tropics. If this is the case, the metaphysical would be the effect, within the event of that which is proper to it, of a veiling of writing concealing itself in accordance with all the implications (historical, political, economic, technical, and psychic as well, as we shall see further on) that we acknowledge while reading the *Essai*. Is it forcing this text to attribute to it this interpretation (itself perhaps metaphysical, by yet another turn) of metaphysics? Let us see. Just when he notes the 'insensible degrees' between the first and last hieroglyphs, an example comes up. It is not just any one. It concerns the hieroglyph (the two hieroglyphs, rather, since there is also a doubling) as it comes 'to mark universal nature.' How is universal nature written? How is the concept written that plays such a role in Warburton's discourse? How is nature, or rather *physis*, written? It is written twice and in two ways: one he calls *physical* (we must still see about this) and the other *metaphysical*, the latter being, in short, only the *enigmatic* refinement of the first trope (*curiological*), the whole of the operation remaining within the *symbolic*: 'One is the figure commonly called *Diana multimammia*; the other is a winged globe with a serpent emerging from it. The first, which is in the simplest taste, is a curiological hieroglyph; and the second, by its mysterious assemblage, is an enigmatic symbol. But observe that, in the first figure, universal nature is considered *physically*; and in the latter, *metaphysically*, according to the different genius of the times in which these two riddles were invented' (*ibid.*).

It will be said: Warburton is here making use of a received opposition, already traditional and itself metaphysical, between the physical and the meta-physical. He does not question it and, particularly, he does not talk about the origins of metaphysics just when he is opposing the physical mark (a metaphor that is moreover coded as feminine and maternal) to the metaphysical mark (a metaphor classified on the masculine and phallic side). So much is true. But if one takes into account the fact 1. that he does not merely turn writing into an auxiliary; 2. that the history of hieroglyphs appears to him indissociable from a history of meaning and knowledge, along with their politico-technico-economic condition; and 3. that metaphor is here being conceived as origi-nary, then one must read in the *Essai* a formal and general description of the metaphysical, of the process of idealization running from the physical to the metaphysical. Whether a cover for or a veiling of *physis*, this can only further urge us on.

But metaphysical supplementarity is not limited to this. Once a refinement of scrypture [*écrypture*] has produced the metaphysical as an effect of enigma (the concentration of a secret narrative), once hieroglyphs 'have ceased to serve to communicate thoughts openly and have become a means of keeping them hidden (*vehicle for secrecy*)' (§ 24), a 'more remarkable change' affects them further ('they suffered a more remarkable change'). It consists in a supplemen-tary and inverse veiling that overturns: a catastrophe of catastrophe, a strophic veiling of the veiling. The abstract metaphysical elements are metaphorized in their turn—not in order to render them accessible to the common man, as one would be naïvely tempted to believe, but 'as an addition made by design to lead the vulgar astray' (*ibid.*). And 'in order to render the matter still more mysterious' (*ibid.*), modes and substances were represented by images.

This gives rise, for example, to an entire zoography (openness: a hare; destruction: a mouse; knowledge: an ant, etc.), which is affected by a supple-mentary complication. It has bearing on a certain passage between this problematic and that of the 'contradictory meaning of primal words'[10] that sought its first examples in Egyptian writing: 'in order to render the matter still more mysterious, one animal served to represent several very contrary moral modes. Thus the falcon signified loftiness, humility, victory, excellence, etc. On the contrary, and for the same reason, a single thing was represented by several and various hieroglyphs . . .' (*ibid.*).

This undecidability will be one of the privileged resources for the workings of mastery and priesthood. The politico-symbolic workings of the master and the priestly interpreter [*l'interprètre (sic)*] come into play between two contrary meanings of the same mark or between two distinct marks with the same meaning.

This is the very status of the priest, it is there that he takes place but also that he takes care not to stand up and show himself or to expose his place. One can have no access to the meaning of priesthood, nor even to the priestly caste itself in the concentration of all its powers (religious, political, scientific, psychic, etc.), without going through this veiling by catastrophes and this contrived undecidability of the mark.

The common man now no longer knows which way to turn, where to find the master-meaning, the repository, or the lay-out of knowledge. He is manipulated, misled, doomed to a wandering controlled from without, a programmed nomad, indeed, and this also holds for future Interpreters of Hieroglyphic Writings. Kircher, for example. They are the victims, a few centuries overdue, of the priestly stratagem, of the same one acting *at a distance*, for such is the nature of its power.

The process is never-ending, by definition. To the supplementary complication of the 'remarkable change' another alteration is yet to be added. Again in order to save *volume*, both time and space, and thus to concentrate the reserve of power and knowledge, Egyptian men of learning substituted abstract 'marks' of the Chinese kind, a sort of 'cursive script,' for hieroglyphs that still retained *representative* value. The abstraction and arbitrariness of these signs added, to be sure, to the effacement of the marking mark in front of the thing signified. This effacement was a 'natural effect.' The use of the mark 'detracted considerably from the attention paid to the symbol and fixed it on the thing signified.' But, paradoxically, what was added to by this was the power of the mark. One had no longer to remember the figuration, the representative figure-head, the content of the symbol—in short, all the knowledge concerning the symbol. The attention was freer to turn to the side of the 'thing signified,' to be sure, but also to dispose of the arbitrary mark in its maximum condensation. Arbitrariness and power unite more successfully than ever under the veil of abstraction. One can even say the arbitrariness-power and, by the same token, the power that holds the arbitrary position. This occurs in the form of differences of force, for example in the attention lent to the concrete symbol. The weakening of this attention always serves priestly mastery. And the apparent freedom opened up by the arbitrariness of the sign is a commandeering [*arraisonnement*] of forces, the diversion of another system of non-semiotic motivation. In this regard, let us say so stenographically, the scope of the *Essai* can not be *simply* exceeded by the Nietzschean and post-Nietzschean period, whether it is a question of power, of force, of writing, of the arbitrariness of the sign, of motivation, of the priest, and therefore of still other themes. Therefore: 'I mean, that its use detracted considerably from the attention paid to the symbol and fixed it on the thing signified. By this means, the study of symbolic writing was much abbreviated, there being then little else to do but to remember the *power* of the symbolic mark, whereas before one had to be instructed in the properties of the thing or animal employed as a symbol. In a word, this reduced this kind of writing to the state that is presently that of the Chinese' (§ 26). Léonard des Malpeines translates faithfully but deletes—as he does regularly, and sometimes at much greater length—that which concerns the institution, the expressions, and the concepts of 'signs of institution,' marks of institution, etc. His last sentence in this paragraph curiously abridged this one: '*this, together with their other* marks *by* institution, *to design mental ideas, would reduce the characters to the present state of the* Chinese.'

The power of the mark thus increases with its degree of arbitrariness. That is to say also insofar as the mark seems to fade away in front of the meaning—whence the devious twist of this power.

Warburton, citing Huntington, describes the monumental example of that powerful, vertical writing which is read from top to bottom, like Chinese. It is Aguglia's Columns or the Columns, as the native inhabitants say simply.

By an 'easy step' and quite 'naturally,' one is thus led from cursive writing (hierographic) to epistolic, to the 'abbreviated method of letters by means of an alphabet: the sublime invention from which epistolic writing was formed.' It was attributed, Léonard des Malpeines recalls, to the Secretary of the King of Egypt. But if he names Theuth (Hermes) in a note, he omits a paragraph in the course of which Warburton cites Plato's *Phaedrus* and the scene of the *pharmakon* (Theuth presenting writing to King Thamus, who declares himself hostile to it in the name of unsound reasons). Léonard nevertheless proposes the word *remedy* in the course of his free adaptation. It was while seeking a remedy that the Secretary invented the alphabet, but a remedy against the equivocality and obscurity of discourse. To ensure proper communication of the orders of the King to generals and provincial governors, it was better to represent words than things. 'I think therefore that our Secretary, in seeking a remedy for this, invented an alphabet, of which he made the letters serve to express words and not things. By this means, all the inconveniences detrimental in these circumstances were avoided, and the writer passed along his instructions with the utmost clarity and precision' (§ 27). This writing of power was at first designed for State secrecy, more precisely for Letters of State, whence the name *epistolic*: '. . . as the government doubtless sought to keep the invention secret, Letters of State were for some time conveyed with all the security of our modern ciphers' (*ibid.*).

What was invented 'for secrecy,' and for political secrecy, would thus be, according to this hypothesis, phonetic writing, that which first professed to be the invisible (imageless) vehicle of a spoken word—and not the hieroglyph in the strict sense, even if the functions could subsequently, in the course of the revolution, be interchanged.

As the political code cannot, by its essence, be kept secret, 'this alphabet, which we may call *political*,' had as it were to be doubled quickly. Whence a 'sacred' alphabet, which was none the less political. Whenever a code is unveiled, disencrypted, made public, the mechanism of power produces another one, secret and sacred, 'profound.' Its *natural* producers are the priests insofar as they have a share in power and knowledge. They secrete the code supplement. This artificial perversion is hence, like the secret/sacred that it engenders, a natural production. It was 'naturally' that the priests made use of the political alphabet and then, when this was divulged, it was 'naturally again' that they added another one. 'This alphabet, which we may call *political*, soon occasioned the invention of a *sacred* alphabet. For the Egyptian priests, having a share in the government, doubtless knew the secret early on; and being then immersed in the study of philosophy and in deep speculations, they naturally made use of it for their hidden doctrines. But the various uses to which this alphabet was put in civil affairs did not permit it to remain a secret long; and when it was known, the priests would, again naturally, invent another one for their use' (§ 28). And this was true (naturally, and hence universally) of the priests of 'nearly all nations,' jealous of power and knowledge, seeking to 'keep learning to themselves' (§ 32) and so, by the same token, to ensure their power.

The growing phonetization of writing multiplies the veil supplements. For the alphabet, in serving to signify words and not things, in 'substituting words for things' (§ 32), is democratized or divulges easily since the language is 'common.' Whence the necessity of a code supplement and another language, of a 'double veil': 'But the simple mystery of a special alphabet, for which the words of a common language would have served, would quickly have been uncovered. It therefore appears that they invented a special language for the use of their alphabet, and that they succeeded in hiding their lore under a double veil (*double cover*).' This supplementary language ('sacred dialect') would then have been formed *on the basis of writing*: ciphered names would be assigned according to the graphic code relating hieroglyphs to the Egyptian language. *Yk* signifies snake in the 'natural' language; the snake denotes a king in hieroglyphs; *Yk* will mean king in the secret language. Warburton, who here borrows from Manetho, can conclude in favor of this graphic origin of language. The natural democratization of writing, for instance its phonetization, immediately requires a crypt supplement, a new language, a new writing, a new language. 'It is in this way that their hieroglyphs became a basis for a wholly new language' (*ibid.*).

Always more veil, 'continual revolution' (*incessant revolutions of things*) since the crypt is uncovered regularly and another must be invented which in turn . . . etc. At each turn, more veil. 'But as a result of the continual revolution of things, these same figures that had at first been invented for clarity and then converted into mystery, at length resumed their initial use' (§ 33).

There is thus a wearing-away of the veil, of the double veil, a double wearing-away of the veil: use deteriorates the veil, makes it more and more common and transparent, but prompts the production of a surplus-value whose wearing-away redistributed in its turn, will call for the more-veil. This revolutionary wearing-away is also the law of language. Warburton turns back a second time to language, 'of which even the slightest progress and changes followed the fate of writing (*ran parallel with writing*).' He follows this parallelism through allegory ('veil and disguise of discourse,' '*covering and disguise to the discourse*'), parable, riddle, and the dark sayings of wisdom. The surplus-value that accrues to writing also increases the power of the priestly interpreter [*l'interprètre*]. 'The veil (*cover*) of this kind of wisdom made it, as such a veil always will, the most high prized of all talents' (§ 34), but also made it, as a Hebrew proverb attests, the 'skill of defrauding and deceiving.'

Need or desire, the movement toward knowledge is not *served* by writing or by language. Rather, it serves them. It is in the service of veil effects sought with a view to power, to all powers. Knowledge is thrown into the bargain, or more precisely it is a market effect in the cryptopolitics of writing. And this last originates in a 'mere need':

> After the art of writing had been perfected to the point of being symbolic, the Egyptians, in order to give it an air of elegance and learning, and a mysterious veil at the same time (*as to cloud it with a variegated obscurity*), studied all the singular properties of beings, and their various relations, so as to make use of them to represent other things. It was the same with the art of speech. Men soon began to adorn the various manners of expressing themselves just mentioned with tropes and figures: for which reason posterity subsequently doubted the origin of figurative expressions, just as it doubted the origin of hieroglyphic painting. But both arts owed their birth to mere need and the coarseness of men; that is, to a want of words and the coarseness of conceptions. (§ 35)

Knowing how (or in order) 'to represent other things'—this is the first action, the first action language as well, dictated by *need*, by that which begins by lacking (words and concepts, for example, that is to say already representatives). Power, the power that the priest commandeers, results from the necessity of 'representing something else'; and it appears at the threshold of representation. When need supplies the lack by representation, a priest is born. And fetishism, too (*as to cloud it* introduces both the theory of fetishism in *The Twilight of the Idols* and the theory of the 'mystic cloud' and of the movements of 'veil' (*mystischen Nebelschleier*) that supports the discourse of *Capital* on merchandise, fetishism, religion, and political economy).[11] The motivation is never interrupted. Arbitrariness is a ruse to conceal motivation and power by creating the illusion of an *internal* system of language or writing in general. One is still taken in by this today, by a supplement of ruse or naïveté—which, by reason of the essential limit that constitutes need, always comes back, somewhere, to

the same thing. In sheltering the inside of a functioning, systematic partition-
ing always conceals the more powerful manoeuvers of motivation—and of
another system. What regularly bursts open this reassuring enclosure is the
duplicity of the functioning that is always possible, even always inevitable, from
within a system. Examples: 1. the pleonastic redundancy that translates the
'lack of words,' the excess of words letting itself be motivated by need and
indigence themselves; 2. the doubling of metaphor which, supplying the deficiencies of the 'coarseness' of the concept, always supersaturates itself with an
esoteric double. Warburton compares metaphors to letters of an alphabet.
Here, too, they are of two kinds: 'one for the use of the public, the other for
the use of the priests.' 'There were clear and intelligible metaphors, and others
that were obscure and mysterious. The writings of the Prophets are full of this
latter kind of metaphor' (§ 36).

Even if they do supersaturate indefinitely a natural and originary process,
Warburton considered all these veilings, until now, as normal, in a way: a
normal complication of the natural norm, a natural revolution in writing.

The sacred crypt, the genealogy of a political religion, the diversion of
power and knowledge—everything that is brewing beneath the veils of a
caste or the robe of priests sinks to depravity or degeneracy only with the
advent of magic, superstition, or charms. Warburton would like this moment
to remain distinct, ulterior, supervenient. He therefore struggles with the
implacable constraint of a dangerous supplementarity that he does not wish
to recognize—and yet has to admit—as coming from without only by virtue
of having already worked within. He must endlessly say (the) 'besides': 'To
conclude, we will observe in the last place that besides all these changes,
which the ancient hieroglyphs underwent, they were finally put to very
depraved use (*a very perverse corruption*) like the Mysteries, that other important
source of Egyptian wisdom, which, in the end, degenerated into magic.
Precisely the same thing befell hieroglyphs' (§ 40). Warburton would like to
see in this a pathological depravation, an unjustifiable negativity, a mere way-
wardness that must be set right—because it leads religion astray, to be sure,
but also science, the modern science of interpretation. It must also, for
example, have induced the hermeneutic aberration of Kircher, who confused
Egyptian wisdom with this refuse of superstition and magic, with the power
of spells, with a 'magical pollution.' These last words disappear in the *Essai*.

Yet the difference between Warburton's theses and those that he professes
to oppose may still seem slim, indeed even imperceptible. It is admitted on all
sides that the power of writing was crypto-gnoseo-political. And Warburton
goes so far as to acknowledge a law in this becoming-cryptic even if he
affirms that writing was not *originarily* devised for secrecy. Can we not raise
this resemblance between the two theses as an objection against Warburton
and propose that he forego a question of origin, the question of an origin

which, as he admits, had to be veiled? Can we not, on the same impulse, judge relative and hence loose the alleged antiquity of Egyptian lore, which War-burton insists on so strongly and which he conceives of in fact as a priority or at least an anteriority?

Warburton pretends to address to himself an objection of this sort: 'Since in asserting that hieroglyphs were not invented for secrecy you agree that they were later put to that use and that they long continued in it even after the invention of letters, it might very well be, one will say, that this profound learning, which authors agree to have been put into hieroglyphics, is the work of centuries later by far than the antiquity that you attribute to it' (§ 42).

Two replies to this objection: the one that Warburton articulates himself and the one that we might develop beyond his stated purpose.

1. If hieroglyphs had not from their beginnings been the treasure-house of learning (the 'repository of so great a treasure of learning' (*ibid.*)), if they had not been inseparable from knowledge, the Egyptians would have abandoned them, by reason of their inconvenience, with the invention of letters. Techno-economic law would have come into play by itself, simply and linearly, in favor of letters, 'if the hieroglyphs had not contained this learning, so highly prized, and if they had been merely records of civil matters.' And the Egyptian nation was the only one 'that continued to write in *marks* after the invention of *letters*.'

This explicit reply already has a general bearing: the power of the archive and of the historico-political order always maintains, within the broadest structures of the apparatus of writing, an irreducible adherence to power that is properly epistemic. Adherence does not mean homogeneity, absolute synchrony, or immediate permeability, but a complex buttressing of all of these, the impossibility of a pure history of knowledge, the necessity of taking into account all the technical, economic, and political apparatus that bind knowledge to its text. Warburton in this way provides himself, at least accord-ing to the principle, with the means to explain or describe the remanences, the stases, the inequalities in development, and the traditional inertias to which he pays a great deal of attention. Despite certain appearances, even the principle of his 'evolutionism' is not simply 'economistic' or 'lineatistic.'

2. By claiming to return to this side of the double veil, and by considering the crypt effect as a historical quasi-event, Warburton precisely avoids natu-ralizing it or taking it to be a primary fact whose constitution or construction, historical process, and techno-political motivation no longer have to be ana-lyzed. A certain naturalism, a certain apologetism as well, permit Warburton to denaturalize the crypt. They give him *in principle* the means to analyze the structure and genesis of this gnoseo-political crypt of writing, and at the same time to appeal to a scientific decipherment of the hieroglyphs. The means to analyze a constructum may also become, under certain conditions, means of

action, with a view to a deconstruction that would not be only theoretical. But it is true that the naturalism implied by any question of ideal origin immediately limits the means that it provides. This limit doubtless has a specific form in the historico-theoretical space that borders the *Essai*. Rousseau's *Discourses*, which are precisely contemporaneous with it, and his *Essay on the Origin of Languages* as well as many others are affected by it. It remains that this schema, which opens questions even while imposing a logic of the *fall* (original sin is only one example) and an accidentalist treatment of the supplement, passes as such far beyond this historico-theoretical configuration.

There is not *one* power, *the* power of *the* mark. This singular would still lead to some mystification: fostering the belief that one can do otherwise than to oppose powers to powers and writings to other writings, or again that the unity of *power* (and of *knowledge*) is always itself, the same, wherever it is and whatever force it represents.

But there are *powers, knowledges,* in every instance interlinked and linked to marking forces in a general agonistics: irenic, apathetic, angelic, or anarchic discourse always answers, too, to the purpose of the priesthood. Whoever situates and settles it at once, limits his movement within a strict margin.

The power of knowledge, State power, economic power, moral power, religious power, etc.—so many *political* institutions of *cryptography*. One more must be named. Without rushing into analogism, some might recognize in this the unvarying features of a system: the *institution linked to the science of dreams*.

When Warburton wishes to demonstrate that oneirocritical science, born wholly of hieroglyphic writing, must have formed part of the treasure of science, he is still speaking, of course, of the theological science reserved for priests and not of the one that today possesses its powers only by virtue of having entered upon the sure course of a science. But if one does not believe in the (political) simplicity of the epistemological-break, is there not something to read, for us today, in this interpretation of the 'art of interpreting dreams'? in what it says about the relations between the science of dreams, writing, knowledge in general, power, the hegemony represented by a priestly caste, etc.?

Warburton, of course, does not believe in the truth or even the effectiveness of Egyptian oneirocritics. He only wants to show, in support of his general thesis, that the oneirocritics possessed their knowledge and their power, without admitting it, from writing. As Freud will later do in the *Traumdeutung*, he refers to Artemidorus, who divided dreams into *speculative* (a simple and direct image of the event foretold) and *allegorical* (a typical and symbolic image requiring an interpretation). Those who consulted the interpreters (who were not 'imposters,' but were sometimes more 'superstitious' than others) were looking for a 'known analogy': 'But what other analogy and what other authority could there be than the *symbolic hieroglyphs*, which had then become a sacred and mysterious thing' (§ 43). The treasure-house of hieroglyphs thus furnished them with the 'materials.' And the symbolic science of the priests 'served as a foundation for their interpretations.' It was moreover the same word (to be translated by *stoikheia* or elements) that served to designate, according to Artemidorus, the 'phantoms seen in dreams,' 'symbolic marks,' and the 'first elements and principles of things.' 'There was nothing so *natural* [my emphasis] as to use the same term to express the same images engraved on stone and in the imagination' (§ 44).

The symbolic marks of writing did not serve as a resource for oneirocritics alone, which was more anxious to interpret dreams by writing than to turn the question around (but is it enough today to turn a cryptographic question around?). These marks furnished animal-religion and idolatry in general with powerful symbolic materials. This is Warburton's conclusion. Here again, as he insists, the cryptographic stratagem presses toward knowledge. In order to occult by writing, *knowledge is needed*. And the substitution of a supplementary crypt, the superencoding *ad infinitum*, takes on a truly compulsive air.

> *The Egyptians worshipped* not only animals but plants as well, and, to say it in a word, every being in which they had noted singular or sovereign qualities: that is, *those same beings that had found their place* in symbolic writing. For when hieroglyphs came to be used for mysterious writing, we have shown that the Egyptians, as soon as a symbol became known, would invent another, more hidden one; and if it was again necessary to change it, they invented a third. So it was necessary to have a nearly complete knowledge of the animal, vegetable, and mineral worlds in order to explain the story of their gods. (§ 45)

Thus the politico-religious power represented by the priests can borrow its forces and its material only from the crypt of writing, but it requires and animates to this end an epistemophilic drive that is always in motion. Nothing is here dissociable.

Priests are not inventors of religion. They accumulate a sort of natural religiosity, commandeer it, divert it for their benefit, for the benefit of the caste and the hegemony it represents. It was 'natural' to worship the mark, to turn 'toward the mark' (§ 46) and toward divine representation. But this natural fetishism of writing was 'favored and fostered' by the priests, who are priests by this very fact, as well as hermetics, esoterics, seeking to make theological science 'more difficult to understand,' to reserve it for interpreters, to keep away the impious 'curious minds' which, 'in enquiring maliciously into the genealogies of the Egyptian gods, had gone back so near to their origin that, in order to counter the danger that their cult was running, the priests could do nothing else than multiply the difficulties of such an enquiry. . . .' Nothing could have been easier, first because of the overmarking and essential plethora that followed from it: 'there were several hieroglyphs to describe each divinity' (§ 47). And whenever a priest wishes to write 'the history of the sciences' and of human discoveries, that of his own hieroglyphic science first of all, he always invokes the intervention of the gods in an immemorial origin (§ 56): 'It was something so opposed to the politics of a pagan priest to ascertain the era of a deification that we cannot believe him guilty of such an error. He was, on the contrary, careful to push this era back beyond familiar time or at least to encourage the belief that immemorial time had since elapsed.'

This process leads them, here again, to multiply the supplements, to 'add new fables to the old theology of the gods' (§ 57). A violent process: by dint of veil, the supplement supplants. This law of supplementary veiling and general cryptography constrains all explanations of origin, that of writing or that of the gods, that of the power of genealogical explanation which the priest appropriates only by pretending to receive it from a divine origin. And however far one goes back toward the limit of the first need, there is always a writing, a religion, already. No first text, not even a virgin surface for its inscription, and if the palimpsest requires a bare, material support for an arche-writing, no palimpsest.

No preface.

This is why the political manoeuver of cryptography does not consist in inventing new religions but in making use of the remanence, in 'taking advantage of those that they [the politicians] find already established' (§ 61). Such is the 'method of politicians.'

Notes

1. Cf. *Of Grammatology*, trans. Gayatri Chakravorty Spivak (Baltimore: Johns Hopkins University Press, 1976), pp. 7, 60ff. [Trans.]
2. As the generalization and dislocation of the notion is constitutive and pervasive in Derrida's project, this 'elsewhere' is scattered and multiple. Cf., for example, 'La Double séance' in *La Dissémination* (Paris: Editions du Seuil, 1972), pp. 207f., n. 7; *Of Grammatology*, p. 86, p. 332, n. 34, pp. 3–93 *passim*. [Trans.]
3. Section numbers refer to the French *Essai* only. [Trans.]
4. Warburton has 'supplying': '. . . supplying the deficiencies of speech by apt and significant signs. Accordingly, in the first ages of the world, mutual converse was upheld by a mixed discourse of words and actions; hence came the eastern phrase of the voice of the signs.' This last sentence, like many others and sometimes whole paragraphs, is omitted in the *Essai*. [Derrida]
5. Though not, as D. will himself point out, in the English original. [Trans.]
6. The father's right to the power of life and death over his children. [Trans.]
7. *Glas* (Paris: Editions Galilée, 1974), pp. 271–2, 115, 120, 124, 215. [Trans.]
8. '*Ce qui ne devait pas arriver devait arriver.*' Derrida here sets into play various meanings of the verb 'devoir' which cannot be rendered by a single word in English.

The possible readings may be schematized as follows:

	a. did not have to happen	a. had to happen
That which	b. was not to happen	b. was to happen
	c. should not have happened	c. should have happened

9. '*Ce qui ne devait pas arriver, ou devait ne pas arriver. . . devait arriver, pouvait arriver, ne pouvait pas ne pas arriver.*'

10. Cf. Freud, *Über den Gegensinn der Urworte, G.W.* VIII regarding Abel's hypothesis. Recourse to the example of hieroglyphs is essential to it. Cf. also Benveniste, *Problèmes de linguistique générale*; Derrida, *Freud et la scène de l'écriture*, in *L'Ecriture et la différence*, Seuil, 1967, p. 326. [Derrida]

11. Cf. J.-M. Rey, *L'Enjeu des signes* (Seuil, 1970); Bernard Pautrat, *Versions du soleil* (Seuil, 1971); Sarah Kofman, *Camera obscura – de l'idéologie* (Galilée, 1973); also *Baubó (perversion théologique et fétichisme chez Nietzsche)* in *Nuova Corriente*, 68–9, 1975–6; Jacques Derrida, *Nietzsche et la question du style*, in *Nietzsche aujourd'hui*, Plon 10/18, 1973; also *Eperons* (Flammarion, 1977); also *Glas* (Galilée, 1974), p. 231 *et seq. passim*. [Derrida]

Chapter 2

The Battle of Proper Names

But how is one to distinguish, in writing, between a man one mentions and a man one addresses. There really is an equivocation which would be eliminated by a vocative mark.—Essay on the Origin of Languages

Back now from *Tristes Tropiques* to the *Essay On the Origin of Languages*, from 'A Writing Lesson' given to the writing lesson refused by the person who was 'ashamed to toy' with the 'trifle[ing]' matter of writing in a treatise on education. My question is perhaps better stated thus: do they say the same thing? Do they do the same thing?

In that *Tristes Tropiques* which is at the same time *The Confessions* and a sort of supplement to the *Supplément au voyage de Bougainville*,[1] the 'Writing Lesson' marks an episode of what may be called the anthropological war, the essential confrontation that opens communication between peoples and cultures, even when that communication is not practiced under the banner of colonial or missionary oppression. The entire 'Writing Lesson' is recounted in the tones of violence repressed or deferred, a violence sometimes veiled, but always oppressive and heavy. Its weight is felt in various places and various moments of the *narrative*: in Lévi-Strauss's account as in the relationship among individuals and among groups, among cultures or within the same community. What can a relationship to writing signify in these diverse instances of violence?

Penetration in the case of the Nambikwara. The anthropologist's affection for those to whom he devoted one of his dissertations, *La vie familiale et sociale des Indiens Nambikwara* (1948). Penetration, therefore, into 'the lost world' of the Nambikwara, 'the little bands of nomads, who are among the most genuinely "primitive" of the world's peoples' on 'a territory the size of France,' traversed by a *picada* (a crude trail whose 'track' is 'not easily distinguished from the bush' [p. 262];[2] one should meditate upon all of the following together: writing as the possibility of the road and of difference, the history of writing and the history of the road, of the rupture, of the *via rupta*, of the path that is broken, beaten, *fracta*, of the space of reversibility and of repetition traced by the opening, the divergence from, and the violent spacing, of nature, of the natural, savage, salvage, forest. The *silva* is savage, the *via rupta* is written, discerned, and inscribed violently as difference, as form imposed on the *hylè*, in the forest, in wood as matter; it is difficult to imagine that access to the possibility of a road-map is not at the same time access to writing). The territory of the Nambikwara is crossed by the line of an autochthonic *picada*. But also by another *line*, this time imported:

> [An abandoned telephone line] obsolete from the day of its completion [which] hung down from poles never replaced when they go to rot and tumble to the ground. (Sometimes the termites attack them, and sometimes the Indians, who mistake the humming of the telegraph wires for the noise of bees on their way to the hive.) [p. 262]

The Nambikwara, whose tormenting and cruelty—presumed or not—are much feared by the personnel of the line, 'brought the observer back to what he might readily, though mistakenly, suppose to be the childhood of our race' [p. 265]. Lévi-Strauss describes the biological and cultural type of this population whose technology, economy, institutions, and structures of kinship, however primitive, give them of course a rightful place within humankind, so-called human society and the 'state of culture.' They speak and prohibit incest. 'All were interrelated, for the Nambikwara prefer to marry a niece (their sister's daughter), or a kinswoman of the kind which anthropologists call "cross-cousin": the daughter of their father's sister, or of their mother's brother' [p. 269]. Yet another reason for not allowing oneself to be taken in by appearances and for not believing that one sees here the 'childhood of our race:' the structure of the language. And above all its *usage*. The Nambikwara use several dialects and several systems according to situations. And here intervenes a phenomenon which may be crudely called 'linguistic' and which will be of central interest to us. It has to do with a *fact* that we have not the means of interpreting beyond its general conditions of possibility, its *a priori*; whose factual and empirical causes—as they open within this determined situation —will escape us, and, moreover, call forth no question on the part of Lévi-Strauss, who merely notes them. This fact bears on what we have proposed about the essence or the energy of the *graphein* as the originary effacement of the proper name. From the moment that the proper name is erased in a system, there is writing, there is a 'subject' from the moment that this obliteration of the proper is produced, that is to say from the first appearing of the proper and from the first dawn of language. This proposition is universal in essence and can be produced *a priori*. How one passes from this *a priori* to the determination of empirical facts is a question that one cannot answer in general here. First because, by definition, there is no general answer to a question of this form.

It is therefore such a *fact* that we encounter here. It does not involve the structural effacement of what we believe to be our proper names; it does not involve the obliteration that, paradoxically, constitutes the originary legibility of the very thing it erases, but of a prohibition heavily superimposed, in certain societies, upon the use of the proper name: "They are not allowed . . . to use proper names' [p. 270], Lévi-Strauss observes.

Before we consider this, let us note that this prohibition is necessarily derivative with regard to the constitutive erasure of the proper name in what I have called arche-writing, within, that is, the play of difference. It is because the proper names are already no longer proper names, because their production is their obliteration, because the erasure and the imposition of the letter are originary, because they do not supervene upon a proper inscription; it is because the proper name has never been, as the unique appellation reserved for the presence of a unique being, anything but the original myth of a transparent legibility present under the obliteration; it is because the proper name was never possible except through its functioning within a classification and therefore within a system of differences, within a writing retaining the traces of difference, that the interdict was possible, could come into play, and, when the time came, as we shall see, could be transgressed; transgressed, that is to say restored to the obliteration and the non-self-sameness [*non-propriété*] at the origin.

This is strictly in accord with one of Lévi-Strauss's intentions. In 'Universalization and Particularization' (*The Savage Mind*, Chapter VI) it will be demonstrated that 'one . . .never names: one classes someone else . . . [or] one classes oneself'[3] A demonstration anchored in some examples of prohibitions that affect the use of proper names here and there. Undoubtedly one should carefully distinguish between the essential necessity of the disappearance of the proper name and the determined prohibition which can, contingently and ulteriorly, be added to it or articulated within it. Nonprohibition, as much as prohibition, presupposes fundamental obliteration. Nonprohibition, the *consciousness* or exhibition of the proper name, only makes up for or uncovers an essential and irremediable impropriety. When within *consciousness*, the name *is called* proper, it is already classified and is obliterated in *being named*. It is already no more than a *so-called* proper name.

If writing is no longer understood in the narrow sense of linear and phonetic notation, it should be possible to say that all societies capable of producing, that is to say of obliterating, their proper names, and of bringing classificatory difference into play, practice writing in general. No reality or concept would therefore correspond to the expression 'society without writing.' This expression is dependent on ethnocentric oneirism, upon the vulgar, that is to say ethnocentric, misconception of writing. The scorn for writing, let us note in passing, accords quite happily with this ethnocentrism. The paradox is only apparent, one of those contradictions where a perfectly coherent desire is uttered and accomplished. By one and the same gesture, (alphabetic) writing, servile instrument of a speech dreaming of its plenitude and its self-presence, is scorned and the dignity of writing is refused to nonalphabetic signs. We have perceived this gesture in Rousseau and in Saussure.

The Nambikwara—the *subject* of 'A Writing Lesson'—would therefore be one of these peoples without writing. They do not make use of what *we* commonly call writing. At least that is what Lévi-Strauss tells us: 'That the Nambikwara could not write goes without saying' [p. 288]. This incapacity will be presently thought, within the ethico-political order, as an innocence and a non-violence interrupted by the forced entry of the West and the 'Writing Lesson.' We shall be present at that scene in a little while.

How can access to writing in general be refused to the Nambikwara except by determining writing according to a model? Later on we shall ask, confronting many passages in Lévi-Strauss, up to what point it is legitimate not to call by the name of writing those 'few dots' and 'zigzags' on their calabashes, so briefly evoked in *Tristes Tropiques*. But above all, how can we deny the practice of writing in general to a society capable of obliterating the proper, that is to say a violent society? For writing, obliteration of the proper classed in the play of difference, is the originary violence itself: pure impossibility of the 'vocative mark,' impossible purity of the mark of vocation. This 'equivocation,' which Rousseau hoped would be 'eliminated' by a 'vocative mark,' cannot be effaced. For the existence of such a mark in any code of punctuation would not change the problem. The death of absolutely proper naming, recognizing in a language the other as pure other, invoking it as what it is, is the death of the pure idiom reserved for the unique. Anterior to the possibility of violence in the current and derivative sense, the sense used in 'A Writing Lesson,' there is, as the space of its possibility, the violence of the arche-writing, the violence of difference, of classification, and of the system of appellations. Before outlining the structure of this implication, let us read the scene of proper names; with another scene, that we shall shortly read, it is an indispensable preparation for the 'Writing Lesson.' This scene is separated from the 'Writing Lesson' by one chapter and another scene: 'Family Life.' And it is described in Chapter 26 [23] 'On the Line.'

> The Nambikwara make no difficulties and are quite indifferent to the presence of the anthropologist with his notebooks and camera. But certain problems of language complicated matters. They are not allowed, for instance, to use proper names. To tell one from another we had to do as the men of the line do and agree with the Nambikwara on a set of nicknames which would serve for identification. Either Portuguese names, like Julio, Jose-Maria, Luisa; or sobriquets such as *Lebre*, hate, or *Assucar*, sugar. I even knew one whom Rondon or one of his companions had nicknamed Cavaignac on account of his little pointed beard—a rarity among Indians, most of whom have no hair on their faces. One day, when I was playing with a group of children, a little girl was struck by one of her comrades. She ran to me for protection and began to whisper something, a 'great secret,' in my ear. As I did not

understand I had to ask her to repeat it over and over again. Eventually her adversary found out what was going on, came up to me in a rage, and tried in her turn to tell me what seemed to be another secret. After a little while I was able to get to the bottom of the incident. The first little girl was trying to tell me her enemy's name, and when the enemy found out what was going on she decided to tell me the other girl's name, by way of reprisal. Thenceforward it was easy enough, though not very scrupulous, to egg the children on, one against the other, till in time I knew all of their names. When this was completed and we were all, in a sense, one another's accomplices, I soon got them to give me the adults' names too. When this [cabal] was discovered the children were reprimanded and my sources of information dried up.

We cannot enter here into the difficulties of an empirical deduction of this prohibition, but we know *a priori* that the 'proper names' whose interdiction and revelation Lévi-Strauss describes here are not proper names. The expression 'proper name' is improper, for the very reasons that *The Savage Mind* will recall. What the interdict is laid upon is the uttering of what *functions* as the proper name. And this function is *consciousness* itself. The proper name in the colloquial sense, in the sense of consciousness, is (I should say 'in truth' were it not necessary to be wary of that phrase)[5] only a designation of appurtenance and a linguistico-social classification. The lifting of the interdict, the great game of denunciation and the great exhibition of the 'proper' (let us note that we speak here of an act of war and there is much to say about the fact that it is little girls who open themselves to this game and these hostilities) does not consist in revealing proper names, but in tearing the veil hiding a classification and an appurtenance, the inscription within a system of linguistico-social differences.

What the Nambikwara hid and the young girls lay bare through transgression, is no longer the absolute idioms, but already varieties of invested common names, 'abstracts' if, as we read in *The Savage Mind* (p. 242) [p. 182], 'systems of appellations also have their "abstracts."'

The concept of the proper name, unproblematized as Lévi-Strauss uses it in *Tristes Tropiques*, is therefore far from being simple and manageable. Consequently, the same may be said of the concepts of violence, ruse, perfidy, or oppression, that punctuate 'A Writing Lesson' a little further on. We have already noted that violence here does not unexpectedly break in all at once, starting from an original innocence whose nakedness is *surprised* at the very moment that the secret of the *so-called* proper names is violated. The structure of violence is complex and its possibility—writing—no less so.

There was in fact a first violence to be named. To name, to give names that it will on occasion be forbidden to pronounce, such is the originary violence of language which consists in inscribing within a difference, in classifying, in suspending the vocative absolute. To think the unique *within* the system, to inscribe it there, such is the gesture of the arche-writing: arche-violence, loss of the proper, of absolute proximity, of self-presence, in truth the loss of what has never taken place, of a self-presence which has never been given but only dreamed of and always already split, repeated, incapable of appearing to itself except in its own disappearance. Out of this arche-violence, forbidden and therefore confirmed by a second violence that is reparatory, protective, instituting the 'moral,' prescribing the concealment of writing and the effacement and obliteration of the so-called proper name which was already dividing the proper, a third violence can *possibly* emerge or not (an empirical possibility) within what is commonly called evil, war, indiscretion, rape; which consists of revealing by effraction the so-called proper name, the originary violence which has severed the proper from its property and its self-sameness [*propriété*]. We could name a third violence of reflection, which denudes the native non-identity, classification as denaturation of the proper, and identity as the abstract moment of the concept. It is on this tertiary level, that of the empirical consciousness, that the common concept of violence (the system of the moral law and of transgression) whose possibility remains yet unthought, should no doubt be situated. The scene of proper names is written on this level; as will be later the writing lesson.

This last violence is all the more complex in its structure because it refers at the same time to the two inferior levels of arche-violence and of law. In effect, it reveals the first nomination which was already an expropriation, but it denudes also that which since then functioned as the proper, the so-called proper, substitute of the deferred proper, *perceived* by the *social* and *moral consciousness* as the proper, the reassuring seal of self-identity, the secret.

Empirical violence, war in the colloquial sense (ruse and perfidy of little girls, *apparent* ruse and perfidy of little girls, for the anthropologist will prove them innocent by showing himself as the true and only culprit; ruse and perfidy of the Indian chief playing at the comedy of writing, *apparent* ruse and perfidy of the Indian chief borrowing all his resources from the Occidental intrusion), which Lévi-Strauss always thinks of as an *accident*. An accident occurring, in his view, upon a terrain of innocence, in a 'state of culture' whose *natural* goodness had not yet been degraded.[6]

Two pointers, seemingly anecdotal and belonging to the decor of the representation to come, support this hypothesis that the 'Writing Lesson' will confirm. They announce the great staging of the 'lesson' and show to advantage the art of the composition of this travelogue. In accordance with eighteenth-century tradition, the anecdote, the page of confessions, the fragment from a journal are knowledgeably put in place, calculated for the purposes of a philosophical demonstration of the relationships between nature and society, ideal society and real society, most often between the *other* society and our *society*.

What is the first pointer? The battle of proper names follows the arrival of the foreigner and that is not surprising. It is born in the presence and even from the presence of the anthropologist who comes to disturb order and natural peace, the complicity which peacefully binds the good society to itself in its play. Not only have the people of the Line imposed ridiculous sobriquets on the natives, obliging them to assume these intrinsically (hare, sugar, Cavaignac), but it is the anthropological eruption which breaks the secret of the proper names and the innocent complicity governing the play of young girls. It is the anthropologist who violates a virginal space so accurately connoted by the scene of a game and a game played by little girls. The mere presence of the foreigner, the mere fact of his having his eyes open, cannot not provoke a violation: the *aside*, the secret murmured in the car, the successive movements of the 'stratagem,' the acceleration, the precipitation, a certain increasing jubilation in the movement before the falling back which follows the consummated fault, when the 'sources' have 'dried up,' makes us think of a dance and a fête as much as of war.

The mere presence of a spectator, then, is a violation. First a pure violation: a silent and immobile foreigner attends a game of young girls. That one of them should have 'struck' a 'comrade' is not yet true violence. No integrity has been breached. Violence appears only at the moment when the intimacy of proper names can be opened to forced entry. And that is possible only at the moment when the space is shaped and reoriented by the glance of the foreigner. The eye of the other calls out the proper names, spells them out, and removes the prohibition that covered them.

At first the anthropologist is satisfied merely to see. A fixed glance and a mute presence. Then things get complicated, become more tortuous and labyrinthine, when he becomes a party to the play of the rupture of play, as he lends an ear and broaches a first complicity with the victim who is also the trickster. Finally, for what counts is the names of the adults (one could say the eponyms and the secret is violated only in the place where the names are attributed), the ultimate denunciation can no longer do without the active intervention of the foreigner. Who, moreover, claims to have intervened and accuses himself of it. He has seen, then heard; but, passive in the face of what he already knew he was provoking, he still waited to hear the master-names. The violation was not consummated, the naked base of the proper was still reserved. As one cannot or rather must not incriminate the innocent young girls, the violation will be accomplished by the thenceforward active, perfidious, and rusing intrusion of the foreigner who, having seen and heard, is now going to 'excite' the young girls, loosen their tongues, and get them to divulge the precious names: those of the adults (the dissertation tells us that only 'the adults possessed names that were proper to them,' p. 39). With a bad conscience, to be sure, and with that pity which Rousseau said unites us with the most foreign of foreigners. Let us now reread the *mea culpa*, the confession of the anthropologist who assumes entire responsibility for a violation that has satisfied him. After *giving* one another *away*, the young girls *gave away* the adults.

> The first little girl was trying to tell me her enemy's name, and when the enemy found out what was going on she decided to tell me the other girl's name, by way of reprisal. Thenceforward it was easy enough, though not very scrupulous, to egg the children on, one against the other, till in time I knew all their names. When this was completed and we were all, in a sense, one another's accomplices, I soon got them to give me the adults' names too [p. 270].

The true culprit will not be punished, and this gives to his fault the stamp of the irremediable: 'When this [cabal] was discovered the children were reprimanded and my sources of information dried up.'

One already suspects—and all Lévi-Strauss's writings would confirm it— that the critique of ethnocentrism, a theme so dear to the author of *Tristes Tropiques*, has most often the sole function of constituting the other as a model of original and natural goodness, of accusing and humiliating oneself, of exhibiting its being-unacceptable in an anti-ethnocentric mirror. Rousseau would have taught the modern anthropologist this humility of one who knows he is 'unacceptable,' this remorse that produces anthropology.[7] That is at least what we are told in the Geneva lecture:

> In truth, I am not 'I,' but the feeblest and humblest of 'others.' Such is the discovery of the *Confessions*. Does the anthropologist write anything other than confessions? First in his own name, as I have shown, since it is the moving force of his vocation and his work; and in that very work, in the name of the society, which, through the activities of its emissary, the anthropologist, chooses for itself other societies, other civilizations, and precisely the weakest and most humble; but only to verify to what extent that first society is itself 'unacceptable' (p. 245).

Without speaking of the point of mastery thus gained by the person who conducts this operation at home, one rediscovers here a gesture inherited from the eighteenth century, from a certain eighteenth century at any rate, for even in that century a certain sporadic suspicion of such an exercise had already commenced. Non-European peoples were not only studied as the index to a hidden good Nature, as a native soil recovered, of a 'zero degree' with reference to which one could outline the structure, the growth, and above all the degradation of our society and our culture. As always, this archeology is also a teleology and an eschatology; the dream of a full and immediate presence closing history, the transparence and indivision of a parousia, the suppression of contradiction and difference. The anthropologist's mission, as Rousseau would have assigned it, is to work toward such an end. Possibly against the philosophy which 'alone' would have sought to 'excite' 'antagonisms' between the 'self and the other.'[8] Let us not be accused here of forcing words and things. Let us rather read. It is again the Geneva lecture, but a hundred similar passages may be found:

> The Rousseauist revolution, pre-forming and initiating the anthropological revolu-
> tion, consists in refusing the expected identifications, whether that of a culture with
> that culture, or that of an individual, member of one culture, with a personage or a
> social function that the same culture wishes to impose upon him. In both cases the
> culture or the individual insists on the right to a free identification which can only
> be realized *beyond* man: an identification with all that lives and therefore suffers; and
> an identification which can also be realized *short of* the function or the person; with
> a yet unfashioned, but given, being. Then the self and the other, freed of an antagonism
> that only philosophy seeks to excite, recover their unity. An original alliance, at last
> renewed, permits them to found together the *we* against the *him*, against a society
> inimical to man, and which man finds himself all the more ready to challenge because
> Rousseau, by his example, teaches him how to elude the intolerable contradictions
> of civilized life. For if it is true that Nature has expelled man, and that society
> persists in oppressing him, man can at least reverse the horns of the dilemma to his
> own advantage, *and seek out the society of nature in order to meditate there upon the nature
> of society.* This, it seems to me, is the indissoluble message of *The Social Contract*, the
> *Lettres sur la botanique*, and the *Reveries*.[9]

'A Little Glass of Rum,' which is a severe criticism of Diderot and a glori-
fication of Rousseau ('[who] of all the *philosophes*, came nearest to being an
anthropologist . . . our master . . . our brother, great as has been our ingratitude
toward him; and every page of this book could have been dedicated to him,
had the object thus proffered not been unworthy of his great memory') concludes thus: '. . . the question to be solved is whether or not these evils are
themselves inherent in that state [of society]. We must go beyond the evidence
of the injustices or abuses to which the social order gives rise and discover the
unshakeable basis of human society.'[10]

The diversified thinking of Lévi-Strauss would be impoverished if it were
not emphatically recalled here that this goal and this motivation do not exhaust,
though they do more than connote, the task of science. They mark it profoundly in its very content. I had promised a second pointer. The Nambikwara,
around whom the 'Writing Lesson' will unfold its scene, among whom evil
will insinuate itself with the intrusion of writing come from *without* (*exothen*,
as the *Phaedrus* says)—the Nambikwara, who do not know how to write, are
good, we are told. The Jesuits, the Protestant missionaries, the American
anthropologists, the technicians on the Line, who believed they perceived
violence or hatred among the Nambikwara are not only mistaken, they have
probably projected their own wickedness upon them. And even provoked the
evil that they then believed they saw or wished to perceive. Let us reread
the end of Chapter 17 [24], entitled, always with the same skill, 'Family Life.'
This passage immediately precedes 'A Writing Lesson' and is, in a certain way,

indispensable to it. Let us first confirm what goes without saying: if we subscribe to Lévi-Strauss's declarations about their innocence and goodness, their
'great sweetness of nature,' 'the most . . . authentic manifestations of human
tenderness,' etc. only by assigning them a totally derived, relative, and empirical
place of legitimacy, regarding them as descriptions of the empirical affections
of the *subject* of this chapter—the Nambikwara as well as the author—if then
we subscribe to these descriptions only as *empirical relation*, it does not follow
that we give credence to the moralizing descriptions of the American anthropologist's converse deploring of the hatred, surliness, and lack of civility of the
natives. In fact these two accounts are symmetrically opposed, they have the
same dimensions, and arrange themselves around one and the same axis. After
having cited a foreign colleague's publication, which is very severe toward the
Nambikwara for their complacency in the face of disease, their filthiness,
wretchedness, and rudeness, their rancorous and distrustful character, Lévi-
Strauss argues:

> When I myself had known them, the diseases introduced by white men had already
> decimated them; but there had not been, since Rondon's always humane endeavors,
> any attempt to enforce their submission. I should prefer to forget Mr. Oberg's har-
> rowing description and remember the Nambikwara as they appear in a page from
> my notebooks. I wrote it one night by the light of my pocket-lamp: 'The camp-fires
> shine out in the darkened savannah. Around the hearth which is their only protec-
> tion from the cold, behind the flimsy screen of foliage and palm-leaves which had
> been stuck into the ground where it will best break the force of wind and rain, beside
> the baskets filled with the pitiable objects which comprise all their earthly belongings,
> the Nambikwara lie on the bare earth. Always they are haunted by the thought of
> other groups, as fearful and hostile as they are themselves, and when they lie
> entwined together, couple by couple, each looks to his mate for support and comfort
> and finds in the other a bulwark, the only one he knows, against the difficulties of
> every day and the meditative melancholia which from time to time overwhelms the
> Nambikwara. The visitor who camps among the Indians for the first time cannot but
> feel anguish and pity at the sight of a people so totally dis-provided for; beaten down
> into the hostile earth, it would seem, by an implacable cataclysm; naked and shivering
> beside their guttering fires. He gropes his way among the bushes, avoiding where he
> can the hand, or the arm, or the torso that lies gleaming in the firelight. But this
> misery is enlivened by laughing whispers. Their embraces are those of couples pos-
> sessed by a longing for a lost oneness; their caresses are in no wise disturbed by the
> footfall of a stranger. In one and all there may be glimpsed a great sweetness of nature,
> a profound nonchalance, an animal satisfaction as ingenuous as it is charming, and,
> beneath all this, something that can be recognized as one of the most moving and
> authentic manifestations of human tenderness' [p. 285].

The 'Writing Lesson' follows this description, which one may indeed read
for what it claims, at the outset, to be: a page 'from my notebooks' scribbled
one night in the light of a pocket lamp. It would be different if this moving

painting were to belong to an anthropological discourse. However, it certainly sets up a premise—the goodness or innocence of the Nambikwara—indispensable to the subsequent demonstration of the conjoint intrusion of violence and writing. Here a strict separation of the anthropological confession and the theoretical discussion of the anthropologist must be observed. The difference between empirical and essential must continue to assert its rights.

We know that Lévi-Strauss has very harsh words for the philosophies that have made the mind aware of this distinction, and which are, for the most part, philosophies of consciousness, of the cogito in the Cartesian or Husserlian sense. Very harsh words also for *L'Essai sur les données immédiates de la conscience*,[11] which Lévi-Strauss reproaches his old teachers for having pondered too much instead of studying Saussure's *Course in General Linguistics*.[12] Now whatever one may finally think of philosophies thus incriminated or ridiculed (and of which I shall say nothing here except to note that only their ghosts, which sometimes haunt school manuals, selected extracts, or popular opinion, are evoked here), it should be recognized that the difference between empirical affect and the structure of essence was for them a major rule. Neither Descartes nor Husserl would ever have suggested that they considered an empirical modification of their relationship with the world or with others as scientific truth, nor the quality of an emotion as the premise of a syllogism. Never in the *Regulae* does one pass from the phenomenologically irrefutable truth of 'I see yellow' to the judgment 'the world is yellow.' Let us not pursue this direction. Never, at any rate, would a rigorous philosopher of consciousness have been so quickly persuaded of the fundamental goodness and virginal innocence of the Nambikwara merely on the strength of an empirical account. From the point of view of anthropological science, this conclusion is as surprising as the wicked American anthropologist's might be 'distressing' (Lévi-Strauss's word). Surprising, indeed, that this unconditional affirmation of the radical goodness of the Nambikwara comes from the pen of an anthropologist who sets against the bloodless phantoms of the philosophers of consciousness and intuition, those who have been, if the beginning of *Tristes Tropiques* is to be believed, his only true masters: Marx and Freud.

The thinkers assembled hastily at the beginning of that book under the banner of metaphysics, phenomenology, and existentialism, would not be recognized in the lineaments ascribed to them. But it would be wrong to conclude that, conversely, Marx and Freud would have been satisfied by the theses written in their name—and notably the chapters that interest us. They generally demanded to see proof when one spoke of 'great sweetness of nature,' 'profound nonchalance,' 'animal satisfaction as ingenuous as it is charming,' and 'something that can be recognized as one of the most moving and authentic manifestations of human tenderness.' They wanted to see proof and would undoubtedly not have understood what could possibly be referred to as 'the original alliance, later renewed,' permitting 'the found[ing] together of the *we* against the *him*' (already quoted), or as 'that regular and, as it were crystalline structure which the best-preserved of primitive societies teach us is not antagonistic to the human condition' (*Leçon inaugurale au Collège de France*, p. 49).[13]

Within this entire system of philosophical kinship and claims of genealogical filiations, not the least surprised might well be Rousseau. Had he not asked that he be allowed to live in peace with the philosophers of consciousness and of interior sentiment, in peace with that sensible cogito,[14] with that interior voice which, he believed, never lied? To reconcile Rousseau, Marx, and Freud is a difficult task. Is it possible to make them agree among themselves in the systematic rigor of conceptuality?

Notes

1. Denis Diderot, *Oeuvres complètes*, Pléiade edition (Paris, 1935), pp. 993–1032; 'Supplement to Bougainville's "Voyage"', *Rameau's Nephew and Other Works*, eds Jacques Barzun and Ralph H. Bowen (Garden City, 1956), pp. 187–239. [Trans.]
2. All page numbers refer to original text. Where page numbers are given in square brackets, these refer to English translations. [Ed.]
3. 'What we have here are thus two extreme types of proper name between which there are a whole series of intermediate cases. At one extreme, the name is an identifying mark which, by the application of a rule, establishes that the individual who is *named* is a member of a preordained class (a social group in a system of groups, a status by birth in a system of statuses). At the other extreme, the name is a free creation on the part of the individual who *gives the name* and expresses a transitory and subjective state of his own by means of the person he names. But can one be said to be really naming in either case? The choice seems only to be between identifying someone else by assigning him to a class or, under cover of giving him a name, identifying oneself through him. One therefore never names: one classifies someone else if the name is given to him in virtue of his characteristics and one classifies oneself if, in the belief that one need not follow a rule, one names someone else 'freely,' that is, in virtue of characteristics of one's own. And most commonly one does both at once' (p. 240) [p. 18l]. Cf. also 'The Individual as A Species' and 'Time Recaptured' (chapters 7 and 8): 'In every system, therefore, proper names represent the quanta of *signification* below which one no longer does anything but point. This brings us to the root of the parallel mistakes committed by Peirce and by Russell, the former's in defining proper names as 'indices' and the latter's in believing that he had discovered the logical model of proper names in demonstrative pronouns. This amounts in effect to allowing that the act of naming belongs to a continuum in which there is an imperceptible passage from the act of signifying to that of pointing. I hope that I

have succeeded in showing that this passage is in fact discontinuous although each culture fixes its thresholds differently. The natural sciences put theirs on the level of species, varieties or subvarieties as the case may be. So terms of different degrees of generality will be regarded each time as proper names' (pp. 285–86) [p. 215].

Radicalizing this intention, it should perhaps be asked if it is any longer legitimate to refer to the pre-nominal 'property' of pure 'monstration'—pointing at—if pure indication, as the zero degree of language, as 'sensible certitude,' is not a myth always already effaced by the play of difference. It should perhaps be said of indication 'proper' what Lévi-Strauss says of proper names: 'At the lower end there is no external limit to the system either, since it succeeds in treating the qualitative diversity of natural species as the symbolic material of an order, and its progress towards the concrete, particular and individual is not even arrested by the obstacle of personal appellations: even proper names can serve as terms for a classification' (p. 288) [p. 218] (cf. also p. 242) [pp. 182–3].

4. [Pp. 269–70]. Since we read Rousseau in the transparence of the texts, why not slide under this scene that other taken out of a *Promenade* (9)? In spelling out all its elements one by one and minutely, I shall be less attentive to the opposition of term to term than to the rigorous symmetry of such an opposition. Everything happens as if Rousseau had developed the reassuring positive whose impression Lévi-Strauss gives us in the negative. Here is the scene: 'But, soon weary of emptying my purse to make people crush each other, I left the good company and went to walk alone in the fair. The variety of the objects there amused me for a long time. I perceived among others five or six boys from Savoy, around a small girl who had still on her tray a dozen meagre apples, which she was anxious to get rid of; the Savoyards, on their side, would have gladly freed her of them; but they had only two or three pence among them all, and that was not much to make a great breach among the apples. This tray was for them the garden of the Hesperides; and the young girl was the dragon who guarded it. This comedy amused me for a long time; I finally created a climax by paying for the apples from the young girl and distributing them among the small boys. I had then one of the finest spectacles that can flatter a man's heart, that of seeing joy united with the innocence of youth, spreading everywhere about me. For the spectators themselves, in seeing it, partook of it, and I, who shared at such cheap expense this happiness had in addition the joy of feeling that it was my work' (*Pléiade*, I, pp. 1092–93; [*The Reveries of a Solitary*, tr. John Gould Fletcher (New York, 1927), pp. 184–85]).

5. Of that word and that concept which, as I had suggested at the outset, has sense only within the logocentric closure and the metaphysics of presence. When it does not imply the possibility of an intuitive or judicative *adequation*, it nevertheless continues in *aletheia* to privilege the instance of a vision filled and satisfied by presence. It is the same reason that prevents the thought of writing to be simply contained within a science, indeed an epistemological circle. It can have neither that ambition nor that modesty.

6. A situation difficult to describe in Rousseauist terms, the professed absence of writing complicating things yet further: *The Essay on the Origin of Languages*

would perhaps give the name 'savagery' to the state of society and writing described by Lévi-Strauss: 'These three ways of writing correspond almost exactly to three different stages according to which one can consider men gathered into a nation. The depicting of objects is appropriate to a savage people; signs of words and of propositions, to a barbaric people, and the alphabet to civilized peoples [*peuples policés*]' [p. 17].

7. 'If the West has produced anthropologists, it is because it was so tormented by remorse' ('A Little Glass of Rum,' *Tristes Tropiques*, chap. 38) [(p. 449) [p. 388]].

8. What one may read between the lines of the second *Discource*: 'It is reason that engenders self-love, and reflection that confirms it: it is reason which turns man back upon himself, and divides him from everything that disturbs or afflicts him. It is philosophy that isolates him, and it is through philosophy that he says in secret, at the sight of the misfortunes of others: "Perish if you will, I am secure"' (p. 60) [p. 184].

9. [*Jean-Jacques Rousseau*,] p. 245. Italics author's.

10. *Tristes Tropiques*, chap. 18. With respect to Diderot, let us note in passing that the severity of his judgment on writing and the book does not in any way yield to Rousseau. The article 'book' [*livre*] which he wrote for the *Encyclopédie* is a most violent indictment.

11. Henri Bergson (Paris, 1889); translated as *Time and Free Will*, by F. L. Pogson (London and New York, 1910). [Trans.]

12. *Tristes Tropiques*, chap. 6. 'How I Became an Anthropologist.'

13. The Scope of Anthropology, trans. Sherry Ortner Paul and Robert A. Paul (London, 1967), p. 49. [Trans.]

14. In the Geneva lecture Lévi-Strauss believes he can simply oppose Rousseau to the philosophies that take their 'point of departure in the cogito' (p. 242).

Chapter 3

The Originary Metaphor

. . . Such is the situation of writing within the history of metaphysics: a debased, lateralized, repressed, displaced theme, yet exercising a permanent and obsessive pressure from the place where it remains held in check. A feared writing must be cancelled because it erases the presence of the self-same [*propre*] within speech . . .

This situation is reflected in the placing of the chapter 'On Script' in the *Essay*. How does Rousseau in fact construct this theory of writing with the help of borrowed elements? He does it after describing the origin of languages. It is the question of a supplement at the origin of languages. This supplement lays bare an additive substitution, a supplement of speech. It is inserted at the point where language begins to be articulated, is born, that is, from falling short of itself, when its accent or intonation, marking origin and passion within it, is effaced under that *other* mark of origin which is articulation. According to Rousseau, the history of writing is indeed that of articulation. The becoming-language of the cry is the movement by which spoken plenitude begins to become what it is through losing itself, hollowing itself out, breaking itself, articulating itself. The cry vocalizes itself by beginning to efface vocalic speech. It is indeed at the moment when it is a question of explaining this originary effacement of what, *properly* speaking, constitutes the spoken of speaking, that is to say the vocalic accent, that Rousseau introduces his chapter on writing. One must deal with the consonant—belonging to the North—and with writing at the same time. 'On Script' must first—in its first paragraph—evoke the *obliteration* of the accent or intonation by consonantal articulation: *effacement* and *substitution* at the same time. We should reread that introduction here:

> Anyone who studies the history and progress of the tongues will see that the more the words become monotonous, the more the consonants multiply; that, as accents fall into disuse and quantities are neutralized, they are replaced [*on supplée*] by grammatical combinations and new articulations. But only the pressure of time brings these changes about. To the degree that needs multiply, that affairs become complicated, that light is shed [knowledge is increased], language changes its character. It becomes more regular and less passionate. It substitutes ideas for feelings. It no longer

speaks to the heart but to reason. For that very reason, accent diminishes, articulation increases. Language becomes more exact and clearer, but more prolix, duller and colder. This progression seems to me entirely natural. Another way of comparing languages and determining their relative antiquity is to consider their script, and reason inversely from the degree of perfection of this art. The cruder the writing, the more ancient the language.

The progress of writing is thus a natural progress. And it is a progress of reason. Progress as regression is the growth of reason as writing. Why is that dangerous progress *natural*? No doubt because it is *necessary*. But also because necessity operates within language and society, according to ways and powers that belong to the state of pure *nature*. A pattern that we have already encountered: it is need and not passion that substitutes light for heat, clarity for desire, precision for strength, ideas for sentiment, reason for heart, articulation for accent. The natural, that which was inferior and anterior to language, acts within language *after the fact*, operates there after the origin, and provokes decadence or regression. It then becomes the posterior seizing the superior and dragging it toward the inferior. Such would be the strange time, the indescribable diagram of writing, the unrepresentable movement of its forces and its menaces.

In what consists the *precision* and the *exactitude* of language, that lodging of writing? Above all in *literalness* [*propriété*]. A precise and exact language should be absolutely univocal and literal [*propre*]: nonmetaphorical. The language is written, and pro-regresses, to the extent that it masters or effaces the figure in itself.

Effaces, that is, its origin. For language is originarily metaphorical. According to Rousseau it derives this from its mother, passion. Metaphor is the characteristic that relates language to its origin. Writing would then be the obliteration of this characteristic, the 'maternal characteristics' . . . It is therefore here that we must discuss 'That the first language had to be figurative' . . ., a proposition that is explicit only in the *Essay*:

> As man's first motives for speaking were of the passions, his first expressions were tropes. Figurative language was the first to be born. Proper meaning was discovered last. One calls things by their true name only when one sees them in their true form. At first only poetry was spoken; there was no hint of reasoning until much later [p. 12].

Epic or lyric, story or song, archaic speech is necessarily poetic. Poetry, the first literary form, is metaphorical in essence. Rousseau belongs therefore — he could not be otherwise, and to make note of it is more than banal — to the tradition which determines literary writing in terms of the speech present in the story or song; literary literality would be a supplementary accessory fixing or coagulating the poem, representing the metaphor. The literary object would have no specificity; at the most that of an unhappy negative of the poetic. In spite of what I have said about literary urgency as he lived it, Rousseau is at ease within this tradition. All that one might call literary modernity tries on the contrary to mark literary specificity against subjugation to the poetic, that is to say to the metaphoric, to what Rousseau himself analyses as spontaneous language. If there is a literary originality, which is by no means a simple certainty, it must free itself if not from the metaphor, which tradition too has judged reducible, at least from the savage spontaneity of the figure as it appears in nonliterary language. This modern protestation can be triumphant or, in Kafka's manner, denuded of all illusion, despairing, and no doubt more lucid: literature, which lives by being outside of itself, within the figures of a language which is primarily not its own, would die as well through a reentry into itself by way of the nonmetaphor. 'From a letter: "During this dreary winter I warm myself by it." Metaphors are one among many things which make me despair of writing [*Schreiben*]. Writing's lack of independence of the world, its dependence on the maid who tends the fire, on the cat warming itself by the stove; it is even dependent on the poor old human being warming himself by the stove. All these are independent activities ruled by their own laws; only writing is helpless, cannot live in itself, is a joke and a despair' (Kafka, *Journal*, 6 November 1921).[1]

'That the First Language Had To Be Figurative:' although this proposition was not peculiar to Rousseau, although he might have encountered it in Vico,[2] although he must not only but surely have read it in Condillac who must not only but surely have taken it from Warburton, we must emphasize the originality of the *Essay*.

'I was, perhaps, the first who discovered his abilities,' says Rousseau of Condillac, remembering their 'tête-à-tête' at the moment that the latter was 'engaged upon his "Essay sur l'Origine des connaissances humaines"' (*Confessions*, p. 347) [pp. 356–7]. Rousseau is closer to Condillac than to Warburton. *The Essay on Hieroglyphics* is certainly governed by the theme of a language originarily figurative and it inspired, among other articles of the *Encyclopaedia*, that on the metaphor, one of the richest. But unlike Vico, Condillac,[3] and Rousseau, Warburton thinks that the originary metaphor does not come from 'the warmth of a Poetic Fancy, as is commonly supposed.' 'The Metaphor arose as evidently from the *Rusticity of Conception*'[4] [Warburton, II: 147]. If the first metaphor is not poetic, it is because it is not sung but acted out. According to Warburton, one passes through a continuous transition from a language of action to a language of speech. That will also be Condillac's thesis. Rousseau is therefore the only one to indicate an absolute break between the language of action or the language of need, and speech or the language of passion. Without criticizing Condillac directly on this point, Rousseau opposes him after a fashion. For Condillac, 'speech succeeding the language of action, retained its character. This new method of communicating our thoughts could not be imagined without imitating the first. In order then to supply the place of violent contorsions of the body, the voice was raised and depressed by very sensible intervals' (II, I, ii, Sec. 13) [pp. 179–80]. This analogy and continuity are incompatible with Rousseau's theses about the formation of languages and local differences. For both Condillac and Rousseau the North certainly inclines toward precision, exactitude, and rationality. But for opposite reasons: for Rousseau the distance from the origin increases the influence of the language of action, for Condillac it reduces it, since for him everything begins through the language of action being continued within speech: 'Precision of style was much sooner received among the northern nations. In consequence of their cold and phlegmatic constitutions, they were readier to part with any thing that resembled the mode of speaking by action. Every where else the influence of this manner of communicating their thoughts subsisted a long time. Even now, in the southern parts of Asia, pleonasms are considered as an elegance of speech.' Sec. 67. 'Style was originally poetical' (p. 149) [p. 228].

Condillac's position is more difficult to maintain. He must reconcile a poetic origin (Rousseau) and a practical origin (Warburton). Through the weaving of these difficulties and differences, Rousseau's intention becomes precise. History goes toward the North as it parts from the origin. But whereas for Condillac this distancing follows a simple, straight, and continuous line, for Rousseau it leads to a place before the origin, toward the nonmetaphoric, the language of needs and the language of action.

In spite of all his borrowings, all his convergences, the system of the *Essay* thus remains original. In spite of all difficulties, the caesura between the gesture and the spoken word, between need and passion, is maintained there:

> It seems then that need dictated the first gestures, while the passions wrung forth the first words. By pursuing the course of the facts with these distinctions we may be able to see the question of the origin of language in an entirely new light. The genius of oriental languages, the oldest known, absolutely refutes the assumption of a didactic progression in their development. These languages are not at all systematic or rational. They are vital and figurative. The language of the first men is represented to us as the tongues of geometers, but we see that they were the tongues of poets [p. 11].

The distinction between need and passion is justified in the last instance only by the concept of 'pure nature.' The functional necessity of this limit-concept and of this juridical fiction also appears from this point of view. For the essential predicate of the state of pure nature is *dispersion*; and culture is always the effect of reconcilement, of proximity, of self-same [*propre*] presence. Need, which manifests itself *in fact before or after passion*, maintains, prolongs, or repeats the original dispersion. As such, and to the extent that it is not born out of an anterior passion that modifies it, it is the pure force of dispersion.

And so it had to be. One does not begin by reasoning, but by feeling. It is suggested that men invented speech to express their needs: an opinion which seems to me untenable. The natural effect of the first needs was to separate men, and not to reunite them. It must have been that way, because the species spread out and the earth was promptly populated. Otherwise mankind would have been crammed into a small area of the world, and the rest would have remained uninhabited [p. 11].

If 'all of this is not true without qualification,' it is because need, structurally anterior to passion, can always in fact succeed it. But is it only a question of fact, of an empirical eventuality? If the principle of dispersion remains active, is it an accident or a residue? In fact, need is necessary to explain the eve of society, what precedes its *constitution*, but it is indispensable in accounting for the *extension* of society. Without need, the force of presence and attraction would play freely, constitution would be an absolute concentration. One would understand how society resists dispersion, one would no longer be able to explain how it distributes and differentiates itself within space. The extension of society, which can in fact lead to the dislocation of the 'assembled people,' does not contribute any the less to the *organization*, the differentiation, and the organic division of the social body. In *The Social Contract*, the ideal dimensions of the city, which must be neither too small nor too large, require a certain extension and a certain distance among citizens. Dispersion, as the law of spacing, is therefore at once pure nature, the principle of society's life and the principle of society's death. Thus, although the metaphoric origin of language can be analyzed as the transcendence of need by passion, the principle of dispersion is not alien to it.

In fact Rousseau cannot, as Warburton and Condillac do, allege the continuity of the language of sounds and the language of action which kept us back in 'crude conceptions.' He has to explain everything in terms of the structure of passion and affectivity. He laboriously helps himself out of the difficulty through a short cut that is very dense and complex under the surface. What is his point of departure in that second paragraph of the third chapter?

Not the difficulty of accounting for metaphor by passion; for him that is self-evident; but the difficulty of making the idea—in effect surprising—of a primitively figurative language acceptable. For do not *good* sense and good *rhetoric*, which agree in considering the metaphor a displacement of style, require that one proceed from the literal [*propre*] meaning in order to constitute and define the figure? Is not the figure a transference of the literal sense? a transport? Did the theoreticians of rhetoric known by Rousseau not define it thus? Is it not the definition given by the *Encyclopaedia*?[5]

To repeat the first springing forth of metaphor, Rousseau does not begin with either good sense or rhetoric. He does not permit himself the use of literal meaning. And, situating himself in a place anterior to theory and common sense, which allow the constituted possibility of what they wish to deduce, he must show us how either common sense or stylistic science is possible. Such is at least his project and the original aim of his psycholinguistics of passions. But in spite of his intention and all appearance to the contrary, he also *starts*, as we shall see, *from the literal meaning. And he does so because the literal* [*le propre*] *must be both at the origin and at the end*. In a word, he restores to the *expression of emotions* a literalness whose loss he accepts, from the very origin, in the *designation of objects*.

Here is the difficulty and the principle of solution:

> However, I feel the reader stopping me at this point to ask how an expression can be figurative before it has a proper meaning, since the figure consists only of a transference of meaning. I agree with that. But, in order to understand what I mean, it is necessary to substitute the idea that the passion presents to us for the word that we transpose. For one only transposes words because one also transposes ideas. Otherwise figurative language would signify nothing [pp. 12–13].

Metaphor must therefore be understood as the process of the idea or meaning (of the signified, if one wishes) before being understood as the play of signifiers. The idea is the signified meaning, that which the word expresses. But it is also a sign of the thing, a representation of the object within my mind. Finally, this representation of the object, signifying the object and signified by the word or by the linguistic signifier in general, may also indirectly signify an affect or a passion. It is in this play of the representative idea (which is signifier or signified according to the particular relationship) that Rousseau lodges his explanation. Before it allows itself to be caught by verbal signs, metaphor is the relation between signifier and signified within the order of ideas and things, according to what links the idea with that of which it is the idea, that is to say, of which it is already the representative sign. Then, the literal or proper meaning will be the relationship of the idea to the affect that it *expresses*. And it is the *inadequation of the designation* (metaphor) which *properly expresses* the passion. If fear makes me see giants where there are only men, the signifier—as the idea of the object—will be metaphoric, but the signifier of my passion will be literal. And if I then say 'I see giants,' that false designation will be a literal expression of my fear. For in fact I see giants and there is a sure truth there, that of a sensible cogito, analogous to what Descartes analyzes in the *Regulae*: phenomenologically, the proposition 'I see yellow' is unexceptionable, error becomes possible only in the judgment 'the world is yellow.'[6]

Nevertheless, what we interpret as literal expression in the perception and designation of giants, remains a metaphor that is preceded by nothing either in experience or in language. Since speech does not pass through reference to an object, the fact that 'giant' is literal as sign of fear not only does not prevent, but on the contrary implies, that it should be nonliteral or metaphoric as sign of the object. It cannot be the idea-sign of the passion without

presenting itself as the idea-sign of the presumed cause of that passion, opening an exchange with the outside. This opening allows the passage to a savage
metaphor. No literal meaning precedes it. No rhetor watches over it.

We must therefore come back to the subjective affect, substitute the phenomenological order of passions for the objective order of designations,
expression for indication, in order to understand the emergence of metaphor,
and the savage possibility of transference. To the objection that the literal
meaning is prior, Rousseau responds with an example:

> Upon meeting others, a savage man will initially be frightened. Because of his fear
> he sees the others as bigger and stronger than himself. He calls them *giants*. After
> many experiences, he recognizes that these so-called giants are neither bigger nor
> stronger than he. Their stature does not approach the idea he had initially attached
> to the word giant. So he invents another name common to them and to him, such
> as the name *man*, for example, and leaves *giant* to the false object that had impressed
> him during his illusion. That is how the figurative word is born before the literal
> word, when our gaze is held in passionate fascination; and how it is that the first idea
> it conveys to us is not that of the truth. What I have said of words and names pre-
> sents no difficulty relative to the forms of phrases. The illusory image presented by
> passion is the first to appear, and the language that corresponded to it was also the
> first invented. It subsequently became metaphorical when the enlightened spirit,
> recognizing its first error, used the expressions only with those passions that had
> produced them [pp. 12–13].

1. The *Essay* thus describes at the same time the advent of the metaphor
and its 'cold' recapture within rhetoric. One cannot, then, speak of metaphor
as a figure of style, as technique or procedure of language, except by a sort of
analogy, a sort of return and repetition of the discourse; then one deliberately
passes through the initial displacement, that which expressed the passion literally. Or rather the representer of the passion: it is not fear itself that the word
giant expresses literally—and a new distinction is necessary which would
infiltrate as far as the literalness [*propre*] of expression—but 'the idea that the
passion presents to us' [*Essay*, p. 13]. The idea 'giant' is at once the literal sign
of the representer of the passion, the metaphoric sign of the object (man) and
the metaphoric sign of the affect (fear). That sign is metaphoric because it is
false with regard to the object; it is metaphoric because it is *indirect* with regard
to the affect: it is the sign of a sign, it expresses emotion only through another
sign, through the representer of fear, namely through the *false* sign. It represents
the affect literally only through representing a false representer.

Subsequently, the rhetor or the writer can reproduce and calculate this
operation. The interval of this repetition separates savagery from civility; it
separates them within the history of the metaphor. Naturally, this savagery and
this civility interrelate within the condition of society opened by passion and
the primitive figures. The 'enlightened spirit,' the cold clarity of reason, turned

toward the North and dragging the corpse of the origin, can, having recognized 'its first error,' handle metaphors as such, with reference to what it knows to be their true and literal meaning. In the south of language, the impassioned spirit was caught within metaphor: the poet relating to the world only in the style of nonliterality. The reasoner, the writer–calculator, and the grammarian, knowingly and coldly organize the effects of the nonliteralness of style. But one must also turn these relationships inside out; the poet has a relationship of truth and literalness with that which he expresses, he keeps himself as close as possible to his passion. Lacking the truth of the object, he speaks himself fully and reports authentically the origin of his speech. The rhetor accedes to objective truth, denounces error, deals with the passions, but all by virtue of having lost the living truth of the origin.

Thus, even while apparently affirming that the original language was figurative, Rousseau upholds the literal [*propre*]: as *arche* and as *telos*. At the origin, since the first idea of passion, its first representer, is literally expressed. In the end, because the enlightened spirit stabilizes the literal meaning. He does it by a process of knowledge and *in terms of truth*. One will have remarked that in the last analysis, it is also in these terms that Rousseau treats the problem. He is situated there by an entire naive philosophy of the idea-sign.

2. Does the example of fear come by chance? Does not the metaphoric origin of language lead us necessarily to a situation of threat, distress, and dereliction, to an archaic solitude, to the anguish of dispersion? Absolute fear would then be the first encounter of the other as *other*: as other than I and as other than itself. I can answer the threat of the other as other (than I) only by transforming it into another (than itself), through altering it in my imagination, my fear, or my desire. 'Upon meeting others, savage men will *initially* be frightened.' Fear would thus be the first passion, the mistaken face of pity of which we spoke above. Pity is the force of reconciliation and presence. Fear would still be turned toward the immediately anterior situation of pure nature as dispersion; the other is *first* encountered at a distance, separation and fear must be overcome so that he may be approached as a fellow-being. From a distance, he is immense, like a master and a threatening force. It is the experience of the small and silent [*infans*] man. He begins to speak only out of these deforming and naturally magnifying perceptions.[7] And as the force of dispersion is never reduced, the source of fear always compounds with its contrary.

The acknowledged influence of Condillac also makes us think that the example of fear is not fortuitous. According to *An Essay on the Origin of Human Knowledge*, anguish and repetition are the double root of language.

As for the language of action. The fact that language was given to man by God does not forbid a search into its natural origin by a philosophic fiction which teaches the essence of what was thus received. It does not suffice 'for a philosopher to say a thing was effected by extraordinary means.' It is 'incumbent upon him to explain how it could have happened according to the ordinary course of nature' [pp. 170–1]. It is the hypothesis of the two children left in the desert after the Flood, 'before they understood the use of any sign'[8] [p. 169]. These two children began to speak only in a moment of fear: to ask for help. But language does not begin in pure anguish or rather anguish signifies itself only through repetition.

It is held between perception and reflection and is here called imitation. Let us italicize:

> Thus by instinct alone they asked and gave each other assistance. I say *by instinct alone*; for as yet there was no room for reflection. One of them did not say to himself, *I must make such particular motions to render him sensible of my want, and to induce him to relieve me*: nor the other, *I see by his motions that he wants such a thing, and I will let him have the enjoyment [jouissance] of it*: but they both acted in consequence of the want which pressed them most . . . For example, he who saw a place in which he had been *frightened, mimicked* those cries and movements which were the signs of fear, in order to warn the other not to expose himself to the same danger.[9]

3. The work which produces the common noun supposes, like all work, the *chilling* and *displacement* of passion. One can substitute the adequate common noun (*man*) for the noun *giant* only after the appeasement of fear and the recognition of error. With this work the number and extension of common nouns (names) multiply. Here the *Essay* is in close accord with the second *Discourse*: the first substantives were not common but proper nouns or names. The absolutely literal [*propre*] is at the origin: one sign to a thing, one repre-senter per passion. It is the moment when the lexical element is as much the more extended as knowledge is limited.[10] But that is true only of categoremes, a fact that ought to raise more than one logical and linguistic difficulty. For the substantive as proper name is not quite the first state of the language. It does not stand alone within the language. It already represents an articulation and a 'division of discourse.' Not that, in Vico's manner, Rousseau makes the noun be born almost at the end, after onomatopoeia, interjections, first names, pronouns, articles, but before verbs. The noun cannot appear without the verb. After a first step, during which discourse is undivided, each word having 'the sense of a whole proposition,' the noun is born at the same time as the verb. It is the first internal rupture of the proposition that opens dis-course. There are no nouns that are not proper, no verbal modes but the infinitive, no tense but the present: 'When they began to distinguish subject and attribute, and noun and verb, which was itself no common effort of genius, substantives were at first only so many proper names; the present infinitive[11] was the only tense of verbs; and the very idea of adjectives must have been developed with great difficulty; for every adjective is an abstract

idea, and abstractions are painful and unnatural operations' (p. 149) [*Discourse*, p. 177].

This correlation of the proper noun and of the infinitive present is important for us. One thus leaves the present and the proper in the same movement: that which—distinguishing the subject from subject with verb—and later distinguishing it from the subject with its attribute—substitutes for the proper noun the common noun and the pronoun—personal or relative—trains the classification within a system of differences and substitutes the tenses for the impersonal present of the infinitive.

Before this differentiation, the moment of languages 'ignorant . . . of the division of discourse' [*Discourse*, p. 77] corresponds to that state suspended between the state of nature and the state of society: an epoch of natural languages, of the neume, of the time of the Isle of St. Pierre, of the festival around the water hole. Between prelanguage and the linguistic catastrophe instituting the division of discourse, Rousseau attempts to recapture a sort of happy pause, the instantaneity of a full language, the image stabilizing what was no more than a point of pure passage: a language without discourse, a speech without sentence, without syntax, without parts, without grammar, a language of pure effusion, beyond the cry, but short of the hinge [*brisure*] that articulates and at the same time disarticulates the immediate unity of meaning, within which the being of the subject distinguishes itself neither from its act nor from its attributes. It is the moment when there are words ('the words first made use of by mankind')—which do not yet function as they do 'in languages already formed' and in which men 'first gave every single word the sense of a whole proposition' [*Discourse*, p. 177]. But language cannot be truly born except by the disruption and fracture of that happy plenitude, in the very instant that this instantaneity is wrested from its fictive immediacy and put back into movement. It serves as an absolute reference point for him who wishes to measure and describe difference within discourse. One cannot do it without referring to the limit, always already crossed, of an undivided language, where the proper-infinitive-present is so welded to itself that it cannot even appear in the opposition of the proper noun and the verb in the infinitive present.

Language in its entirety, then, plunges into that breach between the proper and the common nouns (leading to pronoun and adjective), between the infinitive present and the multiplicity of modes and tenses. All language will substitute itself for that living self-presence of the proper, which, as language, already supplanted things in themselves. Language *adds itself* to presence and supplants it, defers it within the indestructible desire to rejoin it.

Articulation is the dangerous supplement of fictive instantaneity and of the good speech: of full pleasure [*jouissance*], for presence is always determined as pleasure by Rousseau. The present is always the present of a pleasure; and pleasure is always a receiving of presence. What dislocates presence introduces difference and delay, spacing between desire and pleasure. Articulated language, knowledge and work, the anxious research of learning, are nothing but the spacing between two pleasures. 'We desire knowledge only because we wish to enjoy' (Second *Discourse*, p. 143 [p. 171]). And in *The Art of Enjoyment*, that aphorism which speaks the symbolic restitution of the presence supplied in the past of the verb: 'Saying to myself, I enjoyed, I still enjoy.'[12] The great project of *The Confessions*, was it not also to 'enjoy [once more] . . . when I desire it' (p. 585) [p. 607]?

Notes

1. *Tagebücher* 1910–23, ed. Max Brod (New York, 1948–9), pp. 550–1; *The Diaries of Franz Kafka* 1914~29 (New York, 1949), vol. 2, pp. 20 1. [Trans.]
2. Vico says that he understood the origin of languages at the moment when, after many difficulties, it appeared to him that the first nations 'were nations of poets; by the same principles, we first identified the true origin of languages' (*Scienza Nuova*, I: 174). The distinction among three languages would correspond, *mutatis mutandis*, to Rousseau's schema; the second language, which marks the appearance of both speech and metaphor, would, strictly speaking, be the moment of origin, when the poetic song is not yet broken into articulation and convention. Let us compare: 'Three kinds of language were spoken which compose the vocabulary of this Science: (1) that of the time of the families when gentile men were newly received into humanity. This, we shall find, was a mute language of signs and physical objects having natural relations to the ideas they wished to express. (2) That spoken by means of heroic emblems, or similitudes, comparisons, images, metaphors, and natural descriptions, which make up the great body of the heroic language which was spoken at the time the heroes reigned. (3) Human language using words agreed upon by the people, a language of which they are absolute lords' (3, 1, p. 32) [Bergin, op. cit., p. 18]. Elsewhere: 'That first language . . . was not a language in accord with the nature of the things it dealt with . . . but was a fantastic speech making use of physical substances endowed with life and most of them imagined to be divine' (3, 1, p. 163) [pp. 114–15]. 'We find that the principle of these origins both of languages and of letters lies in the fact that the early gentile peoples, by a demonstrated necessity of nature, were poets who spoke in poetic characters. This discovery, which is the master key of this Science, has cost us the persistent research of almost all our literary life' (3, *Idea of the Work*, I: 28–9) [p. 19]. 'Men vent great passions by breaking into song, . . . that . . . they were inexpressive save under the impulse of violent passions— [lead to the conjecture that] their first languages must have been formed in singing' (3, I: 95 [J.-B. Vico, *Oeuvres choisies*], tr. [J.] Chaix Ruy [Paris, 1946]) [p. 69]. 'All that has been reasoned out seems clearly to confute the common error of the grammarians, who say that *prose speech came first and speech in verse afterward*. And within the *origins of poetry*, as they have here been disclosed, we have found

the origins of languages and letters' (Book II, *Poetic Wisdom*, Chap. V, § 5, [*Oeuvres choisies de Vico,*] tr. [J.] Michelet [(Paris, 1893–9), vol. 27] (p. 430) [p. 142]. For Vico, as for Rousseau, the progress of language follows the progress of articulation. Thus, language suffers a fall and humanizes itself through the loss of its poetry and its divine character: 'The language of the gods was almost entirely mute, only very slightly articulate; the language of the heroes, an equal mixture of articulate and mute, . . . the language of men, almost entirely articulate and only very slightly mute' (3, I: 178, tr. Chaix-Ruy) [p. 134].

[For clarification of references throughout this and following notes, the reader is referred to the notes in *Of Grammatology* (pp. 317–54), full details of which are given in the bibliography at the end of the reader. Ed.]

3. Condillac recognized the convergence of his and Warburton's thoughts, rather than his debt to the latter. Yet this convergence, as we shall immediately see, is not complete: 'This section was near finished, when I happened to light on an essay on hieroglyphics, extracted from the second volume of Dr. Warburton's Divine Legation of Moses; a work equally distinguished for strength of reasoning and variety of erudition. With pleasure I found that this author's notions and mine coincided, in supposing that language must, from its first beginning, have been very figurative and metaphysical. My own reflections had led me to observe, that writing at first could be no more than a simple picture; but I had not as yet made any attempt to discover by what progress mankind arrived at the invention of letters, and it seemed difficult to me to succeed in the inquiry. The task has been exceedingly well executed by Dr. Warburton, of whom the greatest part of this chapter has been borrowed' (Chap. 13, 'Of Writing,' § 127, p. 177) [p. 273 n.]

4. . . . 'This way of *Speaking* by *Simile*, we may conceive to answer to the *Chinese Marks* or Characters in *Writing*; and as from such Marks proceeded the abbreviated Method of *Alphabetic Letters,* so from the *Similitude,* to make a Language still more explicit and elegant, came the METAPHOR; which is indeed but a *Similtude* in little: For Men so conversant in matter still wanted sensible Images to convey abstract Ideas' (*Essai sur les hiéroglyphes,* pp. 85–6) [p. 94]. 'This, and not the Warmth of a Poetic Fancy, as is commonly supposed, was the true Original of figurative Expression. We see it even at this Day in the Style of the *American* Barbarians, tho' of the coldest and most flegmatic Complexions . . . Their *Phlegm* could only make their Stile *concise,* not take away the *Figures*: and the Conjunction of these different Characters in it, shews plainly that Metaphors were from Necessity, not Choice. . . . Thus we see it has ever been the way of Man, both in *Speech* and *Writing,* as well as in *Clothes* and *Habitations,* to turn his Wants and Necessities into Parade and Ornament' (pp. 195–7) [pp. 147–8].

    [For Derrida's discussion of the French language edition of Bishop William Warburton's essay (trans. as *Essai sur les hiéroglyphes des Egyptiens,* trans. M.-A. Léonard des Malpeines (Paris, 1977)), see Ch. 1, 'Scribble (writing-power)' above. Derrida's essay precedes the introduction to the reissue of Warburton's essay. Ed.]

5. METAPHORE, S. F. (gram.). 'M. du Marsais says that it is a figure by which the proper signification of a noun (I would prefer to say a *word*) is carried over, so to speak, to another signification which is not appropriate to it except by virtue of a comparison which is in the mind. A word taken in its *metaphoric* sense loses its

proper signification, and acquires a new one that presents itself to the mind only by the comparison undertaken between the proper meaning of the word and what one compares it to: for example, when one says that falsehood often decks itself in the colors of truth.' And after long quotations from Marsais:'I have some-times heard M. du Marsais reproached for being a little prolix; and I realize that it is possible, for example, to give fewer examples of *metaphor*, and to develop them less extensively; but who has no wish at all for such a happy prolixity? The author of a dictionary of language cannot read this article on the metaphor with-out being struck by the astonishing exactitude of our grammarian in distin-guishing the proper meaning from a figurative one, and in assigning to one the foundation of the other.'

6. On this point, Rousseau's doctrine is most Cartesian. It is itself interpreted as a justification of Nature. The senses, which are natural, never deceive us. On the contrary, it is our judgment that misleads us and plays Nature false.'Nature never deceives us; we deceive ourselves'—a passage from *Emile* (p. 237) [p. 166] which the autograph manuscript replaces with the following:'I say it is impossible for our senses to deceive us because it is always true that we feel what we feel.' The Epicureans are praised for having recognized this but criticized for having main-tained that 'the judgments that we made about our sensations were never false.' 'We sense our sensations, but we do not sense our judgments.'

7. Here again we are reminded of a Viconean text:'The poetic characters, in which the essence of the fables consists, were born of the need of a nature incapable of abstracting forms and properties from subjects. Consequently they must have been the manner of thinking of entire peoples, who had been placed under this natural necessity in the times of their greatest barbarism. It is an eternal property of the fables always to magnify the ideas of particulars. On this there is a fine passage in Aristotle's *Ethics* in which he remarks that men of limited ideas erect every particular into a maxim. The reason must be that the human mind, which is indefinite, being constricted by the vigor of the senses, cannot otherwise express its almost divine nature than by thus magnifying particulars in imagina-tion. It is perhaps on this account that in both the Greek and the Latin poets the images of gods and heroes always appear larger than those of men, and that in the returned barbarian times the paintings particularly of the Eternal Father, of Jesus Christ and of the Virgin Mary are exceedingly large' (*Scienza Nuova*, 3, II: 18, tr. Chaix-Ruy) [p. 279].

8. II.I, pp. 11–12 [pp. 168, 171]. This is also Warburton's procedure in the remark-able paragraphs that he devotes to the 'Origin and Progress of Language' (I: 48f.) [pp. 81f.]. Thus:'In judging only from the nature of things, and without the surer aid of revelation, one should be apt to embrace the opinion of Diodorus Siculus (lib.ii) and Vitruvius (lib.ii, cap.I) that the first men lived for some time in woods and caves, after the manner of beasts, uttering only confused and indistinct sounds, till, associating for mutual assistance, they came, by degrees, to use such as were articulate, for the arbitrary signs or marks, mutually agreed on, of those ideas in the mind of the speaker, which he wanted to communicate to others. Hence the diversity of languages; for it is agreed on all hands that speech is not innate.' And yet, 'nothing being more evident from scripture, than that language had a

different original. God, we there find, taught the first man religion; and can we think he would not, at the same time, teach him language?' [Condillac, p. 170].

9. II.I. 2, 3, p. 113 [pp. 172–3]. We have italicized only 'frightened' and 'mimicked.' The same examples are reconsidered in the chapter on 'The Origin of Poetry:' 'For example, in the mode of speaking by action, to give an idea of a person that had been frightened, they had no other way than to mimic the cries and natural signs of fear' (§ 66, p. 148) [pp. 227–8].

10. 'Every object at first received a particular name without regard to genus or species, which these primitive originators were not in a position to distinguish; . . . so that, the narrower the limits of their knowledge of things, the more copious their dictionary must have been. . . . Add to this, that general ideas cannot be introduced into the mind without the assistance of words, nor can the understanding seize them except by means of propositions. This is one of the reasons why animals cannot form such ideas or ever acquire that capacity for self-improvement [*perfectibilité*] which depends on them. . . . We must then make use of [. . .] language [*parler*] in order to form general ideas. For no sooner does the imagination cease to operate than the understanding proceeds only by the help of words. If then the first inventors of speech could give names only to ideas they already had, it follows that the first substantives could be nothing more than proper names' (pp. 149–50 See also the editor's notes) [pp. 177–8].

11. 'The present of the infinitive' (edition of 1782).

12. Vol. I, p. 1174.

Chapter 4

The Retrait *of Metaphor**

to Michel Deguy

What is happening, today, with metaphor?

      Qu'est-ce qui se passe, aujourd'hui, avec la métaphore?
And without metaphor what is happening?

      Et de la métaphore qu'est-ce qui se passe?
It is a very old subject. It occupies the West, inhabits it or lets itself be inhabited: representing itself there as an enormous library in which we would move about without perceiving its limits, proceeding from station to station, going on foot, step by step, or in a bus (we commute already with the 'bus' that I have just named, in translation and, according to the principle of translation, between *Übertragung* and *Übersetzung, metaphorikos* still designating today, in what one calls 'modern' Greek, that which concerns means of transportation). *Metaphora* circulates in the city, it conveys us like its inhabitants, along all sorts of passages, with intersections, red lights, one-way streets, crossroads or crossings, patrolled zones and speed limits. We are in a certain way—metaphorically of course, and as concerns the mode of habitation—the content and the tenor of this vehicle: passengers, comprehended and displaced by metaphor.

A strange statement to start off—you might say. Strange at least to imply that we might know what *inhabit* means, and *circulate*, and *to transport oneself,* to *have* or *let* oneself be transported. In general and in this case. Strange too because it is not only metaphoric to say that we inhabit metaphor and that we circulate in it as in a sort of vehicle, an automobile. It is not simply metaphoric. Nor anymore proper, literal or usual, notions that I do not confound in bringing them together, it being better to specify this immediately. Neither metaphoric nor a-metaphoric, this 'figure' consists singularly in changing the places and the functions: it constitutes the so-called subject of statements (*sujet des énoncés*) (the speaker (*locuteur*) or the writer (*scripteur*)

---

*The lecture here reprinted in its initial form was read on June 1, 1978, at the University of Geneva during a Colloquium ('Philosophy and Metaphor') in which Roger Dragonetti, André de Muralt and Paul Ricoeur also participated. But through its reading it will be proved that I would first have sent to Michel Deguy the draft approximating this detour, *Umriss* in the other language, to say proximity in a parallel way.

whom we say to be, or anyone who would believe himself to be *making use* of metaphors and speaking *more metaphorico*) into the *content* or into the (both still partial, and always already 'embarked,' 'aboard') *tenor* of a vehicle which comprehends the subject, carries him away, displaces him at the very moment when this subject believes he is designating it, saying it, orienting it, driving it, governing it 'like a pilot in his ship.'

Like a pilot in his ship.

I have just changed the principle and means of transport. We are not in metaphor like a pilot in his ship. With this proposition, I drift. The figure of the vessel or of the boat, which was so often the exemplary vehicle of rhetorical pedagogy, of discourse teaching rhetoric, makes me veer towards a quotation of Descartes whose displacement in turn would draw me much further away than I can allow at this moment.

Therefore I ought to decisively interrupt the drifting or skidding. I would do it if it were possible. But what have I just been doing? I skid and I drift irresistibly. I am trying to speak *about* metaphor, to say something proper or literal on this subject, to *treat* it as my subject, but through metaphor (if one may say so) I am obliged to speak of it *more metaphorico*, to it in its own manner. I cannot *treat it (en traiter)* without *dealing with it (sans traiter avec elle)*, without negotiating with it the loan I take from it in order to speak of it. I do not succeed in producing a *treatise (un traité)* on metaphor which is not *treated with (traité avec)* metaphor which suddenly appears *intractable (intraitable)*.

That is why just now I have been moving from digression to digression *(d'écart en écart)*, from one vehicle to another without being able to brake or stop the autobus, its automaticity or its automobility. At least, I can brake only by skidding, in other words, letting my control over the steering slip up to a certain point. I can no longer stop the vehicle or anchor the ship, master completely *(sans reste)* the drifting or skidding (I had recalled somewhere that the word 'skid,' before its greatest metaphoric skidding, had to do with a certain play of the anchor in nautical language, or rather the language of the fleet.) At least, I can only stop the engines of this floating vehicle which is here my discourse, which would still be the best means of abandoning it to its most unforseeable drifting. The drama, for this is a drama, is that even if I had decided to no longer speak metaphorically about metaphor, I would not achieve it; it would continue to go on without me in order to make me speak, to ventriloquize me, metaphorize me. Other ways of saying, other ways of responding to, rather, my first questions. What is happening *with* metaphor? Well, everything: there is nothing that does not happen with metaphor and by metaphor. Any statement concerning anything that happens, metaphor included, will be produced *not without* metaphor. There will not have been a meta-metaphorics consistent enough to dominate all its statements. And what gets along *without* metaphor? Nothing, therefore, and rather it should be said that metaphor gets along without anything else, here without me, at the very moment when it appears to pass through me. But if it gets by without everything that does not happen without it, maybe in a bizarre sense it does without itself, it no longer has a name, a literal or proper meaning, which could begin to render the double figure of my title readable to you: in its withdrawal (*retrait*), one should say in its withdrawals, metaphor perhaps retires, withdraws from the world scene, withdrawing from it at the moment of its most invasive extension, at the instant it overflows every limit. Its withdrawal would then have the paradoxical form of an indiscreet and overflowing insistence, of an over-abundant remanence, of an intrusive repetition, always marking with a supplementary trait, with one more turn, with a re-turn and with a *withdrawal* (*retrait*) the trait that it will have left in the text itself.

So even if I wanted to interrupt the skidding, I would fail (*échouerais*: run aground). And that at the very moment when I shall refrain from letting it be noticed.

The third of the little sentences by which I seemed to attack my subject, and which in sum I have been explaining and quoting for a while, was 'Metaphor is a very old subject.' A subject which is at once sure and dubious, according to the direction in which this word 'subject' will displace itself in its sentence, its discourse, its context, and according to the metaphoricity to which it will itself be subjected, for nothing is more metaphoric than this subject-value. I drop the subject in order to interest myself, rather, in its predicate, in the predicate of the subject 'subject,' namely its age. If I said old, it is for at least two reasons.

And there I begin: another way of saying that I am going to make the greatest possible effort to slow the skidding.

The first reason is astonishment before the fact that a subject so old in appearance, a character or an actor so tired, so used up, should return today to take the stage—and the Western scene—of this drama with so much force and insistence in the last few years in a way which seems to me fairly new. Already a socio-bibliography might show the articles and (national and international) colloquia set up around metaphor alone for about a decade, perhaps a little less, and even this year: in these last months there have been at least three international colloquia on this subject, if I am well informed, two in the U.S. and this one, all international and interdisciplinary, which is no less significant (the one at the University of California-Davis having for its title 'Interdisciplinary Conference on Metaphor').

What is the historical or historial scope (as far as the value itself of historiality or epochality) of this preoccupation and of this uneasy convergence? Where does this pressure come from? What is at stake here? What is happening today with metaphor? So many questions whose necessity and size I was hoping only to mark, it being understood that I could only make a token gesture in their direction. The astonishing youthfulness of this old subject is important and, truthfully speaking, somewhat staggering. Metaphor— Western also, in this respect—is retiring, it is in the evening of its life. 'Evening of life,' for 'old age': this is one of the examples Aristotle chooses in his *Poetics* for the fourth type of metaphor, the one that proceeds *kata to analagon*, the first, which goes from genus to species, *apo genous epi eidos*, having as an example, as if by chance: '"Here stands my ship" (*neus de moi ed esteke*), for to be anchored is one among many ways of being stopped' (1457b). The example is already a citation from the *Odyssey*. In the evening of its life, metaphor is still a very liberal (*genereux*), inexhaustible subject which cannot be stopped, and I could comment indefinitely on the inscription, the pre-appurtenance of each of these statements to a metaphoric corpus, and even—whence the double trait (*re-trait*)—to a metaphoric corpus of statements on the subject of this old subject, of metaphoric statements on metaphor. I stop this movement here.

The other reason which has drawn me towards the expression 'old subject' is a value of apparent wear which has appeared to me necessary to recognize once again. An old subject is an apparently worn, exhausted subject, worn to the bone or threadbare. Now this value of wear and tear, but first of all of use, this value of the value of use, utility, of use or utility as being *useful* or as being *usual*, in short this whole semantic system that I will abbreviate under the title of *us* will have played a determinant role in the traditional problematic of metaphor. Metaphor is perhaps not only a subject worn to the bone, it is a subject which will be kept in an essential relation to *us*, or to *usance* (usance being an old word, a word out of use today, whose polysemy would merit a whole analysis in itself). Now perhaps what is worn out today in metaphor is perhaps precisely this *us*-value that has determined its whole traditional problematic.

Consequently, why return to the us of metaphor? And why in this return do we privilege the text signed with Heidegger's name? And how does this question of *us* adjoin the necessity of privileging the Heideggerian text in this *epoch* of metaphor, a suspensive withdrawal and return supported by the line (*trait*) delimiting a contour? This question is sharpened by a paradox. The Heideggerian text has appeared impossible to get around, for others and for myself,[1] from the moment it was a question of thinking the international epoch of metaphor in which we say we are, while Heidegger has only very allusively treated metaphor as such and by this name. And this very rarity will not have been insignificant. That is why I speak of the Heideggerian *text*:I do so to underscore by a supplementary line (*trait*) that it is not only a question for me of considering the stated propositions, the themes and theses on the subject of metaphor as such, the content of his discourse treating rhetoric and this trope, but of his writing, his treatment of language and, more rigorously, his treatment of the trait, of 'trait' in every sense, and more rigorously still of 'trait' as a word in his language, and of the trait as a tracing incision (*entame*) of language.

Heidegger will therefore have spoken very little about metaphor. Two places are always cited (*Der Satz vom Grund* and *Unterwegs zur Sprache*[2]) where he seems to take a position with respect to metaphor—or more precisely with respect to the rhetorico-metaphysical concept of metaphor—, and still he does so as if in passing, briefly, laterally, in a context where metaphor does not occupy the center. Why would such an elliptical text, in appearance so ready to elude the question of metaphor, have something so necessary to perform with respect to metaphorics? Or moreover, reversing the same question, why will a text inscribing something so decisive with respect to metaphorics have remained so discreet, scant, reserved, withdrawn from metaphor as such and by this name, by its proper and literal name, so to speak? For if we always spoke metaphorically or metonymically of metaphor, how might we determine the moment when we would make it into our proper theme, in our proper name? Would there then be an essential relation between this withdrawal, this reserve, this withholding and what is written, metaphorically or metonymically, about metaphor under the signature of a Heidegger?

Taking into account the size of this question and of all the limits imposed upon on us here, beginning with the one of time, I will not claim to propose anything other than a brief note, and to narrow down my topic even more, a *note on a note*.[3] I hope to convince you along the way that if the citation of this note on a note is to be found in a text signed with my name, 'White Mythology: Metaphor in the Text of Philosophy,'[4] I do not refer to it as does an author who cites himself in order to indecently steer things back to himself. My gesture is all the less complacent, I hope, in that it is because it is from a certain insufficiency of this note that l will take my departure. And I do so for reasons of economy, to save time, so as to reconstruct as quickly as possible a context as broad and as strictly determined as possible. It happens in fact that (1) this Note (19, p. 269)[5] concerns Heidegger and cites at length one of the principle passages where he seems to take a position with respect to the concept of metaphor; (2) a second contextual trait: this note is called for by a development concerning *us* (the usual, usage, wear and tear or usury) and the recourse to this *us*-value in the dominant philosophical interpretation of metaphor; (3) a third contextual trait: this note cites one of Heidegger's sentences ('*Das Metaphorische gibt es nur innerhalb der Metaphysik,*' 'The metaphoric exists only within the boundaries of metaphysics'), which Paul Ricoeur 'discusses'—the word is his—in *Live Metaphor*, precisely in the 'Eighth Study: Metaphor and Philosophical Discourse.'[6] And this sentence, which he regularly calls a saying (*adage*), Paul Ricoeur also places in 'epigraph'—again, the word is his—for what he defines, following the discussion of Heidegger, as a 'second navigation,' which is to say the critical reading of my essay of 1971, 'White Mythology.' I prefer to cite here the third paragraph of the introduction to the Eighth Study:

> *A completely different—and even inverse—manner of involving philosophy in the theory of metaphor must also be considered. It is the inverse of that investigated in the two earlier sections, insofar as it establishes philosophical presuppositions at the very source of the distinctions that make a discourse on metaphor possible. This hypothesis does more than reverse the order of priority between metaphor and philosophy: it reverses the manner of philosophical argumentation. Our earlier discussion will be seen to have been situated at the level of stated intentions of speculative—even onto-theological—discourse, and thus to have had at issue only the order of its argumentation. For another 'reading,' it is the unavowed movement of philosophy and the unseen play of metaphor that are in complicity. Instructed by Heidegger's assertion that* 'the metaphoric exists only within the boundaries of the metaphysical,' *we shall take Jacques Derrida's essay 'White Mythology' as our guide in this 'second navigation.'* (pp. 324–5/258–9)

Without even reckoning with the implication which is common to us, Paul Ricoeur and myself, in this colloquium, the three contextual elements that I have just brought up may suffice to justify that we should return, here, once again, to Heidegger's short sentence, and by the same stroke they engage me in developing the Note that I had devoted to it seven or eight years ago.

Paul Ricoeur seems to me to have neglected the place and scope of this Note in his discussion; and if I may permit myself to recall it as a quite preliminary heading, this is not at all in a polemical spirit, to defend or attack any positions, but only in order better to illuminate the premises of the reading of Heidegger which I am about to attempt. I regret that I must limit myself, for lack of time, to a few principal indications; it will be impossible to proportion my argument in view of the wealth of *Live Metaphor*, and by a detailed analysis (however it may accentuate disagreement) to bear witness to my indebtedness toward Paul Ricoeur. When I say 'disagreement,' as will be seen, I am simplifying. Its logic is sometimes disconcerting: it is because I sometimes subscribe to some of Ricoeur's propositions that I am tempted to protest when I see him turn them back against me as if they were not already evident in what I have written. I will limit myself, as examples, to two of the most general lines (*traits*) which steer all of Ricoeur's reading in order to resituate the place of a possible debate, rather than re-open it, still less to close it. Whoever would wish to engage in it now has available in this respect an ample and detailed corpus.

First trait: Ricoeur inscribes his entire reading of 'White Mythology' in dependence on his reading of Heidegger and on this 'saying,' as if I had attempted no more than an extension or a *continuous* radicalization of the Heideggerian movement. Whence the function of the epigraph. Everything takes place as if I had only generalized what Ricoeur calls Heidegger's 'limited criticism' and as if I had stretched it inordinately, beyond all bounds. A passage, Ricoeur says, 'from the limited criticism of Heidegger to Jacques Derrida's unbounded "deconstruction" in "White Mythology"' (p. 362/284). A little further on, in the same gesture of assimilation or at least of continuous derivation, Ricoeur resorts to the figure of a 'theoretical core common to Heidegger and to Derrida, namely, the supposed collusion between the metaphoric couple of the proper and the figurative and the metaphysical couple of the visible and the invisible' (p. 373/294).

This continuist assimilation or setting into filiation surprised me. For it is precisely on the subject of these couples and particularly of the couple 'visible /invisible,' 'sensible/intelligible' that I had marked, in my Note on Heidegger, a clear and unequivocal reservation; a reservation which, at least in letter, even resembles that of Ricoeur. Thus I see myself the object, after being assimilated to Heidegger, of an objection whose principle I had myself formulated previously. Here it is (excuse these auto-citations, they are useful for the clarity and the economy of this colloquium), coming at the first line of Note 19: 'This explains the mistrust that the *concept* of metaphor inspires in Heidegger [I underline: the *concept* of metaphor]. In *Der Satz vom Grund*, he stresses especially the "sensible/non-sensible" opposition, an important trait but not the only, nor doubtless the first to appear, nor the most determinant for the value of metaphor.'

Is not this reservation clear enough to exclude, on this point in any case, both the 'common theoretical core' (not to mention that here, for essential reasons, there is no core and especially no theoretical core) and the complicity between the two couples in question? In this respect I hold to what is clearly said in this note. I do so in interest of conciseness, for in reality the whole of 'White Mythology' constantly puts in question the current and currently philosophical interpretation (in Heidegger as well) of metaphor as a transfer from the sensible to the intelligible, as well as the privilege accorded this trope (by Heidegger as well) in the deconstruction of metaphysical rhetoric.

Second trait: the whole reading of 'White Mythology' proposed in *Live Metaphor* is bound around what Ricoeur distinguishes as 'two assertions in the tight fabric of Derrida's demonstration' (p. 362/285). One of these two would therefore be that of which we have just spoken, namely, says Ricoeur, 'the deep-seated unity of metaphoric and analogical transfer of visible being to intelligible being.' I have just emphasized that this assertion is not mine but the one I am treating in, let's say for sake of speed, a deconstructive mode. The second assertion would concern the *us* and what Ricoeur calls the 'efficacy of worn-out metaphor.' In a first movement, Ricoeur had recognized that the tropical play on *usure* in 'White Mythology' was not being limited to 'wear and tear' (*usure*) as erosion, impoverishment or exhaustion, to the wear and tear of usage, of the worn or of the worn out. But then Ricoeur no longer takes into consideration that what the twist brings into action is what he himself calls a 'diversionary tactic' (*tactique déroutante*) and which does not correspond to some manipulative or triumphant perversity on my part, but to the intractable structure in which we are implicated and deflected from the outset. Ricoeur then does not at all take into consideration this twist and reduces my entire statement to the assertion which I am precisely putting into question, far from assuming it: namely, that the relation of metaphor to concept, and the process of metaphoricity in general would be understood under the concept or the scheme of *usure* (wear and tear) as a becoming-worn or becoming-worn-out, and not as *usure* (usury) in another sense, as the production of surplus value (*plus-value*) according to laws other than those of a continuous and linearly accumulative capitalization; this not only drove me into other problematic regions (let's say, for the sake of speed: psychoanalytic, economico-political, genealogical in the Nietzschean sense) but to deconstruct what is already dogmatized or accredited in these regions. Now Ricoeur devotes a long analysis to criticism of this motif of 'worn-out' metaphor to demonstrate that 'the hypothesis of a specific fecundity of worn out metaphor is strongly contested by the semantic analysis developed in preceding studies (. . .) the study of the lexicalization of metaphor by Le Guern contributes much to dissipate the false enigma of worn-out metaphor. . . .' (p. 368/290).

Here as well, it is to the extent that I subscribe to this proposition that I am not in agreement with Ricoeur when he attributes statements to me in order to contest them with statements which I had begun by putting into question myself. I did so constantly in 'White Mythology' and even to a degree of literal explication beyond all doubt, starting with the 'Exergue' (from the chapter entitled 'Exergue' on), then again in the immediate context of the Note on Heidegger, in the very paragraph where the citation for this Note is found. The 'Exergue' announces clearly that it is not a question of accrediting the schema of the *us* but of deconstructing a philosophical concept, a philosophical construction erected on this schema of worn out metaphor or privileging, for significant reasons, the trope named metaphor.

> *It was also necessary to subject this value of* wear and tear *to interpretation. It seems to have a systematic link with the metaphoric perspective. It will be found again any place where the theme of metaphor is privileged. It is also a metaphor which carries with itself a presupposition of continuity: the history of a metaphor would not essentially take the form of a displacement, with ruptures, reinscriptions in a heterogeneous system, mutations, digressions without origin, but that of a progressive erosion, of a regular semantic loss, of an uninterrupted exhaustion of original meaning. An empirical abstraction without extraction beyond its native soil. (. . .) This trait—the concept of wear and tear—no doubt does not belong to a narrow historico-theoretical configuration, but most certainly to the concept of metaphor itself and to the long metaphysical sequence which it determines or which determines it. It is with this sequence that we will concern ourselves initially.* (pp. 256/13–14)

The expression 'long metaphysical sequence' well indicates that for me it was not a question of taking 'metaphysics' (*'la' métaphysique*) as the homogeneous unity of an ensemble. I have never believed in the existence or in the consistency of something like metaphysics *itself* (la *métaphysique*). I bring this up again in order to respond to another of Ricoeur's doubts. Keeping in account such and such a demonstrative sentence or such a contextual constraint, if I happened to say 'metaphysics' or 'the' closure of 'metaphysics' (an expression which is the target of *Live Metaphor*), very often, elsewhere, but also in 'White Mythology,' I have put forward the proposition according to which there would never be 'metaphysics,' 'closure' not being here a circular limit bordering a homogeneous field but a more twisted structure which today, according to another figure, I would be tempted to call: 'invaginated.' Representation of a linear and circular closure surrounding a homogeneous space is, precisely, the theme of my greatest emphasis, an autorepresentation of philosophy in its onto-encyclopedic logic. I could multiply the citations from as far as 'Differance' where it was said, for example, that 'the text of metaphysics' is 'not surrounded but traversed by its limit,' 'marked on its inside by the multiple track of its margin,' 'a simultaneously traced and effaced trace, alive and dead simultaneously' (p. 25/156). I shall limit myself to these few lines of 'White Mythology' in the vicinity of the Note 19:

> *Each time a rhetoric defines metaphor, it implies not only a philosophy but a conceptual network within which philosophy as such constitutes itself. Each thread, in this network, forms in addition a turn of speech, one might say a metaphor if this notion were not too derivative here. The defined is therefore implicated in the defining agent of the definition. As is self-evident, there can be no appeal here to some sort of homogeneous continuum, one which would ceaselessly relate tradition to itself, that of metaphysics as well as that of rhetoric. Nevertheless, if we did not begin by paying attention to more durable constraints which have had their effects through a very long systematic chain, if we did not take the trouble to delimit their general functioning and their effective limits, one would run the risk of taking the most derivative effects for the original traits of a historical substructure, of a hastily identified configuration, of an imaginary or marginal mutation. Through an empiricist and impressionistic precipitancy towards supposed differences, in fact towards principally linear and chronological breaks (découpages), one would go from discovery to discovery. A rupture at each step! One could present, for example, as a physiognomy proper to the rhetoric of the '18th Century,' an ensemble of traits (such as the privilege of the name) passed down, although not in a direct line and with all sorts of deviations and inequalities of transformation, from Aristotle or from the Middle Ages. Here we are led back to the program, in its entirety yet to be elaborated, of a new delimitation of corpora, and a new problematic of signatures.* (pp. 274–5/30)

The 'privilege of the name' having been indicated between parentheses, I must take advantage of it in order to emphasize that, like Paul Ricoeur, I have constantly—in 'White Mythology' and elsewhere, and with an insistence that might be judged tiresome but which in any case cannot be neglected—put in question the privilege of the name and the word, like all those 'semiotic conceptions which' Ricoeur says precisely, 'impose the primacy of denomination' (p. 368/290). To this primacy I have regularly opposed attention to the syntactic motif dominant in 'White Mythology' (cf. p. 317/68 for instance). I was therefore once again surprised to see myself criticized from the same place where I had already carried the critique. If I had time I would even venture the same and *a fortiori* for the problem of etymologism or the interpretation of the Aristotelian *idion*. All these misunderstandings form a system with the attribution, to 'White Mythology,' of a thesis and of a thesis which would be confounded with the presupposition, which I have been precisely dead set against, namely, a concept of metaphor dominated by the concept of wear and tear as *being-worn-out* or *becoming worn-out*, with the entire system of its implications. In the ordered array of these implications, one finds a series of oppositions which include precisely those of living and dead metaphor. To say, as Ricoeur does, that 'White Mythology' makes death or dead metaphor its watchword is to abuse that text by marking it with what it clearly marks itself off from, for example, by saying that there are two deaths or two auto-destructions of metaphor (and when there are two deaths, the problem of death *itself* is infinitely complicated), or for yet another example, to be done with this apparent *pro domo*, in this paragraph where is situated this Note which today calls for another Note:

> *To the value of wear and tear* [Abnutzung: wear and tear, erosion, depreciation; Hegel's word on which, far from 'depending,' as Ricoeur would have it, I have brought to bear a deconstructive analysis: I lean on it as one does on a patiently studied text but I do not depend on it myself] *whose implications we have already recognized, here corresponds the opposition between effective metaphors and effaced metaphors. This is a very nearly constant trait of discourses on philosophical metaphor: there would be inactive metaphors, to which all interest can be denied, since the author* was not thinking of them *and since the metaphoric effect is studied inside the field of consciousness. To the difference between effective and extinct metaphors corresponds the traditional opposition between living metaphors and dead metaphors.* (pp. 268–9/25)

I have just said a while ago why it seemed necessary, outside of any plea *pro domo*, for me to begin by resituating the Note on Heidegger which today I would like to annotate and put forth once again. In showing in what way, in his most general premises, Paul Ricoeur's reading of 'White Mythology' appeared to me, let's say, too metaphorically or metonymically lively, I did not want, of course, either to polemicize or to extend my questions to a vast systematic no longer limiting itself to this Eighth Study of *Live Metaphor*, a systematic which 'White Mythology' does not enclose by the two isolated assertions that Ricoeur wanted to attribute to it. Taking up once again Ricoeur's watchword, the 'intersection' which I have just situated does not focus into one point the difference, indeed, the incommensurable distance of the paths crossing there, like parallel lines which, Heidegger will say in a short while, can intersect at infinity. I would be the last to reject a criticism under the pretext that it is metaphoric or metonymic or both at the same time. Every reading is so, in one way or another, and the partition does not pass between a figurative reading and an appropriate or literal, correct or true reading, but between capacities of tropes. Thus leaving aside, intact in reserve, the possibility of a quite different reading of these two texts ('White Mythology' and *Live Metaphor*), I finally come to the promised Note on a Note.

A problem is now imposed upon me which I seek to entitle as briefly as possible. I seek, by reasons of economy, a title for it, as formalizing and thus as economical as possible: well, precisely, it is *economy*. My problem is: economy. How, taking into account the (first of all temporal) constraints of this Colloquium, to determine the most wide-reaching and most entangling (*enchevêtrant*) conducting thread possible through so many virtual passages in Heidegger's immense corpus, as one says, and in his involved writing (*écriture enchtevêtrée*)? How to order the readings, interpretations or re-writings which I would be tempted to put forth? I could have chosen, among many other possibilities, the one which has just been presented to me under the name of entanglement, interlacing— which has been of interest to me for a long time and on which I am currently working in another manner. In the German noun, *Geflecht*, it plays a discreet but irreducible role in 'Der Weg zur Sprache'[7] in order to designate this singular, unique interlacing between *Sprache* (a word I will not translate, so as not to have to choose between *langue* [language] and *parole* [speech]) and path (*chemin; Weg, Bewegung, Bewegen*, etc.). It is a question here of a binding-unbinding interlacing (*entbindende Band*) back towards which we would be incessantly steered according to a circle which Heidegger proposes that we think or practice other than as a regression or vicious circle. Just like *path*, *Geflecht* is not a figure among others. We are implicated in advance, interlaced in advance when we wish to speak of *Sprache* and of *Weg* which are 'already in advance of us' (*uns stets schon voraus*).

But after a first anticipation, I had to decide to leave this theme withdrawn (*en retrait*): it would not have been economical enough. Now I must speak here economically of economy. For at least four reasons, I name them algebraically.

a. Economy in order to articulate what I am going to say about the other possible tropical system (*tropique*) of *usure* (usury), the one of interest, of surplus value, of fiduciary calculus or of usury rate which Ricoeur indicated but left in the dark, although it comes as a heterogeneous and discontinuous supplement, in a tropical divergence (*ecart*) irreducible to that of being-worn-out or worn.

b. Economy in order to articulate this possibility about the law-of-the-house and the law of the proper, *oiko-nomia*, which had made me reserve a particular status for the two motifs of light and home ('Borrowed home,' says Du Marsais in citation in his metaphoric definition of metaphor: 'Metaphor is a species of Trope: the word which one uses in metaphor is taken in another sense than the proper meaning, *it is*, so to speak, *in a borrowed home*, says an ancient; this is common and essential to all Tropes.' *Des Tropes*, Ch. 10).

c. Economy in order to steer, if one may say so, towards this value of *Ereignis*, so difficult to translate and whose entire family (*ereignen, eigen, eigens, enteignen*) intermingles with increasing density, in Heidegger's last texts, with the themes of the proper, of propriety, of propriation, of de-propriation on one hand, with that of light, of the clearing, of the eye on the other (Heidegger says to implicate *Er-aügnis* in *Ereignis*[8]); and finally, in current usage, with what happens as event: what is the place, the taking-place, or the metaphoric event, or of the metaphoric? What is happening, today, with metaphor?

d. Economy finally, because the economic consideration appears to me to have an essential relation with these determinations of passage or of fraying (*frayage*) according to the modes of the trans-fer or of the trans-lation (*Übersetzen*) which I believe I must link here to the question of metaphoric transfer (*Übertragung*). By reason of this economy of economy, I proposed to give this discourse the title of *retrait*. Not economies in the plural, but withdrawal (*retrait*).

Why withdrawal and why withdrawal of metaphor?

I speak in what I call, or rather, in what is called *my* language or, in an even more obscure fashion, my 'mother tongue.' In 'Sprache und Heimat'[9] (a 1960 text on Hebbel from which we will hear much on the subject of metaphor, of the *Gleich* (same) of *Vergleich* (comparison) and of *Gleichnis* (allegory), etc. but which lends itself poorly to the acceleration of a colloquium), Heidegger says that *das Sprachwesen* (the essence or being of language) takes root in dialect (another word for *Mundart*, idiom), and if the idiom is the mother tongue, '*das Heimische des Zuhaus, die Heimat*' (the homeliness of being at home, of native country) also takes root there. And he adds, '*Die Mundart ist nicht nur die Sprache der Mutter, sondern zugleich und zuvor die Mutter der Sprache*' (Dialect is not only the language of the mother, but is at the same time and firstly the mother of language) (p. 28). According to a movement whose law we will analyze, this inversion would induce us to think that not only the *idion* of the *idiome* (the proper of the dialect) is given as the mother of language but that, far from knowing before this what a mother is, such an inversion alone allows us perhaps to approach the essence of maternity. A mother tongue would not be a metaphor in order to determine the meaning of language (*le sens de la langue*), but the essential turn in order to understand what 'mother' means.

And the father? What is called the father? He would be tempted to occupy the place of form, of formal language. This place is untenable, and he can therefore only *attempt* to occupy it, only speaking in this measure the father's language, for form's sake. It is in sum this place and this impossible project that Heidegger would be designating in the beginning of 'Das Wesen der Sprache'[10] under the name of 'metalanguage' (*Metasprache, Übersprache, Metalinguistik*)— or of Metaphysics. Since, finally, one of the dominant names for this impossible and monstrous project of the father—as for this mastery of form for form's sake—is indeed Metaphysics. Heidegger insists on it: 'metalinguistics' does not 'resound' only as 'metaphysics,' for it is *the* metaphysics of the 'technicalization' integral to all languages; it is intended to produce a 'single, both functional and interplanetary instrument of information.' *Metasprache* and *Sputnik* . . . are the same' (p. 160/58). Without plunging into all these pressing questions here, I will first of all remark that in my language the word *retrait* is endowed with a rather rich polysemy. For the moment I leave open the question of knowing whether this polysemy is governed or not by the unity of a focus or of a horizon of meaning which promises it a totalization or a systematic adjoinment. This word imposed itself on me for economic reasons (again, the law of the *oikos* and the idiom), taking, or attempting to take, into account its capacities of translation, of capture or of translative captation, of translation or of transfer (in the traditional and ideal sense of the transport of an intact signified in the vehicle of another language and of another fatherland or motherland), or even in the more disquieting and more violent sense of a captating, seductive, and transformative capture (more or less regulated and faithful, but what then is the law of this violent fidelity?) of a language, discourse, and text by another language, another discourse, and another text which can at once (as will be the case here) violate in the same gesture their proper mother tongue at the moment of importing to it and exporting from it the maximum of energy and of information. I presumed the word *retrait*—at once intact (and forced, except in my language) and simultaneously altered—to be the most proper to capture the greatest quantity of energy and information in the Heideggerian text (inside the context which here is our own, and only within the limits of this context). The testing of such a transfer (at the same time as your patience) is just what I will try here with you, in an obviously schematic and programmatic form. I begin.

1. *First trait.* I depart again from these two apparently allusive and digressive passages where Heidegger posits very quickly the appurtenance of *the* concept of metaphor, as if there were only one, to metaphysics *itself*, as if there were only one and as if it were one. The first passage which I brought up a while ago is the one I cite in the Note ('*Das Metaphorische gibt es nur innerhalb der Metaphysik.*' 'The metaphoric exists only within the boundaries of metaphysics.'). The other, in the triple lecture 'The Nature of Language' (1957),

says, notably: '*Wir blieben in der Metaphysik hängen, wollten wir dieses Nennen Hölderlins in der Wendung "Worte wie Blumen" für eine Metapher halten.*' (We would remain suspended in metaphysics if we wished to take Hölderlin's nomination in the turn of phrase, 'words like flowers,' for a metaphor.) (p. 206/100).

Probably because of their univocal and sententious form, these two passages have constituted the sole focus for analysis and discussion employed on metaphor in Heidegger, on the one hand, in an article by Jean Greisch, 'Les mots et les roses: La métaphore chez Martin Heidegger' (*Revue des Sciences Théologiques et Philosophiques*, 57:3 (July, 1973), pp. 443–56), and on the other, in *Live Metaphor* (1975). These two analyses are oriented differently. Greisch's essay seems to be closer to the movement begun by 'White Mythology.' Nevertheless, the two texts have the following motifs in common which I bring up quickly, without coming back to what I said a while ago about *Live Metaphor*. The first motif, with which I do not feel at all in agreement but on which I will not expand—having done it and having had to do it elsewhere (notably in *Glas*, 'Le sans de la coupure pure,' 'Survivre,' etc.[11]—is the onto-anthological motif of the flower. Both identify what I say of dried flowers at the end of 'White Mythology' with what Heidegger reproaches Gottfried Benn for saying in order to transform Hölderlin's poem into a 'herbarium,' into a collection of dried plants. Greisch speaks of a kinship between Benn's attitude and my own. And Ricoeur uses this motif of the herbarium and Benn's interpretation as a transition to the topic of 'White Mythology.' For multiple reasons that I do not have time to enumerate, I would read that quite differently. Of more importance to me for the moment is the other of the two motifs common to Greisch and Ricoeur, namely, that the metaphoric power of the Heideggerian text is richer, more determinant than his thesis on metaphor. The metaphoricity of Heidegger's text would overflow what he says thematically, in the mode of simplificatory denunciation, of the so-called 'metaphysical' concept of metaphor (Greisch, p. 441ff.; Ricoeur, p. 359/282). I would quite willingly subscribe to this assertion. What remains to be determined, however, is the meaning and necessity which link this apparently univocal, simplifying and reductive denunciation of the 'metaphysical' concept of metaphor on the one hand, and, on the other, the apparently metaphoric power of a text whose author no longer wishes that what happens in that text and what claims to get along without metaphor there be understood precisely as 'metaphoric,' nor even under any concept of metalinguistics or rhetoric. The first schematic response that I will make, under the title of *retrait*, would be the following. The so-called 'metaphysical' concept of metaphor would belong to metaphysics *itself* insofar as the latter corresponds, in the epochality of its epochs, to an *epoché*, in other words, to a suspensive withdrawal of Being, to what is often translated as withdrawal, reserve, shelter, whether it is a question of *Verborgenheit* (being-hidden), of dissimulation or of veiling (*Verhüllung*).

Being withholds itself, gives way, escapes itself, *withdraws (sich entzieht)* in this movement of withdrawal which is indissociable, according to Heidegger, from the movement of withdrawal. With drawing in displaying itself or being determined *as* or *under* this mode of Being (for example as *eidos* according to the divergence or opposition of the 'invisible/visible' which constructs the Platonic *eidos*), which therefore is determined as *ontôs on* in the form of *eidos* or in any other form, Being is already submitted, *autrement dit, sozusagen, so to speak*, to a sort of metaphorico-metonymic displacement. This whole of this aforesaid history of Western metaphysics would be a vast structural process where the *epoché* of Being withholding itself, holding itself in withdrawal, would take or rather *would present* an (interlaced) series of guises, of turns, of modes, that is to say, of figures or of tropical aspects (*allures*) which we could be tempted to describe with the aid of rhetorical conceptuality. Each of these words—form, guise, turn, mode, figure—would already be in a tropical situation. To the extent of this *temptation*, 'metaphysics' would not only be the enclosure in which *the* concept of metaphor *itself* would be produced and enclosed. Metaphysics *itself* would not only have constructed and treated (*traité*) *the* concept of metaphor, for example by way of a determination of being as *eidos*; it would itself be in a tropical position with respect to Being or the thought of Being. This metaphysics *as* a tropical system and singularly as a metaphoric detour would correspond to an essential *withdrawal* of Being: unable to reveal itself, to present itself except in dissimulating itself under the 'species' of an epochal determination, under the species of an *as* which obliterates its *as such* (Being *as* eidos, *as* subjectity, *as* will, *as* work, etc.), Being would only allow itself to be named in a metaphorico-metonymical divergence (*écart*). One would then be tempted to say: the metaphysical, which corresponds in its discourse to the withdrawal of Being, tends to reassemble, in resemblance, all its metonymic divergences in a great metaphor of Being or of the thought of Being. This bringing together is *the* language of metaphysics *itself*.

What, then, would happen with metaphor? Everything: the totality of what is (*l'étant*). And it would happen that we should get along without it, without being able to dispense with it (*il se passerait ceci qu'on devrait se passer d'elle sans pouvoir s'en passer*), and this defines the structure of withdrawals which interests me here. On the one hand, we must be able to dispense with it because the relation of (ontotheological) metaphysics to the thought of Being, this relation (*Bezug*) which marks the withdrawal (*retrait, Entziehung*) of Being, can no longer be named—*literally*—metaphoric as soon as the usage (I do say usage, the becoming-usual of the word and not its original meaning to which no one has ever referred, in any case not me) was fixed by way of this couple of metaphysical opposition to describe relations among beings. Being being nothing, not being a being, it can not be expressed or named *more metaphorico*.[12] And therefore it does not have, in such a context of the dominant metaphysical usage of the word 'metaphor,' a proper or literal meaning which could be alluded to (*visé*) metaphorically by metaphysics. Consequently, if we cannot speak metaphorically on its subject, neither can we speak properly or literally. We will speak of being only *quasi*-metaphorically, according to a metaphor of metaphor, with the surcharge of a supplementary trait, of a double trait (*re-trait*), of a supplementary fold of metaphor articulating this withdrawal, repeating the intra-metaphysical metaphor in displacing it, the very one that the withdrawal of Being would have made possible. The graphics of this withdrawal would then take the following turn (*allure*), which I describe very dryly:

1. What Heidegger calls metaphysics *itself* corresponds to a withdrawal of Being. Therefore metaphor, as a so-called metaphysical concept, corresponds to a withdrawal of Being. Metaphysical discourse, producing and containing the concept of metaphor, is itself quasi-metaphoric with respect to Being: therefore it is a metaphor englobing the narrow-restrained-strict concept of metaphor which itself therefore has only strictly metaphoric sense.

2. The so-called metaphysical discourse can only be exceeded (*débordé*), insofar as it corresponds to a withdrawal of Being, according to a withdrawal of metaphor as a metaphysical concept, according to a withdrawal of metaphysics, a withdrawal of the withdrawal of Being. But as this withdrawal of the metaphoric leaves no place free for a discourse of the proper or the literal, it will have at the same time the sense of a re-fold (*re-pli*), of what retreats like a wave on the shoreline, and of a re-turn (*re-tour*), of the overcharging repetition of a supplementary trait, of yet another metaphor, of a double trait (*re-trait*) of metaphor, a discourse whose rhetorical border is no longer determinable according to a simple and indivisible line, according to a linear and indecomposable trait. This trait has the internal multiplicity, the folded-refolded structure of a double trait (*re-trait*). The withdrawal of metaphor gives place to an abyssal generalization of the metaphoric—metaphor of metaphor in two senses—which splays (*évase*) the borders, or rather, invaginates them. I do not wish to be overabundant in the developments of this paradox; I only draw from it, very quickly, two provisional conclusions.

1. The word *retrait*, which is 'French' up to a certain point, is not too abusive, I believe, as a translation of *Entziehung*, the *Sich-Entziehen* of Being, insofar as, suspending, dissimulating, giving way, and veiling itself, etc., Being withdraws into its crypt. To the extent of being 'not too abusive' (a 'good' translation must always *abuse*), the French word is suitable in order to designate the essential and in itself double, equivocal movement which makes possible all that I am speaking about at this moment in the text of Heidegger. The withdrawal of Being, in its being-withdrawn, gives place to metaphysics as onto-theology producing the concept of metaphor, coming forth and naming itself in a quasi-metaphoric manner. In order to think Being in its withdrawal

it would be necessary to allow a withdrawal of metaphor to come forth or to *vanish away* (*se reduire*) which however (leaving room for nothing which might be *opposed*, opposable to the metaphoric) will spread out without limit and will charge any metaphoric trait with supplementary surplus value. Here the word *re-trait* (a trait in addition to supplement the subtracting withdrawal, the *re-trait* expressing at once, at one stroke [*d'un trait*] the plus and the minus) designates the generalizing and supplementary return only in a sort of quasi-catachrestic violence, a sort of abuse I impose on language, but an abuse that I hope is overjustified by necessity of good, economic formalization. *Retrait* is neither a translation nor a non-translation (in the current sense) in relation to the text of Heidegger; it is neither proper nor literal, neither figurative nor metaphoric. 'Withdrawal of Being' cannot have a literal and proper sense to the extent that Being is not *something*, a determinate being which one might designate. For the same reason, the withdrawal of Being giving place both to the metaphysical concept of metaphor and to its withdrawal, the expression 'withdrawal of Being' is not *stricto sensu* metaphoric.

2. Second provisional conclusion: because of this chiasmatic invagination of borders—and if the word *retrait* functions here neither literally nor by metaphor—I do not know what I mean (*veux dire*) before having thought, so to speak, the withdrawal of Being *as* withdrawal of metaphor. Far from proceeding by way of a word or a known or determinate meaning (the withdrawal) to think where the question of Being or of metaphor stands, I will come to comprehend, understand, read, think, allow the withdrawal in general to manifest itself, only from the withdrawal of Being as a withdrawal of metaphor in all the polysemous *and* disseminal potential of withdrawal. In other words: if one wished that *withdrawal-of* be understood as a metaphor, this would be a curious, inverting—one would say almost *catastrophic*, catastrophical—metaphor: its end would be to state something new, something still unheard of about the vehicle and not about the apparent subject of the trope. *Withdrawal-of-Being-or-of-metaphor* would be by way less of leading us to think Being or metaphor than the Being or the metaphor *of withdrawal*, by way of leading us to think about the way and the vehicle, or their fraying. Habitually, usually, a metaphor claims to procure access to the unknown and to the indeterminate by the detour of something recognizably familiar. 'The evening,' a common experience, helps us to think 'old age,' something more difficult to think or to live, as 'the evening of life,' etc. According to this common schema, we would know in a familiar way what *withdrawal* means, and we would try to think the withdrawal of Being or of metaphor by way of it. Now what arises here is that for once we can think of the trait of *re-trait* only from the thought of this ontico-ontological difference on whose withdrawal would have been traced—with the borders of metaphysics—the current structure of metaphoric usage.

Such a catastrophe inverts therefore the metaphoric passage at the moment when, having become excessive, metaphoricity no longer allows itself to be contained in its so-called 'metaphysical' concept. Would this catastrophe produce a general dilapidation, a destruction of discourse—for example that of Heidegger—or a simple conversion of meaning/direction (*sens*), repeating in its depth the circulation of the hermeneutic circle? I do not know if that is an alternative, but were it one, I would not be able to respond to this question, and not solely for reasons of time: a text, for example that of Heidegger, necessarily entails and crosses the two motifs within itself.

II. I will therefore underline only—this will be the *second* great *trait* announced—what unites (their hyphen [*trait d'union*], if you wish) Heidegger's statements on the so-called metaphysical concept of metaphor, and, on the other, his own text insofar as it appears more 'metaphoric' or *quasi*-metaphoric than ever, at the very moment when he defends himself from it. How is that possible?

In order to find the path, the form of the path, between the two, it is necessary to glimpse what I have just called the generalizing catastrophe. I will draw two examples from among a number of possibilities. It is still a question of these typical moments when, resorting to formulas which one would be tempted to accept as metaphors, Heidegger specifies that these are not metaphors and throws suspicion on what we believe assured and clear in this word. He makes that gesture not only in the two passages cited by Ricoeur or Greisch. In the 'Letter on Humanism,'[13]a movement which I cannot reconstitute here includes this sentence: '*Das Denken baut am Haus des Seins*,' 'Thought works at (constructing) the house of Being,' the adjoinment of Being (*Fuge des Seins*) coming to assign, enjoin (*verfugen*) man to inhabit the truth of Being. And a little further, after a citation from Hölderlin:

> Discourse about the house of Being (Die Rede vom Haus des Seins) *is not a metaphor* (Übertragung) *transporting the image of the 'house' toward Being, but* [*by implication: inversely*] *it is by way of appropriating thinking the essence of Being* (sondern aus dem sachgemäss gedachten Wesens des Seins) *that we will one day be able to think what 'house' and 'to inhabit' are.* (pp. 189/236–7)

'House of Being' would not operate, in this context, in the manner of a metaphor in the current, usual, that is to say, literal meaning (*sens*) of metaphor, if there is one. This current and cursive meaning—I understand it also in the sense of direction[14]—would transport a familiar predicate (and here nothing is more familiar, familial, known, domestic and economic, one would think, than the house) towards a less familiar, more remote, *unheimlich* (uncanny) subject, which it would be a question of better appropriating for oneself, becoming familiar with, understanding, and which one would thus designate by the indirect detour of what is nearest—the house. Now what happens here *with* the quasi-metaphor of the house of Being, and what does *without* metaphor in its cursive direction, is that it is Being which, from the very moment of its withdrawal, would let or promise to let the house or the habitat be thought. One would be tempted to use all kinds of terms and technical schemes borrowed from this or that meta-rhetoric in order to master *formaliter* that which resembles, in this bizarre *Übertragung*, a tropical inversion in the relations between the predicate and subject, signifier and signified, vehicle and tenor, discourse and referent, etc. One could be tempted to formalize this rhetorical inversion where, in the trope 'house of Being,' Being says more to us, or promises more about the house than the house about Being. But this would be to miss what is most strictly proper in what the Heideggerian text would say in this place. In the inversion considered, Being has not become the proper of this supposedly known, familiar, nearby being, which one believed the house to be in the common metaphor. And if the house has become a bit *unheimlich*, this is not for having been replaced, in the role of 'what is nearest,' by 'Being.' We are therefore no longer dealing with a metaphor in the usual sense, nor with a simple inversion permutating the places in a usual tropical structure. All the more since this statement (which moreover is not a judicative statement, a common proposition, of the constative type, S *is* P) is no longer a statement among others bearing on relations between predicates and ontic subjects. First of all because it implies the economic value of the domicile and of the proper both of which often (or always) intervene in the definition of the metaphoric. Then the statement speaks above all *of* language and therefore in it *of* metaphoricity. In fact, the house of Being, we will have read above in the 'Letter,' is *die Sprache* (a particular language or language in general):

> *The only thing* (Das Einzige) *which the thought seeking for the first time to express itself in* Being and Time, *would like to achieve, is something simple* (etwas Einfaches). *As such* [*simple, unique*], *Being remains mysterious* (geheimnisvoll), *the simple proximity of a non-constraining power. This proximity* west *(is, is essenced) as* die Sprache selbst (language itself) . . . (p. 164/212)

Another way of saying that one will be able to think the proximity of the near (which, itself, is not near or proper: proximity is not near, propriety is not proper) only from and within language. And further down:

> *That is why it is proper to think* das Wesen der Sprache (the essence/being of language) *according to the correspondence to Being and as this correspondence, which is to say as* Behausaung des Menschen-wesens *(the house sheltering the essence of man). But man is not only a living being who, along with other aptitudes, also possesses* die Sprache *(language).* Die Sprache *is rather the house of Being, in which living there man ek-sists, in that he belongs to the truth of Being by assuming its guardianship.* (p. 164/213)

This movement is no longer simply metaphoric. 1. It bears on language in general and on a particular language as an element of the metaphoric. 2. It bears on being which is nothing and which one must think according to ontological difference which, with the withdrawal of Being, makes possible both its metaphoricity and its withdrawal. Consequently there is no term which may be proper, usual and literal in the separation without divergence (*dans l'écart sans écart*) of this phrasing. Despite its aspect (*allure*) or resemblance, this phrasing is neither metaphoric nor literal. Stating non-literally the condition of metaphoricity, its frees both its unlimited extension and its withdrawal. Withdrawal by which what is distanced (*entfernt*) in the non-near of proximity is withdrawn and sheltered in it. As said at the beginning of 'The Nature of Language,' no more metalanguage, no more metalinguistics, therefore no more meta-rhetoric, and no more metaphysics. Always another metaphor when metaphor withdraws in expanding (*évasant*) its limits.

This torsion, this twist of the gait and of the step, this *detour* of the Heideggerian path: one finds their trace everywhere where Heidegger writes and writes about the path. Its trail can be followed everywhere and can be deciphered according to the same rule which is neither simply from a rhetoric nor from a tropical system. I will situate only one other occurrence, because it enjoys some privileges. 1. In 'The Nature of Language' (1957–8), it precedes, from quite a distance, the passage cited a while ago on '*Worte wie Blumen*' (words like flowers). 2. It concerns not only the claimed metaphoricity of some statements on language in general, and on metaphor in language. It initially pursues an ostensibly metaphoric discourse bearing on the relation between thought and poetry (*Denken und Dichten*). 3. It determines this relation as one of neighborliness (*voisinage, Nachbarschaft*), according to this type of proximity (*Nähe*) called neighborhood, in the space of the home and the economy of the house. Now there again, to call metaphor, as if we knew what it was, any value of neighborliness between poetry and thought, to act as if one were first of all assured of the proximity of proximity and of the neighborliness of neighborhood (*voisinage du voisinage*), is to close oneself to the necessity of the other movement. Inversely, in renouncing this security of what we believe we recognize under the name of metaphor and of neighborhood, we will perhaps approach the proximity of neighborliness. Not that neighborliness (*le voisinage*) might be strange to us before this access to what there is between *Denken* (thought, thinking) and *Dichten* (poetry). Nothing is more familiar to us than this, and Heidegger brings it up immediately. We reside and move in neighborliness. But it is necessary (and this is what is most enigmatic about this circle) to come back to where we are without properly being there (see p. 184/79 and *passim*). Heidegger has just named 'neighborliness' the relation marked by the 'and' between *Dichten und Denken*. By what right, he then asks, can one speak here of 'neighborliness'? The neighbor

(*Nachbar*) is he who lives in proximity (*in der Nähe*) of another and with another (Heidegger does not exploit the chain *vicus*, *veicus* which perhaps refers to *oikos* and to the Sanskrit *veca* (house), which I note in reserve as a supplementary inquiry). Neighborliness is thus a relation (*Beziehung*)—let us be attentive to this word—which results from one's drawing (*zeiht*) the other into one's proximity so it may settle down there. We could believe, then, that in the case of *Dichten und Denken*, this relation, this trait which draws one into the neighborhood of the other, is named in a '*bildlicher Redeweise*' (imagistic style). That would be reassuring indeed. Unless, Heidegger then notes, by that we have not already said something about the very thing, namely, about what it is essential to think, that is, neighborliness, whereas it still remains 'indeterminate for us what *Rede* (speech) is, and what is *Bild* (image), and up to what point *Die Sprache in Bildern spricht* (language speaks in images), if even it speaks in general in that manner' (p. 187/82).

III. Hastening my conclusion in this *third* and last *trait*, I would now like to come not to the last word, but to this plural word *trait* itself. And not to come to it but to come back to it. Not to the withdrawal of metaphor but to what could first of all resemble the metaphor of withdrawal. Would there not be, in the last instance, behind all this discourse—sustaining it more or less discreetly, in withdrawal—a metaphor of withdrawal which would authorize speaking about ontological difference and, by way of it, about the withdrawal of metaphor? To this question, slightly formal and artificial in appearance, one could respond just as quickly that this would at least confirm the de-limitation of the metaphoric (there is nothing metametaphoric because there are only metaphors of metaphors, etc.) and would also confirm what Heidegger says of the meta-linguistic project as meta-physics, of its limits, and indeed of its impossibility. I will not be satisfied with this form of response, even if in its principle it is adequate.

There is—and in a decisive way in the instance of the 'there is,' of the *es gibt* which one thus translates—the trait/line, an outline or a tracing of the trait operating discreetly, underlined by Heidegger, but each time in a decisive place, and incisive enough to lead us to think that he precisely names the most grave, engraved, and engraving signature of the decision. Two families, so to speak, of words, nouns, verbs and syncatagoremes, form an alliance, engage, cross each other in this contract of the trait in the German language. It is on the one hand the 'family' of *Ziehen* (*Zug, Bezug, Gezüge, durchziehen, entziehen*), and on the other, the 'family' of *Reissen* (*Riss, Aufriss, Umriss, Grundriss*, etc.). To my knowledge the role which this crossing plays has never been remarked or at least thematized. Now this lexicon (more or less a lexicon since it will come to name the trait or the differential traction as a possibility of language, of *logos*, of the language and of *lexis* in general, of spoken inscription just as much as written) forces itself very early upon Heidegger, at least it seems to

me (with reservation made for a more systematic inquiry), from the time of
'The Origin of the Work of Art' (1935–6).[15] But for this first marking out, in
order to avoid accumulation, I will restrict myself to three types of remarks.

1. I remark at the outset something about the 'neighboring' (*avoisinant*)
trait. The neighborhood (*voisinage*) between *Denken* and *Dichten* gave us access
to neighborliness (*voisinage*), to the proximity of neighborliness, by a way,
according to a path, a path which, no longer being either metaphoric or literal, would re-open the question of metaphor. The 'neighboring' trait, I will
say the 'approximate' trait, the proper trait which relates (*bezieht*) one to the
other— *Dichten* (which must not be translated, without precaution, as 'poetry')
and *Denken* (thought) in their neighboring proximity (which divides them
and which they both share)—this common differential trait which reciprocally, even while signing their irreducible difference, is *the trait: Riss*, a tracing
of fraying which cuts, tears, marks the divergence, the limit, the margin, the
mark (Heidegger somewhere names 'march' [*marche*], '*Mark*' as limit, *Grenze*,
Grenzland, [border, borderland], p. 171/67). And this trait (*Riss*) is a *cut* which
the two neighbors (*Denken und Dichten*) make themselves somewhere in
infinity. In the notch of this cut they open one to another, one could say,
with/from their difference and even, to use a word whose use I have already
attempted to regulate, *re-cut* themselves (*se recoupent*: re-intersect) with/off from
their trait and thus with/from their respective withdrawal (*re-trait*). This trait
(*Riss*) of recutting relates one to the other but belongs to neither. This is why
it is not a common trait or a general concept, nor a metaphor anymore. We
could say of the trait that it is more originary than the two (*Dichten* and
Denken) which it splits and re-cuts/re-intersects, that the trait is their common
origin and the seal of their alliance, remaining in this singular and different
from them, if a trait could be something, could be properly and fully originary.
Now, insofar as it frays a differential splitting, a trait is neither fully originary
and autonomous, nor, as fraying, purely derivative. And to the extent that such
a trait frays the possibility of naming in language (written or spoken, in the
accepted meaning of these words), it is not itself nameable as separation,
neither literally, properly, nor metaphorically. *The trait is nothing approximate*
(*approchant*) *as such*.

At the end of the second part of 'The Nature of Language,' Heidegger has
just marked how, in the *es gibt das Wort*, '*es, das Wort, gibt*,' (there is the word; it,
the word, gives) but in such a way that the gem (*Kleinod*) of the poem which
one is reading ('The Word' by Stefan George), what the poem gives as a present and which is none other than a certain relation of the word to the thing,
this gem which remains unnamed withdraws (*das Kleinod entzieht sich*). The *es
gibt* withdraws what it gives, giving itself only to withdraw; and to whoever
knows how to renounce. The jewel withdraws into the 'astonishing secret,'
where secret (*geheimnisvol*) comes to qualify the astonishing (*das Erstaunende*,

was staunen lässt) and designates the intimacy of the house as the place of withdrawal (*geheimnisvoll*). Coming back then to the theme of neighborliness between *Denken* and *Dichten*, on their irreducible alterity, Heidegger speaks of their 'tender,' delicate (*zarte*) but 'clear' difference which must leave no place for confusion whatsoever. *Dichten* and *Denken* are parallels (*para allelôn*), one beside or along the other, but not separate, if separate signifies 'to be distanced in the un-related' (*être eloigné dans le sans-rapport, ins Bezuglose abseschieden*), and they are not without the traction of this trait (*Zug*), of this *Bezug* (relation) which relates or transports one towards the other.

What therefore is the trait (*Riss*) of this *Bezug* between *Denken* and *Dichten*? It is the trait of an 'incision' (*entame*), of a tracing, *fraying* opening (the word *Bahnen* (path, groove) appears often in this context with the figures of *Bewegen* [to open a way]), of an *Aufriss*. The word *incision* which I have used a good deal elsewhere, appears to me the most approximate (*approchant*) for translating *Aufriss*, a decisive word, a word of decision in this context of the non-'voluntary' decision, and one that French translators render sometimes by *tracé-ouvrant* (opening sketch) and sometimes by *gravure* (engraving).

Incised, the two parallels cut each other at infinity, re-cut, split and sign in some way the one in the body of the other, the one in the place of the other, the contract without contract of their neighborliness. If the parallels cut one another (*schneiden sich*: intersect) at infinity (*im Un-endlichen*), this cut, this split (*entaille, Schnitt*), they do not make them to themselves, they re-cut without touching each other, without affecting each other, without wounding each other. They only incise each other and are cut (*geschnitten*) in the incision (*Aufriss*) of their proximity (*avoisinement*), of their neighboring essence (*nachbarlichen Wesens*). And via this incision which leaves them intact, they are *eingezeichnet*, 'signed' as the published French translation says: designed, characterized, assigned, consigned. Heidegger then says, *Diese Zeichnung ist der Riss*. It incises (*er reisst auf*), it traces in opening *Dichten* and *Denken* in the approximating (*approchement*) of one to the other. This approximating does not draw them into proximity again from another place where they would already be themselves and then would allow themselves to be drawn (*ziehen*) to each other. The approximating is the *Ereignis* which sends *Dichten* and *Denken* back into the proper (*in das Eigene*) of their essence (*Wesen*). The trait of the incision, therefore, marks the *Ereignis* as propriation, as an event of propriation. It does not precede the two properties which it causes to come to their propriety, for it is nothing without them. In this sense it is not an autonomous, originary instance, itself proper in relation to the two which it incises and allies. Being nothing, it does not appear itself, it has no proper and independent phenomenality, and in not disclosing itself it withdraws, it is structurally in withdrawal, as a divergence (*écart*: splitting aside), opening, differentiality, trace, border, traction, effraction, etc. From the moment that it withdraws in drawing itself out, the trait is *a priori* withdrawal, unappearance, and effacement of its mark in its incision.

Its inscription, as I have attempted to articulate it in the trace or in differance, *succeeds only in being effaced (n'arrive qu'à s'effacer)*.

It happens and comes about only in effacing itself. Inversely, the trait is not derived. It is not secondary, in its arrival in relation to the domains, or the essences, or to the existences that it cuts away, frays, and refolds in their re-cut. The *re-* of *re-trait* is not an accident occurring to the trait. It rises up (*s'en-lève*) in allowing any propriety to rise up, as one says of a figure on a ground. But it is lifted neither before nor after the incision which permits it to be lifted up, neither substantially, accidentally, materially, formally, nor according to any of the oppositions which organize so-called metaphysical discourse. If metaphysics had a unity, it would be the regime of these oppositions which appears and is determined only *by way of* (*à partir de*) the withdrawal of the trait, of the withdrawal of the withdrawal, etc. The 'by way of' is engulfed in it (*s'y abîme*). We thus have recognized the relation between the *re-* of *retrait* (which states no less violently the repetition of the incision than the negative suspension of the *Ent-Ziehung* [with-drawal] of the *Ent-fernung* [dis-stancing]) and the *Ereignen* of the *Es gibt* which focusses all of Heidegger's 'late' thinking, in precisely this trait where the movement of the *Enteignen* (dispropriation, retraction of propriety) happens to empty out all *Ereignis* (*Dieses enteignende Vereignen ist das Spiegelspiel des Gevierts, Das Ding, in fine*; This dis-propriating appropriation is the mirrorplay of the Fourfold, the thing, *in fine*).

2. I remark, secondly, the performance or, in a very open sense of this word, the performative of writing by which Heidegger names, calls *Aufriss* (*entame*, incision), what he decides, decrees or allows himself to call *Aufriss*, what is called according to him *Aufriss*, and whose translation I sketch according to the traction of an equally performing gesture, by *incision*. The trenchant decision to call *Aufriss* what was in a certain way still unnamed or unknown under its name is already in itself an incision; it can only be named, be auto-named, and be incised in its proper writing. Heidegger often makes the same gesture, for example with *Dasein* at the beginning of *Being and Time*.[16] Neither neologism nor meta-writing in the gesture that *there is* here (*dans le geste qu'il y a ici*).

Here is what is signed and incised under Heidegger's signature. It is at the time when, in 'The Way to Language,' he has just suggested that the unity of *Sprache* still remains *unnamed* (*unbennant*). Traditional names have always stopped the essence on such and such an aspect or predicate. Heidegger thus opens a new paragraph: '*Die gesuchte Einheit des Sprachwesens heisse der Aufriss*,' 'Let the unity sought of the essence of *Sprache*, be called incision' (p. 251/ 121). Heidegger does not say: I arbitrarily decide to baptize it 'incision,' but 'let it be called,' in the decisive language, incision. And better yet, this name, it is not called, it calls us, it calls us to . . . Let us continue: '*Der Name heisst uns*' (this name calls us) to glimpse (*erblicken*, as in *Der Satz vom Grund*, at the moment of the declaration on metaphor) more distinctly (*deutlicher*) the proper (*das Eigene*) of the *Sprachewesens* (essence/being of language). *Riss ist dasselbe Wort wie ritzen* ('Trait is the same word as 'to mark' [*rayer*]').

Now, continues Heidegger, we often know *Riss* only under the 'devalued' (*abgewerteten*) form that it has in the expressions 'to mark a wall' 'to plow' and 'to cultivate a field' (*einen Acker auf- und Umreissen*), in order to trace furrows (*Furchen ziehen*) so that the field will shelter, and keep in it (*berge*) the seeds and the growth. The incision (*Aufriss*) is the totality of the traits (*das Ganze der Züge*), the *Gefüge* (adjoining) and the *Gezüge* (drawing together) of this *Zeichnung* (inscription, engraving, signature) which thoroughly *adjoins* (artic-ulates, splits aside [*écarte*], and holds together) the opening of *Sprache*. But this incision remains veiled (*verhüllt*) as long as one does not remark properly (*eigens*) in what sense the spoken and speaking are spoken of (*il est parlé du parlé et du parler*). The trait of the incision is therefore veiled, withdrawn, but it is also the trait that brings together and separates (*écarte*) at once the veiling *and* the unveiling, the *withdrawal* and the *withdrawal of the withdrawal*.

3. We have just glimpsed the trait contracting with itself, withdrawing, crossing and intersecting itself across these two neighboring circumscriptions of *Reissen* and *Ziehen*. The intersection crosses and allies—after having drawn them together in language—the two heterogeneous *genealogies* of the trait, the two words or 'families' of words, of 'logies.' In the intersection, the trait is itself remarked while withdrawing, it succeeds in effacing itself in an other, in re-inscribing itself there, *in a parallel way*, hence *heterologically*, and *allegorically*. The trait is withdrawn (*le trait est retrait*). We can no longer even say *is*, we can no longer submit withdrawal to the instance of an ontological copula whose very possibility it conditions, like *es gibt*. As Heidegger does for *Ereignis* or *Sprache*, we should say in a non-tautological fashion: the trait treats or is treated, traces the trait, therefore retraces and retreats (*re-traite*) or withdraws the withdrawal (*retire le retrait*), contracts, is contracted and signs with itself, with the with-drawal of itself, a strange contract, which for once, no longer precedes its own signature, *and therefore carries it off*. We ought to therefore, right here, perform, incise, trace, tract, track not only this, or that, but the capture of this crossing from one language into another, the capture (at once violent and faithful, pas-sive however and leaving safe [*sauf*]) of this crossing aligning *Reissen* and *Ziehen*, translating them already *in* what one calls the German language. This capture would affect the captor himself, translating him into the other, since in French *retrait* has never usually meant *re-tracing*. In order to incise this comprehensive captation and this deal (*tractation*) or this transaction with the other's language, and in order to conclude I will underline this: the deal *works*, it is already *at work* in the other's language, I would say in the other's

languages. For there is always more than one language in language. The text
of Heidegger which, to my knowledge, seems for the first time to have called
(in the sense of *heissen*) for this crossing of *Ziehen* and *Reissen*, is 'The Origin
of the Work of Art' in this exact place where truth is stated *as non-truth: Die
Wahrheit ist un-Wahrheit.* In this non-withdrawal of truth as truth, in its *Un-
verborgenheit* (unconcealment), the *Un-* bars, impedes, defends or splits (*fend*) in
a twofold way. The truth is this originary combat (*Urstreit*) in which what
belongs to the essence of truth is submitting to or feeling what Heidegger
calls the *attraction* of the work, the attraction towards the work (*Zug zum
Werk*), as its significant possibility (*ausgezeichnete Möglichkeit*). In particular, the
work has been defined above as *sumballein* and *allegoreuein*. In this appeal
(*attrait*), truth deploys its essence (*west*) as a battle between opening (*éclaircie*)
and reserve or withdrawal (*Verbergung*), between world and earth. Now this
combat is not a trait (*Riss*) as *Aufreissen* incising a simple abyss (*blossen Kluft*)
between adversaries. Combat attracts the adversaries in the attraction of a
reciprocal appurtenance. It is a trait which attracts them to the provenance of
their unity by way of common ground, *aus dem einigen Grunde zusammen*. In
this sense it is a *Grundriss*: fundamental plan, project, design, sketch, outline. A
series of locutions is then printed, whose current, usual, 'literal' sense, so to
speak, is found re-activated as it is simultaneously, discreetly, re-inscribed,
dis-placed, put back into play in what works in this context. The *Grundriss* is
Aufriss ('incision' and in the current sense, an 'essential profile,' a 'schema,' a
'projection') which designs (*zeichnet*) the fundamental traits (*Grundzüge*), that
here intersect the two systems of traits in order to say *trait* in the language of
the opening of being. The trait (*Riss*) does not split the adversaries, rather it
attracts adversity to the unity of a contour (*Umriss*), of a frame, of a framework. The trait is '*einheitliche Gezüge von Auffriss und Grundriss, Durch- und
Umriss*,' the united, adjoined (*Ge-*) ensemble of reassembled traits, the contraction or the contract between these forms of traits, these apparent modifications or properties of *Riss* (*Auf-, Grund-, Durch-, Um-,* etc.) among all these
traits of the trait which do not come upon it as predicative modifications to
a subject, a substance, or a being (which the trait is not) but on the contrary
which open the delimitation, the de-marcation from which ontological discourse on substance, predicate, proportion, logic and rhetoric, can then be
stripped away. I arbitrarily interrupt my reading here, I cut it with a slash (*trait*)
at the moment when it would lead us to the *Ge-stell* (framing) of the *Gestalt*
in the adjoinment of which (*Gefüge*), *der Riss sich fügt* (the trait joins itself).

The trait is therefore nothing. The incision of the *Aufriss* is neither passive
nor active, neither one nor multiple, neither subject nor predicate; it does not
separate more than it unites. All the oppositions of value have their proper
possibility in differance, in the between of its divergence which brings together
as much as it demarcates. Can one say that the lexicon and syntax in French,

in German or between the two which encircle this possibility are metaphoric? Will they be formalized according to some other rhetorical schema? Whatever may be the pertinence, indeed the fecundity of a rhetorical analysis determining everything which happens along such a way of thought or of language, in this fraying of fraying, there will, necessarily, have been a line *divided furthermore*, where the rhetorical determination will have encountered, in the trait, that is to say, in its withdrawal (*retrait*) its own possibility (differentiality, divergence *and* resemblance). This possibility will not be able to be strictly understood in its entirety (*dans son ensemble*), in the ensemble which it makes possible; however, it will not dominate it. Rhetoric will be able then to state itself and its possibility only by getting carried away in the supplementary trait of a rhetoric of rhetoric, and for example, of a metaphor of metaphor, etc. When trait or *retrait* is said in a context where truth is in question, 'trait' is no longer a metaphor of what we usually believe we recognize by this word. It does not however suffice to invert the proposition and say that the withdrawal (*re-trait*) of truth as non-truth is the proper or the literal by way of which current language will be in a position of divergence, of abuse, of tropical detour in any form. Withdrawal is no more proper or literal than figurative. It can no more be confounded with the words which it makes possible in their delimitation or cutting (*découpe*) (including French or German words crossed or grafted here) than it is foreign to words as a thing or a referent. Withdrawal is neither thing, nor being, nor meaning. It *withdraws* itself both from the Being of being as such and from language, without being or being said elsewhere; it *incises* ontological difference itself. It withdraws *itself* (*se retire*) but the ipseity of the pronominal *se* (itself) by which it would be related to itself with a trait or line does not precede it and already supposes a supplementary trait in order to be traced, signed, withdrawn, retraced in its turn. *Retraits* thus writes itself in the plural, it is singularly plural in itself, divides itself and reassembles in the withdrawal of withdrawal. It is what I have elsewhere tried to name *pas*.[17] It is a question here of the path again, of what passes there, of what passes the path by, of what happens there, or not. (*Il y va ici du chemin, encore, de ce qui y passe, le passe, s'y passe, ou pas*).

What is happening? will I have asked in opening this discourse.

Qu'est-ce qui se passe? aurai-je demandé en entamant ce discours. Nothing, no response, if not that withdrawal of/from metaphor happens and with(out) itself.

Rien, pas de réponse, sinon que de la métaphore le retrait se passe et de lui-même.

Notes

1. See Derrida, 'Différance,' in *Marges de la philosophie* (Paris: Minuit, 1972), p. 22; an earlier version is in *Speech and Phenomena and Other Essays on Husserl's Theory of Signs*, trans. D. Allison (Evanston: Northwestern University Press, 1973), p. 153. [Trans.]

2. Pfullingen: Neske, 1957 and 1959. The latter has been trans. by P. Hertz, in part, as *On the Way to Language* (New York: Harper& Row, 1971). [Trans.]

3. It is of interest as well to note that an earlier text by Derrida, concerning Heidegger's thinking on time, had also taken this form: 'Ousia et grammè: Note sur une note de *Sein und Zeit*,' in *Marges*, pp.31–78; 'Ousia and Grammè: A Note on a Footnote in *Being and Time*,' trans. E. Casey, in *Phenomenology in Perspective*, ed. F. Smith (The Hague: Nijhoff, 1970), pp. 54–93. [Trans.]

4. 'La Mythologie blanche. La métaphore dans le texte philosophique,' in *Marges*, pp. 247–324 trans. by F. Moore in *New Literary History*, 6:1 (Autumn, 1974), pp. 5–74. Here and elsewhere: (I) if a translation is available, paginations will dually cite from the original/English translation; (2) citations from other translations have been modified. [Trans.]

5. In the English translation this note becomes number 22, p. 25. [Trans.]

6. *La métaphore vive* (Paris: Seuil, 1975); trans. as *The Rule of Metaphor*, trans. R. Czerny (Toronto: University of Toronto Press, 1977). We have kept to a literal translation of its title (*Live Metaphor*) throughout this text. [Trans.]

7. In *Unterwegs zur Sprache*, pp. 239–68, and as 'The Way to Language' in *On the Way to Language*, pp. 109–36. [Trans.]

8. The play in German here depends on phonic similarity and the neological grafting of *Auge* (eye) into *Ereignis* (appropriation). [Trans.]

9. In *Hebbel-Jahrbuch*, 1960, pp. 27–50. [Trans.]

10. In *Unterwegs zur Sprache*, pp. 157–216, and as 'The Nature of Language' in *On the Way to Language*, pp. 57–108. [Trans.]

11. Paris: Galilée, 1974; *Digraphe*, no. 3 (1974), pp. 5–31; trans. forthcoming as 'Living On: Border Lines' in a collection to be published at Yale University Press. [Trans.]

12. The sense and the play of this sentence depends on the distinction drawn by Heidegger between particular entities or beings (the field of ontics), and Being (the object of ontological thinking). In French, the pair is: *l'étant* and *l'être*; in this text, the convention of distinguishing these as 'being/Being' has been followed. [Trans.]

13. Heidegger, 'Brief über den "Humanismus"' (1947), rpt. in *Wegmarken* (Frankfurt: Klostermann, 1967), pp. 145–94; trans. by F. Capuzzi in Heidegger, *Basic Writings* (New York: Harper & Row, 1977), pp. 193–242. [Trans.]

14. *Sens* means in French 'direction' as well as 'meaning' or 'sense.' [Trans.]

15. *Der Ursrprung des Kunstwerkes* (Stuttgart: Reclam, 1960); partial trans. by A. Hofstadter in *Basic Writings*, pp. 149–87. [Trans.]

16. *Sein und Zeit* (1927; Tubingen: Niemeyer, 1972); trans. by J. Macquarrie and E. Robinson (New York: Harper & Row, 1962). [Trans.]

17. See 'Pas,' in *Gramma*, no. 3/4 (1976), pp. 111–215. [Trans.]

Chapter 5

The Time before First

'... However, *somebody* killed *something*: that's clear, at any rate—'

'But oh!' thought Alice, suddenly jumping up, 'if I don't make haste, I shall have to go back through the Looking-glass, before I've seen what the rest of the house is like! Let's have a look at the garden [*le parc*] first!'

You are retracing your steps. The last vestiges lead you deeper into the park; you are advancing backward, toward it natively.'The triangle with its point downward, the lower part of Solomon's seal, is a traditional symbol of the feminine principle, exploited extensively in *Finnegans Wake*. It goes without saying that the value of the letter V is more justly derived from a vague, vast group of associations. The classic Mallarméan example is found in "Hérodiade"...'

All oppositions based on the distinction between the original and the derived, the simple and the repeated, the first and the second, etc., lose their pertinence from the moment everything 'begins' by following a vestige. *I.e.* a certain repetition or text. Better than ever you will have understood this in reading *Numbers*.

Everything there goes on *beyond* the opposition between *one* and *two* (etc.); everything plays itself out despite or against the distinction between perception and dream, perception and memory, consciousness and the unconscious, the real and the imaginary, story and discourse, etc. Beyond these oppositions or *between* these terms, but not in total confusion. In a different distribution. *Two* is no more an accident of *one* than *one* is a secondary surplus of *zero* (or vice versa), unless we reconsider our whole notion of the values of accident, secondariness, and surplus: the sole condition for being able at last to consider the text, in the movement of its constellation, which always proceeds by number.

Far from being simply erased, the oppositions deactivated by this arithmetical theater are, in the same blow, reactivated, thrown back into play, but this time as effects, not rules, of the game. Since the trace can only imprint itself by referring to the other, to another trace ('the trace of its reflection'), by letting itself be upstaged and forgotten, its force of production stands in necessary relation to the energy of its erasure. The power of expropriation never produces itself as such but only arises through an alteration of the effects of property. Upon the historical stage of the fourth surface, disappropriation is misapprehended, and necessarily so ('*4.52 . . . There is a law for this misapprehension*');[1] it is violently confiscated within the domestic organization and representative economy of property. Coming to terms with desire (the desire for the proper), and taking into account the contradictions among its forces (for properness limits disruption, guards against death, but also regards death closely; absolute property, one's undifferentiated proximity to oneself, is another name for death; the space of property thereby also coincides with the 'dead surface'), the text, quite squarely, makes the stage spin. Expropriation operates by violent revolution. Writing lays bare that which '*dies and comes back to life in a thought that in reality belongs from the beginning to no one*' (4 and 4.100); it modulates expropriation, repeats it, regularly displaces it, and tirelessly enumerates it, '*. . . and I was thus one mark among other marks . . . But no one was any more myself; what was going to happen, in fact happened for no one; there was nothing but this series of ciphers counting and recording and voiding the whole of the outside*—' (3. 7).

Other suns, another revolution, a different arithmetic: 'Something counts inside me, adds I, rounds out the critical number which the chariots of the sun are waiting for in order to fill up the harness. I know that I have been constructed in order to measure . . .'

Expropriation is not ciphered merely by the mark of numbers, whose nonphonetic operation, which suspends the voice, dislocates self-proximity, a living presence that would hear itself represented by speech. The 'stilled melodic encipherment'—as *Music and Letters* puts it—is the violent death of the subject, the reading subject or the writing subject, in the mute substitution of *Numbers*, in the dream of its fastened clasp, in its silent strongbox. Your own. ('*1.5. . . . Upon touching this sequence, I understood that a single murder was constantly in progress, that we were coming from it only to return to it via this detour . . .*') But this encipherment is *melodic*; a kind of chant or song beats out the measures of all the marks in *Numbers*. In all senses of the word, it is a cadence that you must follow.

The 'stilled ode,' in *Mimique*, seals only the decease of a certain voice, a particular function—the representative function—of speech, the reader's voice or the authorial voice that would be there only for the purpose of representing the subject in his inner thoughts, so as to designate, state, express the truth—or presence—of a signified, to reflect it in a faithful mirror, to let it show through untouched, or to become one with it. Without any screen, without any veil, or with excellent tain. But the death of that representative voice, that voice which is already dead, does not amount to some absolute silence that would at last make way for some mythical purity of writing, some finally isolated graphy. Rather, it gives rise to an authorless voice, a phonic tracing that no ideal signified or 'thought' can entirely cover in its sensible stamp without leaving something out. A numerous pounding here subjects all representative outcroppings to the effects of its rhythm; and that pounding is itself adapted to the cruel, ordered deployment and theatrical arithmography of a text that is no more 'written' than 'spoken' in the sense of *'the alphabet henceforth outmoded for us'* (2.22). The disappearance of the 'authorial voice' ('The Text speaking there of itself and without the voice of an author,' as Verlaine was told) triggers off a power of inscription that is no longer verbal but phonic. Polyphonic. The values of vocal spacing are then regulated by the order of that tainless voice, not by the authority of the word or the conceptual signified, which the text, moreover, does not fail to utilize, too, in its own way.

A 'poem silenced,' following those *Variations on a subject* ('Everything becomes suspense, fragmentary disposition with alternation and face-to-face, concurring in the total rhythm, which would be the poem silenced, in the blanks'), *Numbers* is also a poem in a fully raised voice. Try it. Note its broad yet controlled, tense, restrained, yet pressing clamor. It is the clamor of a song that puts the vowel on stage, along with the articulation whose prior echo it precipitates onto the wall surfaces, reflecting, from one panel to the other, in hundredfold repercussion, each bounce. This occurs in a different metal each time; it is the sculpting of another liquid, the traversing of some unheard-of material. An authorless voice, a full-throated writing, a song sung out at the top of the lungs:

> '3 . . . *and the voice was saying so, now, and it really was my voice being raised from the colored vision or rather from the burning background of the colors; it was my voice I heard modulating a pressing, fluid conspiracy in which the vowels lined up, changed places, and seemed to apply themselves to the text through my breath. Their sequence acted directly on each detail, repulsed the hostile elements, formed a rhythmic chain, a specter that collected and distributed the roles, the facts, and this game was using me as one figure among others; I was for it simply a grain picked up and hurled . . . The vocal relief of the letters inserted into the detailed inscription—which, without them, would have remained stable, opaque, undecipherable—; the activity of these atoms which thus enabled me to intervene by reversing the operation of which I was the object; the emission and projection whose discreet power I had returned in mid-flight; all that was opening up the distance, the outside—and I can again see the sounds penetrating the purple sky down to the bottom of the eyes. The formula could be stated thus: I-O-U-I-A-I provided one straightway impresses upon it a kind of constant undulation, something that sounds drunk . . . —And that is how my voice left me . . .'*

This loss of voice is sung elsewhere in the transformed recurrence of the same sequence, following a *'partition of water'* and a *'sun that comes to set it on fire,'* *'and there was this moment before the collapse, this moment that takes off in the song: a pressing conspiracy in which the vowels lined up, changed places; a formula that could have been stated I-O-U-I-A provided one straightway impresses upon it a kind of constant undulation, something that sounds drunk, precipitous . . .' (3.55).* You will have remarked the cadence, and, in the second occurrence, the dropping of the I at the end, '*the last note held for a long time*' in the first occurrence; where you would see the announcement of a certain dismemberment if you went back to look, just before the mark according to which the organ of '*my voice left me*.'

'. . . red I, etc. . . . of course, one can't attribute color to a consonant. But isn't it obvious that each of them, and each letter in general, has a different dynamism, that each one does not *work* in the same way, that it can be compared to a mechanical device which, having a single form, can nevertheless be used in all sorts of different ways? . . . Just recently I was reading in a book . . . that the letter D, the Delta (Δ), is, according to Plato, the first and most perfect of all the letters in the alphabet, the one out of which all the others are born, since it is composed of equal sides and angles. And we are also told that in the Law the Savior did not come in order to remove that dot, that apex, which is located on the top of the I.'

Expropriation thus does not proceed merely by a ciphered suspension of voice, by a kind of spacing that punctuates it or rather draws its shafts from it, or at it; it is also an operation *within* voice. Mainly, if thought belongs from the beginning to no one, if 'impersonification' is what is initial, then this is quite simply because the text never in fact begins. Not that its rifts are erased or its 'positive' ruptures blurred and blended into the continuum of something always-already-there. But precisely because the rifts in it never stand as origins: they always transform a preexisting text. No archeology of *Numbers* is possible from the moment they are read. You find yourself being indefinitely referred to bottomless, endless connections and to the indefinitely articulated regress of the beginning, which is forbidden along with all archeology, eschatology, or hermeneutic teleology. All in the same blow. '*The new text without end or beginning*' (3.99) can be neither maintained nor contained in the clasp of a book. The text is out of sight when it compels the horizon itself to enter the frame of its own scene, so as to 'learn to embrace with increased grandeur the horizon of the present time.'

Thus, for example: *Numbers* does seem to begin at the beginning: with the one of the first sequence. Yet on the eve of this opening:

1. the initial capital letter is suspended by the three dots that precede it; the origin is suspended by this multiple punctuation and you are immediately plunged into the consumption of another text that had already, out of its double bottom, set this text in motion. It is a citation, an inchoative in-citation, which gets the organization of everything cited [*de chaque cité*, also = 'of every city'] moving again;

2. this cited text, this prior past that is still to come, isn't it precisely itself not only consumed but indeed the consummate statement of consumption or

consummation as such? Its theoretical statement, as they say? and quite expert at that? For example: the 'beginning' of *Numbers* is but a propagation, rolled up in the same flame, of the last burning page of *Drama*. You can read: '*I . . . the paper was burning, and it was a matter of all the sketched and painted things being projected there in a regularly distorted manner, while a sentence was speaking: "here is the outer surface." Before the eyes or rather as if retreating from them: this page or surface of browned wood curling up consumed.*'

The 'last' page of *Drama*:

'thinking that he will still have to write:

"one ought to be able to consider that the book is washed up here— (burns) (erases itself) (in a thought that has no last thought—'more numerous than the grass'—'the agile one, the one most rapid of all, the one that leans upon the heart')—."'

Writing, fire, erasure, the 'without end,' the number, the innumerable, the grass, are all citations and cited statements about the necessity of these citational effects. These effects do not describe the line of a simple relation between two texts or two fiery consumptions; they carry you off in the displacement of a constellation or labyrinth. They no longer fit 'inside the frame of this piece of paper.' Not only are the references infinite, but they conduct you through texts and referral-structures that are heterogeneous to each other. Sometimes the citations are 'quotations' of 'quotations' (you are still reading this word in quotation marks before subjecting it, when the time comes, to a thorough examination); the references can be lateral or direct, horizontal or vertical; they are almost always doubled, and most often presented on the bias. One example from out of the number: the fire in this paper does not spread merely from *Drama* to *Numbers*; it has as one focus [*foyer*, also = 'hearth'], a focus more virtual than real, another such 'burning paper' yearning for dawn [*en mal d'aurore*, cf. 'Maldoror'], which is in turn consumed—'cited'—('symbolic figures traced upon burning paper, like so many mysterious signs living with latent breath') in *Logics*, which, in a mode that is no longer simply theoretical but perhaps repeats the attending surface of the tetralogy (*Le Parc, Drame, Nombres, Logiques*), sets forth the 'transfinite' motion of writing: the 'generalized putting-in-quotation-marks of language' which, 'with respect to the text, within it . . . becomes entirely citational.'

No event, then, is being recounted; everything happens in the intertext; only one principle is observed: that 'in the final analysis, what happens is nothing.' There is always another book beginning to burn at the moment 'he closes the book—blows out the candle with that breath of his which contained chance: and, crossing his arms, he lies down on the ashes of his ancestors.'

The duality between original text and quotation is thus swept away. In the process of squaring. And as of the second square, you have been warned: '*1. 5. . . . something had begun, but this beginning in turn revealed a deeper layer of*

beginning; there was no longer any before or after; it was impossible to turn around . . .
—'

Any statements about the pre-beginning, about the fiction of the origin, about the indeterminacy of the seminal imperfect into which the pluperfect of some event without a date, of some immemorial birth, is inserted ('something had begun . . .') cannot themselves escape the rule they set forth. They recite themselves, leading you back for example to the native enclosure of the *Park*: '. . . read the beginning of a sentence: "The exercise-book is open on the table," make quite sure that it contains nothing that I wanted to give it (nothing that might be compared with the original project), that one word is not enough to save the rest, that this whole complacent, numbing succession of words must be destroyed; tear it up, tear it up, throw it away, make a clean sweep, recreate the space that will gradually extend and expand in every direction.'

This 'beginning of a sentence' creates a relation of attraction between a certain piece of paper and a certain 'surface of browned wood' on which *Numbers* will be tabled. But they have already followed a path marked above in *The Park*: 'The exercise-book is open on the table of brown wood feebly lit by the lamp. The cover is already a bit torn and the pages, covered one after another by small, fine handwriting in blue-black ink, follow each other slowly, progress over white squared [*quadrille*] paper, making it impossible to go back, to begin again this meticulous and useless work that demands to be completed to the yet distant final page, where one day it will stop of its own accord.'

Like this graph paper in *The Park*, the checkerboard in *Drama* houses, from the very outset of the game, the impossibility of beginning, which is also the impossibility of '*turning around*' (*Numbers*), of 'going back' (*The Park*): 'All contaminated, significant. No beginning can provide the necessary guarantees of neutrality.' This contamination of origins will also have been indicated by the 'poison' in *Numbers*.

From where you stand, please note, in an angle of the graph paper (*The Park*) in the checkerboard squares (*Drama*), in the squares or cubes (*Numbers*), this opening paradoxically wrought like a thing that closes, the one playing itself off against the other. The necessary exit lays siege; it surrounds the text indefinitely, and also imperfectly, by referring—by exiting—toward another text. A false exit extends out of sight. The mirror is shown the door. Or squared. The enclosure—the grille—in *The Park*, *Drama*, and *Numbers*, is shaped like an opening, a little opening where the key can be inserted, an innumerable opening since it is but a grid (a relation between the lines and angles in the network). It is therefore both necessary and impossible. Urgent and impracticable, literally obsessive, as this will already have been situated and reserved in the *Park;* 'Flat on my belly, my face buried in the pillow, I must attempt the experiment again. All the elements, if I wish, have been known for all time; I know, I can know; I could get out, find the imperceptible crack; the way out that nobody before me has been able to attempt.'

Further on, still in the *Park*, you will have trodden on the numerous grass from *Drama* and *Numbers* as you plunge deeper into the place beyond the mirror which divides up the entire geometry of the text to come:'Quite near, behind me, beyond the mirror where, when I lower my eyes, I can see myself sitting on this chair, the grass is thick in spite of the pebbles, the dead leaves, and the twigs; in spite of the winter and cold, the grass is unalterably green, barely a tad less green.'

This text full of keys harbors no secret. Nothing in sum need be deciphered except the sum the text itself is. There is nothing inside the clasp. Nothing behind the mirror. The obsessive quest for the way out is due, all other motivation being excluded, particularly that of some 'author,' solely to the structure of the text. And to that bunch of keys it provides, which you don't know what to do with. The obsession will always have been a textual one. 'He said it was necessary to tie me to a fence.' Textuality is obsidional. It is an undecidable process of opening/closing that re-forms itself without letup. Under orders and in order (*arithmos*).

It will be said—but things are not so certain if one takes a good look—that this minute, useless, obstinate, tireless composition of uneven squares that don't mean anything, that don't show anything but their regular irregularity, their frames and their colors, doesn't make up a very jolly world. This may be, but it is not a matter of psychology here, or of an author's world, his 'world view' (or yours), or of some 'experiment' to be performed, or of some spectacle to be described or recounted. Not a sight to do with it.

Such will have been the fence in this undecipherable text. A text latticed in the mirror. There are still other grille designs made to foil all deciphering and keep you constantly sidetracked by throwing switch after switch. The geometry of this text's grid has the means, within itself, of extending and complicating itself beyond measure, of its own accord, taking its place, each time, within a set that comprehends it, situates it, and regularly goes beyond its bounds after first being reflected in it. The history of the text's geometries is a history of irrefutable reinscriptions and generalizations.

An example, once again from among so many others: *The Park* 'began' thus, with a blue that was later to clear up: 'The sky above the long, gleaming avenues is dark blue.' In the curling in which the volume of *Numbers* is consumed, you will have read: '*3. 15. . . . Also saying: "the palace is furnished with fifty doors. These are open upon all four sides, forty-nine in number. The last door is not on any side and it is not known whether it opens upward or downward . . . All these doors have a single lock and there is only one little opening into which the key can be introduced, and that spot is indicated only by the trace of the key . . . It contains, opens, and closes the six directions of space"* . . . *Thus understanding that we would have to go through a goodly number of series before directly reaching the return of the architecture into the medium from which it had arisen* . . . *With its terraces, its domes, its gardens, its inhabitants, its ceremonies* . . . *"The sky above the long, gleaming avenues is dark blue": that, in sum, was the sentence from which I took off—.*

In the same way, the 'first' sentence of *Drama* is reconstituted in one of the fourth sequences in *Numbers*, where you will have been able to read it, in the present, without knowing where it comes from: '*4.32. (. . . "Firstly (first draft, lines, engravings, the game begins) it is perhaps the stablest element that is concentrated behind his head and forehead . . ." . . .).*' The text thus trussed up (twisted, bent inward) always leads you back to the whole bundle, stringing you along in its ring of keys.

3. The first sequence of *Numbers* is not merely older than itself, like the wake of a prior text (which already, itself, etc.). If it is straightway plural, divided or multiplied, this is also because of its power of germination or seminal differentiation, which will proceed to engender or will have given birth to a whole chain of other sentences that are both similar and dissimilar, sentences that reflect and transform each other in a regularly irregular way, throughout the length of the text to come, separated each time by the mark or margin of some small difference. In 4. 12, for example, the entire first sequence is modified by a preceding 'as if.' The '*Grand space already extending beyond measure*' has become, in another key, a '*Grand harmony already extending beyond measure.*' The '*Grand object dropped and undone*' has been changed to a '*Grand volume dropped and undone.*' These 'numbered rephrasings' could be multiplied indefinitely.

What you have thus ascertained about the 'first' or 'last' sentences can also be demonstrated of the pre-first words of the text, the epigraphs or dedications, those fictive extratexts which also come to be violently reinscribed within the system of *Numbers*. The epigraph, a sentence from 'Lucretius' (quoted in his originally foreign language: *Seminaque innumero numero summaque profunda*), ceases to be a quotation, pinned or glued to the superficial front of the book, from the moment it is worked over and itself sets to work inside the very body of the text ('*4.80. (. . . / "Desire appeared first, wandering about over everything. It already existed before the germ of any thought" / . . . Germs, seeds sown in innumerable number, and the sum of which reaches the depths in which the word "you" and the thought "you" are carving out a passageway through chance toward you)— . . .' '1. 81. . . . past and future germs . . . Germs, grouped and disseminated, formulae that are more and more derivative . . .*'

The epigraph does not stand outside the text [*hors d'oeuvre*]. Neither does the dedication, even though it presents itself as a proper name ['for ЮАИЯ '] (marked in its originally foreign writing, brought in from the East, like the Chinese characters sown throughout the text) whose vowels compose an ideogrammatic formula which *Numbers* will in several senses decompose and recompose, impressing a kind of constant undulation upon it, by expropriation and anagrammatical reappropriation, translating it, transforming it into a common noun, playing with the vowels that compose it (and '*4.32 (. . . "Consonants are heard only through the air that makes the voice, or vowel" /)*—' marking the color of each one, insisting on the I, which is red like the '*red moment of history.*' But these writing-effects, which will henceforth be called paragrammatical effects, are much more numerous than these examples might lead one to believe.

4. The 'first' sequence, therefore, is not a discourse, a present speech (in the beginning *was* the number, not the word, nor, in what presently amounts to the same, the act); or rather the apparently 'present' statement is not the statement of any present, not even of any past present, of any past defined as having taken place, as having been present. Far from any essence, you are straightway plunged by the imperfect into the already opened thickness of another text. And what is said or written (the 'signified') is already the performing of a cut within a graphic substance that retains and distorts traces of all sorts: forms, sketches, colors, half-silent ideograms and spoken words, etc.:

> '*I. . . . the paper was burning, and it was a matter of all the sketched and painted things being projected there in a regularly distorted manner, while a sentence was speaking: "here is the outer surface." Before the eyes or rather as if retreating from them: this page or surface of browned wood curling up consumed.*'

Just as in *The Park* the total milieu in which the book is written (the bedroom, the 'former room' that keeps reappearing, the table, the exercise-book, the ink, the pen, etc.) is constantly being reinscribed and thrown back into play in *Drama* and *Numbers*. Each time, writing appears as disappearance, recoil, erasure, retreat, curling-up, consumption. This is how *The Park* closes (you will note the reflection of the trace of the key): 'dark; while another day, with the exercise-book on a table in the sun or, this evening, taken out of the drawer of which she alone has the key, the exercise-book will be read for a moment, then closed; the exercise-book with the orange cover, patiently filled, heavily written over with regular handwriting and leading to this page, this sentence, this period, by the old pen frequently and mechanically dipped into the blue-black ink.'

There remains this column of ink, after, before the final period. Dipped mechanically, ready to light into another text.

Drama, which ends where *Numbers* begins, nevertheless begins at the same point ('and we can say that he begins in fact at the point where he ends'), with the already-there-ness of a text that also carves out the space of a game: 'Firstly (first draft, lines, engravings—the game begins). . .'

Note

1. The numbering following the quotation from Sollers' novel, *Nombres* (1968: full bibliographic details given in note 43 of the Introduction to the reader, above), refers to the sectional numbering in the novel discussed in the Introduction, and is taken from the French text. [Ed.]

Chapter 6

From Specters of Marx

June, 1848, was, let us hasten to say, a thing apart, and almost impossible to class in the philosophy of history.... But, at bottom, what was June, 1848? A revolt of the people against itself...; let us then be permitted for a moment to arrest the reader's attention upon the two absolutely unique barricades of which we have just spoke... these two frightful masterpieces of civil war.... The barricade Saint Antoine was monstrous.... Ruin. You might say: who built that? You might also say: who destroyed that?.... It was great and it was little. It was the bottomless pit parodied upon the spot by chaos come again.... This barricade was furious.... It was huge and living; and, as from the back of an electric beast, there came from it a crackling of thunders. The spirit of revolution covered with its cloud that summit whereon growled this voice of the people which is like the voice of God; a strange majesty emanated from that titanic hodful of refuse. It was a garbage heap and it was Sinaï.

As we have said before, it attacked in the name of the Revolution, what? the Revolution....

A mile from there, at the corner of the Rue du Temple ... rose this obstruction, which made of the street a cul-de-sac; an immovable and quiet wall; nobody could be seen, nothing could be heard; not a cry, not a sound, not a breath. A sepulchre ... the chief of that barricade was a geometer or a spectre....

The barricade St. Antoine was the tumult of thunders, the barricade du Temple was silence. There was between these two redoubts the difference between the terrible and the ominous. The one seemed a gaping mouth; the other a mask.

Admitting that the gloomy and gigantic insurrection of June was composed of an anger and an enigma; you felt in the first barricade the dragon, and behind the second the sphinx.

WHAT CAN BE DONE IN THE ABYSS BUT TO TALK

Sixteen years tell in the subterranean education of the émeute, and June 1848 understood it far better than June 1832....

There were no longer giants against colossi. It resembled Milton and Dante rather than Homer. Demons attacked, spectres resisted....

A voice from the most obscure depths of the groups, cried ... 'Citizens, let us offer the protest of corpses....'

The name of the man who thus spoke was never known ... that great anonymous always found in human crises and in social births....

140

After the man of the people, who decreed 'the protest of corpses,' had spoken and given the formula of the common soul, from all lips arose a strangely satisfied and terrible cry, funereal in meaning and triumphant in tone: 'Long live death! Let us all stay!'

'Why all?' said Enjolras.

'All! All!'. . . .

—Victor Hugo, *Les Misérables*

Specters of Marx: The title of this lecture would commit one to speak first of all about Marx. About Marx himself. About his testament or his inheritance. And about a specter, the shadow of Marx, the *revenant* whose return so many raised voices today are attempting to conjure away. For it does resemble a conjuration or conspiracy, because of the agreement or the contract signed by so many political subjects who subscribe to the more or less clear or more or less secret clauses (the point is always to conquer or to keep the keys to a power), but first of all because such a conjuration is meant to conjure away. One must, magically, chase away a specter, exorcise the possible return of a power held to be baleful in itself and whose demonic threat continues to haunt the century.

Since such a conjuration today insists, in such a deafening consensus, that what is, it says, indeed dead, remain dead indeed, it arouses a suspicion. It awakens us where it would like to put us to sleep. Vigilance, therefore: the cadaver is perhaps not as dead, as simply dead as the conjuration tries to delude us into believing. The one who has disappeared appears still to be *there*, and his apparition is not nothing. It does not do nothing. Assuming that the remains can be identified, we know better than ever today that the dead must be able to work. And to cause to work, perhaps more than ever. There is also a mode of production of the phantom, itself a phantomatic mode of production. As in the work of mourning, after a trauma, the conjuration has to make sure that the dead will not come back: quick, do whatever is needed to keep the cadaver localized, in a safe place, decomposing right where it was inhumed, or even embalmed as they liked to do in Moscow. Quick, a vault to which one keeps the keys! These keys would be nothing other than those of the power that the conjuration would like thus to reconstitute upon the death of Marx. [. . .] The logic of the key in which I hoped to orient this keynote address was one of a politico-logic of trauma and a topology of mourning. A mourning in fact and by right interminable, without possible normality, without reliable limit, in its reality or in its concept, between introjection and incorporation. But the same logic, as we suggested, responds to the injunction of a justice which, beyond right or law, rises up in the very respect owed to whoever *is not*, no longer or not yet, living, presently living.

Mourning always follows a trauma. I have tried to show elsewhere that the work of mourning is not one kind of work among others. It is work itself, work in general, the trait by means of which one ought perhaps to reconsider the very concept of production—in what links it to trauma, to mourning, to the idealizing iterability of exappropriation, thus to the spectral spiritualization that is at work in any *tekhnē*. There is the temptation to add here an aporetic postscript to Freud's remark that linked in a same comparative history three of the traumas inflicted on human narcissism when it is thus de-centered: the *psychological* trauma (the power of the unconscious over the conscious ego, discovered by psychoanalysis), after the *biological* trauma (the animal descent of man discovered by Darwin—to whom, moreover, Engels alludes in the Preface to the 1888 *Manifesto*), after the *cosmological* trauma (the Copernican Earth is no longer the center of the universe, and this is more and more the case one could say so as to draw from it many consequences concerning the limits of geopolitics). Our aporia would here stem from the fact that there is no longer any name or teleology for determining the Marxist *coup* and its subject. Freud thought he knew, for his part, what man and his narcissism were. The Marxist blow is as much the projected unity of a thought and of a labor movement, sometimes in a messianic or eschatological form, as it is the history of the totalitarian world (including Nazism and fascism, which are the inseparable adversaries of Stalinism). This is perhaps the deepest wound for mankind, in the body of its history and in the history of its concept, still more traumatizing than the 'psychological' lesion (*Kränkung*) produced by the blow of psychoanalysis, the third and most serious in Freud's view.[1] For we know that the *blow* struck enigmatically in the name of Marx also accumulates and gathers together the other three. It thus presupposes them today, even if such was not the case in the last century. It carries beyond them by carrying them out, just as it bears the name of Marx by exceeding it infinitely. The century of 'Marxism' will have been that of the techno-scientific and effective decentering of the earth, of geopolitics, of the *anthropos* in its onto-theological identity or its genetic properties, of the *ego cogito*—and of the very concept of narcissism whose aporias are, let us say in order to go too quickly and save ourselves a lot of references, the explicit theme of deconstruction. This trauma is endlessly denied by the very movement through which one tries to cushion it, to assimilate it, to interiorize and incorporate it. In this mourning work in process, in this interminable task, the ghost remains that which gives one the most to think about—and to do. Let us insist and spell things out: to do and to make come about, as well as to let come (about).

But the specters *of* Marx come on stage from the other side. They are named according to the other path of the genitive—and this other grammar says more than grammar. The specters *of* Marx are also his. They are perhaps first of all the ghosts that inhabited him, the *revenants* with which Marx himself will have been occupied, and which he will have wanted in advance to make his thing; which does not mean that he knew their secrets, nor even that he thematized in his turn the obsessive recurrence of what would be a theme if one could say of the *revenant* that it lets itself be *posed there, exposed before you,* as a theme or a system, a thesis or a synthesis ought to do. All of these values are disqualified by the specter; if there is any.

The specters of Marx: with these words we will name from now on certain figures whose coming Marx will have been the first to apprehend, sometimes to describe. Those that herald the best and whose event he will have greeted, those that arise from or threaten the worst, whose testimony he will have rejected. There are several times of the specter. It is a proper characteristic of the specter, if there is any, that no one can be sure if by returning it testifies to a living past or to a living future, for the *revenant* may already mark the promised return of the specter of living being. Once again, untimeliness and disadjustment of the contemporary. In this regard, communism has always been and will remain spectral: it is always still to come and is distinguished, like democracy itself, from every living present understood as plenitude of a presence-to-itself, as totality of a presence effectively identical to itself. Capitalist societies can always heave a sigh of relief and say to themselves: communism is finished since the collapse of the totalitarianisms of the twentieth century and not only is it finished, but it did not take place, it was only a ghost. They do no more than disavow the undeniable itself: a ghost never dies, it remains always to come and to come-back.

In the *Manifesto of the Communist Party,* let us recall, a first noun returned three times on the same first page, the noun 'specter' (*Gespenst*): 'A specter is haunting Europe,' says Marx in 1848, 'the specter of communism [*Ein Gespenst geht um in Europa—das Gespenst des Kommunismus*]'. Marx, unless it is the other one, Engels, then puts on stage, for the time of a few paragraphs, the terror that this specter inspires in all the powers of old Europe. No one speaks of anything anymore but this specter. All phantasms are projected onto the screen of this ghost (that is, on something absent, for the screen itself is phantomatic, as in the television of the future which will have no 'screenic' support and will project its images—sometimes synthetic images—directly on the eye, like the sound of the telephone deep in the ear). One watches for the signals, the tables that turn, the dishes that move. Is it going to answer? As in the space of a salon during a spiritualist séance, but sometimes that space is what is called the street, one looks out for one's goods and furniture, attempting to adjust all of politics to the frightening hypothesis of a visitation.[2] Politicians are seers or visionaries. They desire and fear an apparition which they know will not present anyone in person but will strike a series of blows to be deciphered. All possible alliances are thus forged to conjure away this common adversary, 'the specter of communism.' The alliance signifies death to the specter. It is convoked to be revoked, everyone swears [*jure*] only on the specter, but in order to conjure it away. No one talks of anything else. But what else can you do, since it is not there, this ghost, like any ghost worthy of the name? And even when it is there, that is, when it is there without being there, you feel that the specter is looking, although through a helmet; it is watching, observing, staring at the spectators and the blind seers, but you do not see it seeing, it remains invulnerable beneath its visored armor. So one speaks of nothing else but in order to chase it away, to exclude it, to exorcise it. The salon, then, is old Europe which is gathering all its forces (*alle Mächte des alten Europas*). If the conspirators attempt to exorcise or conjure away the specter; it is without knowing at bottom what or whom they are talking about. For the conspirators, communism is a name, the holy alliance is a holy hunt: 'All the powers of old Europe have joined [*verbündet*] into a holy hunt [*zu einer heiligen Hetzjagd*] against this specter [*gegen dies Gespenst*].'

Who could deny it? If an alliance is in the process of being formed against communism, an alliance of the old or the new Europe, it remains a holy alliance. The paternal figure of the Holy Father the Pope, who is then cited by Marx, still figures today in a prominent place in this alliance, in the person of a Polish bishop who boasts, and in this he is confirmed by Gorbachev, that he was not for nothing in the collapse of communist totalitarianism in Europe and in the advent of a Europe that from now on will be what it should always have been according to him, a Christian Europe. As in the Holy Alliance of the nineteenth century, Russia could once again take part. That is why we insisted on the neo-evangelism—Hegelian neo-evangelism—of a rhetoric of the 'Fukuyama' type. It was a Hegelian neo-evangelism that Marx denounced with great verve and vehemence in the Stirnerian theory of ghosts. We will get to this later, but already here we must point out the intersection. We believe it is significant.

The specter that Marx was talking about then, communism, was there without being there. It was not yet there. It will never be there. There is no *Dasein* of the specter, but there is no *Dasein* without the uncanniness, without the strange familiarity (*Unheimlichkeit*) of some specter. What is a specter? What is its history and what is its time?

The specter, as its name indicates, is the *frequency* of a certain visibility. But the visibility of the invisible. And visibility, by its essence, is not seen, which is why it remains *epekeina tes ousias*, beyond the phenomenon or beyond being. The specter is also, among other things, what one imagines, what one thinks one sees and which one projects—on an imaginary screen where there is nothing to see. Not even the screen sometimes, and a screen always has, at bottom, in the bottom or background that it is, a structure of disappearing apparition. But now one can no longer get any shut-eye, being so intent to watch out for the return. Whence the theatricalization of speech itself and the spectacularizing speculation on time. The perspective has to be reversed, once again: ghost or *revenant*, sensuous-non-sensuous, visible-invisible, the specter first of all sees *us*. From the other side of the eye, *visor effect*, it looks at us even before we see *it* or even before we see period. We feel ourselves observed, sometimes under surveillance by it even before any apparition. Especially— and this is the event, for the specter is *of* the event—it sees us during a *visit*. It (re)pays us a visit [*Il nous rend visite*]. Visit upon visit, since it returns to see us and since *visitaire*, frequentative of *visere* (to see, examine, contemplate), translates well the recurrence or returning, the frequency of a visitation. The latter does not always mark the moment of a generous apparition or a friendly vision; it can signify strict inspection or violent search, consequent persecution, implacable *concatenation*. The social mode of haunting, its original style could also be called, taking into account this repetition, *frequentation*. Marx lived more than others, we are going to make this clear, in the frequentation of specters.

The specter *appears* to present itself during a visitation. One represents it to oneself, but it is not present, itself, in flesh and blood. This non-presence of the specter demands that one take its times and its history into consideration, the singularity of its temporality or of its historicity. When, in 1847–48, Marx names the specter of communism, he inscribes it in an historical perspective that is exactly the reverse of the one I was initially thinking of in proposing a title such as 'the specters of Marx.' Where I was tempted to name thereby the persistence of a present past, the return of the dead which the worldwide work of mourning cannot get rid of, whose return it runs away from, which it *chases* (excludes, banishes, and at the same time pursues), Marx, for his part, announces and calls for a presence to come. He seems to predict and prescribe: What for the moment figures only as a specter in the ideological representation of old Europe must become, in the future, a present reality, that is, a living reality. The *Manifesto* calls, it calls for this presentation of the living reality: we must see to it that in the future this specter—and first of all an association of workers forced to remain secret until about 1848—becomes a *reality*, and a *living* reality. This real life must show itself and manifest itself, it must *present itself* beyond Europe, old or new Europe, in the universal dimension of an International.

But it must also manifest itself in the form of a manifesto that will be the *Manifesto* of a party. For Marx already gives the party form to the properly political structure of the force that will have to be, according to the *Manifesto*, the motor of the revolution, the transformation, the appropriation then finally the destruction of the State, and the end of the political as such. (Since this singular end of the political would correspond to the presentation of an absolutely living reality, this is one more reason to think that the essence of the political will always have the inessential figure, the very anessence of a ghost.)

Here is perhaps one of the strange motifs we should talk about this evening: What tends perhaps to disappear in the political world that is shaping up, and perhaps in a new age of democracy, is the domination of this form of organization called the party, the party-State relation, which finally will have lasted, strictly speaking, only two centuries, barely longer than that, a period to which belong as well certain determined types of parliamentary and liberal democracy, constitutional monarchies, Nazi, fascist, or Soviet totalitarianisms. *Not one* of these regimes was possible without what could be called the axiomatics of the party. Now, as one can see foreshadowed, it seems, everywhere in the world today, the structure of the party is becoming not only more and more suspect (and for reasons that are no longer always, necessarily, 'reactionary,' those of the classical individualist reaction) but also radically unadapted to the new—tele-techno-media—conditions of public space, of political life, of democracy, and of the *new* modes of representation (both parliamentary and non-parliamentary) that they call up. A reflection on what will become of Marxism tomorrow, of its inheritance or its testament, should include, among so many other things, a reflection on the finitude of a certain concept or of a certain reality of the party. And, of course, of its State correlative. A movement is underway that we would be tempted to describe as a deconstruction of the traditional concepts of State, and thus of party and labor union. Even though they do not signify the withering away of the State, in the Marxist or Gramscian sense, one cannot analyze their historical singularity outside of the Marxist inheritance—where inheritance is more than ever a critical and transformative filter, that is, where it is out of the question to be for or against the State in general, its life or its death *in general.* There was a moment, in the history of European (and, of course, American) politics, when it was a reactionary gesture to call for the end of the party, just as it was to analyze the inadequation of existing parliamentary structures to democracy itself. Let us put forward here with many precautions, both theoretical and practical, the hypothesis that this is no longer the case, *not always* the case (for these old forms of struggle against the State may survive for a long time); one must do away with this equivocation so that it will no longer be the case. The hypothesis is that this mutation has already begun; it is irreversible.

The universal Communist Party, the Communist International will be, said the *Manifesto* in 1848, the final incarnation, the real presence of the specter, thus the end of the spectral. This future is not described, it is not foreseen in the constative mode; it is announced, promised, called for in a performative mode. From the symptom, Marx draws a diagnosis and a prognosis. The symptom that authorizes the diagnosis is that the fear of the communist ghost *exists.* One gets signs of this if one observes the Holy European Alliance. These signs must mean something, namely that the European powers recognize, through the specter, the power of communism ('Communism is already acknowledged by all European powers to be itself a power [*als eine Macht*]').

As for the prognosis, it does not consist in merely foreseeing (a gesture of the constative type) but in calling for the advent, in the future, of a manifesto of the communist party which, precisely in the performative form of the call, will transform the legend of the specter not yet into the reality of communist society but into that other form of real event (between the legendary specter and its absolute incarnation) that is the Manifesto of the Communist Party. Parousia of the manifestation of the manifest. As party. Not as party that in addition would be, in this case, communist, or whose communism would be only a predicate. But as party that would accomplish the essence of the party as communist party. Here is the call, namely the Manifesto in view of the Manifesto, the self-manifestation of the manifesto, in which consists the essence of any manifesto that calls itself: by saying 'it is time,' time rejoins and adjoins itself here, now, a now that happens to itself in the act and the body of this manifestation: it is 'high time' that I become manifest, that become manifest the manifesto that is no other than this one here, now, me, the present is coming to pass, itself conjoined witness, here precisely is the manifesto that I am or that I operate in the work, in an act, I am myself but this manifestation, at this very moment, in this book, here I am: 'It is high time [*Es ist hohe Zeit*] that communists should openly, in the face of the whole world, publish their views, their aims, their tendencies, and meet [or oppose:*entgegenstellen*] this nursery tale of the specter of communism [*den Märchen vom Gespenst des Kommunismus*] with a Manifesto of the party itself.' What does this manifesto testify to? And who testifies to what? In which languages? The following sentence speaks of the multiplicity of languages: not of all languages but of a few, and of communists of different nationalities gathered in London. *The Manifesto*, says *The Manifesto* in German, will be published in English, French, German, Italian, Flemish, and Danish. Ghosts also speak different languages, national languages, like the money from which they are, as we shall see, inseparable. As circulating currency, money bears local and political character, it 'uses different national languages and wears different national uniforms.'[3] Let us repeat our question of the manifesto as speech or language of testimony. Who testifies to what? In what way does the 'what' determine the 'who,' the one never preceding the other? Why does this absolute manifestation of self *attest* to itself [s'*atteste-t-elle elle-même*], while taking the side of the party, only by contesting and detesting the ghost? What about the ghost, therefore, in this struggle? The ghost that finds itself called upon to take sides, as well as to testify, with the helmet and visor effect?

The structure of the event thus called for remains difficult to analyze. The legend of the specter, the story, the fable (*Märchen*) would be abolished in the *Manifesto*, as if the specter itself, after having embodied a spectrality in legend and without becoming a reality (communism itself, communist society), came out of itself, called for an exit from the legend without entering into the reality of which it is the specter. Since it is neither real nor legendary, some 'Thing' will have frightened and continues to frighten in the equivocation of this event, as in the singular spectrality of this performative utterance, namely, of Marxism itself (and the question this evening could be summed up as follows: what is a Marxist utterance? a so-called Marxist utterance? or more precisely: what *will be from now on* such an utterance? and who could say 'I am a Marxist' or 'I am not a Marxist'?).

To make fear, to make oneself fear.[4] To cause fear in the enemies of the *Manifesto*, but perhaps also in Marx and the Marxists themselves. For one could be tempted to explain the whole totalitarian inheritance of Marx's thought, but also the other totalitarianisms that were not just by chance or mechanical juxtaposition its contemporaries, as a reaction of panic-ridden fear before the ghost in general. To the ghost that communism represented for the capitalist (monarchist, imperial, or republican). States of old Europe in general, came the response of a frightened and ruthless war and it was only in the course of this war that Leninism and then Stalinist totalitarianism were able to constitute themselves, harden themselves monstrously into their cadaverous rigor. But since Marxist ontology was *also* struggling against the ghost in general, in the name of living presence as material actuality, the whole 'Marxist' process of the totalitarian society was also responding to the same panic. We must, it seems to me, take such an hypothesis seriously. Later, between Stirner and Marx, we will get around to this essential ineluctability of the reflexive reflex, of the 'make oneself fear' in the experience of the ghost. It is as if Marx and Marxism had run away, fled from themselves, and had scared themselves. in the course of the same *chase*, the same persecution, the same infernal pursuit. Revolution against the revolution as the figure of *Les Misérables* suggests. More precisely, given the number and the *frequency*, it is as if they had been frightened by *someone* within themselves. They should not have done so, we might think a little hastily. Nazi and fascist totalitarianisms found themselves now on one side, now on the other in this war of ghosts, but in the course of a sole and same history. And there are so many ghosts in this tragedy, in the charnel houses of all the camps, that no one will ever be sure of being on a single and same side. It is better to know that. In a word, the whole history of European politics at least, and at least since Marx, would be that of a ruthless war between solidary camps that are equally terrorized by the ghost, the ghost of the other, and its own ghost as the ghost of the other. The Holy Alliance is terrorized by the ghost of communism and undertakes a war against it that is still going on, but it is a war against a camp that is itself organized by the terror of the ghost, the one in front of it and the one it carries within itself.

There is nothing 'revisionist'[5] about interpreting the genesis of totalitarianisms as reciprocal reactions to the fear of the ghost that communism inspired beginning in the last century, to the terror that it inspired in its adversaries but that it turned inside out and felt sufficiently within itself to precipitate the monstrous realization, the magical effectuation, the animist incorporation of an emancipatory eschatology which ought to have respected the promise, the being-promise of a promise—and which could not have been a simple ideological phantasm since the critique of ideology itself was inspired by nothing else.

For, finally we must get around to this, the *revenant* was the persecution *of* Marx. As it was that *of* Stirner. *Both of them*, as is quite understandable, kept on persecuting their persecutor, their own persecutor, their most intimate stranger. Marx loved the figure of the ghost, he detested it, he called it to witness his contestation, he was haunted by it, harassed, besieged, obsessed by it. In him, but of course in order to repulse it, outside of him. In him outside of him: this is the place outside of place of ghosts wherever they feign to take up their abode. More than others, perhaps, Marx had ghosts in his head and knew without knowing what he was talking about ('Mensch, es spukt in Deinem Kopfe!' one might say to him in a parody of Stirner). But for this very reason he also did not love the ghosts he loved. And who loved him—and observed him from beneath the visor. He was doubtless *obsessed* by them [. . .] but, as he did against the adversaries of communism, he waged a merciless battle against them.

Like all obsessives, he harassed the obsession. There are countless signs of this, each one more explicit than the other. To cite only two very different examples from this rich spectrology, one could evoke in passing his 1841 Dissertation (*The Difference in the Philosophy of Nature of Democritus and Epicurus*). There the very young Marx signs a filial dedication (for it is always to the father, the secret of a father that a frightened child calls for help against the specter: 'I am thy Fathers Spirit . . . I am forbid/ To tell the secrets of my Prison-House'). In this dedication, Marx addresses himself as son to Ludwig von Westphalen, 'personal adviser to the government' in Trier, this 'very dear paternal friend [*seinen theuren väterlichen Freund*].' He then speaks of a sign of filial love (*diese Zeilen als erste Zeichen kindlicher Liebe*) as regards someone before whom 'all the spirits of the world are called to appear [*vor dem alle Geister der Welt erscheinen*]' and who never recoiled in fear from the shadows of retrograde ghosts (*Schlagschatten der retrograden Gespenster*) or from skies often covered with dark clouds. The last words of this dedication name the spirit (*Der Geist*) as the 'great magical physician [*der grosse Zauberkundig Arzt*]' to whom this spiritual father entrusted himself (*anvertraut*) and from whom he draws all his strength to struggle against the evil of the ghost. It is the spirit against the specter. In this adoptive father, in this hero of the struggle against retrograde ghosts (which Marx seems implicitly to distinguish from the specter of progress that communism will be for example), the young Marx sees the living and visible proof (*argumentum ad oculas*) that 'idealism is not a fiction but a truth.'

Youthful dedication? Conventional language? Surely. But the words are not so common, they appear calculated and the statistical accounting can begin. Frequency counts. The experience, the apprehension of the ghost is tuned into *frequency*: number (more than one), insistence, rhythm (waves, cycles, and periods). The youthful dedication continues to speak and to proliferate itself, it appears more significant and less conventional when one notices, in the years that follow, the relentless determination to denounce, that is, to conjure (away), and with great verve, but also with great fascination, what *The German Ideology* will call the history of ghosts (*Gespenstergeschichte*). We will come back to this text in a moment, it is crawling with them, a crowd of *revenants* are waiting for us there: shrouds, errant souls, clanking of chains in the night, groanings, chilling bursts of laughter, and all those heads, so many invisible heads that look at us, the greatest concentration of all specters in the history of humanity. Marx (and Engels) try to straighten things out, they seek to identify, they pretend to count. They have trouble.

A little later, in fact, *The Eighteenth Brumaire of Louis Bonaparte* deploys once again, on the same frequency, something like a spectropolitics and a genealogy of ghosts, more precisely a *patrimonial* logic of the *generations of ghosts*. Marx never stops conjuring and exorcising there. He separates out the good from the bad 'ghosts.' Sometimes in the same sentence, he desperately tries to oppose (but how difficult it is and how risky), the 'spirit of the revolution [*Geist der Revolution*]' to its specter (*Gespenst*). Yes, it is difficult and risky. Because of the lexicon, first of all: like *esprit* and like 'spirit,' *Geist* can also signify 'specter' and Marx thinks he can exploit, even as he controls, its rhetorical effects. The semantics of *Gespenst* themselves haunt the semantics of *Geist*. If there is some ghost, it is to be found precisely where, between the two, reference hesitates, undecidably, or else no longer hesitates where it should have. But if it is so difficult and risky, beyond any possible mastery, if the two remain indiscernible and finally synonymous, it is because, in Marx's own view, the specter will first have been necessary, one might say even vital to the historical unfolding of spirit. For, first of all, Marx himself *inherits* from the Hegelian remark on the repetition of history, whether one is talking about great events, revolutions, or heroes (the remark is well known: first tragedy, then farce). Victor Hugo was also attentive, as we have seen, to the revolutionary repetition. A revolution repeats, and it even repeats the revolution against the revolution. *The Eighteenth Brumaire* concludes from this that men make their *own* history, that is the condition of *inheritance*. Appropriation in general, we would say, is *in the condition of the other* and of the *dead* other, of more than one dead, a generation of the dead. What is said about appropriation is also valid for freedom, liberation, or emancipation.

Men make their own history [*ihre eigene Geschichte*] but they do not make it just as they please [*aus freien Stücken*]; they do not make it under circumstances chosen by themselves, but under circumstances directly encountered, given and transmitted from the past [*überlieferten Umständen*]. The tradition of all the dead generations [*aller toten Geschlechter*] weighs [*lastet*] like a nightmare on the brain of the living.

(Marx writes 'lastet wie ein Alp,' that is, weighs like one of those ghosts that give nightmares; the French translation reads simply 'pèse d'un poids très lourd,' weighs very heavily; as often happens in translations, the ghost drops off into oblivion or, in the best of cases, it is dissolved into approximate figures, for example 'phantasmagoria,' a word that moreover is generally relieved of its literal sense which links it to speech and to public speech.)

And just when they seem engaged in revolutionizing themselves and things, in creating something that has never yet existed [*noch nicht Dagewesenes zu schaffen*], precisely in such periods of revolutionary crisis they anxiously conjure up [*beschwören sie ängstlich*] the spirits of the past to their service [*die Geister der Vergangenheit zu ihrem Dienste herauf*] and borrow [*entlehnen*] from them *names*, battle-cries [*Schlachtparole*] and costumes in order to present the new scene of world history in this time-honoured disguise and this *borrowed language* [*mit dieser erborgten Sprache*].[6]

It is indeed a matter of convoking or conjuring (*beschwören*) the spirits as specters in a gesture of positive conjuration, the one that swears in order to call up and not to drive away. But can one uphold this distinction? For if such a conjuration seems welcoming and hospitable, since it calls forth the dead, makes or lets them come, it is never free of anxiety. And thus of a movement of repulsion or restriction. Not only is the conjuration characterized by a certain anxiety, it does not let itself be determined merely *in addition* by this anxiety (as the word *ängstlich* suggests), it is destined to the anxiety *that it is*. The conjuration is anxiety from the moment it calls upon death to invent the quick and to enliven the new, to summon the presence of what is not yet there (*noch nicht Dagewesenes*). This anxiety in the face of the ghost is properly revolutionary. If death weighs on the living brain of the living, and still more on the brains of revolutionaries, it must then have some spectral density. To weigh (*lasten*) is also to charge, tax, impose, indebt, accuse, assign, enjoin. And the more life there is, the graver the specter of the other becomes, the heavier its imposition. And the more the living have to answer for it. *To answer for the dead, to respond to the dead*. To correspond and have it out with [*s'expliquer avec*] obsessive haunting, in the absence of any certainty or symmetry. Nothing is more serious and nothing is more true, nothing is more exact [*juste*] than this phantasmagoria. The specter weighs [*pèse*], it thinks [*pense*], it intensifies and condenses itself within the very inside of life, within the most living life, the most singular (or, if one prefers, individual) life. The latter therefore no longer has and must no longer have, insofar as it is living, a pure identity to itself or any assured inside: this is what all philosophies of life, or even philosophies of the living and real individual, would have to weigh carefully.[7]

The paradox must be sharpened: the more the new erupts in the revolutionary crisis, the more the period is in crisis, the more it is 'out of joint,' then the more one has to convoke the old, 'borrow' from it. Inheritance from the 'spirits of the past' consists, as always, in borrowing. Figures of borrowing, borrowed figures, figurality as the figure of borrowing. And the borrowing *speaks*: borrowed language, borrowed names, says Marx. A question of credit, then, or of faith. But an unstable and barely visible dividing line crosses through this law of the fiduciary. It passes between a parody and a truth, but one truth as incarnation or living repetition of the other, a regenerating reviviscence of the past, of the spirit, of the spirit of the past from which one inherits. The dividing line passes between a mechanical reproduction of the specter and an appropriation that is so alive, so interiorizing, so assimilating of the inheritance and of the 'spirits of the past' that it is none other than the life of forgetting, life as forgetting itself. And the forgetting of the maternal in order to make the spirit live in oneself. These are Marx's words. It is his language, and the example of the language is not just any example among others. It designates the very element of these rights of succession.

> Thus Luther donned the mask of the Apostle Paul, the revolution of 1789 to 1814 draped itself alternately as the Roman Republic and the Roman Empire, and the revolution of 1848 knew nothing better to do than to parody [*parodieren*], now 1789, now the revolutionary tradition of 1793 to 1795. In like manner a beginner who has learnt a new language always translates it back into his mother tongue, but he has assimilated [appropriated: *hat er sich nur angeeignet*] the spirit of the new language and can freely express himself in it [produce in it: *in ihr produzieren*] only when he finds his way in it without recalling the old and forgets his native tongue in the use of the new. (p. 104)

From one inheritance to the other. The living appropriation of the spirit, the assimilation of a new language is already an inheritance. And the appropriation of another language here figures the revolution. This revolutionary inheritance supposes, to be sure, that one ends up forgetting the specter, that of the primitive or mother tongue. In order to forget not what one inherits but the pre-inheritance on the basis of which one inherits. This forgetting is only a forgetting. For what one must forget will have been indispensable. One must pass through the pre-inheritance, even if it is to parody it, in order to appropriate the life of a new language or make the revolution. And while the forgetting corresponds to the moment of living appropriation, Marx nevertheless does not valorize it as simply as one might think. Things are very complicated. One must forget the specter and the parody, Marx seems to say, so that history can continue. But if one is content to forget it, then the result is bourgeois platitude: life, that's all. So one must not forget it, one must remember it but while forgetting it enough, in this very memory, in order to 'find again the *spirit* of the revolution without making its *specter* return [*den Geist der revolution wiederzufinden, nicht ihr* Gespenst *wieder umgehen machen*; emphasis added].'. . .

• • •

[. . .] these ghosts are bound to the categories of bourgeois economy. [. . .] We do not know if Marx thought to be done with the ghost in general, or even if he really wanted that, when he declares unequivocally that this ghost here, this *Spuk* which *Capital* takes as its object, is only the effect of the market economy. And that, as such, it ought to, it will have to disappear with other forms of production.

> The categories of bourgeois economics consist precisely of forms of this kind [i.e., delirious, Marx has just said]. They are forms of thought which are socially valid, and therefore objective, for the relations of production belonging to this historically determined mode of social production, i.e. commodity production. The whole mystery of commodities, all the magic and necromancy that surrounds the products of labour on the basis of commodity production, vanishes therefore as soon as we come to [escape to: *flüchten*] other forms of production [*Aller Mystizismus der Warenwelt, all der Zauber und Spuk, welcher Arbeitsprodukte auf Grundlage der Warenproduktion umnebelt, versehwindet daher sofort, sobald wir zu andren Produktionsformen fluchten*] (Ibid.)

This translation, like so many others, manages to efface the literal reference to the ghost (*Spuk*).[8] One must also underscore the instant immediacy with which, as Marx would like at least to believe or make us believe, mysticism, magic, and the ghost would disappear: they *will vanish* (indicative), they will dissipate in truth, according to him, as if by magic, as they had come, at the very second in which one will (would) see the end of market production. Assuming even, along with Marx, that the latter will ever have a possible end. Marx does indeed say: 'as soon as,' *sobald*, and as always he is speaking of a disappearance to come of the ghost, the fetish, and religion as cloudy apparitions. Everything is veiled in mist, everything is enveloped in clouds (*umnebelt,*), beginning with truth. Clouds on a cold night, landscape or setting of *Hamlet* upon the apparition of the ghost ('It is past midnight, bitterly cold, and dark except for the faint light of the stars').

Even if *Capital* had thus opened with a great scene of exorcism, with a bid to raise the stakes of conjuration, this critical phase would not be at all destroyed, it would not be discredited. At least it would not annul everything about its event and its inaugurality. For we are wagering here that thinking never has done with the conjuring impulse. It would instead be born of that impulse. To swear or to conjure, is that not the chance of thinking and its destiny, no less than its limit? The gift of its finitude? Does it ever have any other choice except among several conjurations? We know that the question itself—and it is the most ontological and the most critical and the most risky of all questions—still protects itself. Its very *formulation* throws up barricades or digs trenches, surrounds itself with barriers, increases the fortifications. It rarely advances headlong, at total risk to life and limb [*à corps perdu*]. In a magical, ritual, obsessional fashion, its *formalization* uses *formulas* which are sometimes incantatory procedures. It marks off its territory by setting out there strategies and sentinels under the protection of apotropaic shields. Problematization itself is careful to disavow and thus to conjure away (we repeat, *problema* is a shield, an armor, a rampart as much as it is a task for the inquiry to come). Critical problematization continues to do battle against ghosts. It fears them as it does itself.

These questions posed, or rather suspended, we can perhaps return to what *Capital* seems to want to say about the fetish, in the same passage and following the same logic. The point is also, let us not forget, to show that the enigma of the 'money' fetish is reducible to that of the 'commodity' fetish once the latter has become visible (*sichtbar*)—but, adds Marx just as enigmatically, *visible or evident* to the point of blinding dazzlement: the French translation to which I am referring here says the enigma of the commodity fetish 'crève les yeux,' literally, puts out one's eyes (*die Augenblendende Rätsel des Warenfetischs*).[9]

Now, as we know, only the reference to the religious world allows one to explain the autonomy of the ideological, and thus its proper efficacy, its incorporation in apparatuses that are endowed not only with an apparent autonomy but a sort of automaticity that not fortuitously recalls the headstrongness of the wooden table. By rendering an account of the 'mystical' character and the secret (*das Geheimnisvolle*) of the commodity-form, we have been introduced into fetishism and the ideological. Without being reducible one to the other, they share a common condition. Now, says *Capital*, only the religious analogy, only the 'misty realm of religion' (*die Nebelregion der religiösen Welt*) can allow one to understand the production and fetishizing autonomization of this form. The necessity of turning toward this analogy is presented by Marx as a consequence of the 'phantasmagoric form' whose genesis he has just analyzed. If the objective relation between things (which we have called *commerce between commodities*) is indeed a phantasmagoric form of the social relation between men, *then* we must have recourse to the *only analogy possible*, that of religion: 'It is nothing but the definite social relation between men themselves which assumes here, for them, the fantastic form of a relation between things.' Consequence: '*In order, therefore, to find an analogy* [my emphasis: *Um daher eine Analogie zu finden*], we must take flight [*flüchten* again or already] into the misty realm of religion' (p. 165).

Needless to say, the stakes are enormous in the relation of fetishism to the ideological and the religious. In the statements that immediately follow, the deduction of fetishism is also applied to the ideological, to its autonomization as well as to its automatization:

> There [in the religious world] the products of the human brain [of the head, once again, of men: *des menschlichen Kopfes*, analogous to the wooden head of the table capable of engendering chimera—in its head, outside of its head—once, that is, *as soon as*, its form can become commodity-form] appear as autonomous figures endowed with a life of their own, which enter into relations both with each other and with the human race. . . . I call this the fetishism which attaches itself [*anklebt*] to the products of labour as soon as they are produced as commodities, and is therefore inseparable from the production of commodities.
>
> As the foregoing analysis has already demonstrated, this fetishism of the world of commodities arises from the peculiar social character of the labour which produces them. (Ibid.)

In other words, as soon as there is production, there is fetishism: idealization, autonomization and automatization, dematerialization and spectral incorporation, mourning work coextensive with all work, and so forth. Marx believes he must limit this co-extensivity to commodity production. In our view, this is a gesture of exorcism, which we spoke of earlier and regarding which we leave here once again our question suspended.

The religious is thus not just one ideological phenomenon or phantomatic production among others. On the one hand, it gives to the production of the ghost or of the ideological phantasm its originary form or its paradigm of reference, its first 'analogy.' On the other hand (and first of all, and no doubt for the same reason), the religious also informs, along with the messianic and the eschatological, be it in the necessarily undetermined, empty, abstract, and dry form that we are privileging here, that 'spirit' of emancipatory Marxism whose injunction we are reaffirming here, however secret and contradictory it appears.

We cannot get involved here in this general question of fetishization.[10] In work to come, it will no doubt be necessary to link it to the question of phantomatic spectrality. Despite the infinite opening of all these borders, one might perhaps attempt to define what is at stake here from at least *three points of view*:

1. Fetishist phantomaticity in general and its place in *Capital*.[11] Even before commodity value makes its stage entrance and before the choreography of the wooden table, Marx had defined the residual product of labor as a phantomatic objectivity (*gespenstige Gegenständlichkeit*).[12]

2. The place of this theoretical moment in Marx's corpus. Does he or does he not break with what is said about the ghost and the ideological in *The German Ideology*? One may have one's doubts. The relation is probably neither one of break nor of homogeneity.

3. Beyond these dimensions, which are not only those of an exegesis of Marx, at stake is doubtless everything which *today* links Religion and Technics in a singular configuration.

A. At stake first of all is that which takes the original form of a return of the religious, whether fundamentalist or not, and which overdetermines all questions of nation, State, international law, human rights, Bill of Rights—in short, everything that concentrates its habitat in the at least symptomatic figure of Jerusalem or, here and there, of its reappropriation and of the system of alliances that are ordered around it. How to relate, but also how to dissociate the two messianic spaces we are talking about here under the same name? If the messianic appeal belongs properly to a universal structure, to that irreducible movement of the historical opening to the future, therefore to experience itself and to its language (expectation, promise, commitment to the event of what is coming, imminence, urgency, demand for salvation and for justice beyond law, pledge given to the other inasmuch as he or she is not present presently present or living, and so forth), how is one to *think* it *with* the figures of Abrahamic messianism? Does it figure abstract desertification or originary condition? Was not Abrahamic messianism but an exemplary prefiguration, the pre-name [*prénom*] given against the background of the possibility that we are attempting to name here? But then why keep the name, or at least the adjective (we prefer to say *messianic* rather than *messianism*, so as to designate a structure of experience rather than a religion), there where no figure of the *arrivant*, even as he or she is heralded, should be pre-determined, prefigured, or even pre-named? Of these two deserts, which one, first of all, will have signalled toward the other? Can one conceive an atheological heritage of the messianic? Is there one, on the contrary, that is more consistent? A heritage is never natural, one may inherit more than once, in different places and at different times, one may choose to wait for the most appropriate time, which may be the most untimely—write about it according to different *lineages*, and sign thus more than one *import*. These questions and these hypotheses do not exclude each other. At least for us and for the moment. Ascesis strips the messianic hope of all biblical forms, and even all determinable figures of the wait or expectation; it thus denudes itself in view of responding to that which must be absolute hospitality, the 'yes' to the *arrivant(e)*, the 'come' to the future that cannot be anticipated—which must not be the 'anything whatsoever' that harbors behind it those too familiar ghosts, the very ones we must practice recognizing. Open, waiting for the event *as* justice, this hospitality is absolute only if it keeps watch over its own universality. The messianic, including its revolutionary forms (and the messianic is always revolutionary, it has to be), would be urgency, imminence but, irreducible paradox, a waiting without horizon of expectation. One may always take the quasi-atheistic dryness of the messianic to be the condition of the religions of the Book, a desert that was not even theirs (but the earth is always borrowed, on loan from God, it is never possessed by the occupier, says precisely [*justement*] the Old Testament whose injunction one would also have to hear); one may always recognize there the arid soil in which grew, and passed away, the living figures of all the messiahs, whether they were announced, recognized, or still awaited. One may also consider this compulsive growth, and the furtiveness of this passage, to be the only events on the basis of which we approach and first of all name the messianic in general, that other ghost which we cannot and ought not do without. One may deem strange, strangely familiar and inhospitable at the same time (*unheimlich*, uncanny), this figure of absolute hospitality whose promise one would choose to entrust to an experience that is so impossible, so unsure in its indigence, to a quasi-'messianism' so anxious, fragile, and impoverished, to an always presupposed 'messianism,' to a quasi-transcendental 'messianism' that also has such an obstinate interest in a materialism without substance: a materialism of the *khōra* for a despairing 'messianism.' But without this latter despair and if one could *count* on what is coming, hope would be but the calculation of a program. One would have the prospect but one would not longer wait for anything or anyone. Law without justice. One would no longer invite, either body or soul, no longer receive any visits, no longer even think to see. To see coming. Some, and I do not exclude myself, will find this despairing 'messianism' has a curious taste; a taste of death. It is true that this taste is above all a taste, a foretaste, and in essence it is curious. Curious of the very thing that it conjures—and that leaves something to be desired.

B. But also at stake, indissociably, is the differantial deployment of *tekhnē*, of techno-science or tele-technology.[13] It obliges us more than ever to think the virtualization of space and time, the possibility of virtual events whose movement and speed prohibit us more than ever (more and otherwise than ever, for this is not absolutely and thoroughly new) from opposing presence to its representation, 'real time' to 'deferred time,' effectivity to its simulacrum, the living to the non-living, in short, the living to the living-dead of its ghosts. It obliges us to think, from there, another space for democracy. For democracy-to-come and thus for justice. We have suggested that the event we are prowling around here hesitates between the singular 'who' of the ghost and the general 'what' of the simulacrum. In the virtual space of all the teletechnosciences, in the general dis-location to which our time is destined—as are from now on the places of lovers, families, nations—the messianic trembles on the edge of this event itself. It is this hesitation, it has no other vibration, it does not 'live' otherwise, but it would no longer be messianic if it stopped hesitating: how to give rise and to give place [*donner lieu*], still, to render it, this place, to render it habitable, but without killing the future in the name of old frontiers? Like those of the blood, nationalisms of native soil not only sow hatred, not only commit crimes, they have no future, they promise nothing even if, like stupidity or the unconscious, they hold fast to life. This messianic hesitation does not paralyze any decision, any affirmation, any responsibility. On the contrary, it grants them their elementary condition. It is their very experience.

As we must hasten the conclusion, let us schematize things. If something seems not to have shifted between *The German Ideology* and *Capital*, it is two axioms whose inheritance is equally important for us. But it is the inheritance of a double bind which, moreover, signals toward the double bind of any inheritance and thus of any responsible decision. Contradiction and secret inhabit the injunction (the spirit of the father, if one prefers). On the one hand, Marx insists on respecting the originality and the proper efficacity, the autonomization and automatization of ideality as finite-infinite processes of differance (phantomatic, fantastic, fetishistic, or ideological)—and of the simulacrum which is not simply imaginary in it. It is an artifactual body, a technical body, and it takes labor to constitute or deconstitute it. This movement will remain valuable, no doubt irreplaceable, provided that it is adjusted, as it will be by any 'good Marxism,' to novel structures and situations. But, on the other hand, even as he remains one of the first thinkers of technics, or even, by far and from afar, of the tele-technology that it will always have been, from near or from far, Marx continues to want to ground his critique or his exorcism of the spectral simulacrum in an ontology. It is a—critical but predeconstructive—ontology of presence as actual reality and as objectivity. This critical ontology means to deploy the possibility of dissipating the phantom, let us venture to say again of conjuring it away as representative consciousness of a subject, and of bringing this representation back to the world of labor, production, and exchange, so as to reduce it to its conditions. Pre-deconstructive here does not mean false, unnecessary, or illusory. Rather it characterizes a relatively stabilized knowledge that calls for questions more radical than the critique itself and than the ontology that grounds the critique. These questions are not destabilizing as the effect of some theoretico-specu-lative subversion. They are not even, in the final analysis, questions but seismic events. *Practical* events, where thought *becomes act* [se fait agir], and body and manual experience (thought as *Handeln*, says Heidegger somewhere), labor but always divisible labor—and shareable, beyond the old schemas of the division of labor (even beyond the one on whose basis Marx constructed so many things, in particular his discourse on ideological hegemony: the division between intellectual labor and manual labor whose pertinence has certainly not disappeared, but appears more limited than ever). These seismic events come from the future, they are given from out of the unstable, chaotic, and dis-located ground of the times. A disjointed or dis-adjusted time without which there would be neither history, nor event, nor promise of justice.

The fact that the ontological and the critical are here pre-deconstructive has political consequences which are perhaps not negligible. And they are doubtless not negligible, to go too quickly here, with regards to the concept of the political, as concerns the political itself.

To indicate just one example among so many others, let us evoke once again in conclusion a passage from *The German Ideology*. It puts to work a schema that *Capital* seems to have constantly confirmed. In it, Marx advances that belief in the religious specter, thus in the ghost in general, consists in autonomizing a representation (*Vorstellung*) and in forgetting its genesis as well as its real grounding (*reale Grundlage*). To dissipate the factitious autonomy thus engendered in history, one must again take into account the modes of production and techno-economic exchange:

> In religion people make their empirical world into an entity that is only conceived, imagined [*zu einem nur gedachten vorgestellten Wesen*], that confronts them as something foreign [*das ihnen fremd gegenübertritt*]. This again is by no means to be explained from other concepts, from 'self-consciousness' and similar nonsense, but from the entire hitherto existing mode of production and intercourse, which is just as independent [*unabhängig*] of the pure concept as the invention of the self-acting mule [in English in the text] and the use of railways are independent of Hegelian philosophy. If he wants to speak of an 'essence' of religion, i.e., of a material basis of this inessentiality, [*d.h. von einer materiellen Grundlage dieses Unwesen*], then he should look for it neither in the 'essence of man' [*im 'Wesen des Menschen'*], nor in the predicates of God, but in the material world which each stage of religious development finds in existence (cf. above *Feuerbach*). All the 'specters' which have filed before us [*die wir Revue passieren liessen*] were representations [*Vorstellungen*]. These representations—leaving aside their real basis [*abgesehen von ihrer realen Grundlage*] (which Stirner in any case leaves aside)—understood as representations internal to consciousness, as thoughts in people's heads, transferred from their objectality [*Gegenständlichkeit*] back into the subject [*in das Subjekt zurückgenommen*], elevated from substance into self-consciousness, are obsessions [*der Sparren*] or *fixed ideas*. (p. 160–61)

If one follows the letter of the text, the critique of the ghost or of spirits would thus be the critique of a subjective representation and an abstraction, of what happens *in the head*, of what comes only out of the head, that is, of what stays there, in the head, even as it has come out of there, out of the head, and survives *outside the head*. But nothing would be possible, beginning with the critique, without the surviving, without the possible survival of this autonomy and this automatism outside the head. One may say that this is where the spirit of the Marxist critique situates itself, not the spirit that one would oppose to its letter, but the one which supposes the very movement of its letter. Like the ghost, it is neither in the head nor outside the head. Marx knows this, but he proceeds as if he did not want to know it. In *The German Ideology*, the following chapter will be devoted to this obsession that made Stirner say: 'Mensch, es spukt in deinem Kopfe!' commonly translated as 'Man, there are specters in your head!' Marx thinks it is enough to turn the apostrophe back against Saint Max (p. 160).

Es spukt: difficult to translate, as we have been saying. It is a question of ghost and haunting, to be sure, but what else? The German idiom seems to name the ghostly return but it names it in a verbal form. The latter does not say that there is some *revenant*, specter, or ghost; it does not say that there is some apparition, *der Spuk*, nor even that it appears, but that 'it ghosts,' 'it apparitions.' *It is a matter* [Il s'agit], in the neutrality of this altogether impersonal verbal form, of something or someone, neither someone nor something, of a 'one' that does not act. *It is a matter* rather of the passive movement of an apprehension, of an apprehensive movement ready to welcome, but where? In the head? What is the head before this apprehension that it cannot even contain? And what if the head, which is neither the subject, nor consciousness, nor the ego, nor the brain, were defined first of all by the possibility of such an experience, and by the very thing that it can neither contain, nor delimit, by the indefiniteness of the 'es spukt'? To welcome, we were saying then, but even while apprehending, with anxiety and the desire to exclude the stranger, to invite the stranger without accepting him or her, domestic hospitality that welcomes without welcoming the stranger, but a stranger who is already found within (*das Heimliche-Unheimliche*) more intimate with one than one is oneself, the absolute proximity of a stranger whose power is singular *and* anonymous (*es spukt*), an unnameable and neutral power, that is, undecidable, neither active nor passive, an an-identity that, *without doing anything*, invisibly occupies places belonging finally neither to us nor to it. Now, all, *this*, *this* about which we have failed to say anything whatsoever that is logically determinable, *this* that comes with so much difficulty to language, *this* that seems not to mean anything, *this* that puts to rout our meaning-to-say, making us speak regularly from the place where we want to say nothing, where we know clearly what we do not want to say but do not know what we would like to say, as if *this* were no longer either of the order of knowledge or will or will-to-say, well, *this* comes back, *this* returns, *this* insists in urgency, and·*this* gives one to think, but *this*, which is each time irresistible enough, singular enough to engender as much anguish as do the future and death, *this* stems less from a 'repetitive automatism' (of the automatons that have been turning before us for such a long time) than it gives us to think all *this*, *altogether other*, *every other*, from which the repetition compulsion arises: that every other is altogether other.[14] The impersonal ghostly returning of the 'es spukt' produces an automatism of repetition, no less than it finds its principle of reason there. In an incredible paragraph of 'Das Unheimliche,' Freud moreover recognizes that he should have begun his research (on the *Unheimliche*, the death drive, the repetition compulsion, the beyond of the pleasure principle, and so forth) with what says the 'es spukt.'[15] He sees there an *example* with which it would have been necessary to begin the search. He goes so far as to consider it the *strongest example* of *Unheimlichkeit* (Wir hätten eigentlich unsere Untersuchung mit diesem, vielleicht stärksten Beispiel von Unheimlichkeit beginnen können,' 'We could, properly speaking, have begun our inquiry with this example of uncanniness, which is perhaps the strongest'). But one may wonder whether what he calls the strongest example lets itself be reduced to an example—merely to the strongest example, in a series of examples. And what if it were the Thing itself, the cause of the very thing one is seeking and that makes one seek? The cause of the knowledge and the search, the motive of history or of the *epistemē*? If it is from there that it drew its exemplary force? On the other hand, one must pay attention to the conjuring mechanism that Freud then puts forward to justify himself for not having thought that he ought to begin from where he *could* have begun, from where he *ought* to have begun, nevertheless, *him* for example (you understand well what I mean: Marx, *him* too).

Freud explains this to us in the serene tone of epistemological, methodological, rhetorical, in truth psychagogical caution: if he had to begin not where he could have or should have begun, it is because with the thing in question (the strongest example of *Unheimlichkeit*, the 'es spukt,' ghosts, and apparitions), one scares oneself too much [one makes oneself fear too much: *on se fait trop peur*]. One confuses what is *heimliche-unheimliche*, in a contradictory, undecidable fashion, with the terrible or the frightful (*mit dem Grauenhaften*). Now, fear is not good for the serenity of research and the analytic distinction of concepts. One should read also for itself and from this point of view all the rest of the text (we will try to do so elsewhere), while crossing this reading with that of numerous other texts of Heidegger.[16] We think that the frequent, decisive, and organizing recourse that the latter has to the value of *Unheimlichkeit*, in *Being and Time* and elsewhere, remains generally unnoticed or neglected. In both discourses, that of Freud and that of Heidegger, this recourse makes possible fundamental projects or trajectories. But it does so while destabilizing permanently, and in a more or less subterranean fashion, the order of conceptual distinctions that are put to work. It should disturb both the ethics and the politics that follow implicitly or explicitly from that order.

Our hypothesis is that the same is true for Marx's spectrology. Is this not our own great problematic constellation of haunting? It has no certain border, but it blinks and sparkles behind the proper names of Marx, Freud, and Heidegger: Heidegger who misjudged Freud who misjudged Marx. This is no doubt not aleatory. Marx has not yet been received. The subtitle of this address could thus have been: 'Marx—*das Unheimliche*.' Marx remains an immigrant *chez nous*, a glorious, sacred, accursed but still a clandestine immigrant as he was all his life. He belongs to a time of disjunction, to that 'time out of joint' in which is inaugurated, laboriously, painfully, tragically, a new thinking of borders, a new experience of the house, the home, and the economy. Between earth and sky. One should not rush to make of the clandestine immigrant an illegal alien or, what always risks coming down to the same thing, to domesticate him. To neutralize him through naturalization. To assimilate him so as to stop frightening oneself (making oneself fear) with him. He is not part of the family, but one should not send him back, once again, him too, to the border.

However alive, healthy, critical, and still necessary his burst of laughter may remain, and first of all in the face of the capital or paternal ghost, the *Hauptgespenst* that is the general essence of Man, Marx, *das Unheimliche*, perhaps should not have chased away so many ghosts too quickly. Not all of them at once or not so simply on the pretext that they did not exist (of course they do not exist, so what?)—or that all this was or ought to remain past ('Let the dead bury their dead,' and so forth). All the more so in that he also knew how to let them go free, emancipate them even, in the movement in which he analyzes the (relative) autonomy of exchange-value, the ideologem, or the fetish. Even if one wanted to, one could not let the dead bury the dead: that has no sense, that is *impossible*. Only mortals, only the living who are not living gods can bury the dead. Only mortals can watch over them, and can watch, period. Ghosts can do so as well, they are everywhere where there is watching; the dead *cannot do so*—it is impossible and they must not do so.

That the without-ground of this impossible can nevertheless *take place* is on the contrary the ruin or the absolute ashes, the threat that must be *thought*, and, why not, exorcised yet again. To exorcise not in order to chase away the ghosts, but this time to grant them the right, if it means making them come back alive, as *revenants* who would no longer be *revenants*, but as other *arrivants* to whom a hospitable memory or promise must offer welcome—without certainty, ever, that they present themselves as such. Not in order to grant them the right in this sense but out of a concern for *justice*. Present existence or essence has never been the condition, object, or the *thing* [chose] of justice. One must constantly remember that the impossible ('to let the dead bury their dead') is, alas, always possible. One must constantly remember that this absolute evil (which is, is it not, absolute life, fully present life, the one that does not know death and does not want to hear about it) can take place. One must constantly remember that it is even on the basis of the terrible possibility of this impossible that justice is desirable: *through* but also *beyond* right and law.

If Marx, like Freud, like Heidegger, like everybody, did not begin where he ought to have 'been able to begin' (*beginnen können*), namely with haunting, before life *as such*, before death *as such*, it is doubtless not his fault. The fault, in any case, by definition, is repeated, we inherit it, we must watch over it. It always comes at a great price—and for humanity precisely. What costs humanity very dearly is doubtless to believe that one can have done in history with a general essence of Man, on the pretext that it represents only a *Hauptgespenst*, arch-ghost, but also, what comes down to the same thing—*at bottom*—to still believe, no doubt, in this capital ghost. To believe in it as do the credulous or the dogmatic. Between the two beliefs, as always, the way remains narrow.

In order for there to be any sense in asking oneself about the terrible price to pay, in order to watch over the future, everything would have to be begun again. But in memory, this time, of that impure 'impure impure history of ghosts.'

Can one, in order to question it, address oneself to a ghost? To whom? To him? To *it*, as Marcellus says once again and so prudently? 'Thou art a Scholler; speake to *it* Horatio. . . . Question *it*.'

The question deserves perhaps to be put the other way: Could one *address oneself in general* if already some ghost did not come back? If he loves justice at least, the 'scholar' of the future, the 'intellectual' of tomorrow should learn it and from the ghost. He should learn to live by learning not how to make conversation with the ghost but how to talk with him, with her, how to let them speak or how to give them back speech, even if it is in oneself, in the other, in the other in oneself: they are always *there*, specters, even if they do not exist, even if they are no longer, even if they are not yet. They give us to rethink the 'there' as soon as we open our mouths, even at a colloquium and especially when one speaks there in a foreign language:

Thou art a scholar; speak to it, Horatio.

Notes

1. Sigmund Freud, 'Eine Schwierigkeit der Psychoanalyse,' *Gesammelte Werke*, Bd. XII, p. 8; *Standard Edition*, Vol. XVII, p. 141.
2. We will approach this scene below [. . .], around a certain table, regarding fetishization as spectralization of exchange-value. It is the very opening, the first scene, if not the primal scene, of *Capital*.
3. *A Contribution to the Critique of Political Economy* (1859), trans. S. W. Ryazanskaya, ed. Maurice Dobb (New York: International Publishers, 1970), p. 107.
4. The expression translated here is 'faire peur'. The translator of *Specters of Marx*, Peggy Kamuf, elsewhere provides the following footnote explaining the translation, which we reproduce in this location (where Kamuf refers back to her own note in the original) for the purposes of clarity [ed.]: 'The idiomatic expression here is '(se) faire peur,' frightens (itself). Literally, however, it says: to make (itself) fright. Later, the text will exploit this literality when it describes a structure of the

self as fear or fright, as that which makes itself into fear. [Trans.]' (*Specters of Marx*, p. 180, n. 40)

5. Perverse logic, abyssal perversity of all 'revisionisms' that mark the end of this century and will doubtless continue into the next. Of course, there must be no let-up in the opposition to the worst revisionisms and negationisms, those whose figure and interests are now fairly well determined, even if their manifestations continually proliferate and get renewed. The task will therefore always be urgent, always something to be reaffirmed. But here and there one sees advance signs of a symmetrical perversity that is no less threatening. Armed with a good conscience that is imperturbable because often enveloped in ignorance or obscurantism, sheltered from any effective right to response in the mass media (I am thinking of a certain recent article by Michiko Kakutani, 'When History and Memory Are Casualties: Holocaust Denial,' *New York Times*, 30 April 1993), there are those who are not content to profit from the ghosts that haunt our most painful memory. They also authorize themselves thereby, in the same élan, to *manipulate* with impunity, without any scruple, the very word 'revisionism.' They are prepared to use it to accuse anyone who poses critical, methodological, epistemological, philosophical questions about history, about the way it is thought, written, or established, about the status of truth, and so forth. Whoever calls for vigilance in the reading of history, whoever complicates a little the schemas accredited by the *doxa*, or demands a reconsideration of the concepts, procedures, and productions of historical truth or the presuppositions of historiography, and so forth, risks being accused today, through amalgamation, contagion, or confusion, of 'revisionism' or at least of playing into some 'revisionism.' This accusation is now at the disposal of the first comer who understands nothing of this critical necessity, who wishes to be protected from it, and wants first of all his or her culture or lack of culture, his or her certainties or beliefs to be left untouched. A very disturbing historical situation which risks imposing an *a priori* censorship on historical research or on historical reflection wherever they touch on sensitive areas of our present existence. It is urgent to point out that entire wings of history, that of this century in particular, in Europe and outside of Europe, will *still* have to be interrogated and brought to light, radical questions will have to be asked and reformulated without there being anything at all 'revisionist' about that. Let us even say: on the contrary.

6. *The Eighteenth Brumaire of Louis Bonaparte*, in Karl Marx, Frederick Engels, *Collected Works*, vol. 11 (New York: International Publishers, 1979), pp. 103–04; emphasis added.

7. We are obviously thinking here of the work of Michel Henry (*Marx* in two volumes [Paris: Gallimard, 1976]) who classifies the *Eighteenth Brumaire*, as well as *The Manifesto of the Communist Party* and a few other works, among the 'political' or 'historico-political' texts. They are, according to Henry, less philosophical, if indeed they are philosophical, because they 'do not bear their principle of intelligibility within themselves' (1, p. 10). (What does it mean, strictly speaking, for a text to *bear a principle of intelligibility within itself*? [Patrice Loraux devotes to this strategy of Michel Henry several very lucid pages of his book (*Les Sous-Main de Marx* [Paris: Hachette, 1986], pp. 34–36) in the foreword titled 'The Theory of

Texts'; in particular, he recalls the tradition of this strategy]; has there ever been an example of it? This is not the place to discuss it—even though the strange and confident belief in such an immanence of intelligibility is not foreign to the concept of life that supports this whole book.) This 'historico-political' dimension (either weakly philosophical or non-philosophical) would be manifest, according to Henry, in the 'case notably of the *Eighteenth Brumaire of Louis Bonaparte*, written for an American newspaper' (I, p. 11). Now, this latter work does not seem to be at all bounded by the closure of 'political' or 'historico-political' texts, assuming that one can accept such a problematic distinction, in particular in the case of a work like that of Marx. Notably one finds again his spectral paradoxology, the one that matters to us here, in the most 'philosophical' and significant texts in Henry's own view, for example, as we will soon see, in *The German Ideology*. By weighing and thinking this spectrology, we are not directly opposing the philosophy of life or of the 'radical subjectivity from which any objectivity is excluded' (I, p. 326), nor its interpretation by Henry (with whom we share at least some concerns, but doubtless from a wholly different point of view, about the way Marx has been read until now). But we are trying to accept the necessity of complicating it in an abyssal fashion, there where the supplement of an internal-external fold forbids simply opposing the living to the non-living. Whoever subscribes, as we would be tempted to do, to the final words of the very last conclusion of Henry's *Marx* ('Marx's thought places us before the abyssal question: what is life?') has indeed to refer to this abyss, which is to say, to re-problematize all the preceding statements of that book which is so wholly about the *living*, the *living* individual, *living* subjectivity, real work as *living* work, and so forth, in other words, the whole critical arsenal of a profoundly polemical work. For it is finally in the name of this univocal reference to the living that it tries, with great violence, to discredit more or less all previous readings of Marx, and especially in their political dimension. One wonders: Why would the question of life be 'abyssal,' precisely? In other words, why this question? Does it not open onto the unthought non-self-identity of the concept or the being called 'life'? Onto the essential obscurity, for both science and philosophy, of what is called life? Does not all of this mark the internal or external limits, the closure or principle of ruin of a philosophy of life? And of subjectivity, however novel its conceptual presentation may be, once it is determined as essentially living? If one integrates into the life of this living subjectivity the work of negativity or of objectivity, the phenomena or rather the non-phenomena of death and so forth, why persist in calling it life? On the other hand, we do not think this interpretation of being or of production as manifestation—or radical immanence—of a living and monadic subjectivity (cf. for example II, pp. 41–42), an interpretation that is found to be widely justified in the letter of numerous texts of Marx, should be opposed by some philosophy of death (which could claim just as many rights and references in the same texts read differently). We are attempting something else. To try to accede to the possibility of this very alternative (life and/or death), we are directing our attention to the effects or the petitions of a survival or of a return of the dead (neither life nor death) on the sole basis of which one is able to speak of 'living subjectivity' (in opposition to its death): to speak of it but also to understand that it can, itself, speak and speak of itself, leave traces or legacies beyond the living present of its life, ask (itself) questions regarding its own subject, in short, also address itself to the other or, if one prefers, to other living individuals, to other 'monads.' For all these questions, and such is the hypothesis of our reading, the work of the specter here weaves, in the shadow of a labyrinth covered with mirrors, a tenuous but indispensable guiding thread.

8. In the French translation cited by the text (ed. Jean-Pierre Lefebvre [Paris: Presses Universitaires de France, 'Quadrige' collection, 1993]), the final sentence of this passage reads: 'Si donc nous nous échappons vers d'autres formes de production, nous verrons disparaître instantanément tout le mysticisme du monde de la marchandise, tous les sortilèges qui voilent d'une brume fantomatique les produits du travail accompli sur la base de la production marchande.' Derrida then comments in his text: 'With the expression "brume fantomatique" [ghostly fog], the recent translation we are citing marks very well the literal reference to the ghost (*Spuk*), there where so many earlier translations regularly effaced it.' [Trans.]

9. The English translation of this passage reads: 'The riddle of the money fetish is therefore the riddle of the commodity fetish, now become visible and dazzling to our eyes' (p. 187). [Trans.]

10. In its general form, I have attempted to approach it elsewhere (cf. in particular *Glas*, pp. 42, 130, 206ff., 237ff.). [Bibliographic details of *Glas* can be found in the bibliography at the end of the reader. Ed.] On the relation between fetishism and ideology, cf. Sarah Kofman *Camera obscura—de l'idéologie* (Paris: Galilée, 1973), in particular what precedes and follows 'La table tournante' (p. 21), and Etienne Balibar, *Cinq études du matérialisme historique*, as concerns the 'theory of fetishism,' pp. 206ff.

11. Cf. Balibar, *Cinq études*, pp. 208ff.

12. In the figure of its sensuous materiality, the proper body of this phantomatic objectivity takes form, hardens, erects, or petrifies itself, *crystallizes* out of a slack and undifferentiated substance, it institutes itself out of an amorphous residue: 'Let us now look at the residue of the products of labour. There is nothing left of them in each case but the same phantom-like objectivity; they are merely congealed quantities [*Gallerte*: gelatin, figure of the homogeneous mass] of homogeneous human labour, i.e., of human labour-power expended without regard to the form of its expenditure. All these things now tell us [all that is presented in them: *Diese Dinge stellen nur noch dar*] is that human labour-power has been expended to produce them, human labour is accumulated in them. As crystals [*Als Kristalle*] of this social substance, which is common to them all, they are values—commodity values' (*Capital*, p. 128).

On this 'phantomatic objectivity' (*gespenstige Gegenständlichkeit*), cf. Samuel Weber (*Unwrapping Balzac*, p. 75) who, between Balzac and Marx, insists quite rightly on the feminine character of the commodity-chimera. There is in fact more than one sign of this. But how to stabilize the sex of a fetish? Does it not pass from one sex to the other? Is it not this movement of passage, whatever may be its stases?

In a text that has just appeared, Thomas Keenan also analyzes, among other things, what gets 'sublimated' in this 'ghostly reality': 'In the rigor of the abstraction, only ghosts survive' ('The Point Is To (Ex)change It,' in *Fetishism as Cultural Discourse*, E. Apter and W. Pietz, eds. [Ithaca: Cornell University Press, 1993], p. 168).

13. For all these motifs, we refer obviously to the work of Paul Virilio, as well as to Bernard Stiegler, *La technique et le temps, La faute d'Épiméthée* (Paris: Galilée, 1994).

14. The palindromic syntax here is: 'tout autre est tout autre,' both 'every other is altogether other,' and 'altogether other is every other.' [Trans.]

15. Why does Freud consider haunting to be 'perhaps the most striking of all [examples],' a kind of prototype, in the experience of *Unheimlichkeit*? Because many people experience 'in the highest degree' (*im allerhöchsten Grade*) the sense of the 'unheimlich' 'in relation to death and dead bodies, to the return of the dead, and to spirits and ghosts' (*Geistern und Gespenstern*). But to the great chagrin of translators, Freud wants to illustrate this assertion by remarking not that 'es spukt' is so difficult to translate (for the reasons we indicated above), but that 'some languages in use to-day can only render the German expression 'ein unheimliches Haus' by a house in which 'es spukt' [*manche moderne Sprachen unseren Ausdruck: ein unheimliches Haus gar nicht anders wiedergeben können als durch dies Umschreibung: ein Haus, in dem es spukt*]' ('Das Unheimliche,' *Gesammelte Werke*, XII, pp. 254–55). In truth, 'unheimliche' is just as untranslatable as 'es spukt.' And this yields awkward and in fact incomprehensible translations. For example: 'plusieurs langues modernes ne peuvent rendre notre expression "une maison *unheimlich*" autrement que par cette circonlocution: une maison hantée' ('L'Inquiétante étrangeté,' trans. M. Bonaparte et E. Marty, in *Essais de psychanalyse appliquée* [Paris: Gallimard, 1933], pp. 194–95); or again: 'some languages in use to-day can only render the German expression "an *unheimlich* house" by "a *haunted* house"' (*Standard Edition*, Vol. XVII, p. 241). As for what Freud then puts forward concerning death itself, we return to it elsewhere in order to relate it to the discourses of Heidegger and Lévinas on this subject (cf. *Aporias*). Another period, another modality, another mode for ghosts: Freud remarks, on the same page, that distinguished lectures on communication with spirits were showing a tendency to proliferate. Subtle minds, he notes, among men of science and especially at the end of their lives, give into the telepathic or mediumistic temptation. He knew what he was talking about. And since *Hamlet* will have been our subject, let us specify that Freud deemed its apparitions wholly devoid of any power of *Unheimlichkeit* (*GW*, p. 265; *SE*, p 251). Like those of Macbeth or Julius Caesar, like those in Dante's Inferno. They may be terrifying (*schreckhaft*) or lugubrious (*düster*), to be sure, but no more *unheimlich* than the world of Homeric gods. Explanation: literature, theatrical fiction. According to Freud, we adapt our judgment to the conditions of *fictive* reality, such as they are established by the poet, and treat 'souls, spirits, and specters' like grounded, normal, legitimate existences (*vollberechtige Existenzen*). A remark that is all the more surprising in that all the examples of *Unheimlichkeit* in this essay are borrowed from literature!

16. Freud and Heidegger. In *The Post Card* (Chicago: Chicago University Press, 1987), the signatory of *Envois* couples them like two specters: 'Here Freud and Heidegger, I conjoin them within me like the two great ghosts of the "great epoch." The two surviving grandfathers. They did not know each other, but

according to me they form a couple, and in fact just because of that, this singular anachrony' (p. 191).

Given that a *revenant* is always called upon to come and to come back, the thinking of the specter, contrary to what good sense leads us to believe, signals toward the future. It is a thinking of the past, a legacy that can come only from that which has not yet arrived—from the *arrivant* itself.

Chapter 7

From Memoirs of the Blind

. . . But let me pick up my story. With the exhibition already envisaged, I have to cancel a first meeting at the Department of Drawings with Françoise Viatte, Régis Michel, and Yseult Séverac.[1] It is July 5th, and I have been suffering for thirteen days from facial paralysis caused by a virus, from what is called *a frigore* (disfiguration, the facial nerve inflamed, the left side of the face stiffened, the left eye transfixed and horrible to behold in a mirror—a real sight for sore eyes—the eyelid no longer closing normally: a loss of the 'wink' or 'blink,' therefore, this moment of blindness that ensures sight its breath). On July 5th this trivial ailment has just begun to heal. It is finally getting better after two weeks of terror—the unforgettable itself—two weeks of vigilant medical attention (superequipped surveillance, if you hear what I mean, with instruments—anoptic or blind—that sound out, that allow one to know *[savoir]* there where one no longer sees *[voir]*: not the luminous rays of radioscopy or radiography but the play of waves and echoes, the electromyogram, by means of 'galvanic stimulation of the orbicular muscles of the eyelids and lips,' the measurement of the 'blinking reflexes' by the 'orbicular recording of the eyelids,' the 'Ultrasonic Cervical Assessment' with a transcranial *doppler*, echotomography searching for the 'intraluminal echo,' the *scanner*'s computer blindly transcribing the coded signals of the photoelectric cells).

—Things certainly do happen to you, day and night.

—You better believe it *[il faut croire]*; I will have seen my share of late, it's true. And all this is documented, I am not the only one who could bear witness to it. And so on July 11th I am healed (a feeling of conversion or resurrection, the eyelid blinking once again, my face still haunted by a ghost of disfiguration). We have our first meeting at the Louvre. That same evening while driving home, the theme of the exhibition hits me. All of a sudden, in an instant. I scribble at the wheel a provisional title for my own use, to organize my notes: *L'ouvre où ne pas voir* [*The Open Where Not To See*],[2] which becomes, upon my return, an icon, indeed a window to 'open' on my computer screen.

As I told you, this must not be read as the journal of an exhibition. From all this I retain only the chance or the place for a thoughtful question: what would a journal of the blind be like? A newspaper or daily of the blind? Or else the more personal kind of journal, a diary or day-book? And what about the day, then, the rhythm of the days and nights without day or light, the dates and calendars that scan memories and memoirs? How would the memoirs of the blind be written? I say memoirs, and not yet songs, or narratives, or poems of the blind—in the great filiation of the night that buries Homer and Joyce, Milton and Borges. Let's let them wait in the background. I am satisfied for the moment with coupling them off two by two—these great, dead-eyed elders of our literary memory—as in the double rivalry of a duel. The author of *Ulysses*, after having written his own odyssey (itself haunted by a 'blindman'), ends his life almost blind, one cornea operation after another. Hence the themes of the iris and glaucoma pervade *Finnegans Wake* ('. . . the shudder-some spectacle of this semidemented zany amid the inspissated grime of his glaucous den making believe to read his usylessly unreadable Blue Book of Eccles, *édition de ténèbres* . . .).[3] The whole Joycean oeuvre cultivates seeing eye canes.

As for Borges, among the blind ancestors whom he identifies or claims in the gallery of Western literature, it is clearly Milton who is his rival; it is with Milton that he would like to identify himself, and it is from Milton that he awaits, with or without modesty, the noble lineage of his own blindness. For this wound is also a sign of being chosen, a sign that one must know how to recognize in oneself, the privilege of a destination, an assigned mission: in the night, by the night itself. To call upon the great tradition of blind writers, Borges thus turns round an invisible mirror. He sketches at once a celebration of memory and a self-portrait. But he describes himself by pointing to the other blind man, to Milton, especially to the Milton who authored that other self-portrait, *Samson Agonistes*. The confession is entitled *Blindness*:

> Wilde said that the Greeks claimed that Homer was blind in order to emphasize that poetry must be aural, not visual. . . . Let us go on to the example of Milton. Milton's blindness was voluntary. He knew from the beginning that he was going to be a great poet. This has occurred to other poets. . . . I too, if I may mention myself, have always known that my destiny was, above all, a literary destiny—that bad things and some good things would happen to me, but that, in the long run, all of it would be converted into words. . . . Let us return to Milton. He destroyed his sight writing pamphlets in support of the execution of the king by Parliament. Milton said that he lost his sight voluntarily, defending freedom; he spoke of that noble task and never complained of being blind. . . . He spent a good part of his time alone, composing verses, and his memory had grown. He would hold forty or fifty hendecasyllables of blank verse in his memory and then dictate them to whomever came to visit. The whole poem was written in this way. He thought of the fate of Samson, so close to his own, for now Cromwell was dead and the hour of the Restoration had come. . . . But when they brought Charles II—son of Charles I, 'The Executed'—the list of those condemned to death, he put down his pen and said, not without

nobility, 'There is something in my right hand that will not allow me to sign a sentence of death.' Milton was saved, and many others with him. He then wrote Samson Agonistes.[4]

A singular genealogy, a singular illustration, an illustration of oneself among all these illustrious blind men who keep each other in memory, who greet and recognize one another in the night. Borges begins with Homer; he then ends with Joyce—and, still just as modestly, with the self-portrait of the author as a blind man, as a man of memory, and this, just after an allusion to castration.

> Joyce brought a new music to English. And he said, valorously (and mendaciously) that 'of all the things that have happened to me, I think the least important was having been blind.' Part of his vast work was executed in darkness: polishing the sentences in his memory. . . . Democritus of Abdera tore his eyes out in a garden so that the spectacle of reality would not distract him; Origen castrated himself. I have enumerated enough examples. Some are so illustrious that I am ashamed to have spoken of my own personal case—except for the fact that people always hope for confessions and I have no reason to deny them mine. But, of course, it seems absurd to place my name next to those I have recalled.[5]

I had you observe that Borges 'begins with Homer.' In truth, he begins with Wilde, who was himself speaking of Homer. Now, Wilde happens to be the author of *The Picture of Dorian Gray*, a tale of murder or suicide, of *ruin* and *confession*. It is also the story of a representation that carries death: a deadly portrait first reflects the progressive ruin on the face of its model who is also its spectator, the subject being thus looked at, then condemned, by his image:

> It was his beauty that had ruined him. . . . There was blood on the painted feet, as though the thing had dripped—blood even on the hand that had not held the knife. Confess? Did it mean that he was to confess? To give himself up, and be put to death?[6]

The literature of murderous works. On the wall of the same exhibition one would have to hang Poe's *The Oval Portrait*: a portrait at once *seen* and *read*, the story of an artist who kills his drawn out, exhausted model—his wife, in fact—after having given her body over to ruin. The experience of a painter coupled with his model is that of a husband who

> . . . *would* not see that the light which fell so ghastlily in that lone turret withered the health and the spirits of his bride, who pined visibly to all but him . . . the painter . . . wrought day and night to depict her who so loved him. . . . And he *would* not see that the tints which he spread upon the canvas were drawn from the cheeks of her who sat beside him. [The portrait just finished, the husband] grew tremulous and very pallid, and aghast, and crying with a loud voice, 'This is indeed *Life* itself!' turned suddenly to regard his beloved:—*She was dead*.[7]

This is not, then, the journal of an exhibition. I was more than just honored by the invitation that was extended to me; I was intimidated, deeply worried even, by it. And I still am, no doubt well beyond what is reasonable. The anxiety was, of course, mixed with an obscure jubilation. For I have always experienced drawing as an infirmity, even worse, as a culpable infirmity, dare I say, an obscure punishment. A double infirmity: to this day I still think that I will never know *either* how to draw *or* how to look at a drawing. In truth, I feel myself incapable of following with my hand the prescription of a model: it is as if, just as I was about to draw, I no longer *saw* the thing. For it immediately flees, drops out of sight, and almost nothing of it remains; it disappears before my eyes, which, in truth, no longer perceive anything but the mocking arrogance of this disappearing apparition. As long as it remains in front of me, the thing defies me, producing, as if by emanation, an invisibility that it reserves for me, a night of which I would be, in some way, the chosen one. It blinds me while making me attend the pitiful spectacle. By *exposing me*, by *showing me up*, it takes me to task but also makes me bear witness. Whence a sort of passion of drawing, a negative and impotent passion, the jealousy of a drawing in abeyance. And which I see without seeing. The child within me wonders: how can one claim to look at both a model and the lines *[traits]* that one jealously dedicates with one's own hand to the thing itself? Doesn't one have to be blind to one or the other? Doesn't one always have to be content with the memory of the other? . . .

• • •

. . . —We are talking here about drawing, not painting. From this point of view, there are, it seems to me, at least *three* types of powerlessness for the eye, or let us say, three *aspects*, to underscore once again with a *trait* that which gives the experience of the gaze (*aspicere*) over to blindness. *Aspectus* is at once gaze, sight, *and* that which meets the eyes: on one side, the spectator, and on the other, the aspect, in other words, the spectacle. In English, *spectacles* are glasses. This powerlessness is not an impotence or failure; on the contrary, it gives to the experience of drawing its *quasi-transcendental* resource.

I would see the *first aspect*—as we will call it—in the *aperspective of the graphic act*. In its originary, pathbreaking *[frayage]* moment, in the *tracing* potency of the *trait*, at the instant when the point at the point of the hand (of the body proper in general) moves forward upon making contact with the surface, the inscription of the inscribable is not seen. Whether it be improvised or not, the invention of the *trait* does not follow, it does not conform to what is presently visible, to what would be set in front of me as a theme. Even if drawing is, as they say, mimetic, that is, reproductive, figurative, representative, even if the model is presently facing the artist, the *trait* must proceed in the night. It escapes the field of vision. Not only because it *is not yet* visible,[8] but because it does not belong to the realm of the spectacle, of spectacular objectivity— and so that which it makes happen or come *[advenir]* cannot in itself be mimetic. The heterogeneity between the thing drawn and the drawing *trait* remains abyssal, whether it be between a thing represented and its represen- tation or between the model and the image. The night of this abyss can be interpreted in two ways, either as the eve or the memory of the day, that is, as a reserve of visibility (the draftsman does not presently see but he has seen and will see again: the aperspective as the anticipating perspective or the anamnesic retrospective), or else as radically and definitively foreign to the phenomenality of the day. This heterogeneity of the invisible to the visible can haunt the visible as its very possibility. Whether one underscores this with the words of Plato or Merleau-Ponty, the visibility of the visible cannot, by definition, be seen, no more than what Aristotle speaks of as the diaphanous- ness of light can be. My hypothesis—remember that we are still within the logic of the hypothesis—is that the draftsman always sees himself to be prey to that which is each time universal and singular and would thus have to be called the *unbeseen*, as one speaks of the unbeknownst. He recalls it, is called, fascinated, or recalled by it. Memory or not, and forgetting as memory, in memory and without memory.

On the one hand, then, *anamnesis: anamnesis of memory itself*. Baudelaire relates the invisibility of the model to the memory that will have borne that model. He 'restores' invisibility to memory. And what the poet of *The Blind* says is all the more convincing in that he speaks of the graphic *image*, of representative drawing. This goes *a fortiori* for the other kind of drawing. One would have to cite here all of *Mnemonic Art*. For example:

> I refer to Monsieur G's method of draftsmanship. He draws from memory and not from the model. . . . [A]ll good and true draftsmen draw from the image imprinted on their brains, and not from nature. To the objection that there are admirable sketches of the latter type by Raphael, Watteau, and many others, I would reply that these are notes—very scrupulous notes, to be sure, but mere notes, none the less. When a true artist has come to the point of the final execution of his work, the model would be more of an embarassment than a help to him. It even happens that men such as Daumier and Monsieur G, long accustomed to exercising their memory and storing it with images, find that the physical presence of the model and its multiplicity of details disconcerts and as it were paralyzes their principal faculty.[9]

Baudelaire, it is true, interprets memory as a natural reserve, without history, tragedy, or event, as, in his words, the *naturally sacrificial* matrix of a visible order that is selected, chosen, filtered. It breaks with the present of visual perception only in order to keep a better eye on drawing. Creative memory, schematization, the time and schema of Kant's transcendental imagination, with its 'synthesis' and its 'ghosts.' 'Duel' is also one of Baudelaire's words, a duel, as in my dream, between two blind men—and for the appropriation of excess: the (no)-more-sight *[le plus-de-vue]*, the visionary vision of the *seer* who sees beyond the visible present, the overseeing, sur-view, or survival of sight. And the draftsman who trusts in sight, in present sight, who fears the suspension of visual perception, who does not want to be done with mourning it, who does not want to let it go, this draftsman begins to go blind simply through the fear of losing his sight. This cripple is already on the road to blindness; he is 'near-sighted or far-sighted.' The Baudelairian rhetoric also makes use of political tropes or figures:

> *In this way a duel* (my emphasis, J. D.) is established between the will to see everything and forget nothing and the faculty of memory, which has formed the habit of a lively absorption of general color and of silhouette, the arabesque of contour. An artist with a perfect sense of form but accustomed to relying above all on his memory and his imagination will find himself at the mercy of a riot of details all clamoring for justice with the fury of a mob in love with absolute equality. All justice is trampled under foot; all harmony *sacrificed* (my emphasis, J. D.) and destroyed; many a trifle assumes vast proportions; many a triviality usurps the attention. The more our artist turns an impartial eye on detail, the greater the state of anarchy. Whether he be nearsighted or far-sighted, all hierarchy and all subordination vanishes. This is an accident that is often conspicuous. . . .

And so, for Baudelaire, it is the *order of memory* that precipitates, beyond present perception, the absolute speed of the instant (the time of the *clin d'œil* that buries the gaze in the batting of an eyelid, the instant called the *Augenblick*, the wink or blink, and what drops out of sight in the twinkling of an eye),[10] but also the 'synthesis,' the 'phantom,' the 'fear,' the fear of seeing *and* of not seeing what one must not see, hence the very thing that one must see, the fear of seeing without seeing the eclipse between the two, the 'unconscious execution,' and especially the figures that substitute one art for another, the analogical or *economic* (i.e., the familial) rhetoric of which we were just speaking —the *trait*-for-a-*trait*.

> Thus two elements are to be discerned in Monsieur G's execution: the first, an intense effort of memory that evokes and calls back to life—a memory that says to everything, 'Arise, Lazarus'; the second, a fire, an intoxication of the pencil or the brush, amounting almost to a frenzy. It is the fear of not going fast enough, of letting the phantom escape before the synthesis has been extracted and pinned down; it is that terrible fear that takes possession of all great artists and gives them such a passionate desire to become masters of every means of expression so that the orders of the brain may never be perverted by the hesitations of the hand and that finally execution, ideal execution, may become as unconscious and *spontaneous* as digestion is for a healthy man after dinner.

By attributing the origin of drawing to memory rather than to perception, Baudelaire is, in turn, making a show of memory. He is writing himself into an iconographic tradition that goes back to at least Charles Le Brun.[11] In this tradition, the origin of drawing and the origin of painting give rise to multiple representations that substitute memory for perception. First, because they are *re*presentations, next, because they are drawn most often from an exemplary narrative (that of Butades, the young Corinthian lover who bears the name of her father, a potter from Sicyon), and finally, because the narrative relates the origin of graphic representation to the absence or invisibility of the model. Butades does not see her lover, either because she turns her back to him — more abiding than Orpheus — or because he turns his back to her, or again, because their gazes simply cannot meet (see, for example, J. B. Suvée's *Butades or the Origin of Drawing*):[12] it is as if seeing were forbidden in order to draw, as if one drew only on the condition of not seeing, as if the drawing were a declaration of love destined for or suited to the invisibility of the other — unless it were in fact born from seeing the other withdrawn from sight. Whether Butades follows the *traits* of a shadow or a silhouette — her hand sometimes guided by Cupid (a Love who sees and, here, is not blindfolded) — or whether she draws on the surface of a wall or on a veil,[13] a *skiagraphia* or shadow writing in each case inaugurates an art of blindness. From the outset, perception belongs to recollection. Butades writes, and thus already loves in nostalgia. Detached from the present of perception, fallen from the thing itself — which is thus divided — a shadow is a simultaneous memory, and Butades' stick is a staff of the blind. Let's follow its course in Regnault's picture (*Butades Tracing the Portrait of Her Shepherd or the Origin of Painting*), as we have done for all the drawings of the blind: it goes back and forth between love and drawing. Rousseau wanted to grant it speech, to give it the floor. In the *Essay on the Origin of Languages*, he writes:

> Love, it is said, was the inventor of drawing. Love might also have invented speech, though less happily. Dissatisfied with speech, love disdains it: it has livelier ways of expressing itself. How many things the girl who took such pleasure in tracing her Lover's shadow was telling him! What sounds could she have used to convey this movement of the stick?[14]

On the other hand, and in anamnesis itself, there is *amnesia*, the orphan of memory, for the invisible can also lose its memory, as one loses one's parents. On a different trail, which perhaps comes down to the same one, the draftsman would be given over to this other invisibility, given over to it in the same way that a hunter, *himself in relentless pursuit*, becomes a fascinating lure for the tracked animal that watches him. In order to be absolutely foreign to the visible and even to the potentially visible, to the possibility of the visible, this invisibility would still inhabit the visible, or rather, it would come to haunt it to the point of being confused with it, in order to assure, from the specter of this very impossibility, its most proper resource. The visible *as such* would be invisible, not as visib*ility*, the *phenomenality or essence* of the visible, but as the singular body of the visible itself, *right on* the visible—so that, by emanation, and as if it were secreting its own *medium*, the visible would produce blindness. Whence a program for an entire rereading of the later Merleau-Ponty. Let us be satisfied, for lack of space, with a few indications from *The Visible and the Invisible*. Rather than recall the 'teleperception' or the four 'layers' of the invisible, which, as Merleau-Ponty explains,[15] cannot be '*logically*' brought together —(1) 'what is not actually visible, but could be,' (2) the framework of the nonvisible existentials of the visible, (3) the tactile or kinesthetic, (4) the sayable, the '*lekta*' or the '*Cogito*'—I would rather have followed the traces of *absolute* invisibility. To be the other of the visible, *absolute* invisibility must neither take place elsewhere nor constitute another visible, that is, something that does not yet appear or has already disappeared—something whose spectacle of monumental ruins would call for reconstitution, regathering from memory, rememberment. This nonvisible does not describe a phenomenon that is present elsewhere, that is latent, imaginary, unconscious, hidden, or past; it is a 'phenomenon' whose inappearance is of another kind; and what we have here seen fit to call transcendentality is not unrelated to what Merleau-Ponty speaks of as 'pure transcendence, without an ontic mask':

> January, 1960. Principle: not to consider the invisible as an *other visible* 'possible,' or a 'possible' visible for an other. . . . The invisible is *there* without being an *object*, it is pure transcendence, without an ontic mask. And the 'visibles' themselves, in the last analysis, they too are only centered on a nucleus of absence—
>
> Raise the question: the invisible life, the invisible community, the invisible other, the invisible culture.
>
> Elaborate a phenomenology of 'the other world,' as the limit of a phenomenology of the imaginary and the 'hidden'[16]—
>
> [May 1960]. When I say that every visible is invisible, that perception is imperception, that consciousness has a '*punctum caecum*,' that to see is always to see more than one sees—this must not be understood in the sense of a *contradiction*—it must not be imagined that I add to the visible . . . a nonvisible. . . . —One has to understand that it is visibility itself that involves a nonvisibility.[17]

And again:

> *What* [consciousness] does not see it does not see for reasons of principle; it is because it is consciousness that it does not see. *What* it does not see is what in it prepares the vision of the rest (as the retina is blind at the point where the fibers that will permit the vision spread out into it).[18]
>
> To touch *oneself*, to see *oneself* . . . is not to apprehend oneself as an ob-ject, it is to be open to oneself, destined to oneself (narcissism)—. . . .
>
> The feeling that one feels, the seeing that one sees, is not a thought of seeing or of feeling, but vision, feeling, mute experience of a mute meaning[19]—

The *aperspective* thus obliges us to consider the objective definition, the anatomico-physiology or ophthalmology of the '*punctum caecum,*' as itself a mere image, an analogical index of vision itself, of vision in general, of that which, seeing itself see, is nevertheless not reflected, cannot be 'thought' in the specular or speculative mode—and thus is blinded because of this, blinded at this point of 'narcissism,' at that very point where it sees itself looking.

—I'll agree that, at its originary point, the *trait* is invisible and the drafts-man is blind to it, but what about afterwards, once the line has been traced?

—Let's look now at the *second aspect.* It is not an aftereffect, a second or sec-ondary aspect. It appears, or rather disappears, without delay. I will name it the *withdrawal [retrait] or the eclipse, the differential inappearance of the trait.* We have been interested thus far in the act of tracing, in the tracing of the *trait.* What is to be thought now of the *trait once traced*? That is, not of its pathbreaking course, not of the inaugural path of the trace, but of that which remains of it? A tracing, an outline, cannot be seen. One should in fact not see it (let's not say however: 'One *must* not see it') insofar as all the colored thickness that it retains tends to wear itself out so as to mark the single edge of a contour: between the inside and the outside of a figure. Once this limit is reached, there is nothing more to see, not even black and white, not even figure/form, and this is the *trait,* this is the line itself: which is thus no longer what it is, because from then on it never relates to itself without dividing itself just as soon, the divisibility of the *trait* here interrupting all pure identification and forming—one will have no doubt understood it by now—our *general hypothec*[20] for all thinking about drawing—inaccessible in the end, at the limit, and *de jure.* This limit is never presently reached, but drawing always signals toward this inaccessibility, toward the threshold where only the surroundings of the *trait* appear—that which the *trait* spaces by delimiting and which thus does not belong to the *trait. Nothing belongs to the trait,* and thus, to drawing and to the thought of drawing, not even its own 'trace.' Nothing even partic-ipates in it. The *trait* joins and adjoins only in separating.

Is it by chance that in order to speak of the *trait* we are falling back upon the language of negative theology or of those discourses concerned with naming the withdrawal *[retrait]* of the invisible or hidden god? The withdrawal of the One whom one must not look in the face, or represent, or adore, that is, idolize under the *traits* or guise of the icon? The One whom it is even dangerous to name by one or the other of his proper names? The end of iconography. The memory of the *drawings-of-the-blind [dessins-d'avengles]*—it has been only too clear for quite some time now—opens up like a God-memory *[mémoire-Dieu].*[21] It is theological through and through, to the point, sometimes included, sometimes excluded, where the self-eclipsing *trait* cannot even be spoken about, cannot even say itself in the present, since it is not gathered, since it does not gather itself, into any present, 'I am who I am' (a formula whose original grammatical form, as we know, implies the future). The outline or tracing separates and separates itself; it retraces only borderlines, intervals, a spacing grid with no possible appropriation. The *experience* or *experimenting* of drawing (and experimenting, as its name indicates, always consists in journeying beyond limits) at once crosses and institutes these borders, it invents the *Shibboleth* of these passages (the chorus of *Samson Agonistes* recalls that which links the *Shibboleth*, this circumcision of the tongue, of language, to the death sentence: '. . . when so many died / Without reprieve adjudged to death, / For want of well pronouncing Shibboleth').[22]

The linear limit I am talking about is in no way *ideal* or *intelligible*. It divides itself in its ellipsis; *by leaving* itself, and starting *from itself*, it takes leave of itself, and establishes itself in no ideal identity. In this twinkling of an eye, the ellipsis is not an object but a blinking of the difference that begets it, or, if you prefer, a *jalousie* (a blind) of *traits* cutting up the horizon, *traits* through which, *between* which, you can observe without being seen, you can see between the lines, if you see what I mean: the law of the inter-view. For the same reason, the *trait* is not *sensible*, as a patch of color would be. Neither intelligible nor sensible. We are speaking here of graphic and not color blindness, of drawing and not painting, even if a certain painting can wear itself out by painting drawing, indeed by representing—in order to make it into a picture—the allegory of an 'origin of drawing.' For if we *left* the Platonic cave a while back, it was not in order finally to see the *eidos* of the thing itself after a conversion, anabasis, or anamnesis. We left the cave behind because the Platonic speleology misses, is unable to take into account if not to see, the inappearance of a *trait* that is neither sensible nor intelligible. It misses the *trait* precisely because it believes that it sees it or lets it be seen. The lucidity of this speleology carries within it another blind man, not the cave dweller, the blind man deep down, but the one who closes his eyes to *this* blindness—*right here*. (Let us leave for another occasion the treatment Plato reserves for those great blind men Homer and Oedipus.)

'Before' *['avant']* all the 'blind spots' that, literally or figuratively, organize the scopic field and the scene of drawing, 'before' all that can happen *to* sight, 'before' all the interpretations, ophthalmologies, and theo-psychoanalyses of sacrifice or castration, there would thus be the ecliptic rhythm of the *trait*, the blind *[jalousie]*, the abocular contraction that lets one see 'from-since' *['depuis']* the unbeseen. 'Before' and 'from-since': these draw in time or space an order that does not belong to them—is this not all too clear?

—If this was indeed the initial idea for the exhibition, one will always be able to say, without fear of self-deception, that you are in fact seeking to transcendentalize, that is, to ennoble an infirmity or an impotence: does not your blindness to drawing respond to a universal necessity? Is it not the response *par excellence* to an essence of the *trait*, to an invisibility inscribed right on the *trait*? Would you not claim in your jealous, even envious passion, in your wounded impotence, to be more faithful to the *trait*, to the *trait* in its most refined end or finality? As for the 'great draftsman'—to follow your suggestion—does he not also try in vain, up to the point of exhausting a *ductus* or stylus, to capture this withdrawal *[retrait]* of the *trait*, to remark it, to sign it finally—in an endless scarification?

—But say I admitted this, would it be enough to disqualify my hypothesis? This rhetoric of avowal or confession in which you would like to confine me leads us to the *third aspect: the rhetoric of the trait.* For is it not the withdrawal *[retrait]* of the line—that which draws the line back, draws it again *[retire]*, at the very moment when the *trait* is drawn, when it draws away *[se tire]*—that which grants speech? And at the same time forbids separating drawing from the discursive murmur whose trembling transfixes it? This question does not aim at restoring an authority of speech over sight, of word over drawing, or of legend over inscription.[23] It is, rather, a matter of understanding how this hegemony could have imposed itself. Wherever drawing is consonant with and articulated by a sonorous and temporal wave, its rhythm composes with the invisible: even before a Gorgon's mask resounds (for a terrible cry sometimes accompanied its gaze), even before it turns you stone blind. It is still by way of figure that we speak of rhetoric, in order to point out with a supplementary trope this huge domain: the drawing of men. For we here reserve the question of what is obscurely called the animal—which is not incapable of traces. The limit that we leave here in the dark appears all the more unstable since it is there that we necessarily come across the 'monstrosities' of the eye, zoo-theo-anthropomorphic figures, shifting or proliferating transplants or grafts, unclassifiable hybrids of which the Gorgons and Cyclopes are only the best known examples. It is said that the sight of certain animals is more powerful, sharper—more cruel, too—than man's, and yet that it lacks a gaze.

The drawing of men, in any case, never goes without being articulated with articulation, without the order being given with words (recall the angel Raphael), without some order, without the order of narrative, and thus of memory, without the order to bury, the order of prayer, the order of names to be given or blessed. Drawing comes in the place of the name, which comes in the place of drawing: in order, like Butades, to hear oneself call the other or be called (by) the other. As soon as a name comes to haunt drawing, even the without-name of God that first opens up the space of naming, the blind are tied in with those who see. An internal duel breaks out at the very heart of drawing.

The *transcendental retrait* or *withdrawal* at once calls for and forbids the self-portrait. Not that of the author and presumed signatory, but that of the 'source-point' of drawing, the eye and the finger, if you will. This point is represented and eclipsed at the same time. It lends itself to the autograph of this wink or *clin d'œil* that plunges it into the night, or rather, into the time of this waning or declining day wherein the face is submerged: it gets carried away, it decomposes itself or lets itself be devoured by a mouth of darkness. Certain self-portraits of Fantin-Latour show this. Or rather, they would be the figures or the de-monstration of this. Sometimes invisibility is *shared out [s'y partage]*, if one can say this, right between the two eyes. There is *on the one hand [d'une part]* the monocular stare of a narcissistic cyclops: a single eye open, the right one, fixed firmly on its own image. It will not let it go, but that's because the prey necessarily eludes it, making off with the lure. The *traits* of a self-portrait are also those of a fascinated hunter. The staring eye always resembles an eye of the blind, sometimes the eye of the dead, at that precise moment when mourning begins: it is still open, a pious hand should soon come to close it; it would recall a portrait of the dying. Looking at itself seeing, it also sees itself disappear right at the moment when the drawing tries desperately to recapture it. For this cyclops eye sees nothing, nothing but an eye that it thus prevents from seeing anything at all. Seeing the seeing and not the visible, it sees nothing. This seeing eye sees itself blind. *On the other hand [d'autre part]*, and this would be, as it were, the eye's nocturnal truth, the *other* eye is already plunged into the night, sometimes just barely hidden, veiled, withdrawn *[en retrait]*, sometimes totally indiscernible and dissolved into a blotch, and sometimes absorbed by the shadow cast upon it by a top hat shaped like an eyeshade. From one blindness, the other. At the moment of the autograph, and with the most intense lucidity, the seeing blind man observes himself and has others observe . . .

Notes

1. They have since then guided my steps, and I owe them, along with Jean Galard, all my thanks for having done it with such clairvoyant generosity. These *Memoirs* are, naturally, dedicated to them as a sign of gratitude.
2. Note that *L'ouvre* is pronounced like 'Louvre.' [Trans.]
3. James Joyce, *Finnegans Wake* (New York: The Viking Press, 1967), p. 179. Compare '. . . spectacle quelque peu frissonnant de ce bouffon semi démenté, par l'épaisse crasse de son antre glauque, que l'on fit semblant de lire son *Initulyssible* parce qu'illisible Livre Bleu de Klee, édition de ténèbres . . .' (French translation, Ph. Lavergne (Paris, 1982), p. 194). Of necessity, the French translation loses much: not only, and this was not inevitable, the fact that 'édition de ténèbres' is in French in the original text, thereby making the original language invisible in translation, invisible in its very 'ténèbres'—in its shadows; but more seriously, it loses its sight,

even better, the allusion to the loss of the eye: 'usylessly,' which is also to say, 'as if without an eye,' eyeless.

4. 'Blindness,' trans. Eliot Weinberger, in *Seven Nights* (New York: New Directions, 1984), pp. 115– 17. To this conference, which ought to be quoted in its entirety, one must append a few pages entitled 'L'auteur,' i.e., 'The Maker' (in *A Personal Anthology*, trans. Alastair Reid (New York: Grove Press, 1967), pp. 112–14). The themes of *memory* and *descent* regularly intersect here, around a memory that was perhaps a dream: 'When he realized that he was going blind, he wept . . . but one morning he awoke, saw (free of shadows) the obscure things surrounding him, and felt . . . that all this had happened to him before. . . . Then he went deep into his memory, which seemed bottomless, and managed from that dizzying descent to retrieve the lost remembrance that shone like a coin in moonlight, perhaps because he had never faced it except possibly in a dream.

'The memory was as follows: another youth had insulted him, and he had gone to his father and told him the story. His father let him talk, appearing neither to listen nor to understand; and then he took down from the wall a bronze dagger, handsome and charged with power, which the boy had secretly coveted. Now he held it in his hands, and the astonishment of possessing it wiped out the hurt he had suffered, but the voice of his father was saying, "Let someone know you are a man," and there was a firmness in his voice. Night obscured the paths. Clasping the dagger, which he felt to be endowed with magic power, he descended the sharp slope surrounding the house and ran to the sea's edge, imagining himself Ajax and Perseus, and peopling the sea-smelling dark with wounds and battles. The precise flavor of that moment was what he was looking for now; the rest did not matter to him—the insults of the quarrel, the cumbersome fight, the return with the bloodstained blade.

'Another memory, also involving night and an expectation of adventure, sprang up from that one. A woman, the first which the gods had offered him, had waited for him in the shade of a hypogeum. . . . In that night of his mortal eyes, into which he was now descending . . . [he had] an inkling of the Odysseys and Iliads which he was destined to create and leave behind, resounding in the concavity of the human memory. We know these things; but not the things he felt as he descended into the ultimate darkness.'

5. 'Blindness,' in *Seven Nights*, p. 119.

6. Oscar Wilde, *The Picture of Dorian Gray and Other Writings* (New York: Bantam, 1982), pp. 190–91.

7. Edgar Allan Poe, 'The Oval Portrait,' in *Great Short Works of Edgar Allan Poe* (New York: Harper & Row, 1970), pp. 358–59.

8. 'What is it to draw?, asks Van Gogh. 'How do we do it? It is the act of clearing a path for oneself through an invisible iron wall.' This letter is cited by Artaud (*Oeuvres Complètes*, 13 :40). In an essay devoted to the drawings and portraits of Antonin Artaud ('Forcener le subjectile,' in *Dessins et portraits d'Antonin Artaud*, ed. Jacques Derrida and Paule Thévenin [Paris: Galliard, 1986]), I try in particular to interpret the relationship between what Artaud calls drawing's necessary awkwardness or *mal-adresse* in the path-clearing of the invisible and the rejection

of a certain theological order of the visible, the rejection of another *maladresse* of God as 'the art of drawing.' It is as if Artaud here countersigned Rimbaud's willful blindness: 'Yes, my eyes are closed to your light. I am not Christian.'

9. Charles Baudelaire, 'Mnemonic Art,' in *The Painter of Modern Life and Other Essays*, trans. and ed. Jonathan Mayne (New York: Da Capo Press, Reprint of Phaidon Press Ltd., 1986), pp. 16–17. Two references have been suggested for the poem *Les aveugles [The Blind]*. For essential reasons, which have to do with the structure of reference and the poem, these must remain nothing more than hypotheses. The first concerns an etching or lithograph after the painting of Bruegel the Elder ('The Parable of the Blind' in the Naples Museum, a copy of which was acquired by the Louvre in 1893). The other hypothesis of reference refers to *Hoffman, Contes posthumes* (1856), a book by Champfleury. In the note that he devotes to this question, Claude Pichois recalls that in this book 'the *I* declares that the blind can be recognized by the way they tilt their heads upwards,' while 'the *Cousin* says to him that the interior eye seeks to perceive the eternal light that shines in the other world' (Pléiade, t. 1: 1021).

10. 'Wink,' 'blink,' and 'in the twinkling of an eye' are all in English in the original. [Trans.]

11. This is the hypothesis of George Levitine, who is trying to refine or rectify the hypotheses of Robert Rosenblum in his very rich study, 'The Origin of Painting: A Problem in the Iconography of Romantic Classicism,' *The Art Bulletin*, vol. 39 (1957). Rosenblum had considered Runciman's *The Origin of Painting* (1771) to have inaugurated this inexhaustible 'iconographic tradition' in memory of Butades, the young Corinthian woman who bore her father's name and who, 'facing a separation from her lover for some time, noticed on a wall the shadow of this young man sketched by the light of a lamp. Love inspired in her the idea of keeping for herself this cherished image by tracing over the shadow a line that followed and precisely marked its outline. This lover's father was a potter from Sicyon named *Butades* . . .' (Antoine d'Origny, cited by Rosenblum, 'Origin of Painting,' n. 21). Let us note that, in the topography that is here traced back, the apparatus of the origin of drawing recalls quite precisely that of the Platonic speleology. In his 'Addenda' to Rosenblum's study (in *The Art Bulletin*, vol. 40 [1958]), Levitine directs us back to some anterior, and thus, in sum, more originary 'origins of drawing.' The first would be an engraving inspired by a drawing of Charles Le Brun (before 1676), the other, an engraving inspired by a drawing of Charles-Nicolas Cochin, Jr. (1769). In both cases, one sees the young Corinthian woman, her lover, and Cupid. In Le Brun's version Cupid guides Butades' hand. On the theme of blind love (*caecus amor, caeca libido. caeca cupido, caecus amor sui*), on the so very paradoxical story of Cupid's 'eyes,' which were not always 'blindfolded,' I can only refer here to Panofsky's fine treatment in *Studies in Iconology*, pp. 151ff.

12. The painting is sometimes referred to in English as *The Daughter of Butades Drawing the Shadow of Her Lover*. [Trans.]

13. Nougaret in fact notes in his *Anecdotes des Beaux-Arts* (1776) that if the roles are sometimes reversed (and it is Butades' lover who is drawing), Butades 'took advantage of her lover's fortunate stratagem' and herself drew the silhouette not

on a wall but on a *veil*, 'which she knew how to *keep* with the greatest of care' (cited by Levitine, *The Art Bulletin*, vol. 40 [1958]: 330. My emphasis (J. D.)).

14. Permit me to refer to a chapter in *Of Grammatology*, trans. Gayatri Chakravorty Spivak (Baltimore: The Johns Hopkins University Press, 1976) that revolves around this text: 'That Movement of the Wand . . . (pp. 229ff.).

15. Maurice Merleau-Ponty, *The Visible and the Invisible*, trans. Alphonso Lingis (Evanston: Northwestern University Press, 1968), p. 257.

16. *The Visible*, p. 229.

17. Ibid., p. 247.

18. Ibid., p. 248.

19. Ibid., p. 249 (in addition to the pages cited, see also pp. 214–19, 225, 242ff.).

20. Though *hypothèque* would be most commonly translated as 'mortgage,' we have opted for the relatively obsolete English term hypothec to preserve the relationship to hypothesis. [Trans.]

21. *Mémoire-Dieu* evokes both *un prie-Dieu*, a low reading desk with a ledge that sometimes opens out for kneeling at prayer, and *mémoire d'yeux*—an eye-memory. [Trans.]

22. *Samson Agonistes*, lines 287–89.

23. *Une légende* is not only a legend but a caption or title of a painting. [Trans.]

Chapter 8

Logic of the Living Feminine

'. . . for there are human beings who lack everything, except one thing of which they have too much—human beings who are nothing but a big eye or a big mouth or a big belly or anything at all that is big. Inverse cripples [*umgekehrte Krüppel*] I call them.

'And when I came out of my solitude and crossed over this bridge for the first time I did not trust my eyes and looked and looked again, and said at last, 'An ear! An ear as big as a man!' I looked still more closely—and indeed, underneath the ear something was moving, something pitifully small and wretched and slender. And, no doubt of it, the tremendous ear was attached to a small, thin stalk—but this stalk was a human being! If one used a magnifying glass one could even recognize a tiny envious face; also, that a bloated little soul was dangling from the stalk. The people, however, told me that this great ear was not only a human being, but a great one, a genius. But I never believed the people when they spoke of great men; and I maintained my belief that it was an inverse cripple who had too little of everything and too much of one thing.'

When Zarathustra had spoken thus to the hunchback and to those whose mouthpiece and advocate [*Mundstück and Fürsprecher*] the hunchback was, he turned to his disciples in profound dismay and said: 'Verily, my friends, I walk among men as among the fragments and limbs of men [*Bruchstücken und Gliedmassen*]. This is what is terrible for my eyes, that I find man in ruins [*zerstrümmert*] and scattered [*zerstreut*] as over a battlefield or a butcher-field [*Schlacht- und Schlachterfeld*]. ('On Redemption,' *Thus Spake Zarathustra*)

I would like to spare you the tedium, the waste of time, and the subservience that always accompany the classic pedagogical procedures of forging links, referring back to prior premises or arguments, justifying one's own trajectory, method, system, and more or less skillful transitions, reestablishing continuity, and so on. These are but some of the imperatives of classical pedagogy with which, to be sure, one can never break once and for all. Yet, if you were to submit to them rigorously, they would very soon reduce you to silence, tautology, and tiresome repetition.

I therefore propose my compromise to you. And, as everyone knows, by the terms of *academic freedom*—I repeat: a-ca-dem-ic free-dom—you can take it or leave it. Considering the time I have at my disposal, the tedium I also want to spare myself, the freedom of which I am capable and which I want

184

to preserve, I shall proceed in a manner that some will find aphoristic or inadmissible, that others will accept as law, and that still others will judge to be not quite aphoristic enough. All will be listening to me with one or the other sort of ear (everything comes down to the ear you are able to hear me with) to which the coherence and continuity of my trajectory will have seemed evident from my first words, even from my title. In any case, let us agree to hear and understand one another on this point: whoever no longer wishes to follow may do so. I do not teach truth as such; I do not transform myself into a diaphanous mouthpiece of eternal pedagogy. I settle accounts, however I can, on a certain number of problems: with you and with me or me, and through you, me, and me, with a certain number of authorities represented here. I understand that the place I am now occupying will not be left out of the exhibit or withdrawn from the scene. Nor do I intend to withold even that which I shall call, to save time, an *autobiographical* demonstration, although I must ask you to shift its sense a little and to listen to it with another ear. I wish to take a certain pleasure in this, so that *you may learn this pleasure from me*.

The said 'academic freedom,' the ear, and autobiography are my objects— for this afternoon.

A discourse on life/death must occupy a certain space between *logos* and *gramme*, analogy and program, as well as between the differing senses of program and reproduction. And since life is on the line, the trait that relates the logical to the graphical must also be working between the biological and biographical, the thanatological and thanatographical.

As you know, all these matters are currently undergoing a reevaluation —all these matters, that is to say, the biographical and the *autos* of the auto-biographical.

We no longer consider the biography of a 'philosopher' as a corpus of empirical accidents that leaves both a name and a signature outside a system which would itself be offered up to an immanent philosophical reading—the only kind of reading held to be philosophically legitimate. This academic notion utterly ignores the demands of a text which it tries to control with the most traditional determinations of what constitutes the limits of the written, or even of 'publication.' In return for having accepted these limits, one can then and on the other hand proceed to write 'lives of philosophers,' those biographical novels (complete with style flourishes and character development) to which great historians of philosophy occasionally resign themselves. Such biographical novels or psychobiographies claim that, by following empirical procedures of the psychologistic— at times even psychoanalystic—historicist, or sociologistic type, one can give an account of the genesis of the philosophical system. We say no to this because a new problematic of the biographical in general and of the biography of philosophers in particular must mobilize other resources, including, at the very least, a new analysis of the proper name and the signature. Neither 'immanent' readings of philosophical systems (whether such readings be structural or not) nor external, empirical-genetic readings have ever in themselves questioned the *dynamis* of that borderline between the 'work' and the 'life,' the system and the subject of the system. This borderline—I call it *dynamis* because of its force, its power, as well as its virtual and mobile potency—is neither active nor passive, neither outside nor inside. It is most especially not a thin line, an invisible or *indivisible* trait lying between the enclosure of philosophemes, on the one hand, and the life of an author already identifiable behind the name, on the other. This divisible borderline traverses two 'bodies,' the corpus and the body, in accordance with laws that we are only beginning to catch sight of.

What one calls life—the thing or object of biology and biography—does not stand face to face with something that would be its opposable ob-ject: death, the thanatological or thanatographical. This is the first complication. Also, it is *painfully difficult* for life to become an object of science, in the sense that philosophy and science have always given to the word 'science' and to the legal status of scientificity. All of this—the difficulty, the delays it entails— is particularly bound up with the fact that the science of life always accommodates a philosophy of life, which is not the case for all other sciences, the sciences of nonlife—in other words, the sciences of the dead. This might lead one to say that all sciences that win their claim to scientificity without delay or residue are sciences of the dead; and, further, that there is, between the dead and the status of the scientific object, a co-implication which *interests* us, and which concerns the desire to know. If such is the case, then the so-called living subject of biological discourse is a part—an interested party or a partial interest —of the whole field of investment that includes the enormous philosophical, ideological, and political tradition, with all the forces that are at work in that tradition as well as everything that has its potential in the subjectivity of a biologist or a community of biologists. All these evaluations leave their mark on the scholarly signature and inscribe the bio-graphical within the bio-logical.

The name of Nietzsche is perhaps today, for us in the West, the name of someone who (with the possible exceptions of Freud and, in a different way, Kierkegaard) was alone in treating both philosophy and life, the science and the philosophy of life *with his name and in his name*. He has perhaps been alone in putting his name—his *names*—and his biographies on the line, running thus most of the risks this entails: for 'him,' for 'them,' for his lives, his names and their future, and particularly for the political future of what he left to be signed.

How can one avoid taking all this into account when reading these texts? One reads only by taking it into account.

To put one's name on the line (with everything a name involves and which cannot be summed up in a *self*), to stage signatures, to make an immense bio-graphical paraph out of all that one has written on life or death—this is perhaps what he has done and what we have to put on active record. Not so as to guarantee him a return, a profit. In the first place, he is dead—a trivial piece of evidence, but incredible enough when you get right down to it and when the name's genius or genie is still there to make us forget the fact of his death. At the very least, to be dead means that no profit or deficit, no good or evil, whether calculated or not, can *ever return again* to the bearer of the name. Only the name can inherit, and this is why the name, to be distinguished from the bearer, is always and *a priori* a dead man's name, a name of death. What returns to the name never returns to the living. Nothing ever comes back to the living. Moreover, we shall not assign him the profit because what he has willed in his name resembles—as do all legacies or, in French, *legs* (understand this word with whichever ear, in whatever tongue you will)—poisoned milk which has, as we shall see in a moment, gotten mixed up in advance with the worst of our times. And it did not get mixed up in this by accident.

Before turning to any of his writings, let it be said that I shall not read Nietzsche as a philosopher (of being, of life, or of death) or as a scholar or scientist, if these three types can be said to share the abstraction of the bio-graphical and the claim to leave their lives and names out of their writings. For the moment, I shall read Nietzsche beginning with the scene from *Ecce Homo* where he puts his body and his name out front even though he advances behind masks or pseudonyms without proper names. He advances behind a plurality of masks or names that, like any mask and even any theory of the simulacrum, can propose and produce themselves only by returning a constant yield of protection, a surplus value in which one may still recognize the ruse of life. However, the ruse starts incurring losses as soon as the surplus value does not return again to the living, but to and in the name of names, the community of masks.

The point of departure for my reading will be what says '*Ecce Homo*' or what says '*Ecce Homo*' of itself, as well as '*Wie man wird, was man ist,*' how one becomes what one is. I shall start with the preface to *Ecce Homo* which is, you could say, coextensive with Nietzsche's entire oeuvre, so much so that the entire oeuvre also prefaces *Ecce Homo* and finds itself repeated in the few pages of what one calls, in the strict sense, the Preface to the work entitled *Ecce Homo*. You may know these first lines by heart:

> Seeing that before long I must confront humanity with the most difficult demand that has ever been made of it, it seems indispensable to me to say *who I am* [*wer ich bin* is italicized]. Really, one should know it, for I have not left myself 'without testi-mony.' But the disproportion between the greatness of my task and the *smallness* of my contemporaries has found expression in the fact that one has neither heard nor even seen me. I live on my own credit [I go along living on my own credit, the cred-it I establish and give myself; *Ich lebe auf meinen eigenen Kredit hin*]; it is perhaps a mere prejudice that I live [*vielleicht bloss ein Vorurteil dass ich lebe*].

His own identity—the one he means to declare and which, being so out of proportion with his contemporaries, has nothing to do with what they know by this name, behind his name or rather his homonym, Friedrich Nietzsche—the identity he lays claim to here is not his by right of some contract drawn up with his contemporaries. It has passed to him through the unheard-of contract he has drawn up with himself. He has taken out a loan with himself and *has implicated us in this transaction through what, on the force of a signature, remains of his text.* '*Auf meinen eigenen Kredit.*' It is also our business, this unlimited credit that cannot be measured against the credit his contemporaries extended or refused him under the name of F.N. Already a false name, a pseudonym and homonym, F.N. dissimulates, perhaps, behind the imposter, the other Friedrich Nietzsche. Tied up with this shady business of contracts, debt, and credit, the pseudonym induces us to be immeasurably wary whenever we think we are reading Nietzsche's signature or 'autograph,' and whenever he *declares*: I, the undersigned, F.N.

He never knows in the present, with present knowledge or even in the present of *Ecce Homo*, whether anyone will ever honor the inordinate credit that he extends to *himself* in his name, but also necessarily in the name of another. The consequences of this are not difficult to foresee: if the life that he lives and tells to himself ('autobiography,' they call it) cannot be *his* life in the first place except as the effect of a secret contract, a credit account which has been both opened and encrypted, an indebtedness, an alliance or annulus, then as long as the contract has not been honored—and it cannot be honored except by another, for example, by you—Nietzsche can write that his life is perhaps a mere prejudice, '*es ist vielleicht bloss ein Vorurteil dass ich lebe.*' A prejudice: life. Or perhaps not so much life in general, but *my* life, this 'that I live,' the 'I-live' in the present. It is a prejudgment, a sentence, a hasty arrest, a risky prediction. This life will be verified only at the moment the bearer of the name, the one whom we, in our prejudice, call living, will have died. It will be verified only at some moment after or during death's arrest.[1] And if life returns, it will return to the name but not to the living, in the name of the living *as* a name of the dead.

'He' has proof of the fact that the 'I live' is a prejudgment (and thus, due to the effect of murder which *a priori* follows, a harmful prejudice) linked to the bearing of the name and to the structure of all proper names. He says that he has proof every time he questions one of the ranking 'educated' men who come to the Upper Engadine. As Nietzsche's name is unknown to any of them, he who calls himself 'Nietzsche' then holds proof of the fact that he does not live presently: 'I live on my own credit; it is perhaps a mere prejudice that I live. I need only speak with one of the "educated" who come to the Upper Engadine . . . and I am convinced that I do *not* live [*das ich lebe nicht*].

Under these circumstances I have a duty against which my habits, even more the pride of my instincts, revolt at bottom—namely, to say: *Hear me! For I am such and such a person* [literally: I am he and he, *ich bin der und der*]. *Above all, do not mistake me for someone else.*' All of this is emphasized.

He says this unwillingly, but he has a 'duty' to say so in order to acquit himself of a debt. To whom?

Forcing himself to say who he is, he goes against his natural *habitus* that prompts him to dissimulate behind masks. You know, of course, that Nietzsche constantly affirms the value of dissimulation. Life is dissimulation. In saying '*ich bin der und der*,' he seems to be going against the instinct of dissimulation. This might lead us to believe that, *on the one hand*, his contract goes against his nature: it is by doing violence to himself that he promises to honor a pledge in the name of the name, in his name and in the name of the other. *On the other hand*, however, this auto-presentative exhibition of the '*ich bin der und der*' could well be still a ruse of dissimulation. We would again be mistaken if we understood it as a simple presentation of identity, assuming that we already know what is involved in self-presentation and a statement of identity ('Me, such a person,' male or female, an individual or collective subject, 'Me, psychoanalysis,' 'Me, metaphysics').

Everything that will subsequently be said about truth will have to be reevaluated on the basis of this question and this anxiety. As if it were not already enough to unsettle our theoretical certainties about identity and what we think we know about a proper name, very rapidly, on the following page, Nietzsche appeals to his 'experience' and his 'wanderings in forbidden realms.' They have taught him to consider the causes of idealization and moralization in an entirely different light. He has seen the dawning of a '*hidden* history' of philosophers—*he does not say of philosophy*—and the 'psychology of their great names.'

Let us assume, in the first place, that the 'I live' is guaranteed by a nominal contract which falls due only upon the death of the one who says 'I live' in the present; further, let us assume that the relationship of a philosopher to his 'great name'—that is, to what borders a system of his signature—is a matter of psychology, but a psychology so novel that it would no longer be legible *within* the system of philosophy as one of its parts, nor within psychology considered as a region of the philosophical encyclopedia. Assuming, then, that all this is stated in the Preface signed 'Friedrich Nietzsche' to a book entitled *Ecce Homo*—a book whose final words are 'Have I been understood? *Dionysus versus the Crucified*' [*gegen den Gekreuzigten*], Nietzsche, Ecce Homo, Christ but not Christ, nor even Dionysus, but rather the name of the *versus*, the adverse or countername, the combat called between the two names—this would suffice, would it not, to pluralize in a singular fashion the proper name and the homonymic mask? It would suffice, that is, to lead all the affiliated threads of the name astray in a labyrinth which is, of course, the labyrinth of the ear. Proceed, then, by seeking out the edges, the inner walls, the passages.

Between the Preface signed F.N., which comes after the title, and the first chapter, 'Why I Am So Wise,' there is a single page. It is an outwork, an *hors d'oeuvre*, an exergue or a flysheet whose *topos*, like (its) temporality, strangely dislocates the very thing that we, with our untroubled assurance, would like to think of as the time of life and the time of life's *récit*,[2] of the writing of life by the living—in short, the time of autobiography.

The page is dated. To date is to sign. And to 'date from' is also to indicate the place of the signature. This page is in a certain way dated because it says 'today' and today 'my birthday,' the anniversary of my birth. The anniversary is the moment when the year turns back on itself, forms a ring or annulus with itself, annuls itself and begins anew. It is here: my forty-fifth year, the day of the year when I am forty-five years old, something like the midday of life. The noon of life, even midlife crisis,[3] is commonly situated at about this age, at the shadowless midpoint of a great day.

Here is how the exergue begins: '*An diesem vollkommhen Tage, wo Alles reift,*' 'On this perfect day when everything is ripening, and not only the grape turns brown, the eye of the sun just fell upon my life [has fallen due as if by chance: *fiel mir eben ein Sonnenblick auf meinen Leben*].'

It is a shadowless moment consonant with all the 'middays' of Zarathustra. It comes as a moment of affirmation, returning like the anniversary from which one can look forward and backward at one and the same time. The shadow of all negativity has disappeared: 'I looked back, I looked forward, and never saw so many and such good things at once.'

Yet, this midday tolls the hour of a burial. Playing on everyday language, he buries his past forty-four years. But what he actually buries is death, and in burying death he has saved life—and immortality. 'It was not for nothing that I buried [*begrub*] my forty-fourth year today; I had the *right* to bury it; whatever was life in it has been saved, is immortal. The first book of the *Revaluation of All Values*, the *Songs of Zarathustra*, the *Twilight of the Idols*, my attempt to philosophize with a hammer—all presents [*Geschenke*] of this year, indeed of its last quarter. *How could I fail to be grateful to my whole life?*—and so I tell my life to myself' ['*Und sō erzähle ich mir mein Leben*'].

He indeed says: I tell my life *to myself*; I recite and recount it thus *for me*. We have come to the end of the exergue on the flysheet between the Preface and the beginning of *Ecce Homo*.

To receive one's life as a gift, or rather, to be grateful to life for what she gives, for giving after all what is *my* life; more precisely, to recognize one's gratitude to life for such a gift—the gift being what has managed to get written and signed with this name for which I have established my own credit and which will be what it has become only on the basis of what this year has given me (the three works mentioned in the passage), in the course of the event dated by an annual course of the sun, and even by a part of its course or recourse, its returning—to reaffirm what has occurred during these forty-four years as having been good and as bound to return eternally, immortally: this is what *constitutes*, gathers, adjoins, and holds the strange present of this auto-biographical *récit* in place. '*Und so erzähle ich mir mein Leben.*' This *récit* that buries the dead and saves the saved or exceptional as immortal is not *auto*-biographical for the reason one commonly understands, that is, because the signatory tells the story of his life or the return of his past life as life and not death. Rather, it is because he tells *himself* this life and he is the narration's first, if not its only, addressee and destination—within the text. And since the 'I' of this *récit* only constitutes itself though the credit of the eternal return, he does not exist. He does not sign prior to the *récit qua* eternal return. Until then, *until now*, that I am living may be a mere prejudice. It is the eternal return that signs or seals.

Thus, you cannot think the name or names of Friedrich Nietzsche, you cannot *hear* them before the reaffirmation of the hymen, before the alliance or wedding ring of the eternal return. You will not understand anything of his life, nor of his life and works, until you hear the thought of the 'yes, yes' given to this shadowless gift at the ripening high noon, beneath that division whose borders are inundated by sunlight: the overflowing cup of the sun. Listen again to the overture of *Zarathustra*.

This is why it is so difficult to determine the *date* of such an event. How can one situate the advent of an auto-biographical *récit* which, as the thought of the eternal return, requires that we let the advent of all events come about in another way? This difficulty crops up wherever one seeks to make a *determination*: in order to date an event, of course, but also in order to identify the beginning of a text, the origin of life, or the first movement of a signature. These are all problems of the borderline.

Without fail, the structure of the exergue on the borderline or of the borderline in the exergue will be reprinted wherever the question of life, of 'my-life,' arises. Between a title or a preface on the one hand, and the book to come on the other, between the title *Ecce Homo* and *Ecce Homo* 'itself,' the structure of the exergue situates the place from which life will be *recited*, that is to say, reaffirmed—*yes, yes, amen, amen*. It is life that has to return eternally (selectively, as the living feminine and not as the dead that resides within her and must be buried), as life allied to herself by the nuptial annulus, the wedding ring. This *place* is to be found neither in the work (it is an exergue) nor in the life of the author. At least it is not there in a simple fashion, but neither is it simply exterior to them. It is in this place that affirmation is repeated: yes, yes, I approve, I sign, I subscribe to this acknowledgment of the debt incurred toward 'myself,' 'my-life'—and I want it to return. Here, at noon, the least shadow of all negativity is buried. The design of the exergue reappears later, in the chapter 'Why I Write Such Good Books,' where Nietzsche's preparations for the 'great noon' are made into a commitment, a debt, a 'duty,' 'my duty of preparing a moment of the highest self-examination for humanity, a *great noon* when it looks back and far forward [*wo sie zurückschaut und hinnausschaut*]" ('Dawn').

But the noon of life is not a place and it does not take place. For that very reason, it is not a moment but only an instantly vanishing limit. What is more, it returns every day, always, each day, with every turn of the annulus. Always before noon, after noon. If one has the right to read F.N.'s signature only at this instant—the instant in which he signs 'noon, yes, yes, I and I who recite my life to myself'—well, you call see what an impossible protocol this implies for reading and especially for teaching, as well as what ridiculous naiveté, what sly, obscure, and shady business are behind declarations of the type: Friedrich Nietzsche said this or that, he thought this or that about this or that subject— about life, for example, in the sense of human or biological existence— Friedrich Nietzsche or whoever after noon, such-and-such a person. Me, for example.

I shall not read *Ecce Homo* with you. I leave you with this forewarning or foreword about the place of the exergue and the fold that it forms along the lines of an inconspicuous limit: There is no more shadow, and all statements, before and after, left and right, are at once possible (Nietzsche said it all, more or less) and necessarily contradictory (he said the most mutually incompatible things, and he said that he said them). Yet, before leaving *Ecce Homo*, let us pick up just one hint of this contradicting duplicity.

What happens right after this sort of exergue, after this date? (It is, after all, a *date*:[4] signature, anniversary reminder, celebration of gifts or givens, acknowledgment of debt.) After this 'date,' the first chapter ('Why I Am So Wise') begins, as you know, with the origins of 'my' life: my father and my mother. In other words, once again, the principle of contradiction in my life which falls between the principles of death and life, the end and the beginning, the high and the low, degeneracy and ascendancy, et cetera. This contradiction is my fatality. And my fatality derives from my very genealogy, from my father and mother, from the fact that I decline, in the form of a riddle, as my parents' identity. In a word, my dead father, my living mother, my father the dead man or death, my mother the living feminine or life. As for me, I am between the two: this lot has fallen to me, it is a 'chance,' a throw of the dice; and at this place my truth, my double truth, takes after both of them. These lines are well known:

> The good fortune of my existence [*Das Glück meines Daseins*], its uniqueness per-
> haps [he says 'perhaps,' and thereby he reserves the possibility that this chancy situation

may have an exemplary or paradigmatic character], lies in its fatality: I am, to express it in the form of a riddle [*Rätselform*], already dead as my father [*als mein Vater bereits gestorben*], while as my mother, I am still living and becoming old [*als meine Mutter lebe ich noch und werde alt*].

Inasmuch as *I am and follow after* my father, I am the dead man and I am death. Inasmuch as *I am and follow after* my mother, I am life that perseveres, I am the living and the living feminine. I am my father, my mother, and me, and me who is my father my mother and me, my son and me, death and life, the dead man and the living feminine, and so on.

There, this is who I am, a certain masculine and a certain feminine. *Ich bin der und der*, a phrase which means all these things. You will not be able to hear and understand my name unless you hear it with an ear attuned to the name of the dead man and the living feminine—the double and divided name of the father who is dead and the mother who is living on, who will moreover outlive me long enough to bury me. The mother is living on, and this living on is the name of the mother. This survival is my life whose shores she overflows. And my father's name, in other words, my patronym? That is the name of my death, of my dead life.

Must one not take this unrepresentable scene into account each time one claims to identify any utterance signed by F. N.? The utterances I have just read or translated do not belong to the genre of autobiography in the strict sense of the term. To be sure, it is not wrong to say that Nietzsche speaks of his 'real' (as one says) father and mother. But he speaks of them '*in Rätselform*,' symbolically, by way of a riddle; in other words, in the form of a proverbial legend, and as a story that has a lot to teach.

What, then, are the consequences of this double origin? The birth of Nietzsche, in the double sense of the word 'birth' (the act of being born and family lineage), is itself double. It brings something into the world and the light of day out of a singular couple: death and life, the dead man and the living feminine, the father and the mother. The double birth explains who I am and how I determine my identity: as double and neutral.

This double descent [*Diese doppelte Herkunft*], as it were, from both the highest and the lowest rungs on the ladder of life, at the same time *décadent* and a *beginning*—this, if anything, explains that neutrality, that freedom from all partiality in relation to the total problem of life, that perhaps distinguishes me. I have a subtler sense of smell [pay attention to what he repeatedly says about hunting, trails, and his nostrils] for the signs of ascent and decline [literally of rising and setting, as one says of the sun: *für die Zeichen von Aufgang und Niedergang*; of that which climbs and declines, of the high and the low] than any other human being before. I am the master *par excellence* for this—I know both, I am both [*ich kenne beides, ich bin beides*].

I am a master, I am the master, the teacher [*Lehrer*] '*par excellence*' (the latter words in French, as is *décadent* earlier in the passage). I know and I am the both of them (one would have to read 'the both' as being in the singular), the dual or the double, I know what I am, the both, the two, life the dead [*la vie le mort*]. Two, and from them one gets life the dead. When I say 'Do not mistake me for someone else, I am *der und der*,' this is what I mean: the dead the living, the dead man the living feminine.

The alliance that Nietzsche follows in turning his signature into riddles links the logic of the dead to that of the living feminine. It is an alliance in which he seals or forges his signatures—and he also simulates them: the demonic neutrality of midday delivered from the negative and from dialectic.

'I know both, I am both.—My father died at the age of thirty-six. He was delicate, kind and morbid, as a being that is destined merely to pass by [*wie ein nur zum Vorübergehn bestimmtes Wesen*]—more a gracious memory of life rather than life itself.' It is not only that the son does not survive his father *after* the latter's death, but the father was *already* dead; he will have died during his own life. As a 'living' father, he was already only the memory of life, of an already prior life. Elsewhere, I have related this elementary kinship structure (of a dead or rather absent father, already absent to himself, and of the mother living above and after all, living on long enough to bury the one she has brought into the world, an ageless virgin inaccessible to all ages) to a logic of the death knell [*glas*] and of *obsequence*. There are examples of this logic in some of the best families, for example, the family of Christ (with whom Dionysus stands face to face, but as his specular double). There is also Nietzsche's family, if one considers that the mother survived the 'breakdown.' In sum and in general, if one 'sets aside all the facts,' the logic can be found in all families.

Before the cure or resurrection which he also recounts in *Ecce Homo*, this only son will have first of all repeated his father's death: 'In the same year in which his life went downward, mine, too, went downward: at thirty-six I reached the lowest point of my vitality—I still lived, but without being able to see three steps ahead. Then—it was 1879—I retired from my professorship at Basel, spent the summer in St. Moritz like a shadow and the next winter, the most sunless of my life, in Naumberg as a shadow. This was my minimum. The *Wanderer and His Shadow* was born at this time. Doubtless I then knew about shadows.' A little further, we read: 'My readers know perhaps in what way I consider dialectic as a symptom of decadence; for example in the most famous case, the case of Socrates.' *Im Fall des Sokrates*: one might also say in his *casus*, his expiration date and his decadence. He is a Socrates, that *décadent par excellence*, but he is also the reverse. This is what he makes clear at the beginning of the next section: 'Taking into account that I am a *décadent*, I am also the opposite.' The double provenance, already mentioned at the beginning of section 1, then reaffirmed and explained in section 2, may also be heard at the opening of section 3: 'This *dual* series of experiences, this access to apparently separate worlds, is repeated in my nature in every respect: I am a *Doppelgänger*, I have a "second" sight in addition to the first. And perhaps also a third.' Second and third sight. Not only, as he says elsewhere, a third ear. Only a moment ago, he has explained to us that in tracing the portrait of the 'well-turned-out person' [*wohlgerathner Mensch*] he has just described himself: 'Well, then, I am the *opposite* of a *décadent*, for I have just described myself.'

The contradiction of the 'double' thus goes beyond whatever declining negativity might accompany a dialectical opposition. What counts in the final accounting and beyond what can be counted is a certain *step beyond*.[5] I am thinking here of Maurice Blanchot's syntaxless syntax in his *Pas au-delà* ['The Step Beyond']. There, he approaches death in what I would call a step-by-step procedure of overstepping or of impossible transgression. *Ecce Homo*: 'In order to understand anything at all of my *Zarathustra*, one must perhaps be similarly conditioned as I am—with one foot *beyond* life.' A foot,[6] and going beyond the opposition between life and/or death, a single step.

Notes

1. *Arrêt de mort*: both death sentence and reprieve from death. [Trans.]
2. Rather than attempt to translate this word as 'account' or 'story' or 'narration,' it has been left in French throughout. [Trans.]
3. 'Le démon de midi'; literally the midday demon. [Trans.]
4. From '*data littera*,' 'letter given,' the first words of a medieval formula indicating the time and place of a legal act. [Trans.]
5. '*Pas au-delà*,' both 'step(s) beyond' and 'not beyond.' [Trans.]
6. The death of the father, blindness, the foot: one may be wondering why I am not speaking here of oedipus or Oedipus. This was intentionally held in reserve for another reading directly concerned with the *thematic* of oedipus and the name of Oedipus.

Chapter 9

Qual Quelle: Valéry's Sources[1]

I—mark(s) first of all a division in what will have been able to appear in the beginning.

'Valéry's Sources,' here, do not entitle those sources on which theses are written. What historians might name 'influences' will not be followed upstream toward their hidden 'sources,' the near or distant, presumed or verified, origins of a 'work,' that is of a 'thought' whose card in the catalogue thereby could be manipulated. Valéry himself warned of this in advance: concerning what is written here, the 'discourse of history' would chatter on about heritages, readings, borrowings, biographical inner springs. The sources could multiply themselves infinitely, but as so many 'sources of error and powers of falsifications.'[2] We will not, as do positive historians, account for all that could have flowed into this text *from the outside*.

But—I mark(s) the division—by taking a different turn, by observing from an excentric place the logic of Valéry's aversions, why not ask ourselves about another outside, about the *sources set aside*, the sources that Valéry could get a glimpse of only on the bias, as in a brief, or rather foreshortened, mirroring, just the time to recognize or reflect himself and immediately to turn away—quickly, decidedly, furtively too, like an about-face to be described according to the gesture of Narcissus. We will analyze this turning away only where it has left marks *within* Valéry's textual system, as a regular crinkling of every page. Here, for example, the names would be those of Nietzsche and Freud.

Further, under this heading one might also have expected a reading of 'In Praise of Water,' with which Valéry, in 1935, prefaced a collection of tributes to the *Source Perrier*.[3] Will academic accusations be made of the resources that Valéry more than once found for his talent? No moral or political lesson could be elaborated whose premises had not already infallibly been recognized by Valéry. In Mallarmé's wake, quite early on, he had analyzed the law that

A lecture given on 6 November 1971 at the Johns Hopkins University on the centennial of Valéry's birth. I am indebted to Michel Lechantre's rereading of Valéry and his discovery of the *Cahiers*. The following pages therefore are naturally dedicated to him.

administers the exchanges between the values of language, philosophy, or literature, for example, and those of political economy. The *Memoirs of the Poet* had compared the febrile agitation of Literature to that of the stock market.[4] And the trials to which he would be subjected still would derive from those 'convictions . . . (that are) naively and secretly murderous' (I, 1129), and which he knew always explain 'the deep meaning of speculative quarrels and even literary polemics' (ibid.).

But—again I mark(s) and multiply (multiplies) the division—we will not forget 'In Praise of Water.' Rather, in pretending that we abandon its subterranean discourse, perhaps we will see it reemerge, both itself and totally other, after several meanders. This discourse already entails that the 'nymph and the spring stand at that holy place where life sits down and looks around her' (2, 10). Further, it announces that the water of the source holds up the tree on its own course. 'Consider a plant, regard a mighty tree, and you will discern that it is none other than an upright river pouring into the air of the sky. By the tree WATER climbs to meet light' (2, 10). The 'amorous form' of the source traverses and divides the tree in its ascent. In the course of his innumerable statements on the tree, the 'supreme beech' [*hêtre suprême*], Valéry will have taken into account a 'blind tree,' and then a tree trembling in that 'there are two *trees* within it.'[5] This is the moment at which the erect, and thus divided, tree, separated from itself within itself, lets itself be cut off from the simple source. This is where we find the incision into the dream of the source. To be cut off from the source, as predicted finally by 'In Praise of Water,' is to let oneself be multiplied or divided by the difference of the other: to cease to be (a) *self*. The lure of the source ('Now comes the HOUR, the thirst, the spring (*la source*) and the siren' *Hour*, 1, 251): to become again present to oneself, to come back to oneself, to find again, along with the pure limpidity of water, the always efficient mirage of the point of emergence, the instant of welling up, the fountain or well surnamed Truth, which always speaks in order to say I: 'Well one knows that pure thirst is quenched only in pure water. There is something exact and satisfactory in this matching of the real desire of the organism with the element of its origin. To thirst is to lack a part of oneself, and thus to dwindle into another. Then one must make good that lack, complete oneself again, by repairing to what all life demands. [*Etre altéré, c'est devenir autre: se corrompre. Il faut donc se desaltérer, redevenir, avoir recours à ce qu'exige tout ce qui vit.* I, 202] The very language is filled with the praise of WATER. We say that we THIRST FOR TRUTH. We speak of a LIMPID discourse' (2, 10–11). And when Valéry ends with an 'I adore WATER,' which resembles, for whoever would be taken in by it, an advertiser's platitude, he is speaking only of speech, insisting on the transition which puts water into the mouth, engenders discourse, oration, incantation.

What does the course of the source become when the course is made into discourse? What, then, of this turning away?

In letting oneself be carried along by the flow, one would rush, under the rubric of sources, toward a thematics of water, a semantics in 'phenomenological' style or a psychoanalysis of material imagination, both spellbound by the unity, which is precisely originary, of a meaning or a theme flowing from the source and affecting itself with forms, modulations, and variations in a discourse. There would be no lack of material for such an inventory, which would filter almost the entirety of Valéry's text, ingenuously following the trail of the 'MULTIFORM WATER' which from the source goes 'down unconquerably to the ocean where she most abides' (2, 9). At the mouth again one would come back to the source of Paul Valéry himself, who often explained himself thus: 'I was born in a port.'

Without pretense of going any further than this thematic or semantic reading, rather let us attempt abstractly to complicate the question of meaning or of the theme; and of what happens to a text—as text—when the source is divided within it, and altered to the point of no longer rejoining the unity of the resources (the *s* divides itself again) that moreover it never will have been. In sum, repeating the critical question, Valéry's very insistent and very necessary question about *meaning* (theme, subject, content, etc.), we will bring the question to a certain heterogeneity of the source: and first, there are sources, the source is other and plural. But by means of this repetition we may be prepared to poison the question of meaning and to calculate the price that Valéry had to pay for the discredit that, to a certain extent and in a certain way, he justifiably threw on the value and authority of meaning. A repetition of Valéry's, doubtless, but perhaps we will not close this reflection in ring form. Or at least it will not return to where it was expected, to its origin, before leaving behind, thereby affecting and infecting itself, some hardly philosophical venom: thus giving us the sketch of a snake, amongst the tree, hissing with its double-edged tongue whose venom, however vile, leaves far behind the well tempered hemlock!

Rebound

I had not reread Valéry for a long time. And even long ago, I was far from having read all of Valéry. This is still true today. But in going back to the texts that I thought I knew, and in discovering others, especially in the *Notebooks*, naturally I asked myself in what ways a certain relationship had changed. Where had the displacement, which in a way prevented me from taking my bearings, been effected? What does this signify here, now? A banal question, a ring once more in the form of the return to the sources which always afflicts the rhetoric of the anniversaries of a birth: Valéry one hundred years later, Valéry for us, Valéry now, Valéry today, Valéry alive, Valéry dead—always the same code. What laws do these rebirths, rediscoveries, and occultations too, obey, the distancing or reevaluation of a text that one naively would like to believe, having put one's faith in a signature or an institution, always remains the same, constantly identical to itself? In sum a 'corpus,' and one whose self identity would be even less threatened than one's own body [*corps propre*]? What must a text be if it can, by itself in a way, turn itself in order to shine again, after an eclipse, with a different light, in a time that is no longer that of its productive source (and was it ever contemporaneous with it?), and then again repeat this resurgence after several deaths, counting, among several others, those of the author, and the simulacrum of a multiple extinction? Valéry also was interested in this power of regeneration. He thought that it—the possibility for a text to yield (itself) several times and several lives—calculates (itself). I am saying *it calculates itself*: such a ruse cannot be machinated in the brain of an author, quite simply, except if he is situated like a spider who is somewhat lost in a corner of its web, off to the side. The web very quickly becomes indifferent to the animal-source, who might very well die without even having understood what had happened. Long afterward, other animals again will come to be caught in its threads, speculating, in order to get out, on the first meaning of a weave, that is of a textual trap whose economy can always be abandoned to itself. This is called writing. It calculates itself, Valéry knew, and coming back to him, to the enormous cardboard web that literally bears his signature, I said to myself that it had, and not only in the form of the *Notebooks*, more than one certain return. Supposing, of course, that a return can ever be certain, which is precisely what is in question, as will be seen. In the calculation of this economy, for it to 'work' (this is Valéry's expression), the price to be paid negotiates with death; with what cuts the *oeuvre* from its source ('thus there is no author'), henceforth imprinting on it a survival duration that is necessarily *discrete* and *discontinuous*. I am borrowing these qualifications from Valéry. When he analyzes what programs the duration and return of a writing, he never does so in terms of genius, meaning, or force, but in terms of 'application of force.'[6]

How does the return *of* the source negotiate—and dissociate—itself?

Let us repeat the question. Was the source a theme for Valéry? A great number of poems, analyses, meditations, and notes regularly seem to come back to the source as to their object or principal subject. There is here something like an overflow. And already, this thematic overabundance, in making the demonstration all too easy, makes us suspect confusion somewhere else. Here, the recurrence announces, as perhaps it always does, that one does not touch a theme, especially a principal theme. The compulsive obstinacy that always leads back toward a place, a locus, signifies that this topos cannot become a theme or the dwelling place of a rhetoric: it rejects any presentation, any representation. It can never be there, present, *posed* before a glance, facing it; it never constitutes a present or hidden unity, an object or a subject supporting, according to the occurrence or position of the theme, a system of variations, of modulations, of transformations whose meaning or substantial content at heart would remain identical to themselves.

The source for Valéry, then, must be that which never could become a theme. If we persist in considering it in this way, then at least we must specify from some angle or fold that this was the theme of that which cannot be thematized.

It is that the source cannot be reassembled into its originary unity. Because—first of all—it has no proper, literal meaning.

And yet if there is a word with a proper, literal meaning, is it not this one?

We are indeed certain that we know what the word *source* means before the intervention of all these metaphors, whose work was always remarked by Valéry.

Is not the source the origin, the point of formation, or rather emergence, of a flowing body of water, brook, stream, river? Nothing is more familiar to us than water, and than the very familiarity of the earth with water, which is sealed here and there, and unsealed in the *point d'eau*—incalculable syntagm[7] —that is called source: *origo fontium*.

But this meaning denominated as proper can appear for us within the element of familiarity only if we already know, or believe that we already know, what we are thinking when we say that the source is the *origin* of a body of water. If there were not an immemorial complicity with the meaning of the word *origin*, with the naked meaning of the word origin in general, could we ever come close to the determined origin that is a source (*origo fontium*), the birth of a body of water, its *nature*, that is the so-called *proper* and unique meaning of the word *source*? Therefore, we *already* would have to understand the meaning of the word *origin* when it designates something totally other than the welling up of a body of water, in order to gain access to that which nevertheless was proposed as the proper meaning of the source. One first would have to fix what *origo* means, the status of the origin or of the 'source' in general, of the *departure* or beginning of anything at all, that is of the departure as ab-solute, of emergence unloosed from any determination, before coming back to what nevertheless would remain the proper meaning of the word *source*: the origin of a body of water, de-parture and *point d'eau*; locutions which are all very near to veering off, in a way that is not fortuitous, toward the figures of drought, the negative, and separation.

Therefore, we should not be surprised if generality (the origin in general) becomes the accomplice of metaphoricity, and if we learn from the trope about the status of literal, proper meaning, the status of that which *gives itself as* proper meaning.

But what is *to give itself*, what is the *as* when the issue is one of the proper (meaning)?

Proper meaning derives from derivation. The proper meaning or the primal meaning (of the word *source*, for example) is no longer simply the source, but the deported effect of a turn of speech, a return or detour. It is secondary in relation to that to which it seems to give birth, measuring a separation and a departure from it. The source itself is the effect of that (for) whose origin it passes. One no longer has the right to assimilate, as I have just pretended to do, the proper meaning and the primal meaning. That the proper is not the primal, that it is not at the source, is what Valéry gives us to read, thereby reawakening en route the debate to which this confusion of the proper and the primal gave rise in the history of classical rhetoric.

Therefore we will not listen to the source *itself* in order to learn what it is or what it means, but rather to the turns of speech, the allegories, figures, metaphors, as you will, into which the source has deviated, in order to lose it or rediscover it—which always amounts to the same.

Often designated as *source*, for Valéry the absolute origin first has the form of the *ego*, the *I*, the 'most naked I,' of 'the pure *I*, that unique and monotonous element of each being, [that] is lost and recovered by itself, but inhabits our senses eternally' as 'the fundamental permanence of a consciousness that depends on nothing' (*Note and Digression*, 8, 101–2). Nothing in the world, or at least nothing that is presented within it, appears as phenomenon, theme, or object, without first being for me, for (an) ego, and without coming back to me as to the opening, the very origin of the world: not as the cause of its existence, but as the origin of its presence, the point of source on whose basis *everything* takes on meaning, appears, delineates, and measures itself. Everything, that is to say everything that is not I. The non-I is *for* the I, appears as non-I for an I and on the basis of an I. Everything: which is to say that the I, the exception to and condition for everything that appears, does not appear. Never being present to itself, the source hardly exists. It is there for no one. For what Valéry here calls the pure I, and what philosophers usually name the transcendental *ego*, is not the 'person,' the ego or empirical consciousness of the psychologists. An unnamable, 'unqualifiable' source, in effect it has no determinable character since it is not in the world and never presents itself.

Valéry encircles, or rather tracks down, this incessant disappearance, among other places, in the *Note and Digression* to the *Leonardo*: 'But what he raises to this high degree is not his precious personal *self*, since he has renounced his personality by making it the object of his thought, and since he has given the place of *subject* to that unqualifiable *I* which has no name or history, which is neither more tangible nor less real than the center of gravity of a ring or that of a planetary system—but which results from the whole, whatever that whole may be' (8, 102–3, Valéry's italics).

The source results here. Valéry would probably have been *irritated* (I am borrowing this word from him for reasons to be given later) if he had been reminded that this proposition—the origin as result—is literally Hegelian, that it reassembles the essence of speculative dialectics whose proposition it properly is. Hegel does not by chance write it in Latin (*Der Anfang ist das Resultat*) at the beginning of the Greater Logic. In *Identity and Difference*, taking his departure from Hegel, Heidegger also analyzes this *ressaut* (*resultare, resilire, resalire*) of the origin in the result, of the founding proposition in the rebound or reflexive counter-motion (*Rückprall*).[8]

The pure I, the source of all presence, thus is reduced to an abstract point, to a pure form, stripped of all thickness, of all depth, without character, without quality, without property, without an assignable duration. This source therefore has no proper meaning. Nothing of that which proceeds from it belongs to it. *Point d'eau*—that is of it. Thus it has no proper name. It is so universal and so abstract a pronoun (*me, I*)[9] that it *replaces, stands for* no proper name of a person in particular: A universal pronoun, but of so singular a universality that it always remains, precisely, singular. The function of this source which *names itself I* is indeed, within and without language, that of a singular universal. In the same text, Valéry describes 'the plurality of the singular, in the contradictory coexistence of mutually independent durations—as many of these as there are persons, *tot capita, tot tempora*—a problem comparable with that of *relativity* in physics, though incomparably more difficult' (8, 103). He also names, as if in resonance with the *Phenomenology of Spirit*, 'the I, the universal pronoun, the appellation of which has no connection with a face' (8, 104).

That has no relation with a *face*: let us understand this equally as with a particular subject, empirically determined, and with the system which defines the face, to be reconsidered further on as a source which can also receive: the eyes, the mouth, the ears which yield (themselves to) sight, speech, hearing. This pure I which is the source, this singular universal above all does not amount to the individual. A pure consciousness, without the least psychic or physical determination, it 'in an instant immolates its individuality' (8, 104). Like the transcendental consciousness described by Husserl, it is constituted, not being *in* the world, neither by a body, which goes without saying, nor even by a soul. The *psyche*, in effect, is a region of that which is in the world (the totality of that which is). But inversely, not being in the world, not belonging to the totality of the things which exist, which are maintained for and before it, this source is nothing, almost nothing. It would be experienced, if it were experienced, as the excess of everything that can be related to it. A relation of nothing to nothing, this relationship is barely a relation. Imagine the God of a negative theology attempting by himself to describe himself, to catch himself in the grid of a determining discourse: he will almost annihilate himself. 'It [this consciousness] feels compelled to define itself by the sum total of things, as the *excess* over that totality of its own power of perception. In order to affirm itself, it had to begin by denying an infinite number of elements an infinite number of times, and by exhausting the objects of its power without exhausting that power—with the result that it differs from nothingness by the smallest possible margin' (8, 96).

Incapable of receiving the imprint of any characteristic, evading all predication, not permitting itself to be attributed any property, this source also will be able to lend itself without resistance to the most contradictory determinations. Valéry grants it, for example, a certain Being, but this is only to deny it all presence. Or almost, the *almost* imprinting with its regular cadence the play which disqualifies, and does so by arbitrating disqualification, confusing oppositions, and dissolving any ontological pertinence. In question is that which in 'blending all the categories is something *that exists and does not exist*' (8, 137). Thus, this I is not an individual, is almost impersonal, very close to being a non-I. Of this consciousness which itself cannot posit itself, itself come before itself, become for itself a thesis or a theme, we cannot even say that it is present for-itself. This source which cannot be made a theme therefore is not a self consciousness, is hardly a consciousness. Is it not unconscious in a certain way or, barely to displace the citation, different from the unconscious by the smallest possible margin?

The analysis of consciousness, therefore, is not a sure thing. Let us not hasten to reproach Valéry for having limited himself to an analysis of consciousness. We are far from having finished with it. Freud says somewhere that what is most enigmatic, finally, is consciousness.

This I which is not an I, this unconscious consciousness, this X which properly has or is nothing, which is not what it is because it is pure, and which therefore is impure because it is pure—will it still be called a source? The source is, and it is in the world. Therefore, it is *for* the I that is called source. Therefore, it remains the deported metaphor of the I. But the I of which it would be the metaphor being intrinsically, properly, improper, that is, non-proper, impure to the extent that it is pure, it is nothing outside its metaphors, nothing except that which transports it outside itself and throws it outside itself at the instant of its birth, as the irruptive welling up, the sometimes discreet, but always violent effraction of the emerging source. As such, this source, in the purity of its waters, is always disseminated far from itself, and has no relation to itself as source. If pure consciousness and the pure I are *like* the source, it is in not being able to come back to it. In their perpetual and instantaneous loss of consciousness, they cannot become themes or give rise to proper or improper definitions, not even, if one might put it thus, to true tropes. Perhaps to the violence of catachreses, which Fontanier says are 'not true figures.'

And yet *there are* effects of theme, of meaning, of figure. The impossible is possible, by means of the abuse of the twisting which is not yet rhetoric in that it opens and furrows the space of rhetoric. The impossible is possible: the 'source,' for example, but equally everything that will place it in the position of a secondary proper meaning in order to bring back into it divisions and turns.

Der sich aufhebende Ursprung or *La Coupe de Source*[10]

But how is the impossible possible? How can the source divide itself—the sources germinal from the title onward—and thus by itself separate from itself in order to be related to itself—which is, as a pure origin, the irreference to itself. And from as soon as the source begins its process, incising itself and escaping itself, is there a *first* metaphor of the origin? A properly originary metaphor? A metaphor in which the source loses itself less than in another metaphor? Or in which, losing itself *even more* it comes back to itself more certainly? In this procession—Plotinus's language imposes itself here—is there a first metaphoric emanation of the One which is the source?

The I has 'no relation with a face.' That which sees and is seen first of all, that which yields (itself to) seeing, the face, then, elevates the source into an initial displacement. In this figure an initial metaphoricity perhaps places on view that which has no *figure*.[11] Perhaps, but let us wait.

In the text to which I have referred, as in many others, the source (of the)– I is often described *as* a glance, as the site of the glance. The eye becomes simultaneously the division that opens and the substance of the source, the point of departure and the *point d'eau*. The allegory immediately becomes theatrical. Everything that separates itself from the source comes to be placed before it, a visible object on a stage. Facing the source in the light is everything that is presented to it which is not present to itself. Presence is objectivity. And if the source has no profile for itself, it is like an absolute glance which being always opened wide and thrown toward the visible, cannot itself perceive itself, never emerging from its night.

Incapable of putting itself onstage, pure consciousness therefore cannot give itself any image of itself; but this itself can be said only if, by means of an ancient and unperceived image, one already has made this consciousness into an eye and the source into a spectator. In order to speak of the source, which remains interdicted, first it has had to be *turned*: by means of a trope, it must yield to being seen and yield to seeing. The trope does not first consist of speaking, but of seeing. And more precisely, of seeing the invisible, that which only is said, in order blindly to say the interdicted.

Such is the reverie: 'The image it brings to mind spontaneously is that of an invisible audience seated in a darkened theater—a presence that cannot observe itself and is condemned to watch the scene confronting it, yet can feel nevertheless how it creates all that breathless and invincibly oriented darkness' (8, 97–98; modified).

The invincible orient, always apprehended as such from its occidental other (*Orientem Versus*), is the source in that it can have but a single meaning. The eye is always turned in the same direction, toward the outside, and everything is related to this orient. Therefore, the misfortune is to have a meaning, a single invincible meaning. It is because it has a meaning that the source has nothing proper to it, a proper meaning permitting it to come back to and be equal to itself, to belong to itself. It is a kind of nature, or rather a threatened God, impoverished and impotent by virtue of its very originality and its independence from the source. As for this negativity which works upon and anguishes the generative god from within, a certain president, whom we are still leaving in the margin, may have shared knowledge of it with an entire mysticism, a theology, and a certain Hegelianism.[12] The text on the originary scene continues: 'Nothing can be born or perish, exist in some degree, possess a time, a place, a meaning, a figure—except on this definite *stage*, which the fates have circumscribed, and which, having separated it from who knows what primordial chaos, as light was separated from darkness on the first day, they have opposed and subordinated to the condition of *being seen*'(8, 97; Valéry's italics).

For the source to become in turn an image, for it to become engaged in a tropic or fantastic system as well as to appear and to receive, for it to see itself as the glance of the origin, it must divide itself. Wherever the mirror intervenes, each time that Narcissus comes on stage in Valéry's text, the source can be found again as an effect of the mirror only by losing itself twice. The mirror, another unfindable theme (but it propagates itself like a theme that does not exist), manifests in this double loss the singular operation of a multiplying division which transforms the origin into effect, and the whole into a part. Valéry has recognized that the specular agency, far from constituting the I in its properness, immediately expropriates it in order not to halt its march. The imaginary is broken up rather than formed here.[13]

Glance of the figure, figure of the glance, the source is always divided, carried away outside itself: before the mirror it does not come back to itself, its consciousness is still a kind of unconscious. As soon as it performs Narcissus's turn, it no longer knows itself. It no longer belongs to itself. Narcissus defends himself from death only by living it, whether he distances himself from the 'venerable fountain' ('Fountain, my fountain, water coldly present' 1, 151), or whether within it he unites himself to his own body in the moment of 'extreme existence' in which the I loves itself to death:

> I love, I love. And who can love any other
> Than himself? . . .
>   You only, body mine, my dear body
> I love, the one alone who shields me from the dead!
>
> . . . .

>   . . . And soon let me break, kiss
> This frail defense against extreme existence
> This quivering, fragile and holy distance
> Between me and the surface . . .
>
>   (*Fragments of the Narcissus*, 1, 158, 160)

Confronted with this menacing turn of the source, subjected to the contradiction of the apotropaic, desire cannot be simple. Implacable when he analyzes mortal division, Valéry is equally unalterable in his thirst for the origin: into which the analysis itself empties, if it decomposes only in going back toward the principle.

If the source cannot maintain itself, look at itself, present itself to itself in daylight, perhaps it lends itself to being heard. If one displaces the metaphor in order to write it according to other characteristics of the face, shutting the eye and the stage, perhaps the source will be permitted to return to itself: following another turn, another allegory of the origin, another *mythical* circuit from self to self. 'In the Beginning Was the Fable.'

Narcissus speaks. The poem that bears this title also says 'the voice of the springs (*sources*)' and the shout 'to the echoes.' I do not see myself, said the source. But it says so at least, and thus hears itself. I say to myself that I do not see myself. I say to myself . . . perhaps again becoming myself between my direct and my indirect object, reassembling in this operation, virtually perfected, the subject, the object, the interlocutor—I, him, you. I—mark(s) the division.

Less well known, because Valéry devoted himself to them above all in the *Notebooks*, are the analyses reserved for the voice, the voice of the origin, the origin of the voice. The latter is heard as close as possible to the place where it sounds; it seems to do without the detour through the exteriority of the mirror or the water, the world, in order immediately to reflect itself in the intimate instantaneousness of resonance. Does not this echo without delay lift Narcissus from the death to which he was exposing himself? If the eye fails to institute itself as origin, perhaps the voice can produce itself, emerge from itself, all the while remaining or coming back to itself, without detour or organ, in the inner instance of what I propose to call 'hearing oneself speak.' Speech, then, would be the authentic exchange of the source with itself. Will it be said that the voice is finally the source? That it says the source? That it lets the source say itself? Or inversely that it produces only an effect of the source? And what does such an *effect* mean? We still must wait.

It belongs to the very structure of speech that it may be, or seem to be, immediately sensible from the source. What appears to be is not an accident here. It belongs to the very production of speech. Between what I say and what I hear myself say, no exteriority, no alterity, not even that of a mirror, seems to interpose itself. Mutism and deafness go hand in hand, and there is nothing less fortuitous. Hence, the interior speech that is not proffered, no longer would be a contingent event, occasionally occurring here or there: it is the condition for speech itself. The voice, it appears, therefore can accomplish the circular return of the origin to itself. In the circle the voice steps beyond the interdiction which made the eye blind to the eye. The true circle, the circle of the truth is therefore always an effect of speech. And Valéry recognized the immense bearing of this autonomous circuit of 'hearing-oneself-speak,' an apparently highly factual phenomenon, which always might be explained by the anatomical configuration of an animal in the world (but which produces, if one wishes to pursue its consequences, even the concept of an origin of the world, thereby disqualifying the alleged regional empiricity of the 'physiological' explanation), and he did so better, without a doubt, than any traditional philosopher, better than Husserl,[14] and better than Hegel, who nevertheless had described phonic vibration as the element of temporality, of subjectivity, of interiorization, and of idealization in general, along with everything which thereby systemically lets itself be carried along in the circle of speculative dialectics.

But, like the lucid source, the sonorous source attempts to rejoin itself only by differentiating itself, dividing, differing, deferring without end. Quite simply, the lure of reappropriation this time becomes more interior, more twisted, more fatal. Valéry, as we will verify in an instant, did describe this movement which goes back to the source and which separates from the source or simultaneously interdicts the source. Which then occupies another position; it is no longer only that approaching which movement exhausts itself, but also that which somewhere eludes, always a bit further on, our grasp. It is born of this very eluding, like a situated mirage, a site inscribed in a directionless field. It is nothing before being sought, only an effect produced by the structure of movement. The source therefore is not the origin, it is neither at the departure or the arrival. Valéry marks in speech both the circle of hearing-oneself-speak, the lure of the source rejoined, and the law which makes such a return to itself an effect. An effect: simultaneously the derivation of that which is not *causa sui*, and the illusion, the trap, or the play of appearance.

Among many others, here are three fragments from the *Notebooks*:
'Linguistics
I is an element of language linked to speech itself. All speech has its source
which is an I. This *I* is mine if that of X if X hears it gives and receives this
speech, and in receiving it recognizes himself as source, i.e. simultaneously an
object among objects and a non-object, a space or world of objects.

'I, You, Him, this triangle—Trinity! The three roles of the same in relation
to the verb, Mouth, ear, thing' (C. 11, p. 604, 1926). A very enigmatic sequence
from 1910, in examining the 'believer' who 'believes he believes,' proposed
what is doubtless the most efficacious formula for every deviation of the
source: 'Thereby, change 3 to 4 in the Trinity' (II, 574).

In the return of the phonic circle, the source appears as such only at the
moment, which is no longer a moment, the barely second second, of the
instant emission in which the origin yields itself to receive what it produces.
The source receives, receives itself, interrupts circulation only in order to
saturate it. Would the circle disjoin itself only in the separation which is in
sum undefinable, and hardly probable, between a voice of the interior and an
effectively proffered voice? Such a separation in effect remains ungraspable in
linguistic, poetic, or phenomenological terms. Neither in the form nor the
content of a statement could we assign an intrinsic difference between the
sentence I am pronouncing here, now, in my so-called speaking voice, which
soon will return to the silence from which it proceeds, very low in my voice
or on my page, and the *same* sentence retained in an inner instance, mine or
yours. The two events are as different as possible as events, but in the qualitative description of events, in the determination of predicative traits, form or
content, the principle of discernibility, the concept of difference evades us.
Like the separation that disjoints the circle, a certain tangency here appears to
be both nul and infinite. Another note from the *Notebooks*, concerning the
point de source: '. . . no (*point de*) "me" without "you." To each his Other, which
is his Same. Or the *I is two*—by definition. If there is *voice*, there is ear.
Internally there is voice, there is no sight of who is speaking. And who will
describe, will define the *difference between the same sentence which is said* and *not
pronounced*, and the *same sentence sounding in the air*. This identity and this difference are one of the essential secrets of the nature of the mind—and who
has pointed it out? Who has "exhibited" it? The same for sight. I believe that
the relationship of these possibilities of double effect is in the power of motil-
ity, which will never sufficiently be thought about. Within it lies the mystery
of time, i.e. the existence of that which is not. Potential and unactual' (C. 22,
p. 304, 1939; Valéry's italics).

Not long after, still as a displacement but from whence the snake again is
sketched in the form of circles drawn in the margin, we have from Valéry's
hand: 'There is nothing more astonishing than this "interior" speech, which is

heard without any noise and is articulated without movement. Like a closed circuit. Everything comes to be explained and thrashed out in this circle similar to the snake biting its tail. Sometimes the ring is broken and emits the internal speech. Sometimes the communication between what is being born and the born is regular, regimented, and the distinction can no longer be felt. Sometimes the communication is only delayed, and the internal circuit serves as a preparation for a circuit of *external intention*: then there is emission to choice' (C. 24, p. 99, 1940).

The difference between internal speech and external speech therefore passes understanding. No concept can make it its own. Its reserve is almost unheard—with what ear could it be heard?—or in any event undescribable. Thirty years earlier: 'How *to write* this singular difference rationally?' (C. 3, p. 483, 1905).[15] How to write it, in effect, if writing, phonetic writing above all, precisely has as its function the restitution of speech to the internal regime, and to act such that in its event effectively proffered speech is but an accident lost for reading? The regime, being regimented, in effect seems to insure the 'normal' communication of the source with itself, thereby regularly circulating between the external event and the internal event, conferring upon the origin the invisible appearing, the calm being near to itself that the glance saw itself refused.

Now here, again, Valéry remarks a cutting difference: not the external prolation which accidentally would come to interrupt the circle, but already the circuit's return to itself: 'Who speaks, who listens [in the interior speech]? It is not exactly the same . . . The existence of the speech from self to self is the sign of a *cut*' (C. 7, p. 615, 1920). The circle turns in order to annul the cut, and therefore, by the same token, unwittingly signifies it. The snake bites its tail, from which above all it does not follow that it finally rejoins itself without harm in this successful auto-fellatio of which we have been speaking all along, in truth.

Cut off from the end as from the origin, the source is no longer anything but an effect of 'reaction' or, if you will, of revolution, in a system that never will have obeyed it. 'I speak *to myself*. The action formulated this way suggests a distinction. And in effect what one says (or shows) to the other I teaches the latter something—or rather excites a reaction—, which becomes an origin' (C. 15, p. 193, 1931). Earlier: 'On the relations of the I and the me. If I *say* something *to myself*, what I say acts on what follows and modifies what I will say to myself—becomes an origin' (C. 12, p. 692, 1928).

The source having *become*—which is the unintelligible itself—time opens itself as the delay of the origin in relation to itself. Time is nothing other. 'What comes to "mind"—to the lips—modifies you yourself in return. What you have just emitted, emits toward you, and what you have produced fecundates you. In saying something without having foreseen it, you see it like a foreign fact, an *origin*—something you had not known. Thus you were delayed in relation to yourself' (C. 12, p. 24, 1926). And elsewhere: 'We are made of two moments, and as if of the *delay* of a "thing" for itself' (*Mauvaises pensées et autres* II, 885. Valéry's italics).

Thus, we have at our disposition, as a paradigm, all the movements by means of which Valéry could *track down* the source. And, for the very reason we have just analyzed, we no longer have to decide if this paradigm is an origin and a model or one example among others. To track down, to set out on the path on which the living signals death, is indeed to repeat without end the indestructible desire which comes back to the source as to the complicity or simplicity of life and death. In the purity of the source the living is the dead. But to track down is also to dispel the illusion, to flush out all the questions and concepts of the origin. It is to unseal at the source the separation of an altering difference.

Among others, three fragments from the *Notebooks*: 'Heaven preserve you from questions of origin' (C. 21, p. 275, 1938). 'We are not origins, but the illusion of being so is with us' (C. 8, p. 895, 1922). 'Some go to the furthest reach of the *origin*—which is the coincidence of *presence* and of the initial event—and attempt to go to find in this separation *gold*, *diamonds*' (C. 15, p. 526, 1931–32; Valéry's italics).

Point de philosophie[16]—Writing

The origin—coincidence of presence and the initial event. Perhaps I will let myself be guided now by the question put this way: can one dissociate the 'initial event' from presence? Can one conceive of an initial event without presence, the value of a *first time* that cannot be thought in the form or category of presence? Would this be the impossible itself? And if so, impossible for whom, for what, according to what space?

Here we come to *philosophy*.

Valéry lays out his entire reading of the history of philosophy according to this snare. The philosopher—it is he of whom Valéry speaks, and whom Valéry summons to appear, rather than philosophy itself—is the person who wears himself out over vain questions of origin: an illusion both transcendental and natural, natural since it invincibly returns to the orient, to 'nature,' to birth, to the source. Everywhere that 'nature' intervenes in philosophical discourse, that is everywhere, Valéry pursues it with ironic apostrophes that never aim at nature alone, but also the entire cortege of distinctions and oppositions that nature activates and regulates.[17]

Let us sketch out the scheme of this critical solicitation of philosophical discourse. It always insists upon a crisis of the origin.

Valéry reminds the philosopher that philosophy is written. And that the philosopher is a philosopher to the extent that he forgets this.

Philosophy is written—producing at least three consequences.

First of all, a break with the regime of hearing-oneself-speak, with self-presence in the meaning of a source whose truth continuously resources itself. Irreversibly, something of this presence of meaning, of this truth which nonetheless is the philosopher's great and only theme, is lost in writing. Hence the philosopher writes against writing, writes in order to make good the loss of writing, and by this very gesture forgets and denies what occurs by his hand. These two gestures must be kept together. As if unknown to each other, they cooperate as soon as one interprets writing as does Valéry in this context. The philosopher writes in order to keep himself within the logo-centric circle. But also in order to reconstitute the circle, to interiorize a continuous and ideal presence which he knows, consciously or unconsciously —which does not matter since in any event he feels the effect—*already* to have been dispelled within the voice itself. Discontinuity, delay, heterogeneity, and alterity already were working upon the voice, producing it from its first breath as a system of differential traces, that is as writing before the letter. Philosophical writing, then, literally comes to bridge this gap, to close the dike, and to dream of virgin continuity.

Whence Valéry's apparently paradoxical argument, which opposes the continuousness of writing, or rather of the graphic, to the discontinuousness of speech. The philosopher intends to come back to the proximity of the speaking source, or rather to the source murmuring its interior speech, and to deny that he is writing. Terrified by the difference within hearing-oneself-speak, by the writing within speech, the philosopher writes—on the page— in order to erase and to forget that when he speaks the evil of the cipher is already there in germ. 'But the nature of language is quite opposed to the happy outcome of this great endeavor to which all the philosophers have devoted themselves. The strongest of them have worn themselves out in the effort to *make their thoughts speak*. In vain have they created or transfigured certain words; they could not succeed in transmitting their inner reality. Whatever the words may be—Ideas or Dynamis or Being or Noumenon or Cogito or Ego—they are all *ciphers*, the meaning of which is determined solely by the context; and so it is finally by a sort of personal creation that their reader—as also happens with readers of poetry—gives the force of life to writings in which ordinary speech is contorted into expressing values that men cannot exchange and that do not exist in the realm of spoken words' (8, 150–51; Valéry's italics).

These philosophical ciphers formalize natural language and tend to forge, by means of the contract of their conventional formality, a kind of chain of security, of quasi-continuous plenitude which occasionally makes these ciphers resemble the thing itself. They tend to erase the breaks, the tremors working within speech and writing in what is called 'natural language,' which is also, from the start, a diastemic organization, a system of 'arbitrary' signs, or in any event of discrete and diacritical signs. Now the paradoxical law that Valéry was able to recognize is that the more the graphic is formalized the more it is naturalized. As an artist of form, which is what he is from Valéry's point of view, the philosopher is still dreaming of nature. Here we might elaborate the motif of a critique of formalist illusion which would complicate what is often considered to be Valéry's formalism somewhat. The complication is due to the fact that formality, far from simply being *opposed* to it, *simultaneously* produces and destroys the naturalist, 'originarist' illusion. Always insufficiently formalized, still too embroiled in natural language, in natural language's vagueness, equivocalness, and metaphoricity, philosophical writing does not support comparison with its model: the rigor and exactitude of a purely formal language. Valéry has just recalled the effort of the philosopher wearing himself out in *making his thoughts speak*: 'Today, in a number of truly remarkable cases, even the expression of things by means of discrete signs, arbitrarily chosen, has given way to lines traced by the things themselves, or to transpositions or inscriptions directly derived from them. The great invention that consists in making the laws of science visible to the eyes and, as it were, readable on sight has been incorporated into knowledge; and it has in some sort *doubled* the world of experience with a visible world of curves, surfaces, and diagrams that translate properties into forms whose inflexions we can follow with our eyes, thus by our consciousness of this movement gaining an impression of values in transition. The *graphic* has a continuity of movement that cannot be rendered in speech, and it is superior to speech in immediacy and precision. Doubtless it was speech that commanded the method to exist; doubtless it is now speech that assigns a meaning to the graphisms and interprets them; but it is no longer by speech that the act of mental possession is consummated. Something new is little by little taking shape under our eyes; a sort of ideography of plotted and diagrammed relations between qualities and quantities, a language that has for grammar a body of preliminary conventions (scales, axes, grids, etc.)' (8, 152–53; modified).[18]

Philosophy is written—second consequence—so that it must reckon with a formal instance, reckon with form, is unable to get away from it: 'I said one day before philosophers: philosophy is an affair of form.'[19]

A task is then prescribed: to study the philosophical text in its formal structure, in its rhetorical organization, in the specificity and diversity of its textual types, in its models of exposition and production—beyond what previously were called genres—and also in the space of its mises en scène, in a syntax which would be not only the articulation of its signifieds, its references to Being or to truth, but also the handling of its proceedings, and of everything invested in them. In a word, the task is to consider philosophy also as a 'particular literary genre,' drawing upon the reserves of a language, cultivating, forcing, or making deviate a set of tropic resources[20] older than philosophy itself. Here we are quite close to Nietzsche, but let us not hasten to compare: 'What becomes of it (philosophy) when—in addition to feeling beset, overrun, and dismayed at every turn by the furious activity of the physical sciences— it is also disturbed and menaced in its most ancient, most tenacious (and perhaps least regrettable) habits by the slow and meticulous work of the philologists and semanticists? What becomes of the philosopher's *I think*, and what becomes of his *I am*? What becomes, or rebecomes, of that neutral and mysterious verb TO BE, which has had such a grand career in the void? From those modest syllables, released to a peculiar fortune by the loss or attrition of their original meaning, artists of great subtlety have drawn an infinite number of answers.

'*If, then, we take no account of our habitual thinking* and confine ourselves to what is revealed by a glance at the present state of intellectual affairs, we can easily observe that philosophy as defined by its product, which is *in writing*, is objectively a particular branch of literature . . . we are forced to assign it a place not far from poetry . . .

'But the artists of whom I was speaking fail to recognize themselves as artists and do not wish to be such. Doubtless their art, unlike that of the poets, is not the art of exploiting the sound values of words; it speculates on a certain faith in the existence of an absolute value that can be isolated from their meaning. "What is reality?" the philosopher asks, or likewise, "What is liberty?" Setting aside and ignoring the partly metaphorical, partly social, and partly statistical origin of these nouns, his mind, by taking advantage of their tendency to slip into indefinable meanings, will be able to produce combinations of extreme depth and delicacy' (8, 139–40)[21]

Perhaps I will be able to state further on how the critical necessity of this aesthetics, of this formalism or conventionalism, if adhered to otherwise than with controlled insistence and a calculated strategic reaction, would risk just as surely leading us back to the places in question.

Philosophy is written—third consequence—as soon as its forms and operations are not only oriented and watched over by the law of meaning, thought, and Being, which speaks in order to say I, and does so as close as possible to the source or the well.

Of this proposition, as of its simulacrum, Descartes here is exemplary. Valéry does not cease to question him, never leaves him; and if his reading of Descartes at the very least might appear uneven to the historians of philosophy, the fact was not unforeseen by Valéry, who interpreted it in advance. We will concern ourselves with this for a while.

What is the operation of the I in the Cogito? To assure itself of the source in the certitude of an invincible self presence, even in the figure—always paternal, Freud tells us—of the devil. This time a *power*[22] is gained in the course of a movement in grand style which takes the risk of enunciating and writing itself. Valéry very quickly suggests that truth is Descartes's last concern. The words 'truth' and 'reality' are once again in quotation marks, advanced as effects of language and as simple citations. But if the 'I think therefore I am' 'has no meaning whatever,'[23] and *a fortiori* no truth, it has 'a very great value,' and like the style is 'entirely characteristic of the man himself.' This value is that of a shattering blow, a quasi-arbitrary affirmation of mastery by means of the exercise of a style, the egotistic impression of a form, the stratagem of a mise en scène powerful enough to do without truth, a mise en scène keeping that much less to truth in its laying of truth as a trap, a trap into which generations of servile fetishists will come to be caught, thereby acknowledging the law of the master, of I, René Descartes.

Valéry insists upon the style: 'It is precisely this that I think I see in the *Cogito*. Neither a syllogism nor even meaning in the literal sense; but a reflex action of the man, or more accurately, the explosion of an act, a shattering blow. There is, in any thinker of such intellectual power, what might be described as a home policy and a foreign policy of thought; he sets up certain 'reasons of state' against which nothing can prevail . . . Never, until he came, had a philosopher so deliberately exhibited himself on the stage of his own thought, risking his own neck, daring to write 'I' for whole pages on end; he does it above all, and in an admirable style, when writing the *Meditations* . . . I have called his style admirable' (9, 55–56).

Further on, and elsewhere, Valéry associates style with the 'timbre' of the voice. Descartes could assert himself, posit his mastery, only by 'paying with his person,' exposing himself in a theater, putting himself on stage and into play 'by risking the *I*.' And henceforth at issue are the *style* of his writing and the *timbre* of his voice.

How are we to reassemble these propositions? Will it be said that Descartes, by means of what is inimitable in his text (timbre and style), has succeeded in imposing the source, in restoring the presence of the origin that is so implacably set aside by the play of signification?

Not at all, and such is the risk of what is at stake. In order to understand this, we must recall that the concepts of style and timbre have a rigorous definition in Valéry's analyses. In its irreplaceable quality, the timbre of the voice marks the event of language. By virtue of this fact, timbre has greater import than the *form* of signs and the *content* of meaning. In any event, timbre cannot be summarized by form and content, since at the very least they share the capacity to be repeated, to be imitated in their identity as objects, that is, in their ideality. ('Now, as far as you are concerned, all I need do is watch you talk, listen to your timbre, the excitement in your voice. The way people talk tells you more than what they say . . . The content in itself has no . . . essential importance.—Odd. That's one theory of poetry,' *Idée Fixe*, 5, 106.) Numerous notes in the *Notebooks* confirm this point. Not lending itself to substitution, is not timbre on the order of a pure event, a singular presence, the very upsurge [*sourdre*] of the source? And is not style the equivalent of this unique vibration in writing? *If there is* one poetic event, it sounds in timbre; *if there is* one literary event, it is inscribed by style. 'Literature, style—it is to write that which will supplement for the absence of the author, for the silence of the absent, for the inertia of the written thing' (C. 12, p. 10, 1926). This proposition, and others[24] along the same lines, appear to be quite classical, and doubtless are so up to a certain point: style, supplementing timbre, tends to repeat the event of pure presence, the singularity of the source present in what it produces, supposing again that the unity of a timbre—immediately it is identifiable— ever has the purity of an event. But, if style supplements timbre, nothing, it appears, can supplement their unique exchange, nothing can repeat the pure event (if at least there is something like the purity of a style and a timbre, which for me remains quite a hypothesis) that style and timbre constitute.

But, if there is a timbre and a style, will it be concluded that here the source *presents itself*?

Point. And this is why *I* loses itself here, or in any event exposes itself in the operation of mastery. The timbre of my voice, the style of my writing are that which for (a) me never will have been present. I neither hear nor recognize the timbre of my voice. If my style marks itself, it is only on a surface which remains invisible and illegible for me. *Point of speculum*: here I am blind to my style, deaf to what is most spontaneous in my voice. It is, to take up again the formulation from above, and to make it deviate toward a lexicographical monstrosity, the *sourdre* of the source.[25] The spontaneous can emerge as the pure initiality of the event only on the condition that it does not itself *present itself*, on the condition of this inconceivable and *irrelevable*[26] passivity in which nothing can present itself to itself. Here we are in need of a paradoxical logic of the event as a *source which cannot present itself, happen to itself*. The value of the event is perhaps indissociable from that of presence; it remains rigorously incompatible with that of self-presence.

The Event and the Regime of the Other: Timbre

To hear oneself is the most normal and the most impossible experience. One might conclude from this, first, that the source is always other, and that whatever hears itself, not itself hearing itself, always comes from elsewhere, from outside and afar. The lure of the I, of consciousness as hearing-oneself-speak would consist in dreaming of an operation of ideal and idealizing mastery, transforming hetero-affection into auto-affection, heteronomy into autonomy. Within this process of appropriation somehow would be lodged a 'regime' of normal hallucination. When I speak (to myself) without moving tongue and lips, I believe that I hear myself, although the source is other; or I believe that we are two, although everything is happening 'in me.' Supported by a very ancient history, traversing all the stations of the relation to the self (sucking, masturbation, touching/touched, etc.), this possibility of a 'normal' double hallucination permits me to give myself to hear what I desire to hear, to believe in the spontaneity of the power which needs no one in order to give pleasure to itself. Valéry perhaps has read into this the essence of poetic power. 'A Poet's Notebook' opens with these words: 'Poetry. Is it impossible, given time, care, skill, and desire, to proceed in an orderly way to arrive at poetry? To end by *hearing* exactly what one wished to hear by means of a skillful and patient management of that same desire?' (7, 173).

At a certain moment in history, for reasons to be analyzed, the poet ceased being considered the prey of a foreign voice, in mania, delirium, enthusiasm, or inspiration. Poetic 'hallucination' is then accommodated under the rubric of the 'regime': a simple elaboration of hearing-oneself-speak, a regulated, normed exchange of the same and the other, within the limits tolerated by a kind of general organization, that is, an individual, social, historical system, etc.

But what happens when this organization, still intolerant somewhere, incriminates 'literally' abnormal hallucination? What happens, for example, when someone hears voices that he *remains alone* to hear, and that he perceives as a foreign source, which proceeds, as is said, from his own interior? Can one settle this problem as being the poet's? Can one content oneself with saying that since the source is transcendentally other, in sum, this hallucination too is normal, more or less, i.e. an exaggeration hardly baring the truth that would be the essential heterogeneity of the source?

Here is announced the question of psychoanalysis. In one of the *Notebooks* of 1918–21, concerning silent discourse, Valéry noted: 'This voice (morbidly) might become entirely foreign' (C. 7, p. 615, 1920). And, during the course of an analysis that is systematically, in detail, to be collated with Freud's analysis of Schreber's *Memoirs*, Valéry slips in, without pausing, an allusion to Swedenborg's father. Then, like Freud, setting aside the hypothesis of a purely delirious disorder, Valéry wonders: '*How is a Swedenborg possible?*' Making his question explicit, he almost could be speaking of Schreber: 'From what premises must we start when we come to study the coexistence in the same person of a scientist and engineer, a high official, a man at once wise in practical affairs and learned in everything, who yet had the characteristics of an Illuminatus, who did not hesitate to write and publish an account of his visions, and who claimed to have been visited by the inhabitants of another world, to be in touch with them, and to have spent part of his life in their mysterious company?' (9, 123).

Valéry indeed must admit that if the source is always other, the alterity of the source, in the case of the mystic or the hallucinated, is of an other alterity; it is no longer the source which 'normally' divides and constitutes the I, if we might put it thus, although for Valéry, as for Freud, the notion of normality appears to be 'cursory and too simple.' Therefore, he takes into account this surplus heterogeneity of alterity. And the word 'source' imposes itself upon Valéry several times.

In the 'normal' regime, the I controls the distinction between an internal alterity, in some way, and an external alterity. Above all, it does not transform 'deviations' that it may 'attribute' to an 'intimate and functional origin' (9, 120; modified) into an absolutely external source. It recognizes what comes from its own desire. 'The mystic, on the contrary, has a sense of the exteriority, or rather extraneousness, of the *source* of the images, emotions, words, and impulses which reach him through some inner channel' (9, 121; Valéry's italics). The question then becomes one of this alienation of the source, the becoming-exterior of an intimate source: 'How can we conceive that a man like Swedenborg, a highly cultivated man . . . could have failed to perceive the part played by his own mind in producing the images, admonitions, "truths" which came to him as though from some secret source?' (9, 121). And of course Valéry also leads these phenomena of the alienation or alteration of the source back to a certain desire of Swedenborg's: he receives from an 'external source' something 'intensely desired' (9, 125).[27]

But here we have only the principle of a description. There is still nothing to permit us to explain the difference between the state of the hallucinated or the mystic and, for example, the state of the poet, that is, whoever finishes 'by *hearing* precisely what he had desired to hear.' Now, Valéry knew that Swedenborg's experience was not homogeneous with 'poetic' experience, that is, with the experience of the alterity of the 'regimented' source. Valéry recognizes this clearly, and even goes to the extent of indicating that the '"subjective" events which were, strictly speaking, hallucinatory,' as narrated by Swedenborg, 'cannot be reduced either to mystic vision or to the admitted existence of a certain sign' (9, 125–26).

The Implex (Question of Formalisms): Nietzsche and Freud

At this point, ceasing to describe, but also renouncing any attempt at explanation, Valéry in his last three pages proposes a purely negative and polemical discourse which can be summarized as a principled objection to any hypothesis of the psychoanalytic type in the name of the ineffable. The central nerve of the argument is the following: one gains access to these hallucinatory or oneiric phenomena only by means of a narrative discourse, a discrete and relational verbal chain of *ex post facto* descriptions, of transcriptions, of translations of transcriptions, etc. which always leave the experience itself out of reach, the experience being '*something which is nameless*' (9, 127; Valéry's italics). And, before coming to any conclusions on what he dubiously calls the 'Swedenborg Mystery,' Valéry had written: 'That is why I am very far from putting confidence in the pretended analysis of dreams which is so fashionable at the present time and in which we seem to have forged a new Key to Dreams' (9, 126).

Here the question of psychoanalysis imposes itself. All the motifs I have emphasized, and still others, to a certain point are in agreement, in any event in their principles, with Freud's motifs: redefinition of the I (the ego) and consciousness as effects in a system, development of the logic of a primary narcissism in relation to a death drive, systematic interest in everything that escapes the control of waking consciousness (Valéry's meditation on dreams was unceasing), etc. One could pursue the correspondence of the two texts a long way. I do not know whether Freud read Valéry, and since it is not his birthday, I leave suspended the question of knowing why, and above all if he can be excused for this. But why did Valéry so nervously reject psychoanalysis? Why did he seize upon the argument of the unnamable that he just as summarily could have used against all science? The connotation of nervousness, of precipitation, and of spasm are not insignificant. Valéry could have offered arguments, showed his disagreement, asked epistemological questions, differentiated his criticisms, vigilantly examined what then could be seen of psychoanalysis: but he did so only by opposing his formalist point of view—which therefore produces an effect of obscurantism here—to what he considered to be Freud's semantic, 'significative' point of view about dreams.[28] But why talk about Freud's 'stupidity'? Why multiply sarcastic remarks against those whom he names 'Freud and Co.'? Most often it is the insistence on sexuality that infuriates him, and without recognizing, wanting or being able to recognize, that Freud's 'sexualism' is much more complex and problematical than it appears, Valéry often gets carried away, losing his *teste*[29] so to speak, when confronted by what he calls the 'dirty ins and outs.' Unless M. Teste's strong point, his cold and pure intellectuality ('Stupidity is not my strong point'), somewhere is constructed in order to resist a certain psychoanalytic 'stupidity.' One also might reread *Idée Fixe* with one's sights set in this direction, on Valéry's rejection; in an instant I will indicate why. Concerning dreams and psychoanalysis, we may point out the following in particular: 'My dear man, I'm so fed up with the whole story and all its dirty ins and outs . . . I've been stuffed to the skin with incestuous narcoses!' (5, 41). And the 'Propositions

Concerning Me' close the door on Proust and Freud with a redoubled negation at odds with 'absurd' analyses, which moreover are reproached for being
too 'significant': 'No! no! I do not at all like to find myself once more in mind
of the ancient pathways of my life. I will not track down Things Past! And
even less would I approve of those absurd analyses which inculcate in people
the most obscene rebuses, that they are already to have composed at their
mothers' breasts' (II, 1506). And in the *Notebooks*, concerning love: 'What is
more stupid than Freud's inventions on these matters?' (C. 22, p. 201, 1939).

Here I am setting aside two questions. Not that I judge them to be without
interest or without pertinence, but in the small amount of time given us here,
they might distract us from a reading which appears more urgent. In the first
place, the issue will not be to improvise by tinkering with something which
might resemble a psychoanalysis of Valéry's resistance to psychoanalysis. In the
conditions under which this might be done, it would be very naive, and
would fall well within Valéry's text, and the problems it elaborates, the questions
it puts to a psychoanalysis of the text, to a psychoanalysis in the text, neither
of which have come close to being articulated, or could not be, except by
means of major transformations. Second, the issue will not be of a historical
analysis explaining why Valéry, at a given date, could not read Freud,[30] read
him as we read him now, or will read him henceforth. One would have to
take into account a large number of elements—the state of the translation and
introduction of Freud in France and elsewhere, a general weave of resistances,
and their relation to a certain state of Freudian theory, the heterogeneity of
the psychoanalytic text in general, etc. It is not certain that Valéry simply
participated in this closing off, that is, that he simply consolidated it. Valéry's
work, his attention to language, to rhetoric, to formal agencies, to the paradoxes of narcissism, his distrust concerning naive semanticism, etc. all have
probably contributed, or in any event belonged, to an entire groundswell
which, after the war, carried along a particular rereading of Freud. As for the
irony directed against the psychoanalytic 'fashion,' the ingenuous rush toward
a mono- or pansexual semanticism for Parisian parlor games or literary futil-
ities (Valéry at the time was thinking primarily of the Surrealists), nothing
could appear less anti-Freudian, whatever Valéry may have thought himself,
and nothing could be more needed.

Having reserved these two questions, we will ask, then, which concepts and
which internal marks are the means with which to recognize, in Valéry's textual system, a certain division and a certain conflict of forces between two
critical operations, at the sharpest and most novel point of two necessarily
heterogeneous discourses: Valéry's and Freud's.

Here we must content ourselves with the most schematic reading. Thus,
without pretending to determine any center in Valéry's text, without defining
some closed fist that everything in a powerful, open, and ceaselessly questioning

work renders improbable, I nevertheless will venture to localize a concept, and even a word, that nothing in what I have read seems to contradict. In question is a focal point of great economic density, the intersection of a great circulation, rather than some theological principle. Implied everywhere, never surprised or exceeded, this focal point seems to bring everything back to itself as if to a source. Thus, you will very quickly be tempted to object: aren't you going to reduce a text to its thematic or semantic center, to its final truth, etc.? I will adduce the singular form of this word-concept, which precisely marks an implication that is not one, an implication that cannot be reduced to anything simple, an implication and complication of the source that in a certain way cannot be disimplicated: thus, the IMPLEX.

The implex: that which cannot be simplex. It marks the limit of every analytic reduction to the simple element of the point. An implication-complication, a complication of the same and the other which never permits itself to be undone, it divides or equally multiplies infinitely the simplicity of every source, every origin, every presence. Throughout the numerous variations and contextual transpositions to which Valéry submits this concept, the same structure is always sketched out: the impossibility for a present, for the presence of a present, to *present itself* as *a source*: simple, actual, punctual, instantaneous. The implex is a complex of the present always enveloping the nonpresent and the other present in the simple appearance of its pointed identity. It is the potentiality or rather the power, the dynamis and mathematical exponentiality of the value of presence, of everything the value of presence supports, that is of everything—that *is*. Among many possible citations, let us focus upon *Idée Fixe*. In question is the present and that which the 'popular conception,' that is philosophy, discerns as past, present, future: 'Thus if you stick the point of the *present* into the actual moment . . . You create the present tense of the present, which you express as: *I am in the process of* . . . You create the future tense of the present: *I am just about to* . . . And so on. The present tense of the present of the present tense, the present tense of the future of the past pluperfect, and so on . . . You could refine on that. A mathematician could . . . You've started exponentiating all by yourself . . . To sum up, what I signify by *Implex* is that by which, and in virtue of which, we remain contingent, conditional' (5, 57–58).

This value of contingency, eventuality, describes what is at stake in the concept. The implex, a nonpresence, nonconsciousness, an alterity folded over in the *sourdre* of the source,[31] envelops the possible of what it is not yet, the virtual capacity of that which presently it is not in act. '. . . Now what about that word, that name? . . . —My name for all that inner potentiality that we were talking about is: the IMPLEX . . . No, the Implex is not an activity. Quite the contrary. It's a *capacity*' (5, 55–56).

This nonconsciousness or nonpresence, this nonsimplicity is *the same as* that which it actually is not; it is homogeneous with present consciousness, that is with the self presence whose dynamic virtuality it opens. Even if, at the limit, it were impossible to make it explicit, it relates perception to self-consciousness as potentiality to act. It belongs to the same system as that which would remain, at the limit, always doubled over within it. Such a system covers that of the classical philosopheme of *dynamis*.

This limit is precisely the one which seems to pass between Valéry's critique of consciousness and Freudian psychoanalysis. The unconscious, that which Freud names in this way, is not a virtual consciousness; its alterity is not homogeneous with the alterity lodged in the implex. Here the *sourdre* is entirely other. And the operation that Freud calls repression, which seems to have no specific place in Valéry's analysis, would introduce, if some such thing exists, a difference irreducible to the difference between the virtual and the actual; even if this virtuality must remain an undecomposable implex. This is what, from the outset, would separate the analysis of Swedenborg from the analysis of Schreber.

But would this be teaching Valéry anything? He indeed knew that such was the site of his resistance to psychoanalysis. If I have chosen to remain within *Idée Fixe*, it is that in this text everything seems to be edified around this center, like a system of fortifications impenetrable by psychoanalysis. The implex represents the major device here. From this strong point, one can throw psychoanalysis back where it comes from, that is, from the sea, into the sea, a movement which could not have been simple for Valéry—such occasionally seems to be the obsidional operation of the *Idée Fixe* itself. When the interlocutor, imprudent soul, proposes to 'open up the Implex,' even risking a rapprochement between the implex and the unconscious, he is simply threatened with being thrown into the sea. All the criticisms that have been addressed to psychoanalysis in France for fifty years, find their resources here: 'We'll have to open up the *Implex*. But wait a moment. Does this Implex of yours amount to any more than what vulgar, common mortals, the masses, philosophers, psychologists, psychopaths, the non-Crusoes—the herd, in fact—call quite simply and crudely the "unconscious" or the "subconscious."'?

'—Do you want me to pitch you into the sea? . . . Don't you know I detest such dirty words? . . . And anyhow, it isn't the same thing at all. They are meant to signify some inconceivable hidden springs of action—at times they stand for sly little inner goblins, marvelous tricksters, who can guess riddles, read the future, see through brick walls, and carry on the most amazing industry inside our hidden workings' (5, 53–56).

Immediately afterward defining the implex as virtuality and general *capacity* ('for feeling, reacting, doing, and understanding'), it is true that Valéry adds to the end of the list the 'capacity for resistance': 'To all that we must add our capacity for resistance' (5, 56).

We will not ask what the *meaning* of this resistance is before pointing out that what Valéry intends to resist is meaning itself. What he reproaches psychoanalysis for is not that it interprets in such or such a fashion, but quite simply that it interprets at all, that it is an interpretation, that it is interested above all in signification, in meaning, and in some principal unity—here, a sexual unity—of meaning. He reproaches psychoanalysis for being a 'symbolics'—this is what he names it—a hermeneutism, a semanticism. Is there not, henceforth, a place where all of Valéry's poetic and linguistic formalism, his very necessary critique of thematicist or semanticist spontaneity, in literature and elsewhere, all the irony with which he paralyzed the prejudices of meaning, theme, subject, content, etc., a place, then, where all of these come to be articulated systematically with his compulsive and obstinate rejection of psychoanalysis, a rejection operating as close as possible to psychoanalysis, and completely opposed to it? Was there not in meaning, to the extent that it is worked upon and afterward constituted by repression, something which above all had not to be dealt with? Something which formally had to be thrown back into the sea?

Above all I will not conclude that this hypothesis disqualifies Valéry's critical formalism. Something within it remains necessary and must be maintained, it seems to me, in opposition to all precritical semanticisms. The psychoanalytic discourses known to us are far from being exempt from this semanticism. Perhaps we here are touching upon a limit at which the opposition of form and meaning, along with all the divisions coordinated to it, loses its pertinence, and calls for an entirely other elaboration.

This elaboration would pass through the rereading of all these texts, of course, and of several others. It demands that one become engaged in it without endlessly circling around the form of these texts, that one decipher the law of their internal conflicts, of their heterogeneity, of their contradictions, and that one not simply cast an aesthete's glance over the philosophical discourse which carries within it the history of the oppositions in which are displaced, although often under cover, both critical formalism and psychoanalytic hermeneutics.

Like Nietzsche, reinterpret interpretation.

I proposed that Nietzsche may have been Valéry's other set-aside source. Everything should have led Valéry back to him: the systematic mistrust as concerns the entirety of metaphysics, the formal vision of philosophical discourse, the concept of the philosopher-artist, the rhetorical and philological questions put to the history of philosophy, the suspiciousness concerning the values of truth ('a well applied convention'),[32] of meaning and of Being, of the 'meaning of Being,' the attention to the economic phenomena of force and of the difference of forces, etc.

Valéry no doubt sensed this perhaps excessive proximity. He was ready to associate Nietzsche with Poe (I, 1781). And yet, in certain letters (see, for example, I, 855), after having rendered homage to Nietzsche, he explains why Nietzsche 'shocked' him, 'irritated' him (this is often his reaction to philosophy). In the course of a rather summary argumentation, he accuses Nietzsche of being 'contradictory' of being a 'metaphysician,' and of 'seeking to create a philosophy of violence.' Elsewhere, in the form of a parody, he composes a false letter by Nietzsche, marked, if one may put it thus, by a Teutonic accent, in which the stiffest, and also most ardent, seriousness seems to be more on Valéry's side (I, 1781–83).

Why does M. Teste again permit himself to be irritated here? Why did Valéry not want, not want to be able, to read Nietzsche? Did he consider him threatening? And why? Too close? And in what way? These two hypotheses are not any more mutually exclusive than the for or the against. Did not Valéry push away Nietzsche for the same reason that made him push away Freud?

This is what Freud thought, and he was well placed to know so. Freud in advance knew that if Valéry could not acknowledge Nietzsche, it is because Nietzsche resembled Freud too much. And he had said so around 1925, or rather whispered it, with an imperturbable confidence.

For one to admire the wicked ruse of a certain *igitur (ja)*, it suffices to make psychoanalysis probable from the very fact of its own *mise en scène (Selbst-darstellung)*: 'Nietzsche, another philosopher whose guesses and intuitions often agree in the most astonishing way with the laborious findings of psycho-analysis, was for a long time avoided by me on that very account; I was less concerned with the question of priority than with keeping my mind unembarrassed.'[33]

Notes

1. As is so often the case for Derrida, this title has multiple meanings whose effects are disseminated throughout the essay. It must be understood that Derrida constantly plays on the meaning of 'source' as both origin and as fountain or spring. The German *Quelle* has the same multiple meanings. The explanation of *qual quelle* will be found in note 12 below. [Trans.]
2. The following system of reference to Valéry's works will be employed. (*a*) References to Valéry's *Oeuvres* (Paris: Gallimard, 1957–60) will be given with a roman volume number (I or II) and a page number. Thus, the reference for this citation is *Discours de l'histoire*, I, 1130. (*b*) References to the *Cahiers* (Paris: Centre National de Recherche Scientifique, 1957) will be given by the letter C. followed by an arabic volume number, a page number, and a year. (*c*) References to works of Valéry translated into English will be to the thirteen-volume Bollingen series *The Collected Works of Paul Valéry*, ed. Jackson Mathews (New York: Bollingen

Foundation, 1960–73). These will be indicated by an arabic volume number and a page number (e.g. 2, 11). [Trans.]

3. This booklet, published by the *Source Perrier* (2, 8ff., or II, 202ff.) contains 'The History of a Source,' by P. Reboux, 'The Therapeutic Benefits of the Perrier Source,' by Dr. Gervais, 'How, and In What Circumstances, To Serve Perrier Water,' by Baron Fouquier. In 1919 Gide had written to Valéry: 'I cannot for an instant believe in the exhaustion of your resources or the drying up of your source: what is difficult is to bottle it, but there is nothing surprising about the fact that you find yourself worn out after the efforts of the winter,' thereby describing everything at stake in the question that concerns us here. Without taking into account that by itself the name of the source in question, in a single word, reassembles the extensible length of a sentence. [*Perrier* in French is pronounced the same way as the sentence 'Pere y est'—'Father is there.']

4. I, 1487. And elsewhere: 'Every doctrine necessarily presents itself as a *scheme more advantageous* than the others. Therefore, it depends upon the others' (II, 690). 'Thought is brutal—no taming it . . . What is more brutal than a thought?' (II, 694).

5. 2, 272 ('For Your "Supreme" Beech'); 2, 161 ('Fragments of the Narcissus'). The dream of the tree always *returns* to a source ('Between them the pure air and a shrub contrive / A living spring (*source vive*)' from 'The Spinner,' 1, 3. 'The tree dreams of being a stream / The tree dreams in the air of being a source' C. 9, p. 428, 1923). 'The tree dreams of being a stream / *The tree dreams in the air of being a living source* . . . / And closer and closer, is changed into *poetry*, in a pure line' ('Arbre' in *Autres Rhumbs*, II, 659). 'Today my soul is making itself into a tree. Yesterday I felt it to be a spring (*source*)' ('Dialogue of the Tree,' 4, 154). We will retain from this work, aside from the play on *hêtre*—beech—and *être*—Being, that it posits, concerning the tree, 'its desireful being, which is certainly feminine in essence,' 4, 153; that it deciphers the tree as a petrification of disseminal waters ('the waters of the dense maternal earth, drawn from the depths for years on end, at last bring this hard substance to the light of day . . . TITYRUS. Substance as hard as stone, and fit like it to carve. LUCRETIUS. Ending in branches too, which end in leaves themselves, and then at last the mast which, fleeing far and wide, will scatter life abroad . . . TITYRUS. I see what you would say. LUCRETIUS. See then in this great being here a kind of river,' 4, 157; 'I have told you that I feel, born and growing in me, a Plantlike virtue, and I can merge myself in the thirst to exist of the hard-striving seed, moving towards an infinite number of other seeds throughout a plant's whole life,' 4, 167; 'What I was going to tell (perhaps to sing) to you would have, I think, dried up the spring (*source*) of words,' 4, 167); that it asserts simultaneously that 'There is no author, then . . . a work without an author is not impossible. No poet organized these phantasms for you,' 4, 166, and that 'In the beginning was the Fable,' 4, 168. That division (itself) is marked in this dream ('And like a slow fiber / Which divides the moment') is what prohibits, for reasons to be seen in a moment, the *tree* from being constituted as a theme or a subject. Whence the trap and the irony of the *Notebooks*, when they underline, 'The Tree—what a fine *subject!*' (C. 25, p. 118). P. Laurette cites them as epigraphs to

his very rich polysemic inventory, *The Theme of the Tree in Paul Valéry* (Klincksieck, 1967).

6. 'The duration of works is the duration of their utility. This is why it is discontinuous. There are centuries during which Virgil is useless' (II, 562). 'To have "genius" and to create a viable work are two profoundly different things. All the transports in the world yield only *discrete* elements. Without a fairly accurate reckoning, the work does not hold— does not *work*. An excellent poem supposes a mass of exact reasoning. A question not so much of forces, but of application of forces. And applied to whom?' (II, 566).

7. *Point d'eau* is an incalculable—and untranslatable—syntagm because it means both a 'source of water' and 'no water at all.' Derrida plays on this double meaning throughout this essay. Whenever he does so, *point* is left untranslated. [Trans.]

8. *Identity and Difference*, trans. Joan Stambaugh (New York: Harper and Row), p. 53. [Trans.]

9. The translation of the critical words *moi* and *je* is particularly difficult in this essay. In general I have followed the practice of the translations of the *Collected Works*. It should be noted, however, that in French *le moi*, which is the term Valéry uses most frequently is variously translated as the I, the me, and the ego (in the psychoanalytic sense). [Trans.]

10. This subtitle is a citation from Hegel, which is explained at the end of note 12 below. [Trans.]

11. *Figure* here has the double meaning of (1) figure of speech, and (2) face, visage. [Trans.]

12. [The 'certain president' referred to is Schreber, whose memoirs of his mental illness were analyzed by Freud. Trans.] Hegel: 'And this negativity, subjectivity, ego, freedom are the principles of evil and pain. Jacob Boehme viewed egoity (selfhood) as pain and torment (*Qual*), and as the fountain (*Quelle*, source) of nature and of spirit.' *Hegel's Philosophy of Mind* (part 3 of the *Encyclopedia*), trans. William Wallace (Oxford: Clarendon Press, 1971), p. 232. In the *Lectures on the History of Philosophy*, after recalling that, for Boehme, negativity works upon and constitutes the source, and that in principle 'God *is also* the Devil, each for itself,' etc., Hegel writes this, which I don't attempt to translate: '*Ein Hauptbegriff ist die* Qualität. *Böhme fängt in der* Aurora (Morgenröte im Aufgang) *von den Qualitäten an. Die erste Bestimmung Böhmes, die der Qualität, ist Inqualieren, Qual, Quelle. In der* Aurora *sagt er:* "Qualität ist die Beweglichkeit, Quallen (Quellen) oder Treiben eines Dinges"' (part 3, sec. 1, B. Jakob Böhme). It is within this context (negativity and division in the principle of things, in the mind or in God) that Hegel's well-known *ein sich Entzweiendes* (one dividing itself in two) also must be read. (See, for example, *Die Philosophie der Weltgeschichte, Allgemeine Einleitung*, II, 1 b.)

The law-of-the-proper, the *economy* of the source: the source is produced only in being cut off (*à se couper*) from itself, only in taking off in its *own* negativity, but equally, *and by the same token*, in reappropriating itself, in order to amortize its own, proper death, to rebound, *se relever*. Reckoning with absolute loss, that is, no longer reckoning, general economy does not cease to pass into the restricted economy of the source in order to permit itself to be encircled. Once more, here, we are reduced to the inexhaustible ruse of the *Aufhebung*, which is unceasingly examined, in these margins, along with Hegel, according to his text, against his text, within his boundary or interior limit: the absolute exterior which no longer permits itself to be internalized. We are led back to the question of dissemination: does semen permit itself to be *relevé*? Does the separation which cuts off the source permit itself to be thought as the *relève* of oneself? And how is what Hegel says of the child to be read in general: 'Der sich aufhebende Ursprung' (*Realphilosophie d'Iena*) or 'Trennung von dem Ursprung' (*Phenomenology of Spirit*)?

13. The reference is to Lacan's theory linking the agency he calls the imaginary to the formation of the ego in the mirror stage. [Trans.]
14. See Michel Lechantre, 'L'hiéroglyphe intérieur,' in *Modern Language Notes*, 1972.
15. 'Ext. speech differs from secret speech only through the functions which are associated and co-ordinated with it—weighing it down with their inertia and their passive resistances, but making it subject to their more arduous and solid—more tied together—world. All exterior speech is reduced to an interior speech by creating these auxiliary functions: 0. This is a projection. But conversely, all int. speech cannot become exterior' (C. 3, p. 483, 1905). On the relationship mouth/ear, see, among other fragments, that of C. 24, p. 107, 1940 (which Valéry accompanies by sketches), and M. Lechantre's work cited above.

    A *Poet's Notebook*, which joins an extreme formalism and a 'verbal materialism' (7, 183), also analyzes poetics on the basis of the same functioning. For example: 'So the poet at work is an expectation . . . He reconstructs what he desired. He reconstructs *quasi-mechanisms capable of giving back to him the energy they cost him and more* (for here the principles are apparently violated). *His ear speaks to him.*

    'We wait for the unexpected word—which cannot be foreseen but must be awaited. We are the first to hear it.

    '*To hear?* but that means *to speak.* One understands what one hears only if one has said it oneself from another motive.

    '*To speak* is to hear.

    'What is concerned, then, is a *twofold* attention. The state of being able to produce what is perceived admits of more or of less by reason of the number of elementary functions involved . . . One gets the idea of a reversible apparatus, like a telephone or a dynamo' (7, 174–75).
16. *Point de* must be understood in the double sense explained in note 7 above. Thus, simultaneously 'point of, source of philosophy' and 'no philosophy.' [Trans.]
17. See e.g., *Orientem Versus* 10, 379ff. and II, 572.
18. 'It is the vice of the ordinary philosophical vocabulary that though it must necessarily put on the appearances of technical language, it is nonetheless necessarily lacking in really precise definitions: for the only precise definitions are *instrumental* (that is to say, reducible to acts, such as pointing at an object or carrying out an operation). It is impossible to convince ourselves that words like *reason, universe, cause, matter,* or *idea* possess single, uniform, unchanging meanings. What usually happens is that every attempt to make the meaning of such terms clearer leads to introducing under the same name a fresh object of thought *which differs from the original object in so far as it is new*' (Swedenborg, 9, 118).

19. 'I meant to talk of philosophers—and to philosophers.

     'I wanted to show that it would be of the greatest profit to them to practice this labor of poetry which leads insensibly to the study of word combinations, not so much through the conformity of the meanings of these groups to an idea or thought that one thinks should be *expressed*, as, on the contrary, through their effects once they are formed, from which one chooses.

     'Generally one tries to "express one's thought," that is, to pass from an *impure* form, a mixture of all the resources of the mind, to a *pure* form, that is, one solely verbal and organized, amounting to a system of arranged acts or contrasts.

     'But the art of poetry is alone in leading one to envisage pure forms in themselves' (7, 178).

     On philosophical writing and the philosophical spider, see also *My Faust*, 3, 123–24.

20. 'But up to the present, literature has not, so far as I am aware, paid much attention to this immense treasure house of subjects and situations . . . What are we to make of terms that cannot be precisely defined unless we re-create them? *Thought, mind* itself, *reason, intelligence, understanding, intuition*, or *inspiration*? . . . Each of these terms is both a means and an end in turn, a problem and a solution, a state and an idea; and each of them, in each of us, is adequate or inadequate according to the function which circumstances impose on it. You are aware that at this point the philosopher becomes a poet, and often a great poet: he borrows metaphor from us and, by means of splendid images which we might well envy, he draws on all nature for the expression of his profoundest thought.

     'The poet is not so fortunate when he tries the corresponding procedure' (9, 19).

     'Philosophy is reduced to a logic and to a rhetoric or poetics' (C. 8, p. 911, 1922). (See also the entirety of *Leonardo and the Philosophers* 8, 110ff.).

21. See also 7, 180; and on prose as the erasure of metaphor, 7, 177.

22. Elsewhere, philosophy is considered precisely as the loss of power; or at least it does not lead to 'establishing any power' (8, 139).

23. 'At this point I am going to take a considerable risk. I say that we can consider it from a very different point of view—we can assert that this brief and pregnant expression of its author's personality *has no meaning whatever*. But I must add that it has *a very great value*, entirely characteristic of the man himself.

     'I maintain that *Cogito ergo sum* has no meaning because that little word *sum* has no meaning. No one dreams of saying or needs to say "I am" unless he is taken for dead and wants to protest that he is not. In any case he would say "I'm alive." But a cry or the slightest movement would be quite sufficient. No, "I am" cannot tell anyone anything and is no answer to any intelligible question. But the remark does correspond here to something else, which I shall explain presently. Furthermore, what meaning can be attributed to a proposition whose negative form would express its content just as well as the positive? If "I am" means anything, "I am not" tells us neither more nor less' (9, 54). In the *Address to the Congress of Surgeons*, Valéry scans the formula: 'At one moment I think; at another I am' (11, 139).

     I have proposed elsewhere an interpretation of the equivalence, 'I am': 'I am living': 'I am dead.' Although made from a very different point of view, this interpretation nevertheless seems to me to intersect with Valéry's. Cf. *Speech and Phenomena*.

24. On voice, writing, and literature, see also II, 549.

25. [Derrida's 'lexicographical monstrosity' involves a play on the word *sourdre* which means to well up, to surge up, as when a source emerges from underground. In this context, i.e. the discussion of being '*deaf* to what is most spontaneous in my voice,' Derrida is playing on the *sourd*, deaf, in *sourdre*. He is forcing *sourdre* to mean 'to make deaf' (which it does not), at the same time as it means to well up, and is playing on the consequences of this 'monstrous' double meaning. Trans.]

Once more, then, the value of the origin must be dissociated from the value of the source. 'One must go back to the *source*—which is not the *origin*. The *origin*, in all, is *imaginary*. The *source* is the fact within which the imaginary is proposed: water wells up there. Beneath, I do not know what takes place?' (C. 23, p. 592, 1940).

Beneath, I do not know what takes place. Although we cannot follow all the implications here, let us indicate that which, within the trope, both retains and brings to the surface what is most strange beneath the most familiar (*heimlich/ unheimlich*). Two examples, themselves cited as examples: 1. 'When, seeking to explain the generation of the operations of the soul, you say, Monseigneur, that they have their source in sensation, and that attention flows into comparison, comparison into judgment, etc., you are comparing all these operation to streams, and the words *source* and *flow* are tropes, which convey your thought in sensory fashion. We use this language on all occasions which present themselves, and you experience daily to what extent it is proper to enlighten you.' (Condillac, *De l'art d'écrire*, in *Oeuvres philosophiques*, ed. Georges Le Roy (Paris: Presses Universitaires de France, 1947), pp. 560–61.) It will have been noticed, among other things, that here the *source* is a trope and a comparison which is possible not at the source of the operations, but at a moment which itself is determinate, derived from the course (of what is compared): comparison. 2. 'Compare: "The Zecks are all 'heim-lich.'" ' "*Heimlich*?" . . . *What do you understand by "heimlich"?*' 'Well, . . . they are like a buried spring (*zugegrabenen Brunnen*) or a dried-up pond. One cannot walk over it without always having the feeling that water might come up there again.' 'Oh, we call it "*unheimlich*."' Freud, *The Uncanny*, in SE XVII, 223.

26. *Irrelevable*, i.e. that which cannot be *relevé*, subjected to the Hegelian operation of the *Aufhebung*. [Trans.]

27. This is the analysis that Valéry proposes of Swedenborg's 'sign.' And, in this case at least, he excludes the hypothesis 'of a vast lie in the grand manner' (9, 124).

28. For example: 'I have been concerned with dreams for centuries. Since then have come the theses of Freud and Co., which are completely different—because it is the possibility and intrinsic characteristics of the phen. which interest me; while for them, it is its meaning, its relation to the subject's history—which I am not worried about.' Valéry had just written: 'The small child of two years is transparent. Its impressions, its psyche, and its acts have very few *waystations*' (C. 19, p. 456, 1936).

'My theories of the dream are completely opposed to those of the day. They are completely "formal," while the latter are completely "significative'" (C. 17, p. 766, 1935). 'Now, I am inclined to think that these words have *no meaning*, that it is useless to look for meaning in them, vain to give them meaning. And the reflex acts of the sleeper are only *linear* responses. The sleeper discharges himself through the brain as through the limbs—without past or future—without additivity. For my way of thinking, it is a mistake to approach dreams by way of the *significative*' (ibid., p. 771). See also p. 770, and the entire chapter 'Le rêve et l'analyse de la conscience,' in Judith Robinson, *L'analyse de l'esprit dans les Cahiers de Valéry* (Paris: Corti, 1963). This semanticist error, if we may put it thus, is what from Valéry's point of view deprives psychoanalysis of all scientificity, if not all efficacity. 'If Freud's theories have therapeutic value, it is highly probable that they have no *scientific* value' (C. 11, p. 476, 1926). 'There are authors (and therefore theories at their service) whose works, consciously founded on the unconscious, are comparable finally to the Flea Market' (C. 17, p. 515, 1934).

As is inevitable in this situation of misconstruing, Valéry, who calls himself 'the least Freudian of men' (cited by Robinson, *L'analyse*, p. 105), occasionally makes statements that Freud would not simply have rejected, at the very moment when it is believed that these statements are in opposition to him. Thus: 'Freud's theories are repulsive to my way of thinking, which would have it that in dreams the ideas of the most *insignificant* things from waking life play a role equal to that played by things which are moving, or would be the most moving' (C. 11, p. 621, 1925–26).

29. [Derrida is playing on *tête*, head, and *teste*, the Latin root of the word, and the name of Valéry's most famous character. Valéry himself plays on this word as will be seen in the citation below. Trans.] Rather than play upon the word *testis*, let us cite several lines from 'Sketches for a Portrait of Monsieur Teste': 'Monsieur Teste is the witness.

'That in us which causes *everything* and therefore nothing—reaction itself, pure recoil . . .

'Conscious—Teste, Testis.

'Given an "eternal" observer whose role is limited to repeating and rehearsing the system of which the *Self* is that instantaneous part which believes it is the Whole.

'The Self (*le Moi*) could never engage itself if it did not believe—it is all.

'Suddenly the *suavis mamilla* that he touches becomes nothing more than what it is.

'The sun itself . . .

'The "stupidity" of everything makes itself felt. Stupidity—that is, particularity opposed to generality. "Smaller than" becomes the terrible sign of the mind' (6, 68).

'The game played with oneself . . . The essential is against life.' ('A Few of Monsieur Teste's Thoughts,' 6, 72, and 78.)

30. Cf. Judith Robinson, *L'analyse*, p. 105, n. 2.

31. See above, note 25. [Trans.]

32. I, 1748. 'Truth is a means. It is not the only one' (1, 380).

33. [*An Autobiographical Study*, SE XX, 60. The title of this work in German is *Selbstdarstellung*, literally 'self-representation,' although representation here has a

theatrical sense of *mise en scène*, direction, that Derrida plays upon here. Trans.]
Selbstdarstellung, 1925, *Gesammelte Werke* (Frankfurt: Fischer Verlag, 1967), vol. 14,
p. 86 ('*Nietzsche, den anderen Philosophen, dessen Ahnungen und Einsichten sich oft in
der erstaunlichsten Weise mit denmühsamen Ergennissen der Psychoanalyse decken, habe
ich gerade darum lange gemieden; an der Priorität lag mir ja weniger als an der Erhaltung
meiner Unbefangenheit.*')

Chapter 10

Khōra

Thus myth puts in play a form of logic which could be called—in contrast to the logic of noncontradiction of the philosophers—a logic of the ambiguous, of the equivocal, of polarity. How can one formulate, or even formalize, these see-saw operations, which flip any term into its opposite whilst at the same time keeping them both apart, from another point of view? The mythologist was left with drawing up, in conclusion, this statement of deficit, and to turn to the linguists, logicians, mathematicians, that they might supply him with the tool he lacked: the structural model of a logic which would not be that of binarity, of the yes or no, a logic other than the logic of the *logos*.

—Jean-Pierre Vernant, 'Raisons du mythe,' *Mythe et societé en Grèce ancienne* (Paris, 1974), p. 250.

Khōra reaches us, and as the name. And when a name comes, it immediately says more than the name: the other of the name and quite simply the other, whose irruption the name announces. This announcement does not yet promise, no more than it threatens. It neither promises nor threatens anyone. It still remains alien to the person, only naming imminence, even only an imminence that is alien to the myth, the time, and the history of every possible promise and threat.

It is well known: what Plato in the *Timaeus* designates by the name of *khōra* seems to defy that 'logic of noncontradiction of the philosophers' of which Vernant speaks, that logic 'of binarity, of the yes or no.' Hence it might perhaps derive from that 'logic other than the logic of the *logos*.' The *khōra*, which is neither 'sensible' nor 'intelligible,' belongs to a 'third genus' (*triton genos*, 48a, 52a). One cannot even say of it that it is *neither* this *nor* that or that it is *both* this *and* that. It is not enough to recall that *khōra* names neither this nor that, or, that *khōra* says this and that. The difficulty declared by Timaeus is shown in a different way: at times the *khōra* appears to be neither this nor that, at times both this and that, but this alternation between the logic of exclusion and that of participation—we shall return to this at length—stems perhaps only from a provisional appearance and from the constraints of rhetoric, even from some incapacity for naming.

The *khōra* seems to be alien to the order of the 'paradigm,' that intelligible and immutable model. And yet, 'invisible' and without sensible form, it 'participates' in the intelligible in a very troublesome and indeed aporetic way (*aporōtata*, 51b). At least we shall not be lying, adds Timaeus, at least we shall not be saying what is false (*ou pseudometha*) in declaring this. The prudence of this negative formulation gives reason to ponder. Not lying, not saying what is false: is this necessarily telling the truth? And, in this respect, what about testimony, bearing witness [*témoignage*]?

Let us recall once more, under the heading of our preliminary approach, that the discourse on the *khōra*, as it is *presented*, does not proceed from the natural or legitimate *logos*, but rather from a hybrid, bastard, or even corrupted reasoning (*logismō nothō*). It comes 'as in a dream' (52b), which could just as well deprive it of lucidity as confer upon it a power or divination.

Does such a discourse derive, then, from myth? Shall we gain access to the thought of the *khōra* by continuing to place our trust in the alternative *logos/mythos*? And what if this thought called *also* for a third genus of discourse? And what if, perhaps as in the case of the *khōra*, this appeal to the third genre was only the moment of a detour in order to signal toward a genre beyond genre? Beyond categories, and above all beyond categorial oppositions, which in the first place allow it to be approached or said?

As a token of gratitude and admiration, here then is homage in the form of a question to Jean-Pierre Vernant. The question is addressed to the one who taught us so much and gave us so much pause for thought about the opposition *mythos/logos*, certainly, but also about the unceasing inversion of poles; to the author of 'Raisons du mythe' and of *Ambiguïté et renversement*: how are we to think that which, while going outside of the regularity of the *logos*, its law, its natural or legitimate genealogy, nevertheless does not belong, *stricto sensu*, to *mythos*? Beyond the retarded or johnny-come-lately opposition of *logos* and *mythos*, how is one to think the necessity of that which, while *giving place* to that opposition as to so many others, seems sometimes to be itself no longer subject to the law of the very thing which it *situates*? What of this *place*? It is nameable? And wouldn't it have some impossible relation to the possibility of naming? Is there something to *think* there, as I have just so hastily said, and to think according to *necessity*?

I

The oscillation of which we have just spoken is not an oscillation among others, an oscillation between two poles. It oscillates between two types of oscillation: the double exclusion (*neither/nor*) and the participation (*both this and that*). But have we the right to transport the logic, the para-logic or the meta-logic of this superoscillation from one set to the other? It concerned first of all types of existent thing (sensible/intelligible, visible/invisible, form/formless, icon, or mimeme/paradigm), but we have displaced it toward types of discourse (*mythos/logos*) or of relation to what is or is not in general. No doubt such a displacement is not self-evident. It depends on a sort of metonymy: such a metonymy would displace itself, by displacing the names, from types [*genres*] of being to types [*genres*] of discourse. But on the one hand it is always difficult, particularly in Plato, to separate the two problematics: the quality of the discourse depends primarily on the quality of the being of which it speaks. It is almost as if a name should only be given to whom (or to what) deserves it and calls for it. The discourse, like the relation to that which is in general, is qualified or disqualified by what it relates to. On the other hand, the metonymy is authorized by passing through *genre*, from one genre to the other, from the question of the genres/types of being to the question of the types of discourse. Now the discourse on the *khōra* is also a discourse on genre/type (*genos*) and on different types of type. Later we will get on to genre as *gens*, or people (*genos*, *ethnos*), a theme which appears at the opening of the *Timaeus*. In the narrow context on which we are dwelling at present, that of the sequence on the *khōra*, we shall encounter two further genres of genre or types of type. The *khōra* is a *triton genos* in view of the two types of being (immutable and intelligible/corruptible, in the process of becoming and sensible), but it seems to be equally determined with regard to the sexual type: Timaeus speaks of 'mother' and 'nurse' in regard to this subject. He does this in a mode which we shall not be in a hurry to name. Almost all the interpreters of the *Timaeus* gamble here on the resources of rhetoric without ever wondering about them. They speak tranquilly about metaphors, images, similes.[1] They ask themselves no questions about this tradition of rhetoric which places at their disposal a reserve of concepts which are very useful but which are all built upon this distinction between the sensible and the intelligible, which is precisely what the thought of the *khōra* can no longer get along with—a distinction, indeed, of which Plato unambiguously lets it be known that this thought has the greatest difficulty getting along with it. This problem of rhetoric—particularly of the possibility of naming—is, here, no mere side issue. Nor is its importance limited to some pedagogic, illustrative, or instrumental dimension (those who speak of metaphor with regard to the *khōra* often add: didactic metaphor). We shall be content for the moment with indicating it, and situating it, but it is already clear that, just like the *khōra* and with just as much necessity, it cannot easily be situated, assigned to a residence: it is more situating than situated, an opposition which must in its turn be shielded from some grammatical or ontological alternative between the active and the passive. We shall not speak of metaphor, but not in order to hear; for example, that the *khōra* is *properly* a mother, a nurse, a receptacle, a bearer of imprints or gold. It is perhaps because its scope goes beyond or falls short of the polarity of metaphorical sense versus proper sense that the thought of the *khōra* exceeds the polarity, no doubt analogous, of the *mythos* and the *logos*. Such at least would be the question which we should like here to put to the test of a reading. The consequence which we envisage would be the following: with these two polarities, the thought of the *khōra* would trouble the very order of polarity, of polarity in general, whether dialectical or not. Giving place to oppositions, it would itself not submit to any reversal. And this, which is another consequence, would not be because it would inalterably be *itself* beyond its name but because in carrying beyond the polarity of sense (metaphorical or proper), it would no longer belong to the horizon of sense, nor to that of meaning as the meaning of being.

After these precautions and these negative hypotheses, you will understand why it is that we left the name *khōra* sheltered from any translation. A translation, admittedly, seems to be always at work, both *in* the Greek language and from the Greek language into some other. Let us not regard any of them as sure. Thinking and translating here traverse the same experience. If it must be attempted, such an experience or experiment [*expérience*] is not only of concern for a word or an atom of meaning but also for a whole tropological texture, let us not yet call it a system, and for ways of approaching, in order to *name* them, the elements of this 'tropology.' Whether they concern the word *khōra* itself ('place,' 'location,' 'region,' 'country') or what tradition calls the figures—comparisons, images, and metaphors—proposed by Timaeus ('mother,' 'nurse,' 'receptable,' 'imprint-bearer'), the translations remain caught in networks of interpretation. They are led astray by retrospective projections, which can always be suspected of being anachronistic. This anachronism is not necessarily, not always, and not only a weakness from which a vigilant and rigorous interpretation would be able to escape entirely. We shall try to show that no-one escapes from it. Even Heidegger, who is nonetheless one of the only ones never to speak of 'metaphor,' seems to us to yield to this teleological retrospection,[2] against which, elsewhere, he so rightly puts us on our guard. And this gesture seems highly significant for the whole of his questioning and his relationship to the 'history-of-philosophy.'

What has just been said of rhetoric, of translation, or of teleological anachronism, could give rise to a misunderstanding. We must dispel it without delay. We would never claim to propose the exact word, the *mot juste*, for *khōra*, nor to name it, *itself*, over and above all the turns and detours of rhetoric, nor finally to approach it, *itself*, for what it will have been, outside of any point of view, outside of any anachronic perspective. Its name is not an exact word, not a *mot juste*. It is promised to the ineffaceable even if what it names, *khōra*, is not reduced to its name. Tropology and anachronism are inevitable. And all we would like to show is that it is structure which makes them thus inevitable, makes of them something other than accidents, weaknesses, or provisional moments. It is this structural law which seems to me never to have been approached *as such* by the whole history of interpretations of the *Timaeus*. It would be a matter of a structure and not of some essence of the *khōra*, since the question or essence no longer has any meaning with regard to it. Not having an essence, how could the *khōra* be [*se tiendrait-elle*] beyond its name? The *khōra* is anachronistic; it 'is' the anachrony within being, or better: the anachrony of being. It anachronizes being.

The 'whole history of interpretations,' we have just said. We will never exhaust the immense literature devoted to the *Timaeus* since antiquity. It is out of the question to deal with it here in its entirety. And, above all, to presuppose the unity or homogeneity of this whole, the very possibility of totalizing it in some ordered apprehension. What we shall presuppose, by contrast, and one could still call it a 'working hypothesis,' is that the presumption of such an order (grouping, unity, totality organized by a *telos*) has an essential link with the structural anachronism of which we spoke a moment ago. It would be the inevitable effect produced by *something like* the *khōra*—which is not something, and which is not *like* anything, not even like what *it* would be, *itself*, there beyond its name.

Rich, numerous, inexhaustible, the interpretations come, in short, to give form to the meaning of *khōra*. They always consist in *giving form* to it by determining it, it which, however, can 'offer itself' or promise itself only by removing itself from any determination, from all the marks or impressions to which we say it is exposed: from everything which we would like to give to it without hoping to receive anything from it . . . But what we are putting forward here of the interpretation of the *khōra*—of Plato's text on the *khōra*—by speaking about a form given or received, about mark or impression, about knowledge as information, etc., all of that already draws on what the text itself says about the *khōra*, draws on its conceptual and hermeneutic apparatus. What we have just put forward, for example, for the sake of the example, on the subject of '*khōra*' in the text of Plato, reproduces or simply brings back, with all its schemas, Plato's discourse on the subject of the *khōra*. And this is true even down to this very sentence in which I have just made use of the word *schemas*. The *skhemata* are the cut-out figures imprinted into the *khōra*, the forms which inform it. They are of it without belonging to it.

Thus there are interpretations which would come to give form to '*khōra*' by leaving on it the schematic mark of their imprint and by depositing on it the sediment of their contribution. And yet, '*khōra*' seems never to let itself be reached or touched, much less broached, and above all not exhausted by these *types* of tropological or interpretative translation. One cannot even say that it furnishes them with the support of a stable substratum or substance. *Khōra* is not a subject. It is not the subject. Nor the support [*subjectile*]. The hermeneutic *types* cannot inform, they cannot give form to *khōra* except to the extent that, inaccessible, impassive, 'amorphous' (*amorphon*, 51a) and still virgin, with a virginity that is radically rebellious against anthropomorphism, it *seems to receive* these types and *give place* to them. But if Timaeus names it as receptacle (*dekhomenon*) or place (*khōra*), these names do not designate an essence, the stable being of an *eidos*, since *khōra* is neither of the order of the *eidos* nor of the order of mimemes, that is, of images of the *eidos* which come to imprint themselves in it—which thus *is not* and does not belong to the two known or recognized genera of being. It is not, and this nonbeing cannot but be *declared*, that is, be caught or conceived, via the anthropomorphic schemas of the verb *to receive* and the verb *to give*. *Khōra* is not, is above all not, is anything but a support or a subject which would *give* place by receiving or by conceiving, or indeed by letting itself be conceived. How could one deny it this essential significance as a receptacle, given that this very name is given to it by Plato? It is difficult indeed, but perhaps we have not yet thought through what is meant by *to receive*, the receiving of the receptacle, what is said by *dekhomai*, *dekhomenon*. Perhaps it is from *khōra* that we are beginning to learn it—to receive it, to receive from it what its name calls up. To receive it, if not to comprehend it, to conceive it.

You will already have noticed that we now say *khōra* and not, as convention has always required, *the khōra*, or again, as we might have done for the sake of caution, the word, the concept, the significance or the value of '*khōra*.' This is for several reasons, most of which are no doubt already obvious. The definite article presupposes the existence of a thing, the existent *khōra* to which, via a common name [*nom commun*, or 'common noun'—Ed.], it would be easy to refer. But what is said about *khōra* is that this name does not designate any of the known or recognized or, if you like, received types of existent, *received* by philosophical discourse, that is, by the *ontological logos* which lays down the law in the *Timaeus*: *khōra* is neither sensible nor intelligible. There is *khōra*; one can even ponder its *physis* and its *dynamis*, or at least ponder these in a preliminary way. But what *there is*, there, is not; and we will come back later to what this *there is* can give us to think, this *there is*, which, by the way, *gives* nothing in giving place or in giving to think, whereby it will be risky to see in it the equivalent of an *es gibt*, of the *es gibt* which remains without a doubt implicated in every negative theology, unless it is the *es gibt* which always summons negative theology in its Christian history.

Instead of *the khōra*, shall we be content to say prudently: the word, the common name, the concept, the signification, or the value of *khōra*? These precautions would not suffice; they presuppose distinctions (word/concept, word-concept/thing, meaning/reference, signification/value, etc.) which themselves imply the possibility, at least, of a *determined* existent, distinct from another, and acts which aim at it, at it or its meaning, via acts of language, designations or sign postings. All of these acts appeal to generalities, to an *order* of multiplicities: genus, species, individual, type, schema, etc. Now what we can read, it seems, of *khōra* in the *Timaeus* is that 'something,' which is not a thing, puts in question these presuppositions and these distinctions: 'something' is not a thing and escapes from this order of multiplicities.

But if we say *khōra* and not *the khōra*, we are still making a name out of it. A proper name, it is true, but a word, just like any common name, a word distinct from the thing or the concept. Besides, the proper name appears, as always, to be attributed to a person, in this case to a woman. Perhaps to a woman; indeed, to a woman. Doesn't that aggravate the risks of anthropomorphism against which we wanted to protect ourselves? Aren't these risks run by Plato himself when he seems to 'compare,' as they say, *khōra* to a mother or a nurse? Isn't the value of receptacle also associated, like passive and virgin matter, with the feminine element, and precisely in Greek culture? These objections are not without value. However, if *khōra* indeed presents certain attributes of the word as proper name, isn't that only via its apparent reference to some uniqueness (and in the *Timaeus*, more rigorously in a certain passage of the *Timaeus* which we will approach later, there is *only one khōra*, and that is indeed how we understand it; there is only one, however divisible it be), the referent or this reference does not exist. It does not have the characteristics of an existent, by which we mean an existent that would be receivable in the *ontologic*, that is, those of an intelligible *or* sensible existent. There is *khōra* but *the khōra* does not exist. The effacement of the article should for the moment suspend the determination, within invisible quotation marks (we cite a saying of Plato's in a certain passage of the *Timaeus*, without knowing yet what it means and how to determine it) and the reference to something which is not a thing but which insists, in its so enigmatic uniqueness, lets itself be called or causes itself to be named without answering, without giving itself to be seen, conceived, determined. Deprived of a real referent, that which in fact resembles a proper name finds itself also called an X which has as its property (as its *physis* and as its *dynamis*, Plato's text will say) that it has nothing as its own and that it remains unformed, formless (*amorphon*). This very singular impropriety, which precisely is nothing, is just what *khōra* must, if you like, *keep*; it is just what *must be kept for it*, what *we* must keep for it. To that end, it is necessary not to confuse it in a generality by properly attributing to it properties which would still be those of a determinate existent, one of the existents which it/she 'receives' or whose image it/she receives: for example, an existent of the female gender—and that is why the femininity of the mother or the nurse will never be attributed to it/her as a property, something of her own. Which does not mean, however—we shall return to this— that it is a case here of mere figures of rhetoric. *Khōra* must not receive for *her own sake*, so she must not *receive*, merely let herself be lent the properties (of that) which she receives. She must not receive, she must receive not that which she receives. To avoid all these confusions, it is convenient, paradoxically, to formalize our approach (to it/her) and always to use the same language about it/her ('ταυτόν αυτὴν ἀει προσπητέον,' 50b). Not so much to 'give her always the same name,' as it is often translated, but to speak of it/her and to call it/her *in the same manner*. In short, faithfully even if this *faith* is irreducible to every other. Is this 'manner' unique or typical? Does it have the singularity of an idiomatic event or the regulated generality of a schema? In other words, does this regularity find, in Plato's text, or rather in a particular passage of the *Timaeus*, its unique and best formulation, or rather one of its examples, however privileged? In what regard, in what sense, will it be said of the *Timaeus* that it is exemplary? And if it is important that the *appellation*, rather than the *name*, should stay the same, will we be able to replace, relay, translate *khōra* by other names, striving only to preserve the regularity of the appellation, namely of a discourse?

This question cannot but resound when we know that we are caught in such a scene of reading, included in advance in the immense history of interpretations and reappropriations which in the course of the centuries come to buzz and hum around *khōra*, taking charge of it/her or overloading it/her with inscriptions and reliefs, giving it/her form, imprinting it/her with types, in order to produce in it/her new objects or to deposit on it/her other sediments [the translation of the French pronoun *elle*, referring to *khōra*, includes both 'her' and 'it,' in order to stress that *elle* could also be understood as a personal feminine pronoun—Ed.]. This interminable theory of exegeses seems to reproduce what, following the discourse of Timaeus, would happen, not with Plato's text, but with *khōra* herself/itself. With *khōra itself/herself* if one could at all speak thus about this X (χ or *khi*) which must not have any proper determination, sensible or intelligible, material or formal, and therefore must not have any identity of its/her own, must not be identical with herself/itself. *Everything happens as if* the yet-to-come history of the interpretations of *khōra* were written or even prescribed in advance, *in advance reproduced and reflected* in a few pages of the *Timaeus* 'on the subject' of *khōra* 'herself' ('itself'). With its ceaseless re-launchings, its failures, its superimpositions, its overwritings and reprintings, this history wipes itself out in advance since it programs itself, reproduces itself, and reflects itself by anticipation. Is a prescribed, programmed, reproductive, reflexive history still a history? Unless the concept of history bears within itself this teleological programming which annuls it while constituting it. In saying, in short, 'this is how one can glimpse *khōra*—in a difficult, aporetical way and as if in a dream—,' someone (Timaeus, Plato, etc.) would have said: this is what henceforth all the interpretations, for all eternity, of what I say here will look like. They will resemble *what I am saying* about *khōra*; and hence what I am saying about *khōra* gives a commentary, in advance, and describes the law of the whole history of the hermeneutics and the institutions which will be constructed *on this subject*, over this subject.

There is nothing fortuitous about that. *Khōra* receives, so as to give place to them, all the determinations, but she/it does not possess any of them as her/its own. She possesses them, she has them, since she receives them, but she does not possess them as properties, she does not possess anything as her own. She 'is' nothing other than the sum or the process of what has just been inscribed 'on' her, on the subject of her, on her subject, right up against her subject, but she is not the *subject* or the *present support* of all these interpretations, even though, nevertheless, she is not reducible to them. Simply this excess is nothing, nothing that may be and be said ontologically. This absence of support, which cannot be translated into absent support or into absence as support, provokes *and* resists any binary or dialectical determination, any inspection of a philosophical *type*, or let us say, more rigorously, of an *ontological* type. This type finds itself both defied and relaunched by the very thing that appears to give it place. Even then we shall have to recall later, insisting on it in a more analytical manner, that *if there is place*, or, according to our idiom, *place given*, to give place here does not come to the same thing as to make a present of a place. The expression *to give place* does not refer to the gesture of a donor-subject, the support or origin of something which would come to be given to someone.

Despite their timidly preliminary character, these remarks permit us perhaps to glimpse the silhouette of a 'logic' which seems virtually impossible to formalize. Will this 'logic' still be a logic, 'a form of logic,' to take up Vernant's saying when he speaks of a 'form of logic' of myth which must be 'formulated, or even formalized'? Such a logic of myth exists, no doubt, but our question returns: does the thought of *khōra*, which obviously does not derive from the 'logic of noncontradiction of the philosophers,' belong to the space of mythic thought? Is the 'bastard' *logos* which is regulated according to it [i.e., according to mythic thought—Tr.]—still a *mythos*?

Let us take the time for a long detour. Let us consider the manner in which Hegel's speculative dialectic inscribes mythic thought in a teleological perspective. One can say of this dialectic that it is and that it is not a logic of noncontradiction. It integrates and *sublates* contradiction as such. In the same way, it sublates mythic discourse as such into the philosopheme.

According to Hegel, philosophy becomes serious—and we are also thinking *after* Hegel and *according to* him, following his thought—only from the moment when it enters into the sure path of logic: that is, after having abandoned, or let us rather say sublated, its mythic form: after Plato, with

Plato. Philosophical logic comes to its senses when the concept wakes up from its mythological slumber. Sleep and waking, for the event, consist in a simple unveiling: the making explicit and taking cognizance of a philosopheme enveloped in its virtual potency. The mytheme *will have been* only a prephilosopheme offered and promised to a dialectical *Aufhebung*. This teleological future anterior resembles the time of a narrative but it is a narrative of the going outside of narrative. It marks the end of narrative fiction. Hegel explains it[3] while defending his 'friend Creuzer' and his book, *Symbolism and Mythology of Ancient Peoples, especially of the Greeks* (1810–12). The mythological *logos*, of course, can emit the pretension of being a species of 'philosophizing' (p. 108). There are philosophers who have used myths in order to bring philosophemes closer to the imagination (*Phantasie*). But 'the content of myth is thought' (*ibid*). The mythic dimension remains formal and exterior. If Plato's myths are 'beautiful,' one would be wrong to think that myths are more 'eminent' (*vortrefflicher*) than the 'abstract mode of expression.' In truth, Plato has recourse to myth only to the extent of his 'impotence' (*Unvermögen*) to 'express himself in the pure modality of thought.' But that is also in part because he does so only in the introduction to the dialogues— and an introduction is never purely philosophical: you know what Hegel thinks of introductions and prefaces in general. When he gets on to the thing itself, to the principal subject, Plato expresses himself quite otherwise. Let us think of the *Parmenides*, for example: the simple determinations of thought do without image and myth. Hegel's dialectical schema here just as much concerns the mythic—the figurative or the symbolic. The *Parmenides* is 'serious,' whereas the recourse to myth is not entirely so. In the form in which, still today, this opposition dominates so many evaluations—and not only in so-called Anglo-Saxon thought—the opposition between the serious and the nonserious overlaps here with that of philosophy *as such* and of its ludico-mythological drift [*dérive*]. The *value* of philosophical thought, which is also to say its *seriousness*, is measured by the nonmythic character of its terms. Hegel here emphasizes value, seriousness, the value of seriousness, and Aristotle is his guarantor. For after having declared that 'the value of Plato, however, does not reside in myths' ('der Wert Platons liegt aber nicht in den Mythen,' p. 109), Hegel quotes and translates Aristotle. It is appropriate to dwell on this. We know, let us recall in passing before approaching this problem directly, how great a weight the Aristotelian interpretation of the *Timaeus* carries in the history of the interpretations. Hegel translates then, or paraphrases, the *Metaphysics*:

περι μὲν τῶν μυτικῶς σοψιζομένων οὐκ ἄξιον μετὰ σπουδης σκοπεῖν

Von denen, welche mythisch philosophieren, ist es nicht der Mühe wert, ernstlich zu handeln.

Those who philosophize with recourse to myth are not worth treating seriously.

Hegel seems to oscillate between two interpretations. In a philosophical text, the function of myth is at times a sign of philosophical impotence, the incapacity to accede to the concept as such and to keep to it, at other times the index of a dialectic and above all didactic potency, the pedagogic mastery of the serious philosopher in full possession of the philosopheme. Simultaneously or successively, Hegel seems to recognize in Plato both this impotence and this mastery. These two evaluations are only apparently contradictory or are so only up to a certain point. They have this in common: the subordination of myth, as a discursive *form*, to the *content* of the signified concept, to the meaning, which, in its essence, can only be philosophical. And the philosophical theme, the signified concept, whatever may be its formal *presentation*—philosophical or mythic—always remains the force of law, the mastery or the dynasty of discourse. Here one can see the thread of our question passing by: if *khōra* has no meaning or essence, if she is not a philosopheme and if, nevertheless, she is neither the object nor the form of a fable of a mythic type, where can she be situated in this schema?

Apparently contradictory, but in fact profoundly coherent, this logico-philosophical evaluation is not *applied* to Plato. It derives already from a certain 'Platonism.' Hegel does not read Plato through Aristotle as if doing something unknown to Plato, as if he [Hegel] were deciphering a practice whose meaning would have remained inaccessible to the author of the *Timaeus*. A certain programme of this evaluation seems already legible in this work, as we shall verify. But perhaps with one reservation, and this supplementary reservation could lodge, shelter, and thereby exceed the said programme.

First, the programme. The cosmogony of the *Timaeus* runs through the cycle of knowledge on all things. Its encyclopedic end must mark the term, the *telos*, of a *logos* on the subject of everything that is: 'καὶ δὴ καὶ τέλος περὶ τοῦ παντὸς νῦν ἤδη τὸν λόγον ἡμῖν ψῶμεν ἔχειν'; 'And now at length we may say that our discourse concerning the Universe has reached its termination' (92c).

This encyclopedic *logos* is a general ontology, treating of all the types of being, it includes a theology, a cosmology, a physiology, a psychology, a zoology. Mortal or immortal, human and divine, visible and invisible things are situated there. By recalling it in conclusion, one picks up the distinction between the visible living thing, for example, the sensible god, and the intelligible god of which it is the image (*eikōn*). The cosmos is the heavens (*ouranos*) as living, visible thing and sensible god. It is unique and alone of its race, 'monogenic.'

And yet, half-way through the cycle, won't the discourse on *khōra* have opened, between the sensible and the intelligible, belonging neither to one nor to the other, hence neither to the cosmos as sensible god nor to the intelligible god, an apparently empty space—even though it is no doubt not *emptiness*? Didn't it name a gaping opening, an abyss or a chasm? Isn't it starting out from this chasm, 'in' it, that the cleavage between the sensible and the intelligible, indeed, between body and soul, can have place and take place? Let us not be too hasty about bringing this chasm named *khōra* close to that chaos which also opens the yawning gulf of the abyss. Let us avoid hurling into it the anthropomorphic form and the pathos of fright. Not in order to install in its place the security of a foundation, the 'exact counterpart of what Gaia represents for any creature, since her appearance, at the origin of the world: a stable foundation, sure for all eternity, opposed to the gaping and bottomless opening of Chaos.'[4] We shall later encounter a brief allusion of Heidegger's to *khōra*, not to the one in the *Timaeus* but, outside of all quotation and all precise reference, the one which in Plato would designate the place (*Ort*) between the existent and being,[5] the 'difference' or place between the two.

The ontologico-encyclopedic conclusion of the *Timaeus* seems to cover over the open chasm in the middle of the book. What it would thus cover over, closing the gaping mouth of the quasi-banned discourse on *khōra*, would perhaps not only be the abyss between the sensible and the intelligible, between being and nothingness, between being and the lesser being, nor even perhaps between being and the existent, nor yet between *logos* and *muthos*, but between all these couples and another which would not even be *their* other.

If there is indeed a chasm in the middle of the book, a sort of abyss 'in' which there is an attempt to think or say this abyssal chasm which would be *khōra*, the opening of a place 'in' which everything would, at the same time, come to take *place* and *be reflected* (for these are images which are inscribed there), is it insignificant that a *mise en abyme* regulates a certain order of composition of the discourse? And that it goes so far as to regulate even this mode of thinking or of saying which must be similar without being identical to the one which is practiced *on the edges* of the chasm? Is it insignificant that this *mise en abyme* affects the forms of a discourse on *places* [*places*], notably political places, a politics of place entirely commanded by the consideration of sites [*lieux*] (jobs in the society, region, territory, country), as sites assigned to types or forms of discourse?

II

Mise en abyme of the discourse on *khōra*, site [*lieu*] of politics, politics of sites [*lieux*], such would be, then, the structure of an overprinting without a base.

At the opening of the *Timaeus*, there are considerations of the guardians of the city, the cultivators and the artisans, the division of labor and education. Let us note in passing, although it is an analogy whose structure is formal and external: those who are raised as guardians of the city will not have anything that is properly their own (*idion*), neither gold nor silver. They 'will receive the salary of their rank from those they protect' (18b). To have nothing that is one's own, not even the gold which is the only thing comparable to it (50a), isn't this also the situation of the site, the condition of *khōra*? This question can be asked, even if one does not wish to take it seriously; however formal it may be, the analogy is scarcely contestable. One can say the same thing about the remark which follows immediately (18c) and touches on the education of women, on marriage, and above all, with the most pronounced insistence, on the community of children. All possible measures must be taken in order to ensure that no-one can know and recognize as his own (*idia*) the children who are born (18c–d). In procreation (*paidopoiia*), any attribution or natural or legitimate property should find itself excluded by the very milieu of the city. If one bears in mind the fact that a moment ago the text had prescribed a similar education for men and for women, who must be prepared for the same activities and for the same functions, one can still follow the thread of a formal analogy, namely, that of the said 'comparison' of *khōra* with the mother and, a supplementary sign of expropriation, with the nurse. This comparison does not assure it/her of any property, in the sense of the subjective genitive or in the sense of the objective genitive: neither the properties of a genetrix (she engenders nothing and, besides, possesses no property at all), nor the ownership of children, those images of their father who, by the way, is no more their owner than is the mother. This is enough to say about the impropriety of the said comparison. But we are perhaps already in a site [*lieu*] where the law of the proper no longer has any meaning. Let us consider even the political strategy of marriages. It manifests a relation of abyssal and analogous reflexivity with what will be said later about *khōra*, about the 'riddles' or sieves (*seiomena*, 52e, 53a) shaken in order to sort or select the 'grain' and the 'seed'; the law of the better is crossed with a certain chance. Now from the first pages of the *Timaeus*, in a purely political discourse, are described the apparatuses intended to bring about *in secret* the arranging of marriages in order that the children will be born with the best possible naturalness. And this does not happen without some drawing of lots (*kléros*, 18d–e).

Let us explain it at once. These formal analogies or these *mises en abyme*, refined, subtle (too subtle, some will think), are not considered here, *in the first place* [*en premier lieu*], as artifices, boldness, or secrets of formal composition: the art of Plato the writer! This art interests us and ought to do so more still, but what is important in this very place [*ici même*], and first of all, independently of the supposed intentions of a composer, are the constraints which produce these analogies. Shall we say that they constitute a *programme*? A *logic* whose authority was imposed on Plato? Yes, up to a point only, and this limit appears in the abyss itself: the being-programme of the programme, its structure of pre-inscription and of typographic prescription forms the explicit theme of the discourse *en abyme* on *khōra*. The latter figures the place of inscription of *all that is marked on the world*. Likewise the being-logical of logic, its essential *logos*, whether it be true, probable, or mythic, forms the explicit theme of the *Timaeus*, as we shall yet have occasion to explain. Thus one cannot calmly, with no further ado, call by the name *programme* or *logic* the form which dictates to Plato the law of such a composition: programme and logic are apprehended in it, *as such*, though it be in a dream, and put *en abyme*.

Having taken this precaution with regard to analogies which might seem imprudent, let us recall the most general trait which both gathers and authorizes these displacements, from one place to the other 'in' the 'same' place [*lieu*]. It is obvious, too obvious even to be noticed, and its generality has, so to speak, no other limit than itself: it is precisely that of the *genos*, of the genus in all genders and genera, of sexual difference, of the generation of children, of the kinds of being and of that *triton genos* which *khōra* is (neither sensible nor intelligible, 'like' a mother or a nurse, etc.). We have just alluded to all these genres of genres, but we have not yet spoken of the *genos* as race,[6] people, group, community, affinity of birth, nation, etc. Now we're there.

Still at the opening of the *Timaeus*, there is recalled an earlier conversation, a discourse (*logos*) of Socrates on the *politeia* and on its better government. Socrates sums it up, and these are the themes of which we have just spoken. In passing, he uses the word *khōra* (19a) to designate the place assigned to children: you must rear the 'children of the good,' transport the others in secret to another country, continue to keep them under observation, and carry out a further sifting operation in attributing to each his place (*khōran*). After this reminder, Socrates declares himself incapable of praising this city and its men. In this he feels himself to be comparable to the poets and imitators. And here is the *genos* or *ethnos*. Socrates claims to have nothing against the people or the race, the tribe of the poets (*poiētikon genos*). But allowing for the place and the conditions of birth as well as the education, the nation, or race of imitators (*mimētikon ethnos*) will have difficulty in imitating what it has remained alien to, namely, that which happens in actions and words (*ergois, logois*) rather than in spectacles or simulacra. There is also the genre or the tribe of the sophists (*tōn sophistōn genos*). Socrates privileges here again the *situation*, the relation to place: the genus of sophists is characterized by the absence of a proper place, an economy, a fixed domicile; these people have no domesticity, no house that is proper to them (*oikēsis idias*). They wander from place to place, from town to town, incapable of understanding these men who, being philosophers and politicians, *have (a) place* [ont lieu; from *avoir lieu*, or 'to take place'—Ed.], that is, act by means of gesture and speech, in the city or at war. *Poiētikon genos, mimētikon ethnos, tōn sophistōn genos*, after this enumeration what remains? Well, then, you, to whom I am speaking now, you who are also a *genos* (19e), and who belong to the genre of those who *have (a) place*, who take place, by nature and by education. You are thus both philosophers and politicians.

Socrates' strategy itself operates from a sort of nonplace, and that is what makes it very disconcerting, not to say alarming. In starting by declaring that he is, a little *like* the poets, the imitators, and the sophists, incapable of describing the philosopher-politicians, Socrates pretends to rank himself among those who feign. He affects to belong to the *genos* of those whose *genos* consists in affecting: in simulating the belonging to a place and to a community, for example, to the *genos* of true citizens, philosophers, and politicians, to 'yours.' *Socrates thus pretends to belong to the genus of those who pretend to belong to the genus of those who have (a) place, a place and an economy that are their own.* But in saying this, Socrates denounces this *genos* to which he pretends to belong. He claims to speak the truth on the subject of it: in truth, these people have no place, they are wanderers. *Therefore I who resemble them, I have no place* [je n'ai pas de lieu]: in any case, as for me I am similar to them, I do not take place [*je n'ai pas lieu*], but if I am similar to them or if I resemble them, that does not mean that I am their fellow. But this truth, namely that they and I, if we seem to belong to the same *genos*, are without a place of our own, is enunciated by me, since it is a truth, from *your* place, you who are on the side of the true *logos*, of philosophy and politics. I address you from your place [*place*] in order to say to you that I have no place [*place*], since I am like those who make their trade out of resemblance—the poets, the imitators, and the sophists, the genus of those who have no place. You alone have place and can say both the place and the nonplace in truth, and that is why I am going to give you back the floor. In truth, give it to you or leave it to you. To give back, to leave, or to give the floor to the other amounts to saying: you have (a) place, have (a) place, come.

The duplicity of this self-exclusion, the simulacrum of this withdrawal, plays on the belonging to the proper place, as a political place and as a habitation. Only this belonging to place authorizes the truth of the *logos*, that is, also its political effectivity, its pragmatic and praxical [*praxique*] efficiency, which Socrates regularly associates with the *logos* in this context. It is the belonging of a *genos* to a proper place which guarantees the truth of its *logos* (effective relation of the discourse to the thing itself, to the matter, *pragma*) and of its action (*praxis, ergon*). The specialists of the nonplace and of the simulacrum (among whom Socrates for a moment affects to rank himself) do not even have to be excluded from the city, like *pharmakoi*; they exclude themselves by themselves, as does Socrates here in giving back the word. They exclude themselves by themselves, or pretend to do so, also, because they quite simply have no room [*pas de place*]. There is no room for them in the political place [*lieu*] where affairs are spoken of and dealt with, the *agora*.

Although the word was already uttered (19a), the question of *khōra* as a general place or total receptacle (*pandekhēs*) is, of course, not yet posed. But if it is not posed as such, it gestures and points already. The note is given. For on the one hand, the ordered polysemy of the word always includes the sense of political place or, more generally, of *invested* place, by opposition to abstract space. *Khōra* 'means': place occupied by someone, country, inhabited place, marked place, rank, post, assigned position, territory, or region. And in fact, *khōra* will always already be occupied, invested, even as a general place, and even when it is distinguished from everything that takes place in it. Whence the difficulty—we shall come to it—of treating it as an empty or geometric space, or even, and this is what Heidegger will say of it, as that which 'prepares' the Cartesian space, the *extensio* of the *res extensa*. But on the other hand, the discourse of Socrates, if not the Socratic discourse, the discourse of Socrates in this precise place and on this marked place, proceeds from or affects to proceed from errancy [*depuis l'errance*], from a mobile or nonmarked place, in any case from a space or exclusion which happens to be, into the bargain, neutralized. Why neutralized? If Socrates pretends to include himself among those whose *genus* is to have no place, he does not assimilate himself to them, he says he resembles them. Hence he holds himself in a third genus, in a way, neither that of the sophists, poets, and other imitators (*of whom he speaks*), nor that of the philosopher-politicians (*to whom he speaks*, proposing only to listen to them). His speech is neither his address nor what it addresses. His speech *occurs* in a third genus and in the neutral space or a place without place, a place where everything is marked but which would be 'in itself' unmarked. Doesn't he already resemble what others, later, those very ones to whom he gives the word, will call *khōra*? A mere resemblance, no doubt. Only a discourse of the sophists' type would be so indecent as to misuse it. But to misuse a resemblance, isn't that to present it as an identity, isn't it to assimilate? One can also ponder the reasons for resemblance as such.

We are in the preamble, our preamble on the preamble of the *Timaeus*. There is no serious philosophy in introductions, only mythology, at most, said Hegel.

In these preambles, it is not yet a question of *khōra*, at least not of the one that gives place to the measure of the cosmos. However, in a singular mode, the very place of the preamble gives place, on the threshold, to a treatment of place, to an assigning of their place to interlocutors who will be brought to treat of it later. And this assignation of places obeys a criterion: that of the place of the *genos* with regard to the *proper place*. Now, one has never, it seems, taken into account, taken particular count of, such a staging [*mise en scène*]. It distributes the marked places and the unmarked places according to a schema analogous to the one which will later order the discourse on *khōra*. Socrates *effaces himself*, effaces in himself all the types, all the genera, both those of the men of image and simulacrum whom he pretends for a moment to resemble and that of the men of action and men of their word, philosophers and politicians to whom he addresses himself while effacing himself before them. But in thus effacing himself, he situates himself or institutes himself as a *receptive addressee*, let us say, as a *receptacle of all* that will henceforth be inscribed. He declares himself to be *ready and all set* for that, disposed to *receive* everything he's offered. The words *kosmos* and *endekhomenon* are not far away: 'πάρειμί τε οὖν δὴ κεκοσμημένος ἐπ' αὐτὰ καὶ πάντων ἑτοιμότατος ὢν δέχεσται'; 'So here I am, all ready to accept it and full of drive for receiving everything that you will have to offer me' (20c). Once more the question returns: what does *receive* mean? What does *dekhomai* mean? With this question in the form of 'what does X mean?' it is not so much a question of meditating on the *sense* of such and such an expression as of remarking the fold of an immense difficulty: the relationship, so ancient, so traditional, so determinant, between the question of sense and the sensible and that of receptivity in general. The Kantian moment has some privilege here, but even before the *intuitus derivativus* or pure sensibility has been determined as receptivity, the intuitive or perceptive relation to *intelligible sense* has always included, in finite being in general, an irreducible receptivity. It is true *a fortiori* for sensory intuition or perception. *Dekhomai*, which will determine the relation of *khōra* to everything which is not herself and which she receives (it/she is *pandekhēs*, 51a), plays on a whole gamut of senses and connotations: to receive or accept (a deposit, a salary, a present), to welcome, to gather, or even to expect, for example, the gift of hospitality, to be its addressee, as is here the case for Socrates, in a scene of gift and counter-gift. It is a matter of returning (*antapodidōmi*) the gift of the hospitality of (the) discourses. Socrates says he is ready to receive in exchange the discourses of which he becomes the welcoming, receptive, grateful addressee (20b–c). We are still in a system of gift and debt. When we get on to *khōra* as *pandekhēs*, beyond all anthropomorphy, we shall perhaps glimpse a beyond of the debt.

Socrates is not *khōra*, but he would look a lot like it/her if it/she were someone or something. In any case, he puts himself in its/her place, which is not just a place among others, but perhaps *place itself*, the irreplaceable place. Irreplaceable and unplaceable place from which he receives the word(s) of those before whom he effaces himself but who receive them from him, for it is he who makes them talk like this. And us, too, implacably.

Socrates does not occupy this undiscoverable place, but it is the one from which, in the *Timaeus* and elsewhere, *he answers to his name*. For as *khōra* he must always 'be called in the same way.' And as it is not certain that Socrates himself, this one here, is someone or something, the play of the proper names becomes more abyssal than ever: What is place? To what and to whom does it give place? What takes place under these names? Who are you, *Khōra*?

III

The permutations, substitutions, displacements don't only touch upon names. The staging unfolds according to an embedding of discourses of a narrative type, reported or not, of which the origin or the first enunciation appears to be always relayed, appearing to disappear even where it appears. Their mythic dimension is sometimes exposed as such, and the *mise en abyme*, the putting *en abyme* is there given to be reflected without limit. We no longer know whence comes at times the feeling of dizziness, on what edges, up against the inside face of what wall: chaos, chasm, *khōra*.

When they explicitly touch on myth, the propositions of the *Timaeus* all seem ordered by a *double motif*. In its very duplicity, it would constitute the philosopheme of the mytheme such as we just saw it being installed, from Plato to Hegel.

1. On the one hand, myth derives from play. Hence it will not be taken seriously. Thus Plato warns Aristotle, he gets in ahead of the serious objection of Aristotle and makes the same use of the opposition play/seriousness (*paidia/ spoudê*), in the name of philosophical seriousness.

2. But on the other hand, in the order of becoming, when one cannot lay claim to a firm and stable *logos*, when one must make do with the probable, then myth is the done thing [*de rigueur*]; it is rigor.

These two motifs are necessarily interwoven, which gives the game its seriousness and the seriousness its play. It's not forbidden and not difficult to discourse (*dialogisasthai*, 59c) on the subject of bodies when one seeks only probability. One can then make do with the form (*idean*) of probable myths (*tōn eikotōn mythōn*). In these moments of recreation, one abandons reasonings on the subject of eternal beings; one seeks what is probable on the subject of becoming. One can then take a pleasure there (*hèdonèn*) without remorse; one can moderately and reasonably enjoy the game (*paidian*, 59d). The *Timaeus* multiplies propositions of this type. The mythic discourse plays with the probable image because the sensory world is itself (an) image. Sensory becoming is an image, a semblance; myth is an image of this image. The demiurge formed the cosmos *in the image* of the eternal paradigm which he contemplates. The *logos* which relates to these images, to these iconic beings, must be of the same nature: merely probable (29b–c–d). We are obliged to accept in this domain the 'probable myth' (*ton eikota mython*) and not to seek any further (29d, see also 44d, 48d, 57d, 72d–e).

If the cosmo-ontologic encyclopedia of the *Timaeus* presents itself as a 'probable myth,' a tale ordered by the hierarchized opposition of the sensible and the intelligible, of the image in the course of becoming and of eternal being, how can one inscribe therein or situate therein the discourse on *khōra*?

It is indeed inscribed there for a moment, but it also has a bearing on a *place of inscription*, of which it is clearly said that it *exceeds* or *precedes*, in an order that is, moreover, alogical and achronic, anachronistic too, the constitutive oppositions of mytho-logic as such, of mythic discourse and of the discourse *on* myth. On the one hand, by resembling an *oneiric* and *bastard* reasoning, this discourse reminds us of a sort of myth within the myth, of an open abyss in the general myth. But on the other hand, in giving to be thought that which belongs neither to sensory being nor to intelligible being, neither to becoming nor to eternity, the discourse on *khōra* is no longer a discourse on being, it is neither true nor probable and appears thus to be heterogeneous to myth, at least to mytho-logic, to this philosopho-mytheme which orders myth to its philosophical *telos*.

The abyss does not open all at once, at the moment when the general theme of *khōra* receives its name, right in the middle [*milieu*] of the book. It all seems to happen just *as if*—and the *as if* is important to us here—the fracture of this abyss were announced in a muted and subterranean way, preparing and propagating in advance its simulacra and *mises en abyme*: a series of mythic fictions embedded mutually in each other.

Let us consider first, in the staging of the *Timaeus*, from the outset, what Marx calls the 'Egyptian model.'[7] Certain motifs, which we could call *typomorphic*, anticipate there the sequence on the *ekmageion*, this print-bearer, that matter always ready to receive the imprint, or else on the imprint and the seal themselves, the imprinted relief (*ektupōma*)—these are so many tricks for approaching the enigma of *khōra*.

First occurrence: to write for the child. Such as it reaches us, borne by a series of fictional relays which we shall analyze later, the speech of the old Egyptian priest puts (something) forward in a way prior to all writing. He opposes it to myth, quite simply. You Greeks, he says to Solon, you are like children, for you have no written tradition. After a cataclysm you have to reinvent everything. Here in Egypt everything is written (*panta gegrammena*) since the most ancient times (*ek palaiou*) (23a), and so too is even your own history, the history of you Greeks. You don't know where your present city comes from, for those who survive the frequent catastrophes die in their turn without having been capable of expressing themselves in writing (23c). Deprived of written archives, you have recourse in your genealogies to 'childish myths' (23b). Since you have no writing, you need myth.

This exchange is not without some formal paradoxes. As the myth of its origin, the memory of a city is seen to be entrusted not only to a writing but to the writing of the other, to the secretariat of another city. It must thus *be made other* twice over in order to be saved, and it is indeed a question of salvation, of *saving* a memory (23a) by writing on the walls of temples. The living memory must be exiled to the graphic vestiges of *another place*, which is also another city and another political space. But the techno-graphic superiority of the Egyptians is nonetheless subordinated to the service of the Greek *logos*: you Greeks, 'you surpassed all men in all sorts of qualities, as befits the scions and the pupils of the gods. Numerous and great were your exploits and those of your city: they are here by writing [*gegrammena*] and are admired' (24d). The memory of a people inspected, appropriated by another people, or even by another culture: a phenomenon in the history of cultures well known as the history of colonization. But the fact appears highly significant here: the memory is deposited, entrusted to a depot on the shores of a people which declares, here at least, its admiration, its dependence, its subordination. The Egyptian is supposed to have appropriated the culture of the Greek masters, who now depend on this *hypomnesis*, on this secretariat's writing, on these monuments: Thoth or Hermes, whichever you prefer. For this discourse of the priest—or Egyptian interpreter—is uttered here and interpreted in Greek, for the Greeks. Will we ever know who is holding this discourse *on* the dialectic of the master and the slave and on the two memories?

Second occurrence: to receive and perpetuate childhood. So Critias reports a tale of Solon, who himself reports the tale which an Egyptian priest told him on the subject of the *mythological* foundation, precisely, in the memory of the Athenians. Still more precisely: Critias repeats a tale which he had already told the night before and in the course of which he reported a conversation between Solon and Critias, his great-grandfather, a conversation which had been recounted to him when he was a child by his ancestor Critias, who himself had heard from Solon the account of the talk which the latter had had in Egypt with the old priest, the same one who explained to him, in short, why all the Greeks are at the mercy of oral tale-telling, of the oral tradition which, by depriving them of writing, destined them to perpetual childhood! So here is a tale-telling about oral tale-tellings, a chain of oral traditions by which those who are subject to it explain to themselves how someone else, coming from a country of writing, explains to them, orally, why they are doomed to orality. So many Greek children, then, ancestors, children and grandchildren, reflecting amongst themselves but thanks to the mediation of someone other, at once foreigner/stranger and accomplice, superior and inferior, the mythopoetics of oral tale-telling. But once again, this will not make us forget (since it is written!) that all this is written in that place which *receives* everything, in this case, namely, the *Timaeus*, and is therein addressed to the one who, as we do, and before us, *receives* everything, in this theory of receptions—Socrates.

At the end of these tales of tales, after these recountings that are mutually inscribed in each other to the point where one often wonders who is, after all, *holding* this discourse, who is *taking up* speech and who is *receiving* it, the young Critias recounts how he remembers all this. A tale about the possibility of the tale, a proposition about origin, memory, and writing. As I most often do, I quote a current translation (here that of Rivaud, in the Budé edition [F. M. Cornford's translation, *Plato's Cosmology: The 'Timaeus' of Plato* (Indianapolis: Bobbs-Merrill, n.d.) has been used, and modified at need, in this English version—Tr.], modifying it or mentioning the Greek word only where our context requires it:

> Accordingly, as Hermocrates has told you, no sooner had I left yesterday than I set about repeating the story to our friends as I recalled it, and when I got home I recovered pretty well the whole of it by thinking it over at night. How true it is, as they say [τὸ λεγόμενον] that what we learn in childhood [τὰ παίδων μαθήματα] has a wonderful hold on the memory [θαυμαστὸν ἔχει τι μνημεῖον]! I doubt if I could recall everything that I heard yesterday; but I should be surprised [θαυμά-σαιμ'] if I have lost any detail of this story told me so long ago. I listened at the time with much childish delight, and the old man was very ready to answer the questions I kept on asking; so it has remained in me, as if painted with wax in indelible letters [ὥστε οἷον ἐγκαύματα ἀνεκπλύτου γραφῆς ἔμμονά μοι γέγονεν].(26b–c)

In the space of so-called natural, spontaneous, living memory, the originary would be better preserved. Childhood would be more durably inscribed in this wax than the intervening times. Effacement would be the figure for the *middle* [*milieu*; Derrida plays on this word with its suggestion of 'half-way place,' 'something that is only half place,' *mi-lieu*—Tr.] both for space and for time. It would affect only second or secondary impressions, average or mediated. The originary impression would be ineffaceable, once it has been engraved in the virgin wax.

Now what is *represented* by a virgin wax, a wax that is always virgin, absolutely preceding any possible impression, always older, because atemporal, than everything that seems to affect it in order to take form *in it*, in it which *receives*, nevertheless, and in it which, for the same reason, is always younger, infant even, achronic and anachronistic, so indeterminate that it does not even justify the name and the form of wax? Let us leave this question suspended until the moment when there will be grounds for [*où il y aura lieu de*] renaming *khōra*. But it was already necessary to show the homology of this schema with the very content of the tales. In truth, each narrative content—fabulous, fictive, legendary, or mythic, it doesn't matter for the moment—becomes in its turn the content of a different tale. Each tale is thus the *receptacle* of another. There is nothing but receptacles of narrative receptacles, or narrative receptacles of receptacles. Let us not forget that receptacle, place of reception or harboring/lodging (*hypodokhè*), is the most insistent determination (let us not say 'essential,' for reasons which must already be obvious) of *khōra*.

But if *khōra* is a receptacle, if it/she gives place to all the stories, ontologic or mythic, that can be recounted on the subject of what she receives and even of what she resembles but which in fact takes place in her, *khōra* herself, so to speak, does not become the object of any *tale*, whether true or fabled. A secret without secret remains forever impenetrable on the subject of it/her [*à son sujet*]. Though it is not a true *logos*, no more is the word on *khōra* a probable myth, either, a story that is reported and in which another story will take place in its turn.

Let us take it up again from farther back. In that fiction which is the *written* ensemble of the dialogue entitled *Timaeus*, someone speaks at first of a dialogue which is said to have taken place 'last night' (*khthes*, 17a). This second fiction (F2) has a content, the fictive model of an ideal city (17c), which is described in a narrative mode. A structure of inclusion makes of the *included* fiction, in a sense the theme of the prior fiction, which is its *including* form, its capable container, let us say its receptacle. Socrates, who, as we have noted, figures as a general addressee, capable of understanding everything and therefore of receiving everything (like ourselves, even here), then affects to interrupt this mythopoetic string of events. But this is only in order to relaunch it even more forcefully:

> I may now go on to tell you how I feel about the State [*politeia*] we have described. I feel rather like a man who has been looking at some beautiful creatures [*zōa kala*], either represented in painting [*hypo graphés*] or really alive but motionless, and conceives a desire to watch them in motion and actively exercising the powers promised by their form. That is just what I feel about the State we have described: I should like to hear an account of it putting forth its strength in such contests as a State will engage in against others, going to war in a manner worthy of, and achieving results befitting, the training and education given to its citizens, both in feats of arms and in negotiation with various other States. (19b–c)

Desire of Socrates, of the one who receives everything, once again: to give life, to see life and movement given to a *graphé*, to see a zoography become animated, in other words, a pictural representation, the description or the dead inscription of the living. To give birth—but this is also war. And therefore death. This desire is also political. How would one animate this representation of the political? How would one set in motion, that is, set walking/marching, a dead representation of the *politeia*? By showing the city in relation to other cities. One will thus describe by words, by discursive painting, a State's movement of going outside of itself. Thanks to a *second graphic fiction*, one will go outside of the first *graphé*. The latter was more dead, less living than the second one to the extent that it described the city in itself, internal to itself, at peace with its own interiority, in its domestic economy. The possibility of war makes the graphic image—the description—of the ideal city go out, not yet into the living and mobile real, but into a better image, a living image of this living and mobile real, while yet showing a functioning that is internal to the test: war. In all the senses of the word, it is a decisive exposition, of the city.[8]

At the moment when he asks that one should at last get out of this graphic hallucination to see the image of the things themselves in movement, Socrates points at, without denouncing them, poets and sophists: by definition they are incapable of getting out of the simulacrum or the mimetic hallucination in order to describe political reality. Paradoxically, it is to the extent that they are always outside, without a place of their own and with no fixed abode, that these members of the *mimetikon ethnos*, or the *genos tōn sophistōn* or of the *poiētikon genos* remain powerless, incapable of speaking of the political reality inasmuch as it is measured *on the outside*, precisely, in the test of war.

At the same time, affecting to rank himself on the side of this *ethnos* or of this *genos*, Socrates confesses that he too is incapable of going outside, by himself and of himself, of his mythomimeticographic dream in order to give life and movement to the city. ('I know myself well enough to know that I will never be capable of celebrating as one should this city and its citizens [in war, negotiation, and movement]. My incapacity is not surprising; but I have formed the same judgment about the poets,' 19d.)

A supplementary irony: Socrates is not content to side for a moment with the men of the zoographic simulacrum; he declares that he does not despise their *genos* or their *ethnos*. This confers on the play between the text and the theme, between what is done and what is declared, as between the successive inclusions of the 'receptacles' for themes and theses, a structure without an indivisible origin.

In this theatre of irony, where the scenes interlock in a series of receptacles without end and without bottom, how can one isolate a thesis or a theme that could be attributed calmly to the 'philosophy-of-Plato,' indeed to *philosophy* as the Platonic thing? This would be to misrecognize or violently deny the structure of the textual scene, to regard as resolved all the questions of topology in general, including that of the places of rhetoric, and to think one understood what it means to receive, that is, to understand. It's a little early. As always.

IV

Should one henceforth forbid oneself to speak of the philosophy of Plato, of the ontology of Plato, or even of Platonism? Not at all, and there would undoubtedly be no error of principle in so speaking, merely an inevitable *abstraction*. *Platonism* would mean, in these conditions, the thesis or the theme which one has extracted by artifice, misprision, and abstraction from the text, torn out of the written fiction of 'Plato.' Once this abstraction has been supercharged and deployed, it will be extended over all the folds of the text, of its ruses, overdeterminations, and reserves, which the abstraction will come to cover up and dissimulate. This will be called Platonism or the philosophy of Plato, which is neither arbitrary nor illegitimate, since a certain force of thetic abstraction at work in the heterogeneous text of Plato can recommend one to do so. It works and presents itself precisely under the name of philosophy. If it is not illegitimate and arbitrary to call it as it is called, that is because its arbitrary violence, its abstraction, consists in making the law, up to a point and for a while, in dominating, according to a mode which is precisely all of philosophy, other motifs of thought which are also at work in the text: for example, those which interest us here both by privilege and from another situation—let us say, for brevity, from another *historical* situation, even though history depends most often in its concept on this philosophical heritage. 'Platonism' is thus certainly one of the effects of the text signed by Plato, for a long time, and for necessary reasons, the dominant effect, but this effect is always turned back against the text.

It must be possible to analyze this violent reversion. Not that we have at our disposal at a given moment a greater lucidity or new instruments. Prior to this technology or this methodology, a new situation, a new experience, a different *relation* must be possible. I leave these three words (*situation, experience, relation*) without complement in order not to determine them too quickly and in order to announce new questions through this reading of *khōra*. To say, for example, situation or topology of being, experience *of being* or relation *to being*, would perhaps be to set oneself up too quickly in the space opened up by the question of the meaning of being in its Heideggerian type. Now, it will appear later, apropos the Heideggerian interpretation of *khōra*, that our questions are also addressed to certain decisions of Heidegger and to their very horizon, to what forms the horizon of the question of the meaning of being and of its epochs.

The violent reversion of which we have just spoken is always interested and interesting. It is naturally at work in this ensemble without limit which we call here *the text*. In constructing itself, in being posed in its dominant form at a given moment (here that of the Platonic thesis, philosophy, or ontology), the text is neutralized in it, numbed, self-destructed, or dissimulated: unequally, partially, provisionally. The forces that are thus inhibited continue to maintain a certain disorder, some potential incoherence, and some heterogeneity in the organization of the theses. They introduce parasitism into it, and clandestinity, ventriloquism, and, above all, a general tone of denial, which one can learn to perceive by exercising one's ear or one's eye on it. 'Platonism' is not only an example of this movement, the first 'in' the whole history of philosophy. It commands it, it commands this *whole* history. A philosophy as such would henceforth always be 'Platonic.' Hence the necessity to continue to try to think what takes place in Plato, with Plato, what is shown there, what is hidden, so as to win there or to lose there.

Let us return to the *Timaeus*. At the point we have now reached, how can we recognize the *present* of the tale? Who is *presented* there? Who holds the discourse there? To whom is the speech addressed? Still to Socrates: we have already insisted on this singular dissymmetry: but that remains still too indeterminate, by definition. At this point, then, three instances of textual fiction are mutually included in one another, each as content given form in the receptacle of another: F1, the *Timaeus* itself, a unit(y) that is already difficult to cut up; F2, the conversation of the evening before (*The Republic, Politeia?* This debate is well known); and F3, its present résumé, the description of the ideal *politeia*.

But this is merely to begin (17a–19b). In front of the dead picture [*tableau mort*, a pun on *tableau vivant*—Tr.] Socrates thus demands that one pass on to life, to movement and to reality, in order to speak at last of philosophy and politics, those things that the *mimētikon ethnos*, the *poiētikon genos*, and the *tōn sophistōn genos* are, somewhat like Socrates, incapable of. He addresses his interlocutors as a different *genos*, and this apostrophe will make them speak while according to them the necessary right and competence for that. In effacing himself and in rendering up the word, Socrates seems also to induce and to program the discourse of his addressees, whose listener and receiver he affects to become. Who will speak henceforth through their mouths? Will it be they, Socrates' addressees? Or Socrates, their addressee? The *genos* of those who by nature and by education participate in the two orders, philosophy and politics ('ἅμα ἀμψοτέρων ψύσει καὶ τροψῇ μετέχον,' 20a), sees itself thus being assigned the word by the one who excludes himself from their *genos* and pretends to belong to the *genos* of the simulators.

So young Critias accepts (F4) to recount a tale which he had already told the night before, on the road, according to old oral traditions (*ek palaias akoès*, 20d). In the course of this tale, which, the night before, already repeated an old and ill-determined tradition, young Critias recounts another tale (F5), which old Critias, his ancestor, had himself told of a conversation which he (said he) had with Solon, a conversation in the course of which the latter relates (F6) in his turn a conversation which he (said he) had with an Egyptian priest and in the course of which the latter relates (F7) in his turn the origin of Athens: according to Egyptian scriptures.

Now it is in this last tale (the first one in the series of narrative events, the last one to be reported in this telling of tellings) that the reference to Egyptian writing returns. In the course of this first-last tale, the most mythic in its form, it is a matter of reminding the Greeks, who have remained children, of what the childhood of Athens was. Now, Athens is a figuration of a city which, though it did not have the correct usage of writing, nonetheless served as a model to the Egyptian city from which the priest came—hence as an exemplary paradigm in the place from which, in short, he advances this tale. That place, which seems to inspire or produce the tale thus has another place, Athens, as its model.

So it is Athens or its people who, as the apparent addressees or receptacles of the tale, would thus be, according to the priest himself, its utterers, producers, or inspirers, its informers.

In fiction F1—itself written, let us never forget that—there is thus developed a theory or a procession of writing referring, *in writing*, to an origin older than itself (F7).

In the center, between F3 and F4, is a sort of reversal, an apparent catastrophe, and the appearance is that we think we're passing then at last into reality, exiting from the simulacrum. In truth, everything still remains confined in the space of the zoographic fiction. We can gauge the ironic ingenuity that Socrates needs in order to congratulate himself here on passing over to serious things and going beyond the inanimate painting to get on to real events at last. Indeed, he applauds when Critias announces to him that he is getting ready to recount what his grandfather told him Solon had told him on the subject of what an Egyptian priest had confided to him about 'the marvelous exploits accomplished by this city' (20e), one of these exploits being 'the greatest of all' (*pantōn de hen megiston*). Therefore, we will say (mimicking the argument of Saint Anselm, unless it be that of Gaunilon): an event which must have been *real*, or else it would not have been the greatest of all. That's well said, replies Socrates in his enthusiasm, *eu legeis*. And he goes on to ask at once what is this exploit, this *effective* work (*ergon*) which was not reported only as a fiction, a fable, something said, something one is content to talk about (*ou legomenon*) but also as a high fact really accomplished (*ontōs*) by that city, in former times about which Solon thus heard tell.

We ought, then, to speak at last of a fact (*ergon*) veritably, really accomplished. Now what happens? Let us note first that the essential would come to us from Solon's mouth, himself quoted by two generations of Critiases.

Now who is Solon? He is hastily presented as a poet of genius. If political urgency had left him the leisure to devote himself to his genius, he would have surpassed Hesiod or Homer (2la–b). After what Socrates has just said about poets, after the 'realist' turn which the text pretended to take, this is a further excess of irony, which destabilizes even more the firmness of the theses and themes. It accentuates the dynamic tension between the thetic effect and the textual fiction, between on the one hand the 'philosophy' or the 'politics' which is here associated with him—contents of identifiable and transmissible meanings like the identity of a knowledge—and on the other hand a textual drift [*dérive*] which takes the form of a myth, in any event of a 'saying' (*legomenon*), whose origin appears always undefined, pulled back, entrusted to a responsibility that is forever adjourned, without a fixed and determinable subject. From one telling to the next, the author gets farther and farther away. So the mythic saying resembles a discourse without a legitimate father. Orphan or bastard, it is distinguished from the philosophical *logos*, which, as is said in the *Phaedrus*, must have a father to answer for it and about it. This familial schema by which one situates a discourse will be found again at work at the moment of situating, if we can still say this, the place [*lieu*] of any site [*site*], namely *khōra*. On the one hand, *khōra* would be the 'receptacle—as it were, the nurse—of any birth' ('πάσης εἶναι γενέσεως ὑποδοχὴν αὐτὴν οἷον τιθήνην,' 49a). As a nurse, she thus drives from that *tertium quid* whose logic commands all that is attributed to it. On the other hand, a little further on, another suitable 'comparison' is proposed to us: 'And it is convenient to compare [*proseikasai prepei*] the receptacle to a mother, the paradigm to a father, and the intermediary nature between the two to a child [*ekgonon*]' (50d). And yet, to follow this other figure, although it no longer has the place of the nurse but that of the mother, *khōra* does not couple with the father, in other words, with the paradigmatic model. She is a third gender/genus (48e); she does not belong to an oppositional couple, for example, to that which the intelligible paradigm forms with the sensible becoming and which looks rather like a father/son couple. The 'mother' is supposedly apart. And since it's only a figure, a schema, therefore one of these determinations which *khōra* receives, *khōra* is *not* more of a mother than a nurse, is no more than a woman. This *triton genos* is not a *genos*, first of all because it is a unique individual. She does not belong to the 'race of women' (*genos gynaikōn*).[9] *Khōra* marks a place apart, the spacing which keeps a dissymmetrical relation to all that which, 'in herself,' beside or in addition to herself, seems to make a couple with her. In the couple outside of the couple, this strange mother who gives place without engendering can no longer be considered as an origin. She/it eludes all anthropo-theological schemes, all history, all revelation, and all truth. Preoriginary, *before* and outside of all generation, she no longer even has the meaning of a past, of a present that is past. *Before* signifies no temporal anteriority. The relation of independence, the nonrelation, looks more like the relation of the interval or the spacing to what is lodged in it to be received in it.

And yet the discourse on *khōra*, conducted by a bastard reasoning without a legitimate father (*logismō tini nothō*; 52b), is inaugurated by a new return [*retour*] to the origin: a new raising of the stakes in the analytic regression. Backward steps [*retours en arrière*] give to the whole of the *Timaeus* its rhythm. Its proper time is articulated by movements which resume from even farther back the things already dealt with farther back. Thus:

If, then, we are really [ὄντως] to tell how the world was born, we must bring in also the Errant Cause [καὶ τὸ τῆς πλανωμένης εἶδος αἰτίας] and in what manner its nature is to cause motion. So we must return upon our steps [πάλιν] thus, and take up again, for these phenomena, an appropriate new beginning [προσήκουσαν ἑτέραν ἀρχήν] and start once more upon our present theme from the beginning, as we did upon the theme of our earlier discourse [νῦν οὕτω περὶ τούτων πάλιν ἀρκτέον ἀπ' ἀρχῆς] (48a–b).

We will not begin again at the beginning. We will not go back, as is stated immediately after, to first principles or elements of all things (*stoikheia tou pantos*). We must go further onward, take up again everything that we were able to consider hitherto as the origin, go back behind and below [*en deçà*] the elementary principles, that is, behind and below the opposition of the paradigm and its copy. And when, in order to do this, it is announced that recourse will be made only to probable affirmations ('τὴν τῶν εἰκότων λόγων δύναμιν,' or again 'τὸ τῶν εἰκότων δόγμα,' 48d–e), it is in order also to propose to 'divide further' the principle (48e): 'Now let us divide this new beginning more amply than our first. We then distinguished two forms [δύο εἴδη] of being; now, we must point out a third [τρίτον ἄλλο γένος ἡμῖν δηλωτέον].'

Let us take things up again from farther back, which can be translated thus: let us go back behind and below the assured discourse of philosophy, which proceeds by oppositions of principle and counts on the origin as on a *normal couple*. We must go back toward a preorigin which deprives us of this assurance and requires at the same time an impure philosophical discourse, threatened, bastard, hybrid. These traits are not negative. They do not discredit a discourse which would simply be interior to philosophy, for if it is admittedly not true, merely probable, it still tells what is necessary on the subject of necessity. The strange difficulty of this whole text lies indeed in the distinction between these two modalities: the true and the necessary. The bold stroke consists here in going back behind and below the origin, or also the birth, toward a *necessity* which is neither generative nor engendered and which carries philosophy, 'precedes' (prior to the time that passes or the eternal time before history) and 'receives' the effect, here the image of oppositions (intelligible and sensible): philosophy. This necessity (*khōra* is its sur-name) seems so virginal that it does not even have the figure of a virgin any longer.

The discourse on *khōra* thus plays for philosophy a role analogous to the role which *khōra* 'herself' plays for that which philosophy speaks of, namely, the cosmos formed or given form according to the paradigm. Nevertheless, it is from this cosmos that the proper—but necessarily inadequate—figures will be taken for describing *khōra*: receptacle, imprint-bearer, mother, or nurse. These figures are not even true figures. Philosophy cannot speak directly, whether in the mode of vigilance or of truth (true or probable), about what these figures approach. The dream is between the two, neither one nor the other. Philosophy cannot speak philosophically of that which looks like its 'mother,' its 'nurse,' its 'receptacle,' or its 'imprint-bearer.' As such, it speaks only of the father and the son, as if the father engendered it all on his own.

Once again, a homology or analogy that is at least formal: in order to think *khōra*, it is necessary to go back to a beginning that is older than the beginning, namely, the birth of the cosmos, just as the origin of the Athenians must be recalled to them from beyond their own memory. In that which is formal about it, precisely, the analogy is declared: a concern for architectural, textual (histological) and even organic composition is presented as such a little further on. It *recalls* the organicist motif of the *Phaedrus*: a well-composed *logos* must look like a living body. Timaeus: 'Now that, like the builders [*tektosin*], we have the materials [*hylè*: material, wood, raw material, a word that Plato never used to qualify *khōra*, let that be said in passing to announce the problem posed by the Aristotelian interpretation of *khōra* as matter—JD] ready sorted to our hands, namely, the kinds of cause [necessary cause, divine cause—JD] we have distinguished, which are to be combined in the fabric [*synyphanthènai*] of reasoning [*logos*] which remains for us to do. Let us go back, then, once more, briefly, to the beginning [*palin ep'arkhēn*], and rapidly trace the steps that led us to the point from which we have now reached the same position once more; and then attempt to crown our story with a completion fitting all that has gone before [*teleutēn tōn mythō kephalèn*]' (69a).

Notes

NOTE: Translated by Ian McLeod. The first version of this text appeared in *Poikilia: Etudes offertes à Jean-Pierre Vernant* (Paris: Ecole des Hautes Etudes en Sciences Sociales, 1987).

1. We hope to come back to this point, one of the most sensitive ones of our problematic, often and at length, in particular by sketching a history and a typology
of the interpretations of *khōra*, or rather, when we shall try to describe the law of
their paradoxes or of their aporias. Let us note for the moment only that in these
two works—which, in the French language and separated by an interval of sev-
enty years, propose a synoptic table and conclude with a general interpretation
of all the past interpretations—the meta-linguistic or meta-interpretative
recourse to these values of metaphor, of comparison, or of image is never questioned for what it is. No question on interpretive rhetoric is posed, in particular,
no question on what it necessarily borrows from a certain Platonic tradition
(metaphor is a sensory detour for acceding to an intelligible meaning), which
would render it little suited to provide a metalanguage for the interpretation of

Plato and in particular of a text as strange as some passages of the *Timaeus* on *khōra*. Rivaud speaks thus of a 'crowd of comparisons and metaphors whose variety is surprising' (p. 296), of 'metaphors' and of 'images' brought back to an 'idea,' that of the 'in what' (p. 298), even if, against Zeller, he refuses to 'see only metaphors in Plato's formulations' (p. 308). ('La Théorie de la khōra et la cosmogonie du *Timée*,' in *Le Problème du devenir et la notion de matière*, 1905, ch. 5).

Luc Brisson in turn speaks of 'the metaphor of the dream used by Plato to illustrate his description' (*Le même et l'autre dans la structure ontologique au Timée de Platon*, 1974, p. 197, cf. also pp. 206, 207). He even systematizes operative recourse to the concept of metaphor and proposes classifying all the said metaphors at the moment of determining what he calls 'the ontological nature of the "spatial milieu" (we shall come back later to this title and to the project it describes): 'This [determining the "ontological nature" of the "spatial milieu"] poses a considerable problem, for Plato only speaks of the spatial milieu by using a totally metaphorical language, which gets away from any technical quality. That is why we shall first analyze two sequences of images: one of them bearing on sexual relations, and the other on artisanal activity' (p. 208, cf. also pp. 211, 212, 214, 217, 222).

Of course, it is not a question here of criticizing the use of the words *metaphor, comparison*, or *image*. It is often inevitable, and for reasons which we shall try to explain here. It will sometimes happen that we too will have recourse to them. But there is a point, it seems, where the relevance of this rhetorical code meets a limit and must be questioned as such, must become a theme and cease to be merely operative. It is precisely the point where the concepts of this rhetoric appear to be constructed on the basis of 'Platonic' oppositions (intelligible/sensible, being as *eidos*/image, etc.), oppositions from which *khōra* precisely escapes. The apparent multiplicity of metaphors (or also of mythemes in general) signifies in these places not only that the proper meaning can only become intelligible via these detours, but that the opposition between the proper and the figurative, without losing all value, encounters here a limit.

2. Heidegger does this in particular in a brief passage, in fact a parenthesis, in his *Introduction to Metaphysics*. Let us do no more than quote here the translation, and we shall come back to it at length in the last part of this work: '(The reference to the passage in *Timaeus* [50d–e] is intended not only to clarify the link between the *paremphainon* and the *on*, between also-appearing [*des Miterscheinens*] and being as permanence, but at the same time to suggest that the transformation of the barely apprehended essence of place [*topos; Ortes*] and of *khōra* into a "space" [*Raum*] defined by extension [*Ausdehnung*] was prepared [*vorbereitet*] by the Platonic philosophy, i.e. in the interpretation of being as *idea*. Might *khōra* not mean: that which abstracts itself from every particular, that which withdraws, and in such a way precisely admits and "makes place" [*Platz macht*] for something else?') (Pp. 50–51; English trans. by Ralph Manheim, Martin Heidegger, *An Introduction to Metaphysics* [Garden City NY: Doubleday, 1961], p. 55, t.m.) Among all the questions posed for us by this text and its context, the most serious will no doubt bear upon all the decisions implied by this 'is prepared' (*vorbereitet*).

3. *Vorlesungen über die Geschichte der Philosophie, Einleitung*, 8, 2b, *Verhältnis der Philosophie zur Religion, Werke* 18 (Frankfurt a. M.: Suhrkamp), p. 103.

4. Marcel Detienne and Jean-Pierre Vernant, *Les Ruses de l'intelligence, la métis des Grecs*, p. 66. Gaia is evoked by the Egyptian priest of the *Timaeus*, in a discourse to which we shall return. It is at the moment when he recognizes the greater antiquity of the city of Athens, which, however, has only a mythic memory and whose written archive is located as if on deposit in Egypt (23d–e). Cf. also Heidegger, *Nietzsche*, 1: 350: 'Chaos, *khaos, khaine*, signifies the yawning [*das Gähnen*], the gaping, that which is split in two [*Auseinanderklaffende*]. We understand *khaos* in close connection with an original interpretation of the essence of the *aletheia* inasmuch as it is the abyss which opens (cf. Hesiod, *Theogony*). The representation of Chaos, in Nietzsche, has the function of preventing a "humanization" [*Vermenschung*] of existence in its totality. The "humanization" includes as much the moral explanation of the world on the basis of the resolution of a Creator, as its technical explanation on the basis of the activity of a great artisan [*Handwerker*] (the Demiurge).'

5. 'An interpretation decisive [*massgebende Deutung*] for Western thought is that given by Plato. He says that between beings and Being there is [*bestehe*] the *khorismos*; the *khōra* is the locus, the site, the place [*Ort*]. Plato means to say: beings and Being are in different places. Particular beings and Being are differently placed [*sind verschieden geortet*]. Thus when Plato gives thought to the *Khorismas*, to the different location of beings and Being, he is asking for the totally different place [*nach dem ganz anderen Ort*] of Being, as against the place of beings.' (*Was heisst Denken?* [Tübingen: Max Niemeyer, 1954], pp. 174–75. English translation by J. Glenn Gray, Martin Heidegger, *What Is Called Thinking?* [New York: Harper & Row, 1968], p. 227, t.m.) Later we shall return at length to this passage and its context.

6. This is one of the motifs which link this essay to the one I wrote on *Geschlecht* in Heidegger. Cf. the introduction to that essay, '*Geschlecht*, différence sexuelle, différence ontologique,' in *Psyché: Inventions de l'autre* (Paris: Galilée, 1987).

7. *Capital*, fourth section, 14, 5. In another context, that of a seminar held at the Ecole Normale Supérieure in 1970 (Theory of Philosophical Discourse: The Conditions of Inscription of the Text of Political Philosophy—the Example of Materialism), these reflections on the *Timaeus* intersected with other questions which here remain in the background and to which I shall return elsewhere. Other texts were studied, in particular those of Marx and Hegel, for the question of their relation to the politics of Plato in general, or of the division of labor, or of myth, or of rhetoric, or of matter, etc.

8. The possibility of war breaks into the ideality, in the ideal description of the ideal city, in the very space of this fiction or of this representation. The vein of this problematic, which we cannot follow here, seems to be among the richest. It might lead us in particular toward an original form of fiction which is *On the Social Contract*. According to Rousseau, the state of war between States cannot give rise to any pure, that is purely civil, law like the one which must reign inside the State. Even if it has its original law, the law of the people (*genos*, race, people,

ethnic group), war makes us come back to a sort of specific savagery. It brings the social contract out of itself. By this suspension, it also shows the limits of the social contract: it throws a certain light on the frontiers of the social contract itself and of the theoretical or fabulous discourse which describes it. Thus it is at the end of the book of this ideal fiction that Rousseau in a few lines gets on to the problems which he is not going to deal with. We would have to analyze closely this conclusion and these considerations on war, the singular relation which they maintain with *the inside* of the social contract at the moment where they open onto its outside. It is both a thematic relation and a formal relation, a problem of composition: Rousseau seems to rub his eyes so as to perceive the outside of the fable or of the ideal genesis. He opens his eyes, but he closes the book: 'Chap. X, *Conclusion*. After having set down the true principles of political law and tried to found the State on this basis, it remains to support it by its external relations: which would include the law of nations, commerce, the law of war and conquest, public law, leagues, negotiations, treaties, etc. But all that forms a new object too vast for my short sight: I should have fixed it ever closer to me.'

9. Cf. Nicole Loraux, 'Sur la race des femmes,' in *Les Enfants d'Athéna* (Paris: 1981, pp. 75ff). In the context which we are here delimiting, see also, in the preceding chapter. 'L'Autochtonie: Une Topique athénienne,' that which concerns Athens in particular: 'nurse (*trophos*), fatherland, and mother at the same time' (*Panegyric* of Isocrates) and the 'rival and complementary poles, *logos* and *mythos*' which 'share the theatrical stage, in mutual confrontation but also in complicity' (pp. 67–72). As for the race of men (*genos anthropōn*), the Egyptian priest of the *Timaeus* assigns 'places' to it: these are the places propitious for memory, for the conservation of archives, for writing and for tradition, these temperate *zones* which provide protection from destruction by excesses of heat and cold (22e–23a).

Chapter 11

Economimesis

Under the cover of a controlled indeterminacy, pure morality and empirical culturalism are allied in the Kantian critique of pure judgments of taste. A politics, therefore, although it never occupies the center of the stage, acts upon this discourse. It ought to be possible to read it. Politics and political economy, to be sure, are implicated in every discourse on art and on the beautiful. But how does one discern the most pointed specificity of such an implication? Certain of its motifs belong to a long sequence, to a powerful traditional chain going back to Plato and to Aristotle. Very tightly interlaced with these, though at first indistinguishable, are other narrower sequences that would be inadmissible within an Aristotelian or Platonic politics of art. But sorting out and measuring lengths will not suffice. Folded into a new system, the long sequences are displaced; their sense and their function change. Once inserted into another network, the 'same' philosopheme is no longer the same, and besides it never had an identity external to its functioning. Simultaneously, 'unique and original' ['*inédits*'] philosophemes, if there are any, as soon as they enter into articulated composition with inherited philosophemes, are affected by that composition over the whole of their surface and under every angle. We are nowhere near disposing of rigorous criteria for judging philosophical specificity, the precise limits framing a corpus or what properly belongs [*le propre*] to a system. The very project of such a delimitation itself already belongs to a set of conditions [*un ensemble*] that remains to be thought. In turn, even the concept of belonging [to a set] is open to elaboration, that is dislocation, by the structure of the *parergon* [Cf. 'Le parergon,' *La verité en peinture* (Paris: Champs Flammarion, 1978]

Production as mimesis

That is what prompts us once again to feign a point of departure in examples, in any case in very particular locations, following a procedure which for reasons already recognized can be neither empirical nor meta-empirical.

These locations, here and now, are two; their choice is motivated by the concept of *economimesis*. It would appear that *mimesis* and *oikonomia* could have nothing to do with one another. The point is to demonstrate the contrary, to exhibit the systematic link between the two; but not between some particular political economy and *mimesis*, for the latter can accommodate itself to political systems that are different, even opposed to one another. And we are not yet defining economy as an economy of circulation (a restricted economy) or a general economy, for the whole difficulty is narrowed down here as soon as—that is the hypothesis—there is no possible *opposition* between these two economies. Their relation must be one neither of identity nor of contradiction but must be other.

The two particular locations are signaled by statements that are economic in the current sense. Each time it is a question of *salary*. Remarks of this kind are rare in the third *Critique*. That is not a reason, quite the contrary, to consider them insignificant. Is it merely an accident of construction, a chance of composition that the whole Kantian theory of *mimesis* is set forth between these two remarks on salary?

One of these remarks is found in section 43 (*On art in general*): it is the definition of free (or liberal: *freie*) art by opposition to mercenary art [*Lohnkunst*]. The other one is in paragraph 51, in a parenthesis, where it is declared that in the Fine-Arts the mind must occupy itself, excite and satisfy itself without having any end [*but*] in view and independently of any salary.

The first remark intervenes in the course of a definition of art in general —a definition that comes rather late in the book. Up to this point, the subject has been beauty and pure judgments of taste, and if examples have been drawn from art, natural beauty might just as well have furnished them for a theory of judgments of taste. In the preceding paragraph, the superiority of natural beauty had been justified from a moral point of view and by recourse to an analogy between judgments of taste and moral judgments. On the basis of this analogy one can read the 'ciphered language' [*Chiffreschrift*] that nature 'speaks to us figurally [*figürlich*] through its beautiful forms,' its real signatures which make us consider it, nature, as art production. Nature lets itself be admired as art, not by accident but according to well-ordered laws. If on this point Hegel seems to say the contrary—that there is nothing beautiful but what is art—the analogy between art and nature here as always provides a principle of reconciliation.

What is art? Kant seems to begin by replying: art is not nature, thus subscribing to the inherited, ossified, simplified opposition between *tekhnè* and *physis*. On the side of nature is mechanical necessity; on the side of art, the play of freedom. In between them is a whole series of secondary determinations. But analogy annuls this opposition. It places under Nature's dictate what is

most wildly free in the production of art. Genius is the locus of such a dictation—the means by which art receives its rules from nature. All propositions
of an anti-mimetic cast, all condemnations leveled against imitation are
undermined at this point. One must not imitate nature; but nature, assigning
its rules to genius, folds itself, returns to itself, reflects itself through art. This
specular flexion provides both the principle of reflexive judgments—nature
guaranteeing legality in a movement that proceeds from the particular—and
the secret resource of *mimesis*—understood not, in the first place, as an imitation of nature by art, but as a flexion of the *physis*, nature's relation to itself.
There is no longer here any opposition between *physis* and *mimesis*, nor
consequently between *physis* and *tekhnè*, or that, at least, is what now needs to
be verified.

Section 43 begins: 'Art is distinguished from nature as doing (*Thun*) (*facere*)
is distinguished from acting (*Handeln*) or working (*Wirken*) generally (*agere*),
and as the product (*Produkt*) or result of the former is distinguished as work
(*Werk*) (*opus*) from the working (*Wirkung*) (*effectus*) of the latter.' [*Critique of
Judgment*, trans. J.H. Bernard (New York: Hafner Press, 1974)]

These proportional analogies are constructed on a certain number of
apparently irreducible oppositions. How are they finally, as they always do,
going to dissolve? And to the advantage of what political economy?

In order to dissolve, as they always do, the oppositions must be produced,
must be propagated and multiplied. The process is one that has to be followed.

Within art in general (one of the two terms of the preceding opposition)
another split engenders a series of distinctions. Their logical structure is not
insignificant: there is no symmetry between the terms, but rather a regular
hierarchy such that any attempt to distinguish between the two is also to
classify one as being more and the other less. The attempt is to define two
distinct sorts of art, but in order to display two phenomena of which one is
more properly 'art' than the other.

Immediately after having distinguished art from nature, Kant specifies that
the only thing one ought to call 'art' is the production of freedom by means
of freedom [*Hervorbringung durch Freiheit*]. Art properly speaking puts free-will
(*Wilkür*) to work and places reason at the root of its acts. There is therefore no
art, in a strict sense, except that of a being who is free and *logon ekon* [has
speech]: the product of bees ['cells of wax regularly constructed'] is not a
work of art. What can be glimpsed in this inexhaustible reiteration of the
humanist theme, of the ontology bound up with it as well, in this obscurantist
buzzing that always treats animality *in general*, under the purview of one or
two scholastic examples, as if there were only a single 'animal' structure that
could be opposed to the human (inalienably endowed with reason, freedom,
sociality, laughter, language, law, the symbolic, with consciousness, or an
unconscious, etc.), is that the concept of art is also constructed with just such

a guarantee in view. It is there to raise man up [*ériger l'homme*], that is, always, to erect a man-god, to avoid contamination 'from below,' and to mark an incontrovertible limit of anthropological domesticity. The whole of economimesis (Aristotle: only man is capable of *mimesis*) is represented in this gesture. Its ruse and its naiveté—the logic of man—lie in the necessity, in order to save the absolute privilege of emergence (art, freedom, language, etc.), of grounding it in an absolute naturalism and in an absolute indifferentialism; somewhere human production has to be renaturalized, and differentiation must get effaced into opposition.

Thus bees have no art. And if one were to name their production a 'work of art,' it would be 'only by analogy' [*nur wegen der Analogie*]. The work of art is always that of man [*ein Werk der Menschen*].

A power, aptitude, property, destiny of man [*Geschicklichkeit des Menschen*], art is distinguished in its turn from science. Scientific knowledge is a power [*un pouvoir*]; art is what it does not suffice to know, in order to know how to do it [*savoir faire*], in order to be able to do it [*pouvoir faire*]. In the region that Kant comes from, the common man is rarely wrong. Solving the problem of the egg of Columbus, that is science: it suffices to know in order to know how. The same may be said of prestidigitation. As for high-wire dancing, that is something else: you have to do it [*faut le faire*] and it does not suffice to know about it (there is a very brief passage of a tightrope walker in a confidential note, '*In meinen Gegenden* . . .' For anyone who would like to take the plunge and put in something of himself: Kant, Nietzsche, Genet).

Distinct from science, art in general (the question of the Fine-Arts has not yet arisen) cannot be reduced to craft [*Handwerk*]. The latter exchanges the value of its work against a salary; it is a mercenary art [*Lohnkunst*]. Art, strictly speaking, is liberal or free [*freie*], its production must not enter into the economic circle of commerce, of offer and demand; it must not be exchanged. Liberal art and mercenary art therefore do not form a couple of opposite terms. One is higher than the other, more 'art' than the other: it has more value for not having any economic value. If art, in the literal sense, is 'production of freedom,' liberal art better conforms to its essence. Mercenary art belongs to art only by analogy. And if one follows this play of analogy, mercenary productivity also resembles that of bees: lack of freedom. a determined purpose or finality, utility, finitude of the code, fixity of the program without reason and without the play of the imagination. The craftsman, the worker, like the bee, does not play. And indeed, the hierarchical opposition of liberal art and mercenary art is that of play and work. 'We regard the first as if it could only prove purposive as play, i.e. as occupation that is pleasant in itself. But the second is regarded as work, i.e. as occupation which is unpleasant (a trouble) in itself and which is only attractive on account of its effect (for example salary) and which can consequently only be imposed on us by constraint (*zwangmässig*).' [§ 43]

Let us follow the law of analogy:

1. If art is the distinguishing property of man as freedom, free art is more human than remunerated work, just as it is more human than the so-called instinctual activity of bees. The free man, the artist in this sense, is not *homo oeconomicus*.

2. Just as everythlng in nature prescribes the utilization of animal organization by man [§ 63], in the same way free man should be able to utilize, were it by constraint, the work of man insofar as it is not free. Liberal art ought thus to be able to use mercenary art (without touching it, that is without implicating itself); an economy must be able to utilize (render useful) the economy of work.

3. The value of play defines pure productivity. With the beautiful and art both proceeding from the imagination, it was still necessary to distinguish between the reproductive imagination and the productive imagination that is spontaneous, free, and playful: 'If we seek the result of the preceding analysis, we find that everything runs up into this concept of taste—that it is a faculty for judging an object in reference to the imagination's *free conformity to law*. Now, if in the judgment of taste the imagination must be considered in its freedom, it is in the first place not regarded as reproductive [*reproductiv*], as subject to the laws of association, but as productive [*productiv*] and spontaneous [*selbstthätig*] (as the author of arbitrary forms of possible intuitions): and although in the apprehension of a given object of sense it is tied [*gebunden*] to a definite form of this object and so far has no free play [*freies Spiel*] (such as that of poetry), yet it may be readily conceived that the object can furnish it with such a form containing a collection of the manifold as the imagination itself, if it were let free, would project [*entwerfen*], in accordance with the *conformity to law of the understanding in general*.' [*General Remark on the First Section of the Analytic*].

Poetry, the summit of fine art considered as a species of art, carries the freedom of play announced in the productive imagination to its extreme, to the top of the hierarchy. *Mimesis* intervenes, however, not only as one would expect in reproductive operations, but in the free and pure productivity of the imagination as well. The latter deploys the brute power of its invention only by *listening* to nature, to its dictation, its edict. And the concept of nature here itself functions in the service of that ontotheological humanism, of that obscurantism of the economy one could call liberal in its era of *Aufklärung*. Genius, as an instance of the Fine-Arts ('Fine-Arts must necessarily be considered arts of *genius*'. § 46) carries freedom of play and the pure productivity of the imagination to its highest point. It gives rules or at least examples but it has its own rules dictated to it by nature: so that the whole distinction between liberal and mercenary art, with the whole machinery of hierarchical subordination that it commands, reproduces nature in its production, breaks with *mimesis*, understood as imitator of what is, only to identify itself with the free unfolding-refolding of the *physis*.

One ought to analyze closely the paragraph that exploits the false opposition between liberal art and craft. Liberal art is an occupation that is agreeable in itself. The liberal artist—the one who does not work for a salary—enjoys and gives enjoyment. Immediately. The mercenary, insofar as he is practicing his art, does not enjoy. But since we are dealing here with a hierarchy inside of a general organization governed by the universal law of nature, the non-enjoyment of the mercenary artist (his work) serves the cause of liberal enjoyment. And what imposes mercenary art by force, in the last analysis, is nature, which commands genius and which, through all sorts of mediations, commands everything. Speaking immediately after of a 'hierarchy' [*Rangliste*] in the grade of the professions, Kant asks whether we ought to consider an occupation such as watchmaking a (free) art or a (mercenary) handicraft. A difficult question that is immediately put aside: it would require 'another point of view', that of the 'proportion of talents.' The rigorous criterion is lacking. Similarly, Kant 'does not want to discuss here' the question whether, among the seven liberal arts, some could be classed as sciences and others as handicrafts. The liberal arts taught in the arts faculties of the Middle Ages (*trivium*: grammar, dialectic, rhetoric; *quadrivium*: arithmetic, geometry, astronomy, music) are the disciplines that depend the most on the mind's work—by contrast with the mechanical arts, which above all require manual labor. And yet in the exercise of a liberal art (of the free spirit) a certain constraint must be at work. Something compulsory ('*zwangmässiges*' is also the word used to designate the constraint imposed on handicraft) must intervene as a 'mechanism' [*Mechanismus*]. Without this coercive constriction, this tight corset [*corsage*], the spirit which must be free in art 'would have no body and would evaporate altogether.' The body, constraint, or mechanism, for example, of poetry, the highest of the liberal arts, would be lexical accuracy or richness [*Sprachrich-tigkeit, Sprachreichtum*], prosody or metrics. The freedom of a liberal art relates to the system of coercions or constraints, to its own mechanism, as the spirit does to the body or the living body to its corset, which as always, as its name indicates, gives body to things. Attention is required here to seize the organic linchpin of the system: the two arts (liberal and mercenary) are not two totalities independent of or indifferent to one another. Liberal art relates to mercenary art as the mind does to the body, and it cannot produce itself, in its freedom, without the very thing that it subordinates to itself, without the force of mechanical structure which in every sense of the word it *supposes*— the mechanical agency, mercenary, laborious, deprived of pleasure. Hence we hear already the well-known reaction against any non-directive pedagogy: 'many modern educators believe that the best way to produce a free art is to remove it from all constraint [*Zwang*] and thus to change it from work into mere play.' [Ibid.]

It was just said that the free play of liberal art, unlike mercenary art, offers enjoyment [*donne à jouir*]. This is still vague. One needs to distinguish pleasure [*plaisir*] from enjoyment [*jouissance*]. In this context and in a slightly conventional fashion, in order to mark two different concepts, Kant opposes *Lust* and *Genuss*. And that precisely at the moment when he defines the Fine-Arts [*Beaux-Arts*], fine art [*schöne Kunst*]. Once again, this definition does not proceed by symmetrical opposition, by classification of gender and species. Fine-Arts are free arts certainly, but they do not all belong to the liberal arts. Certain among these belong to the Fine-Arts, others to the Sciences.

What then characterizes the 'Fine-Arts'?[1]

This locution, despite being so familiar, is not self-evident. Is there a reason for terming 'fine' or 'beautiful' an art that produces the beautiful? The beautiful is the object, the *opus*, the form produced. Why then would art be fine or beautiful? Kant never asks this question. It seems called for by his critique. If one transfers to art a predicate which, in all rigor, seems to belong to its product, it is because the relation to the product cannot, structurally, be cut off from the relation to a productive subjectivity, however indeterminate, even anonymous it may be: we have here the implication of signature which should not be confused with the extrinsic demands of some empiricism (whether psychological, sociological, historical, etc.) The beautiful would always be the work [*l'œuvre*] (as much the act as the object), the art whose signature remains marked at the limit of the work, neither in nor out, out and in, in the parergonal thickness of the frame. If the beautiful is never ascribed simply to the product *or* to the producing act, but to a certain passage to the limit between them, then it depends, provided with another elaboration, on some parergonal effect: the Fine-Arts are always of the frame and the signature. Kant doubtless would not endorse these propositions which nevertheless do not appear to be entirely incompatible with his problematic of aesthetic subjectivity.

When one says that an art is fine or beautiful, one is not referring to a singularity, to some productive act or to some unique production. The generality (music is a fine art, the art of some composer) implies, within the totality of the operation's subjective powers, a repetition, a possibility of beginning again. This iterability belongs to the very concept of the 'Fine-Arts.'

The repetition is of a pleasure. Whence the answer to the question: can a science be beautiful? No, says Kant. 'A beautiful science' would be an absurdity, a non-sense, a nonentity [*Unding*]: nothing. One can certainly find beautiful things around scientific activity; an artist can also put scientific knowledge to work. But as such, an act or an object of science, for example a scientific statement, could not be called beautiful—any more than one could speak of the scientific value of an art. That would just be idle talk [*bavardage*]. The beauty of a scientific statement would be of the order of the *Bonmot*: 'tasteful witticisms' [*geschmacksvolle Ausspruche (Bonmots)*].

If *Witz* as such can have no scientific value, science must do without it in order to be what it is. It must therefore do without art, without beauty, and indissolubly, without pleasure. It must not proceed from (in view of) pleasure, must neither take nor give any.

A remark in passing, in the *Introduction*, nevertheless recognizes pleasure at the distant origin of knowledge: 'but this pleasure has certainly been present at one time, and it is only because the commonest experience would be impossible without it that it is gradually confounded with mere cognition and no longer arrests particular attention.'

If in an immemorial time, which cannot be a time of consciousness, pleasure does not allow itself to be separated from knowledge, one can no longer exclude science from all relation to beauty, to *Witz*, as well as to the whole economy of pleasure (return to the self-same, reduction of the heterogeneous, recognition of the law, etc.) [Cf. 'Le parergon' (II) (*Le sans de la coupure pure*), p. 27.] Moreover, one has to admit that in the *bon mot*, the force of *Witz* leads back into the buried or repressed origin of science, that is to the science of science, to the point where all the distinctions, oppositions, limits remarked by the Kantian critique lose their pertinence. It is important to take note of the sweeping consequences [*enjeu*] of this problem in the place where the Kantian text itself allows the effacement of that pertinence to be announced.

Let us return to the point where the limits are firmly inscribed, even if this inscription remains derived. The Fine-Arts are not at all scientific, sciences are not at all beautiful or artistic. The Fine-Arts proceed from and give pleasure, not enjoyment [*jouissance*], science, neither pleasure or enjoyment; fine art, pleasure without enjoyment. Nevertheless, not every art procures pleasure. A new series of distinctions intervenes.

An art that conforms to the knowledge of a possible object, which executes the operations necessary to bring it into being, which knows in advance that it must produce and consequently does produce it, such a *mechanical art* neither seeks nor gives pleasure. One knows how to print a book, build a machine, one avails oneself of a model and a purpose. To mechanical art Kant opposes aesthetic art. The latter has its immediate end in pleasure.

But aesthetic art in turn splits into two hierarchic species. Not every aesthetic art is a fine or beautiful art. There is thus aesthetic art that has no relation to the beautiful. Among aesthetic arts, certain of them, the agreeable arts, have enjoyment [*jouissance, Genuss*] as their aim. The Fine-Arts seek pleasure [*Lust*] without enjoyment. Kant defines them first in two stringent lines without parentheses after having leisurely described the art of enjoyment (fourteen lines including a long parenthesis), the art of conversation, jest, laughter, gaiety, simple-minded entertainment, irresponsible gossip around the table, the art of serving, the management of music during the meal, party games, etc. All these are directed to enjoyment. 'On the other hand, fine or beautiful art is a mode of representation which is purposive for itself and which, although devoid of purposes [*ohne Zweck*], yet furthers the culture of the mental powers in reference to social communication.' [§ 44]

Sociality, universal communicability: that can only be pleasure, not enjoyment. The latter involves an empirical sensibility, includes a kernel of incommunicable sensation. Pure pleasure, without empirical enjoyment, therefore belongs to judgment and reflection. But the pleasure of judgment and reflection must be *without* concept, for the reasons already recognized.

This pleasure dispenses with [*faire son deuil de*] both concept and enjoyment. It can only be given in reflective judgment. And according to the order of a certain *socius*, of a certain reflective intersubjectivity.

So what is the relation with *economimesis*? To be able to take pleasure in a reflective pronouncement [*prédication*] without enjoying and without conceiving, belongs, of course, to the essence [*le propre*] of man, of free man— capable of pure, that is non-exchangeable productivity. Non-exchangeable in terms of sensible objects or signs of sensible objects (money for example), non-exchangeable in terms of enjoyment—neither as a use value nor as exchange value.

And nevertheless this pure productivity of the inexchangeable liberates a sort of immaculate commerce. Being a reflective exchange, universal communicability between free subjects opens up space for the play of the Fine-Arts. There is in this a sort of pure economy in which the *oikos*, what belongs essentially to the definition [*le propre*] of man, is reflected in his pure freedom and his pure productivity.

Why then *mimesis* here? The productions of the Fine-Arts are not productions of nature, that, as Kant repeatedly recalls, goes without saying. *Facere* and not *agere*. But a certain *quasi*, a certain *als ob* re-establishes analogical *mimesis* at the point where it appears detached. The works of the Fine-Arts must have the appearance of nature and precisely in so far as they are productions (fashionings) of freedom. They must resemble *effects* of natural *action* at the very moment when they, most purely, are works [*opera*] of artistic confection. 'In a product of the Fine-Arts, we must become conscious that it is art and not nature; but yet the purposiveness in its form must seem [*scheinen*] to be as free from all constraint [*Zwang*] of arbitrary rules as if [*als ob*] it were a product of pure nature. On this feeling of freedom in the play of our cognitive faculties, which must at the same time be purposive, rests that pleasure [*Lust*] which alone is universally communicable, without being based on concepts.' [§ 45].

What is the scope of the *as if*?

Pure and free productivity must resemble that of nature. And it does so precisely because, free and pure, it does not depend on natural laws. The less it depends on nature, the more it resembles nature. *Mimesis* here is not the representation of one thing by another, the relation of resemblance or of identification between two beings, the reproduction of a product of nature by a product of art. It is not the relation of two products but of two productions. And of two freedoms. The artist does not imitate things in nature, or, if you will, in *natura naturata*, but the acts of *natura naturans*, the operations of the *physis*. But since an analogy has already made *natura naturans* the art of an author-subject, and, one could even say, of an artist-god, *mimesis* displays the identification of human action with divine action—of one freedom with another. The communicability of pure judgments of taste, the (universal, infinite, limitless) exchange between subjects who have free hands in the exercise or the appreciation of fine art, all that presupposes a commerce between the divine artist and the human one. And indeed this commerce is a *mimesis*, in the strict sense, a play, a mask, an identification with the other on stage, and not the imitation of an object by its copy. 'True' *mimesis* is between two producing subjects and not between two produced things. Implied by the whole third *Critique*, even though the explicit theme, even less the word itself, never appears, this kind of *mimesis* inevitably entails the condemnation of imitation, which is always characterized as being servile.

As the first effect of this anthropo-theological *mimesis*, a divine teleology secures the political economy of the Fine-Arts, the hierarchical opposition of free art and mercenary art. *Economimesis* puts everything in its place, starting with the instinctual work of animals without language and ending with God, passing by way of the mechanical arts, mercenary art, liberal arts, aesthetic arts and the Fine-Arts.

We are now at the point where the structure of *mimesis* effaces the opposition between nature and art, *agere* and *facere*. And perhaps we rediscover here the root of that pleasure which, before having been reserved for art and for the beautiful, used to belong to knowledge. As for Aristotle, *mimesis* is that which belongs to the essential definition [*le propre*] of man. Kant speaks of imitation as 'aping' (*singerie*) [§ 49]; the ape knows how to imitate, but he does not know how to mime in the sense in which only the freedom of a subject mimes itself. The ape is not a subject and has no relation—not even that of subjection—to the other as such. And the *Poetics* places *mimesis* at the conjoined origin of knowledge and pleasure: 'Poetry does seem to owe its origin to two causes, and two natural causes [*physikai*]. To imitate [*mimeisthai*] is natural [*symphyton*: innate, congenital] for men and shows itself from infancy—man differs from other animals in that he is very apt at imitation [*mimetikôtaton*] and it is by means of this that he acquires his first knowledge [*mathesis protas*], and secondly in that all men take pleasure in imitations [*khairein tois mimemasi pantas*]' [1448 b].

It must still be explained, in order to carry the analysis of a traditional link as far as possible, why the *Poetics* associates pleasure and knowledge while, in the same space of *mimesis*, the third *Critique* appears to disassociate them. In the first place it is because here, as we have seen, the unity of pleasure and knowledge was not excluded but merely re-assigned to the unconsciousness of some immemorial time. And in the second, because nature, the object of knowledge, will turn out to have been an art, an object of pleasure; and natural beauty will have been the production of a natural art. A strange imperfect tense signals it, referring either to an 'above-in-the-text' or to some originary production. Following an *als ob*: 'On this feeling of freedom in the play of our faculties of knowledge, which must at the same time be purposive, rests that pleasure which alone is universally communicable, without however being based on concepts. Nature was beautiful when it simultaneously was seen as art [*Die Natur war schön, wenn sie zugleich als Kunst aussah*] and art cannot be called beautiful unless we are conscious that it is art while yet it is seen, by us, as nature.' [§ 45]

The only beauty therefore remains that of productive nature. Art is beautiful to the degree that it is productive *like* productive nature, that it reproduces the production and not the product of nature, to the degree that nature may once have been (was), before the critical disassociation and before a still to be determined forgetfulness, beautiful. The analogy leads back to this precritical time, anterior to all the disassociations, oppositions, and delimitations of critical discourse, 'older' even than the time of the transcendental aesthetic.

The beautiful brings productive nature back to itself, it qualifies a spectacle that artist-nature has given itself. God has given himself to be seen in a spectacle, just as if he had masked—had shown—himself: a theomime, a physiomime, for the pleasure of God—an immense liberality which however can only give itself to itself to be consumed.

If *economimesis* institutes a specular relation between two liberties, readable in reflective judgment and in *gustus reflectans*, how can man's freedom be said to resemble the freedom of God? Do we know what freedom is, what *freedom* means before having conceived of *physis* as *mimesis*? Before the fold God gives himself in a mirror? How can man's freedom (in a liberal economy) resemble God's freedom which resembles itself and reassembles itself in it. It resembles it precisely by not imitating it, the only way one freedom can resemble another.

The passage of *mimesis* cannot proceed by concepts but only—between freedoms—by exemplars with reflective value, quasi-natural productions which will institute the non-conceptual rules of art.

The original agency here is the figure of genius. It capitalizes freedom but in the same gesture naturalizes the whole of *economimesis*. 'Fine art is the art of genius' [§ 46]. *Ingenium* is natural, it is a natural talent, a gift of Nature [*Naturgabe*]. A productive and donative instance, genius is itself produced and given by nature. Without this gift of nature, without this present of a productive freedom, there would not be any fine art. Nature produces what produces, it produces freedom [*for*] itself [*elle se produit la liberté*] and gives it to itself. In giving non-conceptual rules to art (rules 'abstracted from the act, that is from the product'), in producing 'exemplars,' genius does nothing more than reflect nature, represent it: both as its legacy or its delegate and as its faithful image. 'Genius is the innate disposition of the spirit [*ingenium*], *by which* nature gives rules to art.' [§ 46.]

The non-conceptual role, readable in the act and off the exemplar, does not derive from imitation (genius is incompatible with 'the spirit of imitation'). Genius is not learned. 'To learn is nothing other than to imitate.' Beyond the fact that with this last proposition (§ 47), one returns to the language of the *Poetics*, the affinity is confirmed by the fact that the originality of genius and the exemplarity of its products must incite a certain imitation. A good imitation: one which is not a servile repetition, which does not reproduce, which avoids counterfeiting and plagiarism. This free imitation of a freedom (that of genius) which freely imitates divine freedom is a point that is 'difficult to explain.' The ideas 'awaken,' stir up, excite 'similar ideas,' neighboring, related, analogical [*ähnliche*] ones. The difficult nuance which relates good to bad imitation, good to bad repetition, is fixed briefly in the opposition between *imitation* and *copy* [*contrefaçon*], between *Nachahmung* and *Nachtmachung*. The indiscernibility of that distinction, which nevertheless pervades everything, is repeated, imitated, counterfeited in the signifier: a perfect anagrammatical inversion, except for a single letter.

Once nature has detached genius in order to represent it and to give its rules to art, everything turns out to be naturalized, immediately or not, everything is interpreted as a structure of naturality: the content of empirical culturalism, the political economy of art, its very particular propositions, going from the verse of Frederick the Great to assertions about salary scales.

The second remark on salary belongs to the chapter 'On the Divisions of the Fine-Arts' [§ 51]: 'Everything which is studied and painful must therefore be avoided [in the Fine-Arts]; for fine art must be free art in a double sense: it is not, of course, in the form of some salaried activity [*Lohngeschäft*], work whose quantity can be evaluated according to a determined measure, which can be imposed [*erzwingen*] or paid for [*bezahlen*]; but at the same time the mind must feel itself occupied, although appeased and excited without looking to any other purpose (independent, that is, of any salary).

'The orator therefore gives something that he does not promise, namely an attractive play of the imagination; but he also cheats a little on what he promises and on what he announces as being properly his business, namely the purposive occupation of the understanding. The poet conversely promises little and announces a mere play with ideas, but he supplies something which has the value of a serious occupation, because he provides in this play food for the understanding and gives life to his concepts by the aid of the imagination: on the whole, the poet thus gives more, and the orator less than he promises.'

At the summit is the poet, analogous (and that precisely by a return of *logos*) to God: he gives more than he promises, he submits to no exchange contract, his overabundance generously breaks the circular economy. The hierarchy of the Fine-Arts therefore signifies that some power supercedes the (circular) economy, governs and places itself above (restricted) political economy. The naturalization of political economy subordinates the production and the commerce of art to a transeconomy.

Economimesis is not impaired by it, on the contrary. It unfolds itself there to infinity. It suffers that transeconomy in order to pass to infinity as 'Kantism' passes into 'Hegelianism.' An infinite circle plays [with] itself and uses human play to reappropriate the gift for itself. The poet or genius receives from nature what he gives, of course, but first he receives from nature (from God), besides the given, the giving, the power to produce and to give more than he promises to men. The poetic gift, content and power, wealth and action, is an add-on [*un en-plus*] given as a [power] to give [*un donner*] by God to the poet, who transmits it in order to permit this supplementary surplus value to make its return to the infinite source—this source which can never be lost (by definition, if one can say that of the infinite). All that must pass through the voice. The genius poet is the voice of God who gives him voice, who gives himself and by giving gives to himself, gives himself what he gives, gives himself the [power] to give (*Gabe* and *es gibt*), plays freely with himself, only breaks the finite circle or contractual exchange in order to strike an infinite accord with himself. As soon as the infinite gives itself (to be thought), the *opposition* tends to be effaced between restricted and general economy, circulation and expendiary productivity. That is even, if we can still use such terms, the *function* of the passage to the infinite: the passage *of* the infinity between gift and debt.

Being what he is, the poet gives more than he promises. More than anyone asks of him. And this more belongs to the understanding: it announces a game and it gives something conceptual. Doubtless it is a plus-law [a more/no-more law] [*un plus-de-loi*], but one produced by a faculty whose essential character is *spontaneity*. Giving more than he promises or than is asked of him, the genius poet is paid for this more by no one, at least within the political economy of man. But God supports him. He supports him with speech and in return for gratitude He furnishes him his capital, produces and reproduces his labor force, gives him surplus value and the means of giving surplus-value.

This is a poetic commerce, because God is a poet. There is a relation of hierarchical analogy between the poetic action of the speaking art, at the summit, and the action of God who dictates *Dichtung* to the poet.

This structure of *economimesis* necessarily has its *analogon* in the city. The poet, when he is neither writing nor singing, is just a man among men, must also eat. He must sustain the (mechanical) labor force which poetry, Kant shows, *cannot* forego. So that he may not forget that his essential wealth comes to him from on high, and that his true commerce links him to the loftiness of free, not mercenary art, he receives subsidies from the sun-king or from the enlightened-and-enlightening monarch, from the king-poet, the analogue of the poet-god: from Frederick the Great, a sort of national fund for letters which serves to lessen the rigors of supply and demand in a liberal economy. But this powerful scheme does not necessarily carry over into another organization of the restricted economy. *Economimesis* itself can still find a way to make a profit [*peut s'y retrouver dans ses comptes*].

Frederick the Great, the 'great king', is almost the only poet quoted by the third *Critique*—a sign of the servile precaution and bad taste on the part of the philosopher, it is often ironically noted. But these poetic lines, like the commentary that surrounds them, very rigorously describe the generous overabundance of a solar source. God, King, Sun, Poet, Genius, etc. give of themselves without counting. And if the relation of alterity between a restricted economy and a general economy is above all not a relation of opposition, then the various helio-poetics—Platonic, Kantian, Hegelian, Nietzschean (up to and including Bataille's)—form an apparently *analogical* chain. No oppositional logic seems fitted to disassociate its *themes*.

'When the great king in one of his poems expresses himself as follows:

> *Oui, finissons sans trouble et mourons sans regret,*
> *En laissant l'universe comblé de nos bienfaits.*
> *Ainsi l'astre du jour au bout de sa carrière,*
> *Répand sur l'horizon une douce lumière,*
> *Et les derniers rayons qu'il darde dans les airs*
> *Sont les derniers soupirs qu'il donne à l'univers,*

> ('Yes, let us finish without disquiet and die without regret
> Leaving the universe overflowing with our benefactions,
> Thus the star of day at the end of its career,
> Spreads over the horizon a soft light,
> And the last rays that it shoots in the air
> Are the last sighs that it gives to the universe.')

he quickens his rational idea of a cosmopolitan disposition at the end of life by an attribute of the imagination.' [§ 49]. Inversely, Kant specifies, an intellectual concept can serve as an attribute for a sensible representation and thus animate it ('the sun arose/as calm from virtue springs', '*Die Sonne quoll hervor, wie Ruh aus Tugend quillt*') on the condition that there be recourse to the perceptible awareness of the suprasensible [*Ibid.*] And in a note: 'Perhaps nothing more sublime was ever said and no sublimer thought ever expressed than the famous inscription on the Temple of Isis (Mother Nature): "I am all that is and that was and that shall be, and no mortal hath lifted my veil."' Between the quotation about the springing sun and the note on the veil of Mother Nature comes the analysis of Kant: 'The consciousness of virtue, if we substitute it in our thoughts for a virtuous man, diffuses in the mind a multitude of sublime and restful feelings, and a boundless prospect of a joyful future, to which no expression that is measured by a definite concept completely attains.'

Exemplorality

Perhaps we are approaching the embouchure [the mouth or outlet], if not the sea.

What is it in an embouchure that could open onto *economimesis*?

We have recognized the fold of *mimesis* at the origin of pure productivity, a sort of gift for itself [*pour soi*] of God who makes a present of himself to himself, even prior to the re-productive or imitative structure (that is foreign and inferior to the Fine-Arts): genius imitates nothing, it identifies itself with the productive freedom of God who identifies himself in himself, at the origin of the origin, with the production of production. Is the very concept of production marked by it everywhere and *in general*? Does it belong, by an irreducible semantic invariant, to this logic of economimesis? Let us allow the question to ferment.

The analogy between the free productivity of nature and the free productivity of genius, between God and the Poet, is not only a relation of proportionality or a relation between two—two subjects, two origins, two productions. The analogical process is also a refluence towards the *logos*. The origin is the *logos*. The origin of analogy, that from which analogy proceeds and towards which it returns, is the *logos*, reason and word, the source as a mouth and as an outlet [*embouchure*].

Now it must be demonstrated.

Nature furnishes rules to the art of genius. Not concepts, not descriptive laws, but rules precisely, singular norms which are also orders, imperative statements. When Hegel reproaches the third *Critique* for staying at the level of the 'you must,' he very well evinces the moral order which sustains the aesthetic order. That order proceeds from one freedom to another, it gives itself from one to the other: and as discourse, it does so through a signifying element. Every time we encounter in this text something that resembles a discursive metaphor (nature says, dictates, prescribes, etc.), these are not just any metaphors but analogies of analogy, whose message is that the literal meaning is analogical: nature is properly [*proprement*] *logos* towards which one must always return [*remonter*]. Analogy is always language.

For example, one reads (at the end of § 46) that 'nature, by the medium of genius, does not prescribe [*vorschreibe*] rules to science but to art . . .' Genius transcribes the prescription and its *Vorschreiben* is written under the dictation of nature whose secretary it freely agrees to be. At the moment it writes, it allows itself literally to be inspired by nature which dictates to it, which tells it in the form of poetic commands what it must write and in turn prescribe; and without genius really understanding what it writes. It does not understand the prescriptions that it transmits; in any case it has neither concept nor knowledge of them. 'The author of a product for which he is indebted to his genius does not know himself how he has come by his ideas; and he has not the power to devise the like at pleasure or in accordance with a plan, and to communicate it to others in precepts [*Vorschriften*] that will enable them to produce [*hervorbringen*] similar products [*Producte*].' Genius prescribes, but in the form of non-conceptual rules which forbid repetition, imitative reproduction.

At the moment it freely gives orders to man through the voice of genius, nature is already, itself, a product, the production of the divine genius. At the moment it dictates, it is already in a situation analogous to that of human genius which, furthermore, itself produces a second nature. Productive imagination has the power to create 'as it were' [*gleichsam*] 'another nature' [*Schaffung einer andern Natur*] [§ 49]. There is an analogy therefore between genius which creates a second nature (for example by prescribing rules to other artists), the first nature which dictates its precepts to genius, and God who creates the first nature and produces the archetype which will serve as example and rule. Such hierarchical analogy forms a society of the *logos*, a sociology of genius, a logoarchy. In any case, at each step of the analogy, it (id) speaks [*ça parle*]: God commands, nature speaks in order to transmit to genius; the highest genius is the speaking one, the poet.

Analogy is the rule. What does that mean [*veut dire*]? It means that it means and that it says that it means that it wants [*ça veut*] and that it wants what it wants, for example. [*Ça veut dire que ça veut dire et que ça dit que ça veut dire que ça veut et que ça veut ce que ça veut par exemple.*]

For example. It is by example that it means that it means and that it says that it means that it wants and that it wants what it wants by example. [*C'est par exemple que ça veut dire que ça veut dire et que ça dit que ça veut dire que ça veut et que ça veut ce que ça veut par exemple.*]

For example, analogy is the rule, that means that the analogy between the rule of art (of fine art) and the moral rule, between the aesthetic order and the moral order, that analogy is the rule. It consists in a rule. There is an 'analogy' [*Analogie*] between the pure judgment of taste which, independent of any interest, provokes a *Wohlgefallen* suitable *a priori* to humanity, and the moral judgment that does the same thing by means of concepts [§ 42, *Of the intellectual interest in the beautiful*]. This analogy confers an equal and immediate interest upon the two judgments. The articulated play of this analogy (*Wohl/Gut*) is itself subject to a law of supplementarity: we admire nature 'which displays itself in its beautiful products as art' and 'as it were designedly' (*ibid.*), but in aesthetic experience the purpose or end of this purposiveness does not appear to us.

It is the purpose-lessness [*le sans-fin*] which leads us back inside ourselves. Because the outside appears purposeless, we seek purpose within. There is something like a movement of interiorizing suppliance [*suppléance interiorisante*], a sort of slurping [*suçotement*] by which, cut off from what we seek outside, from a purpose suspended outside, we seek and give within, in an autonomous fashion, not by licking our chops, or smacking our lips or whetting our palate, but rather (what is not entirely something else) by giving ourselves orders, categorical imperatives, by chatting with ourselves through universal schemas once they no longer come from the outside.

Kant describes this movement of idealizing interiorization: 'To this is to be added our admiration for nature, which displays itself in its beautiful products as art, not merely by chance, but as it were designedly, in accordance with a regular arrangement and as purposiveness without purpose. This latter, as we never meet with it outside ourselves, we naturally seek in ourselves and, in fact, in that which constitutes the ultimate purpose of our being [*Dasein*], viz. our moral destination [*moralischen Bestimmung*]. (Of this question as to the ground of possibility of such natural purposiveness we shall first speak in the teleology.)' [§ 42.]

Not finding in aesthetic experience, which here is primary, the determined purpose or end from which we are cut off and which is found too far away, invisible or inaccessible, over there, we fold ourselves back towards the purpose of our Da-sein. This interior purpose is at our disposal, it is ours, ourselves, it calls us and determines us from within, we are *there* [*da*] so as to respond to a *Bestimmung*, to a vocation of autonomy. The *Da* of our *Dasein* is first determined by this purpose which is present to us, and which we present to ourselves as our own and by which we are present to ourselves as what we are: a free existence or presence [*Dasein*], autonomous, that is to say moral.

That is what our *Da* is called and it passes through the mouth. The *Da* of the *Sein* gives itself what it cannot consume outside, while not-to-consume forms the condition of possibility of taste understood as what relates us to purpose-lessness.

Moreover it is in this chapter that 'analogies' multiply concerning the language of nature. It is a matter of explaining why we ought to take a moral interest in the beautiful in nature, a moral interest in this disinterested experience. It must be that nature harbors in itself a principle of harmony [*Übereinstimmung*] between its productions [*Producte*] and our disinterested pleasure. Although the latter is purely subjective and remains cut off from all determined purpose or end, a certain agreement must nevertheless reign between the purposiveness of nature and our *Wohlgefallen*. The *Wohl*, would not be explicable but for this harmony. As this agreement cannot be shown nor demonstrated by concepts, it must be announced otherwise.

How is it announced? How does one announce, in other words, the adherence between adherence and non-adherence?

By means of signs. Here we recognize the proper site, the primary place of *signification* in the third *Critique*. All subsequent signification will depend on it. Nature, then, announces to us by signs and traces (not to be distinguished for the moment) that there must be a harmonious agreement [*un accord*], a correspondence, concert, reciprocal understanding [*Übereinstimmung*], between the purposiveness of its own productions and our disinterested *Wohlgefallen* precisely as it appears cut off from any purpose. 'But it also interests reason that the ideas (for which in moral feeling it arouses an immediate interest) should have objective reality, i.e. that nature should at least show a trace [*Spur*] or give an indication [*Wink*: a sign that one rather makes silently, a signal or wink, a brief and discreet hint instead of a discourse] that it contains in itself a ground for assuming a regular agreement [*Übereinstimmung*] of its products with our entirely disinterested satisfaction (which we recognize *a priori* as a law for everyone, without being able to found it on proofs). Hence reason must take an interest in every expression [*Äusserung*] on the part of nature of an agreement of this kind. Consequently the mind cannot ponder upon the beauty of nature without finding itself at the same time interested therein. But this interest is akin to a moral interest [*der Verwandtschaft nach moralisch*].'

Meditation on a disinterested pleasure therefore provokes a moral interest in the beautiful. It is a strange motivation, this interest taken in disinterestedness, the interest of the interestlessness [*le sans-intérêt*], a moral revenue drawn from a natural production that is without interest for us, from which one takes wealth without interest, the singular moral surplus value of the *without* [*le sans*] of pure detachment—all that maintains a necessary relation with the trace [*Spur*] and the sign [*Wink*] of nature. The latter leaves us signs so that we might still feel assured, in the *without* of pure detachment, of banking on our own account, of satisfying our purpose, of seeing our stocks and our values on the moral rise.

And in order to respond to those who might find this argument subtle, specious, and studied [*studiert*], Kant specifies the nature of the analogy between judgment of taste and moral judgment: 'It will be said that this account [*Deutung*] of aesthetical judgments, as akin to the moral feeling, seems far too studied to be regarded as the true interpretation [*Auslegung*] of that cipher [*Chiffreschrift*] through which nature speaks to us [*uns spricht*] figuratively [*figürlich*] in her beautiful forms. However . . .' [§42.]

Beautiful forms, which signify nothing and have no determined purpose are therefore *also, and by that very fact*, encrypted signs, a figural writing set down in nature's production. The *without* of pure detachment is in truth a language that nature speaks to us—she who loves to encrypt herself and record her signature on things. Try to improvise an epistemic framework for this proposition which is common to Heraclites, to the field of the *signatura rerum* and to the configuration of the third *Critique*, and you will observe that it does not fit all by itself and that it causes the *parergon* to strain.

Thus the in-significant non-language of forms which have no purpose or end and make no sense, this silence is a language between nature and man.

It is not only beautiful forms, purely formal beauties which seem to converse, it is also the adornments and charms that too often, mistakenly, says Kant, we confuse with beautiful forms. He is referring, for example, to colors and sounds. It all seems as if these charms had some 'higher sense' [*ein höhern Sinn*], as if these changes in meaning [*Modificationen der Sinne*] had a more elevated sense and possessed 'as it were a language' [*gleichsam eine Sprache*]. The white color of lilies seems to 'dispose' [*stimmen*] the mind to ideas of innocence; the seven colors, in order from red to violet, seem respectively to suggest the ideas of sublimity (red then), intrepidity, candor, friendliness, modesty, constancy, tenderness.

These meanings are not posited as objective truths. The moral interest that we take in beauty, moreover, presupposes that the trace and the wink of nature do not have to be objectively regulated by conceptual science. We interpret colors like a natural language and it is this hermeneutic *interest* that matters: it is not a matter of knowing whether nature speaks to us and means to tell us this or that, but rather of our interest in its doing so, in involving it necessarily, and of the intervention of this *moral* interest in aesthetic disinterestedness. It belongs to the structure of this interest that we believe in the sincerity, the loyalty, the authenticity of the ciphered language, even if it remains impossible to control objectively. And Kant will say the same thing later about poetry: it is not what it is in the absence of loyalty and sincerity. That which speaks through the mouth of the poet as through the mouth of nature, that which, having been dictated by their voice, is written in their hand, must be veridical and authentic. For example, when the voice of the poet celebrates and glorifies the song of the nightingale, in a lonely copse, on a still summer evening by the soft light of the moon, the mouth to mouth or beak to beak of the two songs must be authentic. If a trickster simulated the song of the nightingale, 'by means of a reed or tube in his mouth,' no one would find it tolerable as soon as we realized that it was a cheat. If the contrary were the case, if you should happen to like that sort of thing, it must be that your feelings are coarse and ignoble. In order to characterize those who are deprived of any '*feeling* for beautiful nature,' Kant again has recourse to an oral example.— And it is a certain examplorality that is being treated here.—We judge to be coarse and ignoble the 'mental attitude' of those who have no feeling for beautiful nature and who 'confine themselves to eating and drinking—to the mere enjoyments of sense.' In the first exemplorality, in the exemplary orality, it is a question of singing and hearing, of unconsummated voice or ideal consummation, of a heightened or interiorized sensibility; in the second case that of a consuming orality which as such, as an interested taste or as actual tasting, can have nothing to do with pure taste. What is already announced here is a certain allergy in the mouth, between pure taste and actual tasting [*dégustation*]. We still have before us the question of where to inscribe disgust. Would not disgust, by turning itself back against actual tasting, also be the origin of pure taste, in the wake of a sort of catastrophe?

The mouth in any case no longer merely occupies one place among others. It can no longer be situated *in* a typology of the body but seeks to organize all the sites and to localize all the organs. Is the *os* of the system, the place of tasting or of consumption but also the emitting production of the *logos*, still a term in an analogy? Could one, by a figure, compare the mouth to this or that, to some other orifice, lower or higher? Is it not itself the analogy, towards which everything returns as towards the logos itself? The *os* for example is no longer a term that can be substituted for the anus, but is determined, hierarchically, as the absolute of every analogon. And the split between all the values that at one moment or another are opposed will pass through the mouth: what it finds good or what it finds bad, according to what is sensible or ideal, as between two means of entering and two means of leaving the mouth, where one would be expressive and emissive (of the poem in the best case), the other vomitive or emetic.

To show this we need to make a detour, through the division of the Fine-Arts [§ 51]. Before this chapter, by an effect of framing that we keep on following, Kant had situated taste as a fourth term which serves to unify the three faculties, imagination, understanding, spirit, that are required by the Fine-Arts: 'The first three faculties only arrive at their *unification* by means of the fourth.'

The chapter on the division of the Fine-Arts will interest us for three of its major motifs. 1. It puts into operation the category of *expression*. 2. It allows itself to be guided by the expressive organization of the human body. 3. For these two reasons it organizes the description of the arts as a hierarchy. These three motifs are inseparable.

Forceful interventions are required, a violent framing activity of which Kant's rhetoric bears the marks. Take the first sentence: 'We may describe beauty in general (whether natural or artificial) as the *expression* of aesthetical ideas.' In the Fine-Arts the concept of the object pre-exists expression; that is not necessary in nature but the absence of the concept does not prevent us from considering natural beauty as the expression of an idea.

Then why *expression*? Why 'we may describe' that as expression? Who, we? By what right? And why as an expression of ideas?

Kant does not say. It goes without saying. He says only what he says, namely that it expresses, and, as it will shortly be confirmed, that the highest form of expression is the spoken, that it says what it expresses and that it passes through the mouth, a mouth that is self-affecting, since it takes nothing from the outside and takes pleasure in what it puts out.

From this dictate which posits as an axiom that the beautiful is expression (even if it signifies nothing), there naturally follows a division of the Fine-Arts with reference to the so-called expressive organs of expression in man. It has been recognized in effect that the Fine-Arts could only be arts of man. In explaining that he is going to classify the arts as a function of the organs of expression in man, Kant clearly senses that the forcing is a little obvious. The signs of his embarrassment multiply: 'If, then, we wish to make a division of the Fine-Arts, we cannot choose a more convenient principle, at least tentatively, than the analogy of art with the mode of expression of which men avail themselves in speech, [*Sprechen*] in order to communicate to one another as perfectly as possible not merely their concepts but also their sensations.' This calls for a note which marks the embarrassment: 'The reader is not to judge this scheme for a possible division of the Fine-Arts as a deliberate theory. It is only one of various attempts which we may and ought to devise.' Another note is added, on the following page, saying exactly the same thing.

The principle therefore is analogy and a very particular analogy: the analogy with *Sprechen*, with language and with its modes. Everything moves back to language; analogy is produced by language which therefore puts everything in relation to itself, as both the reason for the relation and the ultimate term of the relation.

Language having been decomposed, we find *word*, *gesture*, and *tone*. There will therefore only be three kinds of Fine-Arts: *speech* [*redende*], the *formative* [*figuratif, bildende*] and the *art of the 'play of sensations'* [*Spiel der Empfindungen*] as external sensible impressions.

Discursive arts in turn are reduced to rhetoric [*éloquence, Beredsamkeit*] and poetry [*Dichtkunst*], a concept whose very great generality explains why there is no question of any other literary art. But also a very pure concept: through complex combinations we will obtain poetic genres like *tragedy, didactic poem, oratorio,* etc. (§ 52). The orator and the poet meet one another and exchange their masks, masks of an *as if.* Both pretend, but the *as if* of one is more and better than the *as if* of the other. In the service of truth, of loyalty, of sincerity, of productive freedom is the *as if* of the poet, who therefore *expresses* more and better. The orator's *as if* deceives and machinates. It is precisely a machine or rather a 'deceitful art' which manipulates men 'like machines' [§ 53]. The orator announces serious business and treats it as if it were a simple play of ideas. The poet merely proposes an entertaining play of the imagination and proceeds as if he were handling the business of the understanding. The orator certainly gives what he had not promised, the play of the imagination, but he also withholds what he had promised to give or to do: namely, to occupy the understanding in a fitting manner. The poet does just the contrary; he announces a play and does serious work [*eines Geschäftes wurdig*]. The orator promises understanding and gives imagination; the poet promises to play with the imagination while he nurtures the understanding and gives life to concepts. These nursing metaphors are not imposed on Kant by me. It is food [*Nahrung*] that the poet brings by playing at understanding, and what he does thereby is give life [*Leben zu geben*] to concepts: conception occurs through the imagination and the ear, while nutrition passes from mouth to mouth and from mouth to ear, overflowing the finite contract by giving more than it promises.

At the summit of the highest of the speaking arts is poetry. It is at the summit [*den obersten Rang*] because it emanates almost entirely from genius. It stands therefore in the greatest proximity, by virtue of its 'origin,' to that free productivity which rivals that of nature. It is the art which *imitates* the least, and which therefore *resembles* most closely divine productivity. It produces more by liberating the imagination; it is more playful because the forms of external sensible nature no longer serve to limit it. Unleashing the productive imagination, poetry blows up the finite limits of the other arts. 'It expands the mind by setting the imagination at liberty and by offering, [*darbietet*], within the limits of a given concept, amid the unbounded variety of possible forms accordant therewith, that which unites [*verknüpft*] the presentation [*Darstellung*] of this concept with a wealth of thought [*Gedankenfülle*] to which no verbal expression [*Sprachausdruck*] is fully adequate [*völlig adäquat*] and so rising [*sich erhabt*] aesthetically to ideas. It strengthens the mind by making it feel its faculty—free, spontaneous, and independent of natural determination.' [§ 53.]

The criteria here are those of *presentation* (*darbieten, darstellen*). Poetry, more and better, presents—the plenitude of thought [*Gedankenfülle*]. It binds presentation (on the side of expression) to a fullness of thought. It better 'binds' the presenting to the presented in its plenitude. Poetry, more and better, presents the fullness, the fullness of conceptual thought or the fullness of the idea, in so far as it frees us from the limits of external sensible nature. By remaining an art, a fine art, it certainly still belongs to the imagination. And like all language, it is still inadequate to the absolute plenitude of the supra-sensible. And Kant immediately speaks of the 'schema' of the supra-sensible. Imagination of course is the locus of schematism and the name of that art which is concealed in the depths of the soul, but here we can better understand why this art should be 'speech' and why it is 'poetic' *par excellence*.

Why does the poetic have this privilege? Beyond what poetry shares with the speaking arts in general and which has to do with the structure (mouth to ear) of hearing oneself speak, what is it that raises it above eloquence?

The answer is its relation to truth, more precisely its authenticity, its sincerity and its loyalty, its faithful adequation to *itself*, to its interior content if not *ad rem*—to what it is that assures in presentation the fullness of meaning, full of presented thought. These values are not narrowly or immediately moral. The moral agency itself derives from or depends on the value of full presence or full speech. When the poet gives more than he promises, he does of course give a present, an authentic gift: a gift of truth and the truth of the gift. He does not deceive since he presents a fullness of thought [*Gedankenfülle*] but also because he declares his exercise to be merely playing with imagination and with inadequate schemes: 'Poetry plays with illusion, which it produces [*bewirkt*] at pleasure, but without deceiving by it; for it declares its exercise to be mere play, which however can be purposively used by the understanding.' [§ 53.] Poetry manages not to deceive by saying that it plays, and what is more its play, auto-affection elaborating appearances without external limitation, 'at pleasure' [*à volonté*], maintains itself seriously in the service of truth. The value of full presence guarantees both the truth and the morality of the poetic. The plenitude can only be achieved within the interiority of hearing oneself-speak [*du s'entendre-parler*] and poetic formalization favors the process of interiorization by doing without the aid of any external sensible content.

Rhetoric on the contrary defines an art of deceiving, of frustrating with beautiful appearances, with artifices of sensible presentation [*sinnliche Darstellung*], with machines of persuasion [*Maschinen der Überredung*]. The classical condemnation of the machine signifies exactly that discourse produces effects on others in the absence of intention, that no intentions intervene to animate and fill up the speech. Hence, the false life and the empty symbolism of these sophistical *tekhnai*.

If art is expressive, if speech expresses more than other modes of expression, poetic speech in turn is the most telling [*la plus parlante*]; interiority is produced there and is better preserved there in its plenitude. And it produces

not only the most moral and the truest disinterested pleasure, which is therefore the most present and the highest, but also the most positive pleasure. A
priceless pleasure. By breaking with the exchange of values, by giving more than
is asked and more than it promises, poetic speech is both out of circulation,
at least outside any finite commerce, without any determinate value, and yet
of infinite value. It is the origin of value. Everything is measured on a scale
on which poetry occupies the absolutely highest level. It is the universal analogical equivalent, and the value of values. It is in poetry that the work of
mourning, transforming hetero-affection into auto-affection, produces the
maximum of disinterested pleasure.

What relation does this exemplorality maintain with the structure of *gustus*
(relation between the palate, lip, tongue, teeth, throat, opposition between
gustus reflectus and *gustus reflectens*, etc.) on the one hand, and with the structure
of hearing-oneself-speak on the other? And what is the place of the negative,
singularly of 'negative pleasure' in this process?

Hearing holds a certain privilege among the five senses. The classification
of the *Anthropology*, places it among the *objective* senses (touch, sight, and
hearing) which gives a *mediate* perception of the object (sight and hearing).
Objective senses put us in relation to an outside—which is not what taste and
smell do. Here the sensible gets mixed in, with saliva for example, and pene-
trates the organ without preserving its objective subsistance. Mediate objective
perception is reserved for sight and hearing which require the mediation of
light or air. As for touch, it is objective and immediate.

There are thus two mediate objective senses, hearing and sight. In what
respect does hearing prevail over sight? By virtue of its relation to air, that is
to vocal production which can cause it to vibrate. A look is incapable of that.
'It is precisely by this element, moved by the organ of voice, the mouth, that
men, more easily and more completely, enter with others in a community of
thought and sensations, especially if the sounds that each gives the other to
hear are articulated and if, linked together by understanding according to
laws, they constitute a language. The form of an object is not given by hearing,
and linguistic sounds [*Sprachlaute*] do not immediately lead to the representation of the object, but by that very fact and because they signify nothing in
themselves, at least no object, only, at most, interior feelings, they are the most
appropriate means for characterizing concepts, and those who are born deaf,
who consequently must also remain mute (without language) can never accede
to anything more than an *analogon* of reason' [*Anthropology*, § 18].

'More easily and more completely': no exterior means is necessary, nothing
exterior poses an obstacle. Communication here is closer to freedom and
spontaneity. It is also more complete, since interiority expresses itself here
directly. It is more universal for all these reasons. Speaking now of tone and
modulation, the third *Critique* discovers in hearing a sort of 'universal tongue.'

And once sounds no longer have any relation of natural representation with external sensible things, they are more easily linked to the spontaneity of the understanding. Articulated, they furnish a language in agreement with its laws. Here indeed we have the arbitrary nature of the vocal signifier. It belongs to the element of freedom and can only have interior or ideal signifieds, that is, conceptual ones. Between the concept and the system of hearing-oneself-speak, between the intelligible and speech, the link is privileged. One must use the term hearing-oneself-speak [*le s'entendre-parler*] because this structure is auto-affective; in it the mouth and the ear cannot be disassociated. And the proof of it, at the juncture of the empirical and the metempirical, is that the deaf are dumb. They have no access to the *logos itself*. With other senses and other organs they can *imitate* the *logos*, establish with it a sort of empty or purely external relation. They can only become *analogons* of that which reg-ulates all analogy and which itself is not analogical, since it forms the ground of analogy, the *logos* of analogy towards which everything flows back but which itself remains without system, outside of the system that it orients as its end and its origin, its embouchure and its source. That is why the mouth may have analogues in the body at each of the orifices, higher or lower than itself, but is not simply exchangeable with them. If there is a vicariousness of all the senses it is *less true* of the sense of hearing; that is, of hearing-oneself-speak. The latter has a unique place in the system of the senses. It is not the 'noblest' of senses. The greatest nobility accrues to sight which achieves the greatest remove from touch, allows itself to be less affected by the object. In this sense, the beautiful has an essential relation with vision in so far as it consumes less. Mourning presupposes sight. *Pulchritudo vaga* gives itself above all to be seen: and, by suspending consumption on behalf of the *theorein*, it forms an object of pure taste in nature. Poetry, as a fine art, presupposes a preliminary concept and occasions a more adherent beauty on a more immediately present horizon of morality.

But if hearing is not the most noble of the senses, it takes its absolute privilege from its status as the least replaceable. It tolerates substitution badly and almost succeeds in resisting all vicariousness.

Is there anything vicarious in the senses [Vicariat der Sinne], *that is, can one sense be used as a substitute for another? There may be. One can evoke by gesture the usual speech from a deaf person, granted that he has once been able to hear. In this, the eyes serve in place of ears. The same thing may happen through observing the movements of his teacher's lips, indeed by seeing the movements of another's organs of speech must convert the sounds, which his teacher has coaxed from him, into a feeling of the movement of his own speech muscles. But he will never attain real concepts* [wirklichen Begriffen], *since the signs necessary to him are not capable of universality. (. . .) Which deficiency* [Mangel] *or loss of sense is more serious, that of hearing or sight? When it is inborn, deficiency of hearing is the least reparable* [ersetzlich]. [Ibid. § 22.]

Hence hearing, by its unique position, by its allergy to prosthesis, by the auto-affective structure that distinguishes it from sight, by its proximity to the inside and to the concept, by the constitutive process of hearing-oneself-speak is not merely one of the senses among others. It is not even, in spite of the conventional classifications, an external sense. It has a relation of evident affinity with what Kant calls internal sense. Now the latter is unique and its element, its 'form' is time. Like hearing-oneself-speak. It does not properly belong, as the other senses do, to anthropology but to psychology. Thus hearing-oneself-speak, in its singular relation to the unique internal sense and by the eminent place it occupies in the third *Critique*, tears the problematic away from its anthropological space in order to make it pass, with all the consequences that can entail, into a psychological space.

> § 24. *The inner sense is not pure apperception, a consciousness of what man does (for the latter belongs to the power of thought) but of what man feels, to the extent he is affected by his own play of thought. Inner intuition, and consequently the relation between representations in time (whether simultaneous or successive), is at the basis of this consciousness. Its perceptions, and the (true or apparent) inner experience resulting from the combination of the perceptions does not simply belong to anthropology, in which one neglects the question of knowing whether or not man has a soul (as a special incorporal substance), but to psychology in which we believe that we perceive such a sense within ourselves, and in which the mind, represented in its quality as a pure faculty of feeling and thinking, is considered as a substance especially inhabiting man. —As a result there is but one inner sense, for there are not various organs by which man receives an inner sensation of himself . . .* [Ibid. § 24].

If hearing-oneself-speak, in so far as it also passes through a certain mouth, transforms everything into auto-affection, assimilates everything to itself by idealizing it within interiority, masters everything by mourning its passing, refusing to touch it, to digest it naturally, but digests it ideally, consumes what it does not consume and *vice versa*, produces disinterestedness in the possibility of pronouncing judgments, if that mouth governs a space of analogy into which it does not let itself be drawn, if it is from the irreplaceable place of this enormous 'phantasm' (but one does not know what a phantasm is prior to the system of *these* effects) that it orders pleasure, what is the border or the absolute overboard [*le bord ou le débord absolu*] of this problematic? What is the (internal and external) border which traces its limit and the frame of its *parergon*? In other words, what is it that does not enter into this theory thus framed, hierarchized, regulated? What is excluded from it and what, proceeding from this exclusion, gives it form, limit, and contour? And what about this over-board with respect to what one calls the mouth? Since the mouth orders a pleasure dependant on assimilation, to ideal auto-affection, what is it that does not allow itself to be transformed into oral auto-affection, taking the *os* for a *telos*? What is it that does not let itself be regulated by examplorality?

There is no answer to such a question. One cannot say, it is this or that, this or that thing. We will see why. And the impossibility of finding examples in this case, Kant's inability to furnish any at a certain moment will be very noticeable. In the same way that we have often had to treat examples preceding the law in a reflective manner, we are now about to discover a sort of law without example; and first of all we shall state our answer in a tautological form, as the inverted duplication of the question.

What this logo-phonocentric system excludes is not even a negative. The negative is its business and its work. What it excludes, what this very work excludes, is what does not allow itself to be digested, or represented, or stated —does not allow itself to be transformed into auto-affection by exemplorality. It is an irreducible heterogeneity which cannot be eaten either sensibly or ideally and which—this is the tautology—by never letting itself be swallowed must therefore *cause itself to be vomited*.

Vomit lends its form to this whole system, beginning with its specific parergonal overflow. It must therefore be shown that the scheme of vomiting, as the experience of disgust, is not merely one excluded term among others.

What then is the relation between disgust and vomit? It is indeed vomit that interests us rather than the act or process of vomiting, which are less disgusting than vomit in so far as they imply an activity, some initiative whereby the subject can at least still mimic mastery or dream it in auto-affection, believing that he *makes himself vomit*. Here, hetero-affection no longer even allows itself to be pre-digested in an act of making-oneself-vomit.

Why vomit then, as a parergon of the third *Critique* considered as a general synthesis of transcendental idealism?

I start from the place of the negative. Kant admits the possibility and the concept of *negative pleasure*. For example the feeling of the sublime. While 'the beautiful directly brings with it a feeling of the furtherance of life, and thus is compatible with charms and with the play of the imagination, the other [the feeling of the sublime] is a pleasure that arises [*entspringt*] only indirectly; viz. it is produced by the feeling of a momentary checking [*inhibition*] (*Hemmung*: an arrest, a retention) of the vital powers and a consequent stronger outflow [*Ergiessung*: pouring out] of them [the corporal scheme here, since there is *Wohlgefallen* and pleasure, is rather that of ejaculation than vomiting which this outflow might at first resemble] so that it seems to be regarded,' continues Kant, 'as emotion—not play, but earnest in the exercise of the imagination. Hence it is not incompatible with charm; and as the mind is not merely attracted by the object but is ever being alternately repelled, the *Wohlgefallen* in the sublime does not so much involve a positive pleasure as admiration or respect, which rather deserves to be called negative pleasure.' (§ 23)

Although repulsive on one of its faces, the sublime is not the absolute other of the beautiful. It still provokes a certain pleasure. Its negativity does indeed provoke a disagreement between the faculties and disorder in the unity of the subject. But it is still productive of pleasure and the system of reason can account for it. A still internal negativity does not reduce to silence; it lets itself be spoken. The sublime itself can dawn in art. The silence it imposes by taking the breath away and by preventing speech is less than ever heterogeneous to spirit and freedom. The movement of reappropriation on the contrary is even more active. That which in this silence works against our senses or in opposition to the interest of sense (*hindrance* and *sacrifice*, says Kant) keeps the extension of a domain and of power in view. *Sacrifice* [*Aufopferung*] and *spoliation* [*Beraubung*], through the experience of a negative *Wohlgefallen*, thus allows for the acquisition of an extension and a power [*Macht*] greater than what is sacrificed to them. (*General Remark upon the Exposition of the Aesthetical Reflective Judgment*) Economic calculation allows the sublime to be swallowed. The same is the case for all sorts of 'negative pleasures,' of pleasures that displease whoever feels them in the present: for example the needy but well-meaning man at becoming the heir of an affectionate but avaricious father; or the widow at the death of her husband (in this latter case her grief is satisfying while the pleasure of the orphan, in the former example, causes him grief.) [§ 54] In all these cases, whether or not they amount to the same thing, there is negative pleasure or a negative of pleasure but still pleasure, and the work of mourning is consequently not absolutely blocked, impossible, excluded.

In the same way, the Fine-Arts can give beauty to ugly or displeasing things and therein lies their superiority. [§ 48.] The ugly, the evil, the false, the monstrous, the negative in general can be assimilated by art. An old *topos*: furies, diseases, the ravages of war, etc. can all furnish beautiful descriptions and 'even be represented in paintings.' The ugly, the evil, the horrible, the negative in general are therefore not unassimilable to the system.

A single 'thing' is unassimilable. It will therefore form the transcendental of the transcendental, the non-transcendentalizable, the non-idealizable, and that is the *disgusting*. It presents itself, in the Kantian discourse, as a 'species' (*Art*) of the hideous or of the hateful, but one quickly observes that it is not a species that would peacefully belong to its genus. 'There is only one kind of ugliness [*Hasslichkeit*] which cannot be represented in accordance with nature without destroying [send to ground: *zu Grunde zu richten*] all aesthetical satisfaction, and consequently artificial beauty, viz., that which excites *disgust* (*Eckel*).' [§ 48.]

Thus it is no longer a question here of one of those negative values, one of those ugly or harmful things that art can represent and thereby idealize. The absolute excluded [*l'exclu absolu*] does not allow itself even to be granted the status of an object of negative pleasure or of ugliness redeemed by representation. It is unrepresentable. And at the same time it is unnameable in its singularity. If one could name it or represent it, it would begin to enter into the auto-affective circle of mastery or reappropriation. An economy would be possible. The disgusting X cannot even announce itself as a *sensible* object without immediately being caught up in a teleological hierarchy. It is therefore in-sensible and un-intelligible, irrepresentable and unnameable, the absolute other of the system.

Nevertheless Kant does speak of a certain representation regarding it: 'For in this singular [*sonderbaren*] sensation, which rests on mere imagination, [therefore there is none], the object is represented as it were [*der Gegenstand gleichsam . . . vorgestellt wird*] obtruding itself for our enjoyment [*als ob er sich zum Genuss aufdränge*: the disgusting, vomit is represented in advance as forcing pleasure, and that is why it disgusts] while we strive against it with all our might [*wider den wir doch mit Gewalt streben*]. And the artistic representation of the object is no longer distinguished from the nature of the object itself in our sensation, and thus it is impossible that it can be regarded as beautiful.'

Vomit is related to enjoyment [*jouissance*], if not to pleasure. It even *represents* the very thing that forces us to enjoy—in spite of ourselves [*notre corps défendant*]. But this representation annuls itself, and that is why vomit remains unrepresentable. [A representation of the irrepresentable, a presentation of the unpresentable, is also the structure of the *colossal*, as it is described, or circumvented, in § 26. Cf. 'Le colossal,' in *La verité en peinture*, p. 136.] By limitlessly violating our enjoyment, without granting it any determining limit, it abolishes representative distance—beauty too—and prevents mourning. It irresistibly forces one to consume; but without allowing any chance for idealization. If it remains unrepresentable or unspeakable—absolutely heterogeneous—it is not because it is this or that. Quite the contrary. By forcing enjoyment, it suspends the suspense of non-consummation, which accompanies pleasure that is bound up with representation [*Vorstellung*], pleasure bound to discourse, to the poetic in its highest form. It can be neither beautiful, nor ugly, nor sublime, give rise neither to positive nor negative, neither to interested nor disinterested pleasure. It gives too much enjoyment [*trop à jouir*] for that and it burns up all work as mourning work.

Let it be understood in all senses that what the word *disgusting* de-nominates is what one cannot resign oneself to mourn [*faire son deuil*].

And if the work of mourning always consists in biting off the bit,[2] the disgusting can only be vomited.

It will be objected that all that is tautological. It is quite normal that the other of the system of taste [*goût*] should be distaste. And if taste metaphorizes exemplorality, then disgust should have the same form, but inverted; nothing has been learned. Certainly. Unless we learn to question this tautological necessity in another way; and to wonder whether the tautological structure is not itself the very form of what the exclusion [of dis-gust] serves to construct.

If it can be confirmed that everything can be said (assimilated, represented, interiorized, idealized) by this logocentric system except vomit, it is only because the oral relation taste/disgust constitutes, other than as a metaphor, this whole discourse on discourse, this whole tautology of the *logos* as self-same-identity [*le même*]. And to confirm it, it must be ascertained that the word disgust [*Eckel*] does not designate the repugnant or the negative in general. It refers precisely to what makes one desire to vomit. But how can anyone desire to vomit? [That is a question (the question precisely of *Eckel*) on which Zarathoustra (in the third passage) endlessly ruminates.]

Moreover, once fixed in its 'literal sense' by the *Anthropology*, the word *disgust* can be seen to be caught up in an analogical derivation. There is worse than the literally disgusting. And if there is worse, it is because the literally disgusting is maintained, as security, in place of the worse. If not of something worse, at least in place of an 'in place,' in place of the replacement that has no proper place, no proper trajectory, no circular and economical return. In place of prosthesis.

All that can no longer take place between 'objective' senses (hearing, sight, touch) but only between subjective 'senses'; and that no longer depends on mechanics but on chemistry:

> § 20 *The senses of taste and smell are both more subjective than objective. The sense of taste is activated when the organ of the tongue, the gullet, and the palate come into touch with an external object. The sense of smell is activated by drawing in air which is mixed with alien vapors; the body itself from which the vapors emanate may be distant from the sensory organ. Both senses are closely related, and he who is deficient in the sense of smell is likewise weak in taste. Neither of the two senses can lead by itself to the cognition of the object without the help of one of the other senses; for example, one can say that both are affected by salts (stable and volatile) of which one must be broken up by liquefaction in the mouth, the other by air which has to penetrate the organ, in order to allow its specific sensation to reach it.*
>
> § 21 *We may divide the sensations of the external senses into those of mechanical and those of chemical operation. To the mechanical belong the three higher senses, to the chemical the two lower senses. The first three senses are those of perception (of the surface), while the other two are senses of pleasure (Genusses) (of innermost sensation). Therefore it happens that nausea, (Eckel) a stimulus to rid oneself* [entledigen] [*by vomiting:* sich zu erbrechen] *of food* [that which has been enjoyed: genossenen] *by the quickest way through the gullet, is given to man as such a strong vital sensation, since such an internal feeling can be dangerous to the animal.*
>
> *However, there is also a pleasure of the intellect* [Geistesgenuss] *consisting in the communication of thought. But when it is forced upon us* [uns aufgedrungen], *the mind finds it repugnant and it ceases to be nutritive as food for the intellect. (A good example of this is the constant repetition of amusing, or witty* [witzig] *quips, which can become indigestible through sameness.) Thus the natural instinct to be free of it is by analogy called nausea, although it belongs to the inner sense.*
>
> *Smell is, so to speak, taste at a distance, and other people are forced to share in the pleasure* [mit zu geniessen] *whether they want to or not. Hence, by interfering with individual freedom, smell is less sociable than taste, when confronted with many dishes and bottles, one can choose that which suits his pleasure without forcing others to participate in that pleasure. Filth seems to awaken nausea less through what is repulsive to eye and tongue than through the stench associated with it. Internal penetration (into the lungs) through smell is even more intimate than through the absorptive vessels of mouth or gullet.*

There is then something more disgusting than the disgusting, than what disgusts taste. The chemistry of smell exceeds the tautology taste/disgust. Disgust is not the symmetrical inverse of taste, the negative key to the system, except in so far as some interest sustains its excellence, like that of the mouth itself—the chemistry of the word—, and prohibits the substitution of any non-oral analogue. The system therefore is interested in determining the other as *its* other, that is, as literally disgusting.

What is absolutely foreclosed is not vomit, but the possibility of a vicariousness of vomit, of its replacement by anything else—by some other unrepresentable, unnameable, unintelligible, insensible, unassimilable, obscene other which forces enjoyment and whose irrepressible violence would undo the hierarchizing authority of logocentric analogy—its power of *identification*.

Vicariousness would in turn be reassuring only if it substituted an identifiable term for an unrepresentable one, if it allowed one to step aside from the abyss in the direction of another place, if it were interested in some other go-around [*interessé à quelque manège*]. But for that it would have to be *itself* and represent itself as such. Whereas it is starting from that impossibility that economimesis is constrained in its processes.

This impossibility cannot be said to be some thing, something sensible or intelligible, that could fall under one or the other senses or under some concept. One cannot name it within the logocentric system—within the name—which in turn can only vomit it and vomit itself in it. One cannot even say: what is it? That would be to begin to eat it, or—what is no longer absolutely different—to vomit it. The question *what is?* already parleys [*arraisonne*] like a *parergon*, it constructs a framework which captures the energy of what is completely inassimilable and absolutely repressed. Any philosophical question already determines, concerning this other, a paregoric *parergon*. A paregoric remedy softens with speech; it consoles, it exhorts with the word. As its name indicates.

The word *vomit* arrests the vicariousness of disgust; it puts the thing in the mouth; it substitutes, but only for example, oral for anal. It is determined by the system of the beautiful, 'the symbol of morality,' as *its* other; it is then for philosophy, still, an elixir, even in the very quintessence of its bad taste.

Notes

1. Fine-Arts has been used throughout to translate *Beaux-Arts*, which translates *Schöne Kunst*. [Trans.]
2. *le mors*: the bit of a bridle, what is bitten or bitten off (*un mor-ceau*), a remainder, a corpse (*un mort*). In Freud, mourning reconciles one to the loss of a beloved object by cannibalizing—incorporating, internalizing, hence idealizing—the dead. [Trans.]

Bibliography

This bibliography is in two sections: a selection of books, contributions to books and articles by Jacques Derrida, in English and French; and works which discuss Derrida, draw on his work, are considered as examples of deconstruction, or, in a few cases, those which are mentioned in Derrida's texts gathered in this reader. The second section of the bibliography is restricted mostly to monographs and collections of essays, although a few chapters and articles are included. This bibliography is not to be considered exhaustive.

For other bibliographies which refer to Derrida's publications in French and other translations (and which also include informative lists of works on, or influenced by, Derrida), the reader is referred to the bibliographies provided by Geoffrey Bennington in *Jacques Derrida* (1993), Peggy Kamuf in *A Derrida Reader: Between the Blinds* (1991), William B. Schultz and Lewis L. B. Fried, *Jacques Derrida: An Annotated Primary and Secondary Bibliography* (1992), Albert Leventure, 'A Jacques Derrida Bibliography 1962–90', *Textual Practice*, 5:1 (Spring 1991), and Joan Nordquist, ed., *Social Theory: A Bibliographic Series*, No. 37, *Jacques Derrida (II): A Bibliography* (1995).

Under the entries for the two other Derrida readers available—Derek Attridge's *Acts of Literature* and Peggy Kamuf's *A Derrida Reader*—I have included the contents of those readers.

For many, the most accessible 'introductions' to Derrida are the numerous interviews with him available in many places. *Points . . .* offers a collection of interviews gathered over a twenty-year period, 1974–94. For, me, a favourite 'introductory' text is 'Letter to a Japanese Friend', which is to be found in Peggy Kamuf's reader, and which discusses the im/possibilities of translating deconstruction. Of Derrida's commentators who have written 'introductions', I would recommend Geoffrey Bennington's 'Derridabase' in *Jacques Derrida* by Geoffrey Bennington and Jacques Derrida, and John D. Caputo's *Deconstruction in a Nutshell*. For those interested in 'virtual Derrida', there are well over 6,000 references to be located on the web, one of the most interesting of which is to be found at www.hydra.umn.edu/derrida

Books and Articles by Jacques Derrida

Derrida, Jacques (trans. and intro.). *L'Origine de la géométrie*, by Edmund Husserl. Paris: Presses Universitaires de France, 1962.

——. *De la grammatologie*. Paris: Minuit, 1967.

——. *L'Ecriture et la différence*. Paris: Seuil, 1967.

——. *La Voix et le phénomène: introduction au problème du signe dans la phénomènologie de Husserl*. Paris: Presses Universitaires de France, 1967.

——. *La dissémination*. Paris: Seuil, 1972.

——. *Marges de la philosophie*. Paris: Minuit, 1972.

——. *Positions: Entretiens avec Henri Ronse, Julia Kristeva, Jean-Louis Houdebine, Guy Scarpetta*. Paris: Minuit, 1972.

——. *Speech and Phenomena and Other Essays on Husserl's Theory of Signs*. Trans. David B. Allison. Evanston: Northwestern University Press, 1973.

——. 'L'Archéologie du frivole', introduction to Condillac. *Essai sur l'origine des connaissances humaines*. Paris: Galilée, 1973.

——. *Of Grammatology*. Trans. Gayatri Chakravorty Spivak. Baltimore: The Johns Hopkins University Press, 1974.

——. *Husserl: L'Origine de la géométrie*. 2nd ed. Paris: Presses Universitaires de France, 1974.

——. *Glas*. Paris: Galilée, 1974. Rpt., Paris: Denoël/Gonthier, 1981, 2 vols.

——. *Adami*. Paris: Galerie Maeght, 1975.

——. *L'Archéologie du frivole*. Paris: Denoël/Gonthier. 1976.

——. *Eperons. Sporen. Spurs. Sproni.* Venice: Corbo e Fiore, 1976.

——. 'Fors: Les mots anglés de N. Abraham et M. Torok', preface to Nicholas Abraham and Maria Torok, *Cryptonymie: Le verbier de l'homme aux loups*. Paris: Aubier–Flammarion, 1976, pp. 7–73.

——. 'Fors'. Trans. Barbara Johnson. *The Georgia Review*. 31 (1977): 64–116.

——. *Edmund Husserl's "Origin of Geometry": An Introduction*. Ed. David B. Allison. Trans. and Preface, John P. Leavey, Jr. Stony Brook: Nicholas Hays, 1978. Rpt. Lincoln: University of Nebraska Press, 1989.

——. *Writing and Difference*. Trans. Alan Bass. London: RKP, 1978.

——. *La Vérité en peinture*. Paris: Flammarion, 1978.

——. 'Scribble (pouvoir/écrire)'. Introduction to William Warburton, *Essai sur les hiéroglyphs*. Paris: Aubier, 1978.

——. 'Coming into One's Own'. Trans. James Hulbert. *Psychoanalysis and the Question of the Text*. Ed. Geoffrey Hartman. Baltimore: The Johns Hopkins University Press, 1978, pp. 114–48. Rpt. in *Sigmund Freud*. Ed. Harold Bloom. New York: Chelsea House, 1985, pp. 129–42.

——. 'Me – Psychoanalysis: An Introduction to the Translation of "The Shell and the Kernel" by Nicholas Abraham". Trans. Richard Klein. *Diacritics*. 9: 2 (1979): 4–12.

——. 'Scribble (writing-power)'. Trans. Cary Plotkin. *Yale French Studies*. 58 (1979): 116–47.

——. *Spurs: Nietzsche's Styles*. Trans. Barbara Harlow. Chicago: University of Chicago Press, 1979.

——. *The Archeology of the Frivolous: Reading Condillac*. Trans. John P. Leavey, Jr. Pittsburgh: Duquesne University Press, 1980.

——. 'La Loi du genre/The Law of Genre'. Trans. Avital Ronell. *Glyph*. 7 (1980): 176–232.

——. *La Carte postale: de Socrate à Freud et au-delà*. Paris: Flammarion, 1980.

——. *Dissemination*. Trans. Barbara Johnson. Chicago: University of Chicago Press, 1981.

——. 'Economimesis'. Trans. Richard Klein. *Diacritics*. 11: 2 (1981): 3–25.

——. *Margins of Philosophy*. Trans. Alan Bass. Chicago: University of Chicago Press, 1982.

——. *Positions*. Trans. Alan Bass. Chicago: University of Chicago Press, 1982.

——. *L'Oreille de l'autre: Otobiographies, transferts, traductions: textes et débats avec Jacques Derrida*. Sous la direction de Claude Lévesque et Christie V. McDonald. Montréal: VLB, 1982.

——. 'The Principle of Reason: The University in the Eyes of its Pupils'. Trans. Catherine Porter and Edward P. Morris. *Diacritics*. 13: 3 (1983): 3–20.

——. 'The Time of a Thesis: Punctuations'. Trans. Kathleen McLaughlin. *Philosophy in France Today*. Ed. Alan Montefiore. Cambridge: Cambridge University Press, 1983, pp. 34–51.

——. *D'un ton apocalyptique adopté naguère en philosophie*. Paris: Galilée, 1983.

——. 'Racism's Last Word'. Trans. Peggy Kamuf. *Critical Inquiry*. 12 (1985): 290–99.

——. 'Deconstruction and the Other'. *Dialogues with Contemporary Continental Thinkers: The Phenomenological Heritage*. Ed. Richard Kearney. Manchester: Manchester University Press, 1984, pp. 107–26.

——. 'My Chances/*Mes Chances*: A Rendezvous with Some Epicurean Stereophonies'. Trans. Irene E. Harvey and Avital Ronell. *Taking Chances: Derrida, Psychoanalysis, and Literature*. Eds Joseph H. Smith and William Kerrigan. Baltimore: The Johns Hopkins University Press, 1984, pp. 1–32.

——. 'No Apocalypse, Not Now' (full speed ahead, seven missiles, seven missives)'. Trans. Catherine Porter and Phillip Lewis. *Diacritics*. 14: 2 (1984): 20–31.

——. *Signéponge/Signsponge*. Trans. Richard Rand. New York: Columbia University Press, 1984.

——. 'Two Words for Joyce'. Trans. Geoff Bennington. *Post–Structuralist Joyce: Essays from the French*. Eds Derek Attridge and Daniel Ferrer. Cambridge: Cambridge University Press, 1984, pp. 145–61.

——. *Otobiographies: l'enseignement de Nietzsche et la politique du nom propre*. Paris: Galilée, 1984.

——. 'Choreographies'. Trans. Christie McDonald. *The Ear of the Other: Otobiography, Transference, Translation*. Trans. Peggy Kamuf et al. Eds Claude Levesque and Christie McDonald. Lincoln: University of Nebraska Press, 1985.

——. 'Letter to a Japanese Friend'. Trans. David Wood and Andrew Benjamin. *Derrida and Différance*. Eds David Wood and Robert Bernasconi. Coventry: Parousia Press, 1985, pp. 1–6.

——. 'Des Tours de Babel'. Trans. Joseph F. Graham. *Difference in Translation*. Ed. Joseph F. Graham. Ithaca: Cornell University Press, 1985, pp. 165–248.

——, et al. *La Faculté de juger*. Paris: Minuit, 1985.

——. 'The Question of Style'. Trans. R. Berezdivin. *The New Nietzsche*. Ed. David B. Allison. Cambridge, MA: MIT Press, 1985, pp. 176–89.

——. 'The Age of Hegel'. Trans. Susan Winnett. *Glyph*. 1 (1986): 3–44.

——. 'Fors: The Anglish Words of Nicholas Abraham and Maria Torok'. Trans. Barbara Johnson. *The Wolf Man's Magic Word: A Cryptonomy*. Nicholas Abraham and

Maria Torok. Trans. Richard Rand. Minneapolis: University of Minnesota Press, 1986.

——. *Glas.* Trans. John P. Leavey, Jr., and Richard Rand. Lincoln: University of Nebraska Press, 1986.

——. *Parages.* Paris: Galilée, 1986.

——. 'Shibboleth (on Paul Celan)'. Trans. Joshua Wilner. *Midrash and Literature.* Eds Geoffrey Hartman and Sanford Budick. New Haven: Yale University Press, 1986, pp. 307–47. Rpt. as 'Shibboleth: For Paul Celan' in *Word Traces: Readings of Paul Celan.* Ed. Aris Fioretos. Baltimore: The Johns Hopkins University Press, 1994, pp. 3–74.

——. *Schibboleth pour Paul Celan.* Paris: Galilée, 1986.

——. 'Forcener le subjectile'. Preface to *Dessins et portraits d'Antonin Artaud.* Paris: Gallimard, 1986.

——. 'Proverb: "He that would Pun"'. Preface to *Glossary,* by John P. Leavey, Jr., and Gregory Ulmer. Lincoln: Nebraska University Press, 1986.

——. *De l'esprit: Heidegger et la question.* Paris: Galilée, 1987.

——. '*Geschlect* II: Heidegger's Hand'. Trans. John P. Leavey, Jr. *Deconstruction and Philosophy: The Texts of Jacques Derrida.* Ed. John Sallis. Chicago: University of Chicago Press, 1987, pp. 161–96.

——. 'The Laws of Reflection: Nelson Mandela, in Admiration'. Trans. Mary Ann Caws and Isabelle Lorenz. *For Nelson Mandela.* Eds Jacques Derrida and Mustapha Tlili. New York: Henry Holt, 1987, pp. 13–42.

——. 'Living On • Borderlines'. Trans. James Hulbert. *Deconstruction and Criticism.* Harold Bloom, Paul de Man, Jacques Derrida, Geoffrey Hartman, J. Hillis Miller. New York: Continuum, 1987, pp. 75–176.

——. *The Post Card: From Socrates to Freud and Beyond.* Trans. Alan Bass. Chicago: Chicago University Press, 1987.

——. The *Retrait* of Metaphor'. Trans. F. Gasdner et al. *Enclitic.* 2: 2 (1987): 5–33.

——. 'Some Questions and Responses'. *The Linguistics of Writing: Arguments between Language and Literature.* Eds Nigel Fabb, Derek Attridge, Alan Durant and Colin MacCabe. Manchester: Manchester University Press, 1987, pp. 252–64.

——. *The Truth in Painting.* Trans. Geoff Bennington and Ian McLeod. Chicago: University of Chicago Press, 1987.

——. *De l'esprit: Heidegger et la question.* Paris: Galilée, 1987.

——. *Feu la cendre.* Paris: des Femmes, 1987.

——. *Psyché: Inventions de l'autre.* Paris: Galilée, 1987.

——. *Ulysse gramophone: Deux mots pour Joyce.* Paris: Galilée, 1987.

——. 'Women in the Beehive: A Seminar with Jacques Derrida'. Eds James Adner, Kate Doyle and Glenn Hendler. *Men in Feminism.* Eds Alice Jardine and Paul Smith. New York: Methuen, 1987, pp. 189–203.

——. 'Ulysses Gramophone: Hear Say Yes in Joyce'. Trans. Tina Kendall and Shari Benstock. *James Joyce: The Augmented Ninth.* Ed. Bernard Benstock. Syracuse: Syracuse University Press, 1988, pp. 27–75.

——. *Limited Inc.* Ed. Gerald Graff. Trans. Samuel Weber and Jeffrey Mehlman. Evanston: Northwestern University Press, 1988.

——. *Mémoires pour Paul de Man.* Paris: Galilée, 1988.

——. 'The Deaths of Roland Barthes'. Trans. Pascale-Anne Brault and Michael Naas.

Continental Philosophy I: Philosophy and Non-Philosophy since Merleau-Ponty.
Ed. Hugh J. Silverman. New York: Routledge, 1988, pp. 259–96. Rpt. as
Philosophy and Non-Philosophy since Merleau-Ponty. Ed. Hugh J. Silverman.
Evanston: Northwestern University Press, 1997.

——. 'The Purveyor of Truth'. (1980) Trans. Alan Bass. *The Purloined Poe: Lacan,
Derrida, and Psychoanalytic Reading.* Eds John P. Muller and William J. Richardson. Baltimore: The Johns Hopkins University Press, 1988, pp. 213–51.

——. *Memoires for Paul de Man.* Revised edition. Trans. Cecile Lindsay, Jonathan Culler,
Eduardo Cadava and Peggy Kamuf. New York: Columbia University Press,
1989.

——. 'Biodegradables: Seven Diary Fragments'. Trans. Peggy Kamuf. *Critical Inquiry.*
15: 4 (1989): 812–73.

——. 'How to Avoid Speaking: Denials'. Trans. Ken Frieden. *Languages of the Unsayable.*
Eds Sanford Budick and Wolfgang Iser. New York: Columbia University Press,
1989, pp. 3–70.

——. 'Introduction: Desistance'. Trans. Christopher Fynsk. *Typography: Mimesis, Philosophy, Politics.* Philippe Lacoue–Labarthe. Trans. Christopher Fynsk et al.
Cambridge: Harvard University Press, 1989, pp. 1–42.

——. *Of Spirit: Heidegger and the Question.* Trans. Geoffrey Bennington and Rachel
Bowlby. Chicago: University of Chicago Press, 1989.

——. 'Psyche: Inventions of the Other'. Trans. Catherine Porter. *Reading de Man Reading.* Eds Wlad Godzich and Lindsay Waters. Minneapolis: University of
Minnesota Press, 1989, pp. 25–65.

——. 'Three Questions to Hans-Georg Gadamer' (1981). Trans. Diane Michelfelder
and Richard Palmer. *Dialogue and Deconstruction: The Gadamer–Derrida Encounter.* Eds Diane P. Michelfelder and Richard E. Palmer. Albany: SUNY Press,
1989, pp. 52–54.

——. 'Interpreting Signatures (Nietzsche/Heidegger): Two Questions'. Trans. Diane
Michelfelder and Richard Palmer. *Dialogue and Deconstruction: The Gadamer–
Derrida Encounter.* Eds Diane P. Michelfelder and Richard E. Palmer. Albany:
SUNY Press, 1989, pp. 58–71.

——. *Du droit à la philosophie.* Paris: Galilée, 1990.

——. 'Some Statements and Truisms about Neologisms, Newisms, Postisms, Parasit-
isms, and Other Small Seismisms'. Trans. Anne Tomiche. *The States of "Theory".*
Ed. David Carroll. New York: Columbia University Press, 1990, pp. 63–94.

——. *Mémoires d'aveugle: L'autobiographie et autres ruines.* Paris: Musée de Louvre, 1990.

——. *Limited Inc.* Présentation et traductions par Elisabeth Weber. Paris: Galilée, 1990.

——. *La problème de la genèse dans la philosophie de Husserl.* Paris: Presses Universitaires
de France, 1990.

——. *Heidegger et la question: De l'esprit et autres essais.* Paris: Flammarion, 1990.

——. 'Sending: On Representation'. Trans. Mary Ann Caws and Peter Caws. *Transforming the Hermeneutic Context: From Nietzsche to Nancy.* Eds Gayle L. Ormiston
and Alan D. Schrift. Albany: SUNY Press, 1990, pp. 107–38.

——. 'At This Very Moment in This Work Here I Am'. Trans. Ruben Berezdivin. *Re-
Reading Lévinas.* Eds Robert Bernasconi and Simon Critchley. Bloomington: Indiana University Press, 1991, pp. 11–50.

——. 'Che cos'è la poesia'. Trans. Peggy Kamuf. *A Derrida Reader: Between the Blinds.*
Ed. Peggy Kamuf. New York: Columbia University Press, 1991, pp. 221–40.

——. *Cinders*. (1987). Trans., ed. and intro. Ned Lukacher. Lincoln: University of Nebraska Press, 1991.

——. '"Eating Well," or the Calculation of the Subject: An Interview with Jacques Derrida'. Trans. Peter Connor and Avital Ronell. *Who Comes After the Subject*. Eds Eduardo Cadava, Peter Connor and Jean-Luc Nancy. London: Routledge, 1991, pp. 96–120.

——. 'This is Not an Oral Footnote'. Trans. Stephen A. Barney and Michael Hanly. *Annotation and its Texts*. Ed. Stephen A. Barney. New York: Oxford, 1991, pp. 192–205.

——. *L'autre cap, suivi de la démocratie ajournée*. Paris: Minuit, 1991.

——. *Circonfession: Cinquante-neuf périodes et périphrases*. In Geoffrey Bennington and Jacques Derrida, *Jacques Derrida*. Paris: Seuil, 1991.

——. *Donner le temps. I. La fausse monnaie*. Paris: Galilée, 1991.

——. *Given Time. I. Counterfeit Money*. Trans. Peggy Kamuf. Chicago: University of Chicago Press, 1991.

——. *Acts of Literature*. Ed. Derek Attridge. New York: Routledge, 1992. Contents: '"This Strange Institution Called Literature": An Interview with Jacques Derrida'; '… That Dangerous Supplement …'; 'Mallarmé'; 'The First Session'; 'Before the Law'; 'The Law of Genre'; 'Ulysses Gramophone: Hear Say Yes in Joyce'; *From* 'Psyche: Invention of the Other'; *From* 'Signsponge'; *From* Shibboleth: For Paul Celan'; 'Aphorism Countertime'.

——. 'Afterw.rds or, at least, less than a letter about a letter less'. Trans. Geoffrey Bennington. *Afterwords*. Ed. Nicholas Royle. Tampere: Outside Books, 1992, pp. 197–217.

——. 'Force of Law: The "Mystical Foundation of Authority"'. Trans. Mary Quaintance. *Deconstruction and the Possibility of Justice*. Eds Drucilla Cornell, Michael Rosenfeld and David Gray Carlson. New York: Routledge, 1992, pp. 3–67.

——. 'Mochlos: or, The Conflict of the Faculties'. Trans. Richard Rand and Ann Wygant. *Logomachia: The Conflict of the Faculties*. Ed. Richard Rand. Lincoln: University of Nebraska Press, 1992, pp. 3–34.

——. 'Onto-Theology of National–Humanism'. *Oxford Literary Review*. 14: 1–2 (1992): 3–24.

——. *The Other Heading: Reflections on Today's Europe*. Trans. Pascale-Anne Brault and Michael B. Naas. Intro. Michael B. Naas. Bloomington: Indiana University Press, 1992.

——. 'Passions: "An Oblique Offering"'. Trans. David Wood. *Derrida: A Critical Reader*. Ed. David Wood. Oxford: Blackwell, 1992, pp. 5–35.

——. 'Post-Scriptum: Aporias, Ways and Voices'. Trans. John P. Leavey, Jr. *Derrida and Negative Theology*. Eds Harold Coward and Toby Foshay. Albany: SUNY Press, 1992, pp. 283–324.

——. "*Donner la Mort*". In *L'Ethique du don: Jacques Derrida et la pensée du don*. Paris: Métailié-Transition, 1992.

——. *Points de suspension: Entretiens*. Choisis et présentés par Elisabeth Weber. Paris: Galilée, 1992.

——. *Aporias*. Trans. Thomas Dutoit. Stanford: Stanford University Press, 1993.

——. 'Back from Moscow, in the USSR'. Trans. Mary Quaintaire. *Politics, Theory, and Contemporary Culture*. Ed. Mark Poster. New York: Columbia University Press, 1993, pp. 197–236.

——. 'Heidegger's Ear: Philopolemology (*Geschlect* IV)'. Trans. John P. Leavey, Jr. *Reading Heidegger: Commemorations*. Ed. John Sallis. Bloomington: Indiana University Press, 1993, pp. 163–218.

——. *Memoirs of the Blind*. Trans. Pascale-Anne Brault and Michael Naas. Chicago: University of Chicago Press, 1993.

——. 'On a Newly Arisen Apocalyptic Tone in Philosophy'. Rev. version. Trans. John P. Leavey, Jr. *Raising the Tone of Philosophy: Late Essays by Immanuel Kant, Transformative Critique by Jacques Derrida*. Ed. Peter Fenves. Baltimore: The Johns Hopkins University Press, 1993, pp. 117–73.

——. *Khōra*. Paris: Galilée, 1993.

——. *Spectres de Marx: l'état de la dette, le travail du deuil et la nouvelle Internationale*. Paris: Galilée, 1993.

——. 'Maddening the Subjectile'. Trans. Mary Ann Caws. *Yale French Studies*. 84 (1994): 154–71.

——. *Force de loi: Le "Fondement mystique de l'autorité."* Paris: Galilée, 1994.

——. 'The Spatial Arts: An Interview with Jacques Derrida'. *Deconstruction and the Visual Arts: Art, Media, Architecture*. Eds Peter Brunette and David Wills. Cambridge: Cambridge University Press, 1994, pp. 9–33.

——. *Specters of Marx: The State of the Debt, the Work of Mourning, and the New International*. Trans. Peggy Kamuf. Intro. Bernd Magnus and Stephen Cullenberg. New York and London: Routledge, 1994.

——. *Politiques de l'amitié: suivi de l'oreille de Heidegger*. Paris: Galilée, 1994.

——. '"To Do Justice to Freud": The History of Madness in the Age of Psychoanalysis'. (1992) Trans. Pascale-Anne Brault and Michael Naas. *Critical Inquiry* 20 (Winter 1994): 227–66.

——. 'Geopsychoanalysis: ... and the Rest of the World'. Trans. Donald Nicholson–Smith. *New Formations*. 26 (1995): 141–62.

——. *The Gift of Death*. Trans. David Wills. Chicago: University of Chicago Press, 1995.

——. *On the Name*. Ed. Thomas Dutoit. Trans. David Wood, John P. Leavey, Jr., and Ian McLeod. Stanford: Stanford University Press, 1995.

——. *Points ... Interviews 1974–1994*. Ed. Elisabeth Weber. Trans. Peggy Kamuf et al. Stanford: Stanford University Press, 1995.

——. 'The Time is Out of Joint'. Trans. Peggy Kamuf. *Deconstruction is/in America: A New Sense of the Political*. Ed. Anselm Haverkamp. New York: New York University Press, 1995, pp. 14–41.

——. 'Sauver le phénomènes: Pour Salvatore Puglia'. *Contretemps*. I (hiver 1995): 14–31.

——. *Moscou aller-retour*. [Suivi d'un entretien avec] Natalia Avtonomova, Valeri Podoroga et Mikhail Ryklin. La Tour d'Aigues: Editions de l'Aube, 1995.

——. *Archive Fever: A Freudian Impression*. Trans. Eric Prenowitz. Chicago: University of Chicago Press, 1996.

——. '"As if I were Dead": an Interview with Jacques Derrida'. *Applying: to Derrida*. Eds John Brannigan, Ruth Robbins and Julian Wolfreys. Basingstoke: Macmillan, 1996, pp. 212–27.

——. *Apories: Mourir – s'attendre aux "limites de la vérité"*. Paris: Galilée, 1996.

——. 'Foi et savoir: Les deux sources de la «religion» aux limites de la simple raison'. In *La Religion: Séminaire de Capri sous la direction de Jacques Derrida et Gianni Vattimo*. Paris: Seuil, 1996.

——. 'Remarks on Deconstruction and Pragmatism'. Trans. Simon Critchley. *Deconstruction and Pragmatism*. Simon Critchley, Jacques Derrida, Ernesto Laclau and Richard Rorty. Ed. Chantal Mouffe. London: Routledge, 1996, pp. 77–88.

——. 'Spectrographies'. *Échographies: de la télévision. Entretiens filmés*. Jacques Derrida and Bernard Stiegler. Paris: Galilée–INA, 1996.

——. *Résistances de la psychanalyse*. Paris: Galilée, 1996.

——. 'oui, mes livres sonts politiques: Entretien avec Didier Eribon'. *Le Nouvel Observateur*. (1633, 22–28 fevrier, 1996): 84–86.

——. *Le Monolinguisme de l'autre ou la Prosthèse d'origine*. Paris: Galilée, 1996.

——. 'il courait mort: Salut salut. Notes pour la courrier aux Tempes Modernes'. *Les Tempes Modernes*. 51e année 587 (1996): 7–54.

——. *The Politics of Friendship*. (1996) Trans. George Collins. London: Verso, 1997.

——. *Deconstruction in a Nutshell: A Conversation with Jacques Derrida*. Ed. with a commentary by John D. Caputo. New York: Fordham University Press, 1997.

——. *Adieu à Emmanuel Lévinas*. Paris: Galilée, 1997.

——. *Cosmopolites de tous les pays encore un effort!*. Paris: Galilée, 1997.

——. 'Architecture Where the Desire May Live (Interview)'. (1986) *Rethinking Architecture: A Reader in Cultural Theory*. Ed. Neil Leach. New York: Routledge, 1997, pp. 319–23.

——. 'Point de Folie – maintenant l'architecture'. (1986) Trans. Kate Linker. *Rethinking Architecture: A Reader in Cultural Theory*. Ed. Neil Leach. New York: Routledge, 1997, pp. 324–335.

——. 'Why Peter Eisenman Writes Such Good Books' (1988). Trans. Sarah Whiting. *Rethinking Architecture: A Reader in Cultural Theory*. Ed. Neil Leach. New York: Routledge, 1997, pp. 336–347.

—— and Peter Eisenman. *Chora L Works*. Eds Jeffrey Kipnis and Thomas Leeser. New York: Monacelli Press, 1997.

——. 'Fourmis'. Trans. Eric Prenowitz. *Hélène Cixous: Rootprints: Memory and Life Writing*. Hélène Cixous and Mireille Calle-Gruber. Trans. Eric Prenowitz. London: Routledge, 1997, pp. 117–27.

——. 'A Silkworm of One's Own (Points of view stitched on the other veil)'. Trans. Geoffrey Bennington. *The Oxford Literary Review: Derridas*. Eds Timothy Clark and Nicholas Royle. 18: 1–2 (1996): 3–65.

——. '"Perhaps or Maybe": Jacques Derrida in conversation with Alexander Garcia Düttman, ICA, 8 March 1996'. *Responsibilities of Deconstruction: PLI Warwick Journal of Philosophy*. Eds Jonathon Dronsfield and Nick Midgley. 6 (Summer 1997): 1–18.

——. '"On Responsibility': an interview with Jacques Derrida, Jonathon Dronsfield, Nick Midgley and Adrian Wilding, May 1993'. *Responsibilities of Deconstruction: PLI Warwick Journal of Philosophy*. Eds Jonathon Dronsfield and Nick Midgley. 6 (Summer 1997): 19–36.

——. 'Writing Proofs'. (1985) Trans. Roland-François Lack. *Responsibilities of Deconstruction: PLI Warwick Journal of Philosophy*. Eds Jonathon Dronsfield and Nick Midgley. 6 (Summer 1997): 38–50.

——, and Anne Duformantelle. *De l'hospitalité*. Paris: Calmann-Lévy, 1997.

Other Works

Abraham, Nicholas, and Maria Torok. *The Wolf Man's Magic Word* (1976). Foreword Jacques Derrida. Trans. Richard Rand. Minneapolis: University of Minnesota Press, 1986.

Adamson, Joseph. 'Deconstruction'. *Encyclopedia of Contemporary Literary Theory: Approaches, Scholars, Terms*. Ed. Irena R. Makaryk. Toronto: University of Toronto Press, 1993, pp. 25–31.

Aichele, George, Jr. *The Limits of Story*. Philadelphia: Fortress Press, 1985.

Altieri, Charles. *Act and Quality*. Amherst: University of Massachusetts Press, 1981.

Arac, Jonathan. *Critical Genealogies: Historical Situations for Postmodern Literary Studies*. New York: Columbia University Press, 1987.

——, Wlad Godzich and W. Martin, eds. *The Yale Critics: Deconstruction in America*. Minneapolis: University of Minnesota Press, 1983.

Argyros, Alex. *A Blessed Rage for Order: Deconstruction, Evolution, and Chaos*. Ann Arbor: University of Michigan Press, 1991.

Atkins, G. Douglas. *Reading Deconstruction, Deconstructive Reading*. Lexington: University Press of Kentucky, 1983.

——. *Quests of Difference: Reading Pope's Poems*. Lexington: University Press of Kentucky, 1986.

Atkins, G. Douglas, and Michael L. Johnson, eds. *Writing and Reading Differently: Deconstruction and the Teaching of Composition and Literature*. Lawrence: University Press of Kansas, 1985.

Attridge, Derek. *Peculiar Language: Literature as Difference from the Renaissance to James Joyce*. London: Methuen, 1988.

—— and Daniel Ferrer, eds. *Post-Structuralist Joyce: Essays from the French*. Cambridge: Cambridge University Press, 1984.

——, Geoff Bennington and Robert Young, eds. *Post-Structuralism and the Question of History*. Cambridge: Cambridge University Press, 1987.

Baker, Peter. *Deconstruction and the Ethical Turn*. Gainesville: University Press of Florida, 1995.

Baldacchino, John. *Post-Marxist Marxism: Questioning the Answer: Difference and Realism after Lukacs and Adorno*. Brookfield: Avebury, 1996.

Bannet, Eve Tavor. *Structuralism and the Logic of Dissent: Barthes, Derrida, Foucault, Lacan*. Urbana: University of Illinois Press, 1989.

Barnes, Trevor J., and James S. Duncan. *Writing Worlds: Discourse, Texts, and Metaphor in the Representation of Landscape*. London: Routledge, 1992.

Barney, Stephen A., ed. *Annotation and Its Texts*. Oxford: Oxford University Press, 1991.

Battaglia, Rosemarie Angela. *Presence and Absence in Joyce, Heidegger, Derrida, Freud*. Albany: SUNY Press, 1985.

Beardsworth, Richard. *Derrida and the Political*. London: Routledge, 1996.

Beeler, Michael. *T. S. Eliot, Wallace Stevens, and the Discourses of Difference*. Baton Rouge: Louisiana State University Press, 1987.

Behler, Ernst. *Confrontations: Derrida, Heidegger, Nietzsche* (1988). Trans. Steven Taubeneck. Stanford: Stanford University Press, 1991.

Bell, Shannon. *Reading, Writing, and Rewriting the Prostitute Body*. Bloomington: Indiana University Press, 1994.

Benedikt, Michael. *Deconstructing the Kimbell: an Essay on Meaning and Architecture.* New York: Sites Books, 1991.

Benjamin, Andrew. *Present Hope: Philosophy, Architecture, Judaism.* London: Routledge, 1997.

Bennington, Geoffrey. 'Derridabase' (1991). *Jacques Derrida.* Geoffrey Bennington and Jacques Derrida. Trans. Geoffrey Bennington. Chicago: University of Chicago Press, 1993. 3–316.

——. *Legislations: The Politics of Deconstruction.* London: Verso, 1994.

——. 'Genuine Gasché (Perhaps)'. *Imprimatur.* 1: 2/3 (Spring 1996): 252–7.

——. 'X'. *Applying: to Derrida.* Eds John Brannigan, Ruth Robbins and Julian Wolfreys. Basingstoke: Macmillan, 1996, pp. 1–21.

Berman, Art. *From the New Criticism to Deconstruction: The Reception of Structuralism and Post-Structuralism.* Urbana: University of Illinois Press, 1988.

Bernasconi, Robert, and Simon Critchley, eds. *Re-Reading Levinas.* Bloomington: Indiana University Press, 1991.

Bernstein, J. M. *The Fate of Art: Aesthetic Alienation from Kant to Derrida and Adorno.* Cambridge: Polity Press, 1992.

Boyne, Roy. *Foucault and Derrida: The Other Side of Reason.* London: Unwin Hyman, 1990.

Brandt, Joan. *Geopoetics: The Politics of Mimesis in Poststructuralist French Poetry and Theory.* Stanford: Stanford University Press, 1997.

Brannigan, John, Ruth Robbins, and Julian Wolfreys, eds. *Applying: To Derrida.* Basingstoke: Macmillan, 1996.

Brock, Bernard L., ed. *Kenneth Burke and Contemporary European Thought.* Tuscaloosa: University of Alabama Press, 1995.

Brunette, Peter, and David Wills, eds. *Screen/Play: Derrida and Film Theory.* Princeton: Princeton University Press, 1989.

——, eds. *Deconstruction and the Visual Arts: Art, Media, Architecture.* Cambridge: Cambridge University Press, 1994.

Budick, Sanford, and Wolfgang Iser, eds. *Languages of the Unsayable: The Play of Negativity in Literature and Literary Theory.* New York: Columbia University Press, 1989.

Butler, Christopher. *Interpretation, Deconstruction, and Ideology: An Introduction to Some Current Issues in Literary Theory.* Oxford: Clarendon Press, 1984.

Butler, Judith. *Bodies that Matter: On the Discursive Limits of "Sex".* New York: Routledge, 1993.

——. *Excitable Speech: A Politics of the Performative.* New York: Routledge, 1997.

——. *The Psychic Life of Power: Theories in Subjection.* Stanford: Stanford University Press, 1997.

Cadava, Eduardo, Peter Connor and Jean-Luc Nancy, eds. *Who Comes After the Subject.* New York: Routledge, 1991.

Caputo, John D. *Radical Hermeneutics: Repetition, Deconstruction and the Hermeneutic Project.* Bloomington: Indiana University Press, 1987.

——. *The Prayers and Tears of Jacques Derrida: Religion without Religion.* Bloomington: Indiana University Press, 1997.

Carlsharme, Steffan. *Language and Time: An Attempt to Arrest the Thought of Jacques Derrida.* Göteborg: Acta Universitatis Gothobergenesis, 1986.

Carroll, David. *Parasthetics: Foucault, Lyotard, Derrida.* London: Methuen, 1987.

——, ed. *The States of "Theory": History, Art, and Critical Discourse.* New York: Columbia University Press, 1991.

Caruth, Cathy. *Unreclaimed Experience: Trauma, Narrative, and History.* Baltimore: The Johns Hopkins University Press, 1996.

—— and Deborah Esch, eds. *Critical Encounters: Reference and Responsibility in Deconstructive Writing.* New Brunswick: Rutgers University Press, 1995.

Cavell, Stanley. *Philosophical Passages: Wittgenstein, Emerson, Austin, Derrida.* Oxford: Blackwell, 1995.

Caws, Peter. *Structuralism: The Art of the Intelligible.* Atlantic Highlands: Humanities Press, 1988.

Champagne, Roland A. *Jacques Derrida.* New York: Twayne Publishers, 1995.

Chang, Briankle G. *Deconstructing Communication: Representation, Subject, and Economies of Exchange.* Minneapolis: University of Minnesota Press, 1996.

Cherryholmes, Cleo H. *Power and Criticism: Poststructural Investigations in Education.* New York: Teachers College, Columbia University, 1988.

Clark, Timothy. *Derrida, Heidegger, Blanchot: Sources of Derrida's Notion and Practice of Literature.* Cambridge: Cambridge University Press, 1992.

Clark, Timothy, and Nicholas Royle, eds. *The Oxford Literary Review: Derridas.* 18: 1–2 (1996).

Corlett, William. *Community without Unity: A Politics of Derridian Extravagance.* Durham: Duke University Press, 1989.

Cornell, Drucilla. *Beyond Accommodation: Ethical Feminism, Deconstruction, and the Law.* New York: Routledge, 1991.

——. *The Philosophy of the Limit.* New York: Routledge, 1992.

——, Michael Rosenfeld and David Gray Carlson, eds. *Deconstruction and the Possibility of Justice.* New York: Routledge, 1992.

Corngold, Stanley. *The Fate of the Self: German Writers and French Theory.* Durham: Duke University Press, 1994.

Coward, Harold. *Derrida and Indian Philosophy.* Albany: SUNY Press, 1990.

—— and Toby Foshay, eds. *Derrida and Negative Theology.* Albany: SUNY Press, 1992.

Critchley, Simon. *The Ethics of Deconstruction: Derrida and Levinas.* London: Blackwell, 1992.

—— and Peter Dews, eds. *Deconstructive Subjectivities.* Albany: SUNY Press, 1996.

Culler, Jonathan. *On Deconstruction: Theory and Criticism after Structuralism.* London: RKP, 1982.

Dasenbrock, Reed Way, ed. *Redrawing the Lines: Analytic Philosophy, Deconstruction, and Literary Theory.* Minneapolis: University of Minnesota Press, 1989.

Davis, Robert Con, and Ronald Schleifer, eds. *Rhetoric and Form: Deconstruction at Yale.* Norman: University of Oklahoma Press, 1985.

de Man, Paul. *Allegories of Reading: Figural Language in Rousseau, Nietzsche, Rilke and Proust.* New Haven: Yale University Press, 1979.

——. *Blindness and Insight: Essays in the Rhetoric of Contemporary Criticism.* Intro. Wlad Godzich. Minneapolis: University of Minnesota Press, 1983.

——. *The Rhetoric of Romanticism.* New York: Columbia University Press, 1984.

——. *The Resistance to Theory.* Foreword Wlad Godzich. Minneapolis: University of Minnesota Press, 1986.

——. *Critical Writings, 1953–1978.* Ed. and intro. Lindsay Waters. Minneapolis: University of Minnesota Press, 1989.

——. *Romanticism and Contemporary Criticism: The Gauss Seminar and Other Papers.* Eds E. S. Burt, Kevin Newmark and Andrzej Warminski. Baltimore: The Johns Hopkins University Press, 1993.

——. *Aesthetic Ideology.* Ed. and intro. Andrzej Warminski. Minneapolis: University of Minnesota Press, 1996.

DeNeef, A. Leigh. *Traherne in Dialogue: Heidegger, Lacan, and Derrida.* Durham: Duke University Press, 1988.

Descombes, Vincent. *Modern French Philosophy* (1979). Trans. L. Scott-Fox and J. M. Harding. Cambridge: Cambridge University Press, 1980.

Deutscher, Penelope. *Yielding Gender: Feminism, Deconstruction and the History of Philosophy.* London: Routledge, 1997.

Dews, Peter. *Logics of Disintegration: Post-Structuralist Thought and the Claims of Theory.* London: Verso, 1987.

Dillon, M. C., ed. *Écart and Différance: Merleau-Ponty and Derrida on Seeing and Writing.* Atlantic Highlands: Humanities Press, 1997.

Dronsfield, Jonathon and Nick Midgley, eds. *Responsibilities of Deconstruction:* PLI *Warwick Journal of Philosophy.* 6 (Summer 1997).

Eagleton, Terry. *Literary Theory: An Introduction.* Oxford: Blackwell, 1983.

Elam, Diane. *Feminism and Deconstruction: Ms. en Abyme.* London: Routledge, 1994.

Eliot, George. *Daniel Deronda* (1876). Ed. Barbara Hardy. London: Penguin, 1986.

Evans, Joseph Claude. *Strategies of Deconstruction: Derrida and the Myth of the Voice.* Minneapolis: University of Minnesota Press, 1991.

Evans, Malcolm. *Signifying Nothing: Truth's True Contexts in Shakespeare's Text.* Athens: University of Georgia Press, 1986.

Feder, Ellen K., Mary C. Rawlinson and Emily Zakin, eds. *Derrida and Feminism: Recasting the Question of Woman.* New York: Routledge, 1997.

Felperin, Howard. *Beyond Deconstruction: The Uses and Abuses of Literary Theory.* Oxford: Clarendon Press, 1985.

Fenves, Peter, ed. *Raising the Tone of Philosophy: Late Essays by Immanuel Kant, Transformative Critique by Jacques Derrida.* Baltimore: The Johns Hopkins University Press, 1993.

Ferry, Luc, and Alain Renaut. *French Philosophy of the Sixties: An Essay on Anti-Humanism* (1985). Trans. Mary Schnakenberg Cattani. Amherst: University of Massachusetts Press, 1985.

Fioretos, Aris, ed. *Word Traces: Readings of Paul Celan.* Baltimore: The Johns Hopkins University Press, 1994.

Flores, Ralph. *The Rhetoric of Doubtful Authority: Deconstructive Readings of Self-Questioning Narratives, St. Augustine to Faulkner.* Ithaca: Cornell University Press, 1984.

Forrester, John. *The Seductions of Psychoanalysis: Freud, Lacan and Derrida.* Cambridge: Cambridge University Press, 1990.

Fynsk, Christopher. *Language and Relation: … That there is Language.* Stanford: Stanford University Press, 1996.

Game, Ann. *Undoing the Social: Towards a Deconstructive Sociology.* Toronto: University of Toronto Press, 1991.

Gasché, Rodolphe. *The Tain of the Mirror: Derrida and the Philosophy of Reflection.* Cambridge: Harvard University Press, 1986.

——. *Inventions of Difference: On Jacques Derrida.* Cambridge, Massachusetts: Harvard University Press, 1994.

Gearhart, Suzanne. *The Open Boundary of History and Fiction: A Critical Approach to the*

French Enlightenment. Princeton: Princeton University Press, 1984.

Gilman, Charlotte Perkins. *The Yellow Wall-Paper and Other Stories.* Ed. Robert Shulman. Oxford: Oxford University Press, 1995.

Graham, Joseph F., ed. *Difference in Translation.* Ithaca: Cornell University Press, 1985.

Guerlac, Suzanne. *Literary Polemics: Bataille, Sartre, Valéry, Breton.* Stanford: Stanford University Press, 1997.

Harland, Richard. *Superstructuralism: The Philosophy of Structuralism and Post-Structuralism.* London: Methuen, 1987.

Hart, Kevin. *The Trespass of the Sign: Deconstruction, Theology and Philosophy.* Cambridge: Cambridge University Press, 1989.

Hartman, Geoffrey. *Saving the Text: Literature / Derrida / Philosophy.* Baltimore: The Johns Hopkins University Press, 1981.

——. 'Preface'. *Deconstruction and Criticism.* Harold Bloom, Paul de Man, Jacques Derrida, Geoffrey Hartman and J. Hillis Miller. New York: Continuum, 1987. vii–ix.

Harvey, Irene E. *Derrida and the Economy of Difference.* Bloomington: Indiana University Press, 1986.

Haverkamp, Anselm, ed. *Deconstruction is/in America: A New Sense of the Political.* New York: New York University Press, 1995.

Heidegger, Martin. *Being and Time.* (1927) Trans. J. Macquarrie and E. Robinson. New York: Harper & Row, 1962.

——. *On the Way to Language* (1959). Trans. P. Hertz. New York: Harper & Row, 1971.

——. 'The Origin of the Work of Art' (1935–36). Trans. A. Hofstadter. *Basic Writings.* New York: Harper & Row, 1977, pp. 149–87.

——. 'Letter on Humanism' (1947). Trans. F. Capuzzi. *Basic Writings.* New York: Harper & Row, 1977, pp. 193–242.

Herman, Luc, Kris Humbeeck and Gert Lernout, eds. *(Dis)Continuities: Essays on Paul de Man.* Amsterdam: Rodopi, 1989.

Hirsch, David. *The Deconstruction of Literature: Criticism After Auschwitz.* Hanover: University Press of New England, 1991.

Holland, Nancy J., ed. *Feminist Interpretations of Jacques Derrida.* University Park: Pennsylvania University Press, 1997.

Jabès, Edmond. *The Book of Margins.* (1975, 1984) Trans. Rosemarie Waldrop. Intro. Mark C. Taylor. Chicago: University of Chicago Press, 1993.

Jefferies, Richard. 'Snowed Up: A Mistletoe Story'. Wolfreys and Baker, eds., pp. 19–29.

Johnson, Barbara. *The Critical Difference: Essays in the Contemporary Rhetoric of Reading.* Baltimore: The Johns Hopkins University Press, 1980.

——, ed. *Freedom and Interpretation.* New York: Basic Books, 1993.

——. *The Wake of Deconstruction.* Oxford: Blackwell, 1994.

Johnson, Christopher. *System and Writing in the Philosophy of Jacques Derrida.* Cambridge: Cambridge University Press, 1993.

Kamuf, Peggy. *Signature Pieces: On the Institution of Authority.* Ithaca: Cornell University Press, 1988.

——, ed. *A Derrida Reader: Between the Blinds.* New York: Columbia University Press, 1991. Contents: Part One: Differance at the Origin: 1. From *Speech and Phenomena*; 2. From *Of Grammatology*; 3. From 'Différance'; 4. 'Signature Event Context'; 5. 'Plato's Pharmacy'; Part Two: Beside Philosophy – "Literature": 6. 'Tympan'; 7. From 'The Double Session'; 8. From 'Psyche: Inventions of the Other'; 9. 'Che cos'è la poesia?'; Part Three: More Than One Language: 10. From 'Des Tours de Babel'; 11. From 'Living On: Border Lines'; 12. 'Letter to a Japanese Friend'; 13. From 'Restitutions of the Truth in Pointing'; Part Four: Sexual Difference in Philosophy: 14. From *Glas*; 15. From *Spurs: Nietzsche's Styles*; 16. '*Geschlect:* Sexual Difference, Ontological Difference'; 17. From 'At This Very Moment in This Work Here I Am'; 18. From 'Choreographies'; Part Five: Tele–Types (Yes, Yes): 19. From 'Le Facteur de la vérité'; 20. From 'Envois'; 21. From 'To Speculate – on "Freud"'; 22. From 'Ulysses Gramophone: Hear Say Yes in Joyce'.

——. *The Division of Literature or the University in Deconstruction*. Chicago: University of Chicago Press, 1997.

Kant, Immanuel. *Critique of Judgment* (1790). Trans. Werner S. Pluhar. Indianapolis: Hackett Press, 1987.

Karasu, Toksoz B. *The Deconstruction of Psychotherapy*. Northvale: J. Aranson, 1996.

Kearney, Richard. *Dialogues with Contemporary Continental Thinkers. The Phenomenological Heritage*. Manchester: Manchester University Press, 1984.

——. *The Wake of Imagination: Toward a Postmodern Culture*. Minneapolis: University of Minnesota Press, 1988.

Keenan, Thomas. *Fables of Responsibility: Aberrations and Predicaments in Ethics and Politics*. Stanford: Stanford University Press, 1997.

Kerruish, Valerie. *Jurisprudence as Ideology*. London: Routledge, 1991.

Kramer, Matthew H. *Legal Theory, Political Theory, and Deconstruction: Against Rhadamanthus*. Bloomington: Indiana University Press, 1991.

Krupnick, Mark, ed. *Displacement: Derrida and After*. Bloomington: Indiana University Press, 1983.

Küchler, Tilman. *Postmodern Gaming: Heidegger, Duchamp, Derrida*. New York: P. Lang, 1994.

Lacoue-Labarthe, Philippe. *Typography: Mimesis, Philosophy, Politics*. Intro. Jacques Derrida. Trans. Christopher Fynsk et al. Cambridge, MA: Harvard University Press, 1989.

——. *Heidegger, Art, and Politics: The Fiction of the Political* (1987). Trans. Chris Turner. Oxford: Blackwell, 1990.

—— and Jean-Luc Nancy. *Retreating the Political* (1979, 1981, 1983). Ed. Simon Sparks. London: Routledge, 1997.

Lawlor, Leonard. *Imagination and Chance: the Difference between the Thought of Ricoeur and Derrida*. Albany: SUNY Press, 1992.

Leach, Neil, ed. *Rethinking Architecture: A Reader in Cultural Theory*. New York: Routledge, 1997.

Lechte, John. *Fifty Key Contemporary Thinkers: From Structuralism to Postmodernity*. London: Routledge, 1994.

Lehmann, Jennifer H. *Deconstructing Durkheim: A Post-Post Structuralist Critique*. London: Routledge, 1993.

Leitch, Vincent B. *Deconstructive Criticism: An Advanced Introduction*. New York: Columbia University Press, 1983.

Lentricchia, Frank. *After the New Criticism*. London: Athlone Press, 1980.

Levinas, Emmanuel. *Proper Names* (1975 and 1976). Trans. Michael B. Smith. Stanford: Stanford University Press, 1996.

Lévi-Strauss, Claude. *Triste Tropiques*. (1955) Trans. John Weightman and Doreen Weightman. New York: Washington Square Press, 1977.

Llewelyn, John. *Derrida on the Threshold of Sense*. London: Macmillan, 1986.

Loesberg, Jonathan. *Aestheticism and Deconstruction: Pater, Derrida and de Man.* Princeton: Princeton University Press, 1991.

Lowe, Walter James. *Theology and Difference: the Wound of Reason.* Bloomington: Indiana University Press, 1993.

Loy, David. *Healing Deconstruction: Postmodern Thought in Buddhism and Christianity.* Atlanta: Scholars Press, 1996.

Lucy, Niall. *Debating Derrida.* Carlton South: Melbourne University Press, 1995.

Lukacher, Ned. *Primal Scenes: Literature, Philosophy, Psychoanalysis.* Ithaca: Cornell University Press, 1986.

Lynn, Steven. *Samuel Johnson After Deconstruction: Rhetoric and the Rambler.* Carbondale: Southern Illinois University Press, 1992.

McCance, Dawne. *Posts: Re Addressing the Ethical.* Albany: SUNY Press, 1996.

McCarthy, Thomas A. *Ideals and Illusions: On Reconstruction and Deconstruction in Contemporary Critical Theory.* Cambridge, MA: MIT Press, 1991.

McKenna, Andrew J. *Violence and Difference: Girard, Derrida, and Deconstruction.* Urbana: University of Illinois Press, 1991.

McKenna, William R., and J. Claude Evans, eds. *Derrida and Phenomenology.* Dordrecht: Kluwer Academic Publishers, 1995.

Madison, Gary B., ed. *Working Through Derrida.* Evanston: Northwestern University Press, 1993.

Magiola, Robert R. *Derrida on the Mend.* West Lafayette: Purdue University Press, 1984.

Martin, Bill. *Matrix and Line: Derrida and the Possibilities of Postmodern Social Theory.* Albany: SUNY Press, 1992.

——. *Humanism and its Aftermath: The Shared Fate of Deconstruction and Politics.* Atlantic Highlands: Humanities Press, 1995.

Marx, Karl. *The German Ideology* (1845–46). Trans. W. Lough, C. Dutt and C. P. Magill. Ed. and intro. C. J. Arthur. London: Lawrence & Wishart, 1970.

——. *The Eighteenth Brumaire of Louis Bonaparte* (1852). Trans. Ben Fowkes. In *Surveys from Exile: Political Writings: Volume 2.* Ed. and intro. David Fernbach. London: Penguin, 1973.

——. *Capital.* Vol. 1 (1867). Trans. Samuel Moore and Edvard Aveling. Ed. Frederick Engels. New York: International Publishers, 1967.

May, Todd. *The Moral Theory of Poststructuralism.* University Park: Pennsylvania State University, 1995.

Megill, Allan. *Prophets of Extremity: Nietzsche, Heidegger, Foucault, Derrida.* Berkeley: University of California Press, 1985.

Melville, Stephen W. *Philosophy Beside Itself: On Deconstruction and Modernism.* Foreword Donald Marshall. Minneapolis: University of Minnesota Press, 1986.

Merleau-Ponty, Maurice. *The Visible and the Invisible.* Ed. Claude Lefort. Trans. Alphonso Lingis. Evanston: Northwestern University Press, 1968.

Merrell, Floyd. *Deconstruction Reframed.* West Lafayette. Purdue University Press, 1985.

Michelfelder, Diane P., and Richard E. Palmer, eds. *Dialogue and Deconstruction: The Gadamer–Derrida Encounter.* Albany: SUNY Press, 1989.

Miller, J. Hillis. *Fiction and Repetition: Seven English Novels.* Oxford: Basil Blackwell, 1982.

——. *The Linguistic Moment: From Wordsworth to Stevens.* Princeton: Princeton University Press, 1985.

——. *The Ethics of Reading: Kant, de Man, Eliot, Trollope, James, and Benjamin*. New York: Columbia University Press, 1987.

——. *Tropes, Parables, Performatives: Essays on Twentieth-Century Literature*. Hemel Hempstead: Harvester Wheatsheaf, 1990.

——. *Versions of Pygmalion*. Cambridge, MA: Harvard University Press, 1990.

——. *Hawthorne and History: Defacing it*. Oxford: Blackwell, 1991.

——. *Theory Now and Then*. Hemel Hempstead: Harvester Wheatsheaf, 1991.

——. *Victorian Subjects*. Durham: Duke University Press, 1991.

——. *Ariadne's Thread: Story Lines*. New Haven: Yale University Press, 1992.

——. 'Deconstruction Now? The States of Deconstruction or Thinking without Synecdoche'. *Afterwords*. Ed. Nicholas Royle. Tampere: Outside Books, 1992, pp. 7–19.

——. *Illustration*. Cambridge, MA: Harvard University Press, 1992.

——. 'The Disputed Ground: Deconstruction and Literary Studies'. *Deconstruction is/in America: A New Sense of the Political*. Ed. Anselm Haverkamp. New York: New York University Press, 1995, pp. 79–86.

——. *Topographies*. Stanford: Stanford University Press, 1995.

——. 'Heart of Darkness Revisited'. *Tropes, Parables, Performatives: Essays on Twentieth-Century Literature*. Hemel Hempstead: Harvester Wheatsheaf, 1990, pp. 181–94. Rpt. in *Heart of Darkness*. Joseph Conrad. Case Studies in Contemporary Criticism. 2nd ed. Ed. Ross C. Murfin. Boston: St. Martin's Press, 1996, pp. 206–220.

Montefiore, Alan, ed. *Philosophy in France Today*. Cambridge: Cambridge University Press, 1983.

Mouffe, Chantal, ed. *Deconstruction and Pragmatism*. London: Routledge, 1996.

Moxey, Keith. *The Practice of Theory: Poststructuralism, Cultural Politics, and Art History*. Ithaca: Cornell University Press, 1994.

Muller, John P., and William J. Richardson, eds. *The Purloined Poe: Lacan, Derrida, and Psychoanalytic Reading*. Baltimore: The Johns Hopkins University Press, 1989.

Naas, Michael B. 'Introduction: For Example'. In *The Other Heading*, Jacques Derrida, 1992, pp. vii–lix.

Nägele, Rainer. *Echoes of Translation: Reading Between Texts*. Baltimore: The Johns Hopkins University Press, 1997.

Nancy, Jean-Luc. *The Muses* (1994). Trans. Peggy Kamuf. Stanford: Stanford University Press, 1996.

——. *The Gravity of Thought* (1993). Trans. François Raffoul and Gregory Recco. Atlantic Highlands: Humanities Press, 1997.

Nealon, Jeffrey T. *Double Reading: Postmodernism After Deconstruction*. Ithaca: Cornell University Press, 1993.

Neel, Jasper P. *Plato, Derrida, and Writing*. Carbondale: Southern Illinois University Press, 1988.

Nietzsche, Friedrich. *On the Genealogy of Morals and Ecce Homo*. Ed. and trans. Walter Kaufmann. New York: Vintage Books, 1967.

Niranjana, Tejaswini. *Siting Translation: History, Post-Structuralism, and the Colonial Context*. Berkeley: University of California Press, 1992.

Norris, Christopher. *Deconstruction: Theory and Practice*. London: Methuen, 1982.

——. *The Contest of Faculties: Philosophy and Theory After Deconstruction*. London: Methuen, 1985.

——. *Derrida*. London: Fontana Press, 1987.

——. 'Deconstruction, Post-modernism and the Visual Arts'. *What is Deconstruction?* Christopher Norris and Andrew Benjamin. London: Academy Editions/St. Martin's Press, 1988, pp. 7–33.

——. *Paul de Man, Deconstruction and the Critique of Aesthetic Ideology.* New York: Routledge, 1988.

——. *Deconstruction and the Interests of Theory.* Norman: University of Oklahoma Press, 1989.

—— and Andrew Benjamin. *What is Deconstruction.* London: Academy Editions, 1988.

Oliver, Kelly. *Womanizing Nietzsche: Philosophy's Relation to the "Feminine".* New York: Routledge, 1995.

Parker, Ian, et al. *Deconstructing Psychopathology.* London: Sage, 1995.

Payne, Michael. *Reading Theory: An Introduction to Lacan, Derrida, and Kristeva.* Oxford: Blackwell, 1993.

Pepper, Thomas. *Singularities: Extremes of Theory in the Twentieth Century.* Cambridge: Cambridge University Press, 1997.

Percesepe, Gary John. *Future(s) of Philosophy: The Marginal Thinking of Jacques Derrida.* New York: Peter Lang Publishing, 1989.

Pheby, Keith C. *Interventions: Displacing the Metaphysical Subject.* Washington, DC: Maisonneuve Press, 1988.

Plotnitsky, Arkady. *In the Shadow of Hegel: Complementarity, History, and the Unconscious.* Gainesville: University Press of Florida, 1993.

——. *Reconfigurations: Critical Theory and General Economy.* Gainesville: University Press of Florida, 1993.

——. *Complementarity: Anti-epistemology After Bohr and Derrida.* Durham: Duke University Press, 1994.

Poster, Mark, ed. *Politics, Theory, and Contemporary Culture.* New York: Columbia University Press, 1993.

Protevi, John. *Time and Exteriority: Aristotle, Heidegger, Derrida.* Lewisberg: Bucknell University Press, 1994.

Rand, Richard, ed. *Logomachia: The Conflict of the Faculties.* Lincoln: Nebraska University Press, 1992.

Rappaport, Herman. *Heidegger and Derrida: Reflections on Time and Language.* Lincoln: Nebraska University Press, 1989.

Reader, Keith. *Intellectuals and the Left in France since 1968.* Basingstoke: Macmillan, 1987.

Readings, Bill. *Introducing Lyotard: Art and Politics.* London: Routledge, 1991.

Ronell, Avital. *The Telephone Book: Technology, Schizophrenia, Electric Speech.* Lincoln: University of Nebraska Press, 1989.

——. *Crack Wars: Literature, Addiction, Mania.* Lincoln: University of Nebraska Press, 1992.

——. *Finitude's Score: Essays for the End of the Millenium.* Lincoln: University of Nebraska Press, 1994.

Rorty, Richard. 'Deconstruction'. *The Cambridge History of Literary Criticism: Volume 8. From Formalism to Poststructuralism.* Ed. Raman Selden. Cambridge: Cambridge University Press, 1995, pp. 166–97.

Roth, Michael. *The Poetics of Resistance.* Evanston: Northwestern University Press, 1996.

Rousseau, Jean-Jacques. *Essay on the Origin of Languages.* Trans. and Afterword John H. Moran and Alexander Gode. Intro. Alexander Gode. Chicago: University of Chicago Press, 1986.

Royle, Nicholas, ed. *Afterwords.* Tampere: Outside Books, 1992.

——. *After Derrida.* Manchester: Manchester University Press, 1995.

Ruthven, K. K. *Nuclear Criticism.* Carlton: Melbourne University Press, 1993.

Ryan, Michael. *Marxism and Deconstruction: A Critical Articulation.* Baltimore: The Johns Hopkins University Press, 1982.

Sallis, John. *Nietzsche and the Space of Tragedy.* Chicago: University of Chicago Press, 1991.

——. *Double Truth.* Albany: SUNY Press, 1995.

——, ed. *Deconstruction and Philosophy: The Texts of Jacques Derrida.* Chicago: University of Chicago Press, 1987.

——, ed. *Reading Heidegger: Commemorations.* Bloomington: Indiana University Press, 1993.

Sartiliot, Claudette. *Citation and Modernity: Derrida, Joyce, and Brecht.* Norman: University of Oklahoma Press, 1993.

Scharlemann, Robert P., ed. *Negation and Theology.* Charlottesville: University Press of Virginia, 1992.

Scheer, Steven C. *Pious Impostures and Unproven Words: The Romance of Deconstruction in Nineteenth-Century America.* Lanham: University Press of America. 1990.

Scholes, Robert E. *Textual Power: Literary Theory and the Teaching of English.* New Haven: Yale University Press, 1985.

Schrift, Alan D. *Nietzsche and the Question of Interpretation: Between Hermeneutics and Deconstruction.* New York: Routledge, 1990.

Schultz, William. *Genetic Codes of Culture? The Deconstruction of Tradition by Kuhn, Bloom, and Derrida.* New York: Brill, 1994.

Schwenger, Peter. *Letter Bomb: Nuclear Holocaust and the Exploding Word.* Baltimore: The Johns Hopkins University Press, 1992.

Seeley, David. *Deconstructing the New Testament.* Leiden: Brill, 1994.

Shumway, David R. 'The Star System in Literary Studies'. *PMLA.* 112: 1 (January 1997): 85–100.

Silverman, Hugh J., ed. *Derrida and Deconstruction.* New York: Routledge, 1989.

——. *Textualities: Between Hermeneutics and Deconstruction.* New York: Routledge, 1994.

——, ed. *Philosophy and Non-Philosophy since Merleau-Ponty.* (1988) Evanston: Northwestern University Press, 1997.

—— and Gary E. Aylesworth, eds. *The Textual Sublime: Deconstruction and its Differences.* Albany: SUNY Press, 1990.

Sim, Stuart. *Beyond Aesthetics: Confrontations with Poststructuralism and Postmodernism.* Toronto: University of Toronto Press, 1992.

Slawek, Tadeusz. *The Outlined Shadow: Phenomenology, Grammatology, Blake.* Katowice: Uniwersytet Slaski, 1985.

Smith, Joseph, and William Kerrigan, eds. *Taking Chances: Derrida, Psychoanalysis, and Literature.* Baltimore: The Johns Hopkins University Press, 1984.

Smith, Robert. *Derrida and Autobiography.* Cambridge: Cambridge University Press, 1995.

Spivak, Gayatri Chakravorty. 'Translator's Preface'. Derrida, *Of Grammatology,* pp. ix–lxxxix.

——. *In Other Worlds: Essays in Cultural Politics.* New York: Routledge, 1988.

——. *The Post-Colonial Critic: Interviews, Strategies, Dialogues.* Ed. Sarah Harasym. New York: Routledge, 1990.

——. *Outside in the Teaching Machine.* New York: Routledge, 1993.

——. 'At the *Planchette* of Deconstruction is/in America'. *Deconstruction is/in America:*

A New Sense of the Political. Ed. Anselm Haverkamp. New York: New York University Press, 1995, pp. 237–49.

Staten, Henry. *Wittgenstein and Derrida*. Lincoln: University of Nebraska Press, 1984.

Stratton, Jon. *Writing Sites: A Genealogy of the Postmodern World*. Ann Arbor: University of Michigan Press, 1990.

Strozier, Robert M. *Saussure, Derrida, and the Metaphysics of Subjectivity*. Berlin: Mouton de Gruyter, 1988.

Subotnik, Rose Rosengard. *Deconstructive Variations: Music and Reason in Western Society*. Minneapolis: University of Minnesota Press, 1996.

Sychrava, Juliet. *Schiller to Derrida: Idealism in Aesthetics*. Cambridge: Cambridge University Press, 1989.

Taylor, Mark C. *Erring: A Postmodern A/Theology*. Chicago: University of Chicago Press, 1984.

——. *Tears*. Albany: SUNY Press, 1990.

——, ed. *Deconstruction in Context: Literature and Philosophy*. Chicago: University of Chicago, 1986.

Tschumi, Bernard. *Architecture and Disjunction*. Cambridge, MA: MIT Press, 1994.

Ulmer, Gregory L. *Applied Grammatology: Post(e)-pedagogy from Jacques Derrida to Joseph Beuys*. Baltimore: The Johns Hopkins University Press, 1985.

Ward, Graham. *Barth, Derrida, and the Language of Theology*. Cambridge: Cambridge University Press, 1995.

Weber, Samuel. *Institution and Interpretation*. Minneapolis: University of Minnesota Press, 1987.

——. *Mass Mediauras: Form Technics Media*. Stanford: Stanford University Press, 1996.

Weedon, Chris. *Feminist Practice and Poststructuralist Theory*. Oxford: Blackwell, 1987.

Wheeler, Kathleen M. *Romanticism, Pragmatism and Deconstruction*. Oxford: Blackwell, 1993.

Wigley, Mark. *The Architecture of Deconstruction: Derrida's Haunt*. Cambridge, MA: MIT Press, 1993.

Wihl, Gary. *The Contingency of Theory: Pragmatism, Expressivism, and Deconstruction*. New Haven: Yale University Press, 1994.

Wills, David. *Prosthetics*. Stanford: Stanford University Press, 1995.

Winquist, Charles E. *Desiring Theology*. Chicago: University of Chicago Press, 1995.

Wolfreys, Julian. *The Rhetoric of Affirmative Resistance: Dissonant Identities from Carroll to Derrida*. Basingstoke: Macmillan, 1997.

——. *Deconstruction • Derrida*. New York: New York University Press, 1998.

—— and William Baker, eds. *Literary Theories: A Case Study in Critical Performance*. Basingstoke: Macmillan, 1996.

Wood, David. *The Deconstruction of Time*. Atlantic Highlands: Humanities Press, 1989.

——, ed. *Derrida: A Critical Reader*. Oxford: Blackwell, 1992.

——, ed. *Of Derrida, Heidegger, and Spirit*. Evanston: Northwestern University Press, 1993.

—— and Robert Bernasconi, eds. *Derrida and Différance* (1985). Evanston: Northwestern University Press, 1988.

Ziarek, Ewa Plonowska. *The Rhetoric of Failure: Deconstruction of Skepticism, Reinvention of Modernism*. Albany: SUNY Press, 1996.